MW00677932

KIERKEGAARD BIBLIOGRAPHY

TOME IV: HUNGARIAN TO KOREAN

Kierkegaard Research: Sources, Reception and Resources
Volume 19, Tome IV

Kierkegaard Research: Sources, Reception and Resources
is a publication of the Søren Kierkegaard Research Centre

Kierkegaard Bibliography

Tome IV: Hungarian to Korean

Edited by
PETER ŠAJDA AND JON STEWART

Routledge
Taylor & Francis Group

LONDON AND NEW YORK

First published 2017
by Routledge
2 Park Square, Milton Park, Abingdon, Oxon OX14 4RN

and by Routledge
711 Third Avenue, New York, NY 10017

Routledge is an imprint of the Taylor & Francis Group, an informa business

British Library Cataloguing in Publication Data
A catalogue record for this book is available from the British Library

Library of Congress Cataloging-in-Publication Data
A catalog record for this book has been requested

ISBN: 978-1-138-20949-7 (hbk)

Typeset in Times New Roman
by Apex CoVantage, LLC

Cover design by Katalin Nun

Printed in the United Kingdom
by Henry Ling Limited

Contents

List of Contributors

Judit Bartha, Eötvös Loránd University (ELTE), Faculty of Humanities, Institute for Art Theory and Media Studies, 1088 Budapest, Múzeum krt 6–8, Hungary.

István Czakó, Pázmány Péter Catholic University, Faculty of Humanities and Social Sciences, Department of Philosophy, 2087 Piliscsaba, Egyetem út 1, Hungary.

Kristian Guttesen, University of Iceland, Institute of Philosophy, Gimli, 3rd floor, 101 Reykjavik, Iceland.

Min-Ho Lee, c/o Søren Kierkegaard Research Centre, Farvergade 27 D, 1463 Copenhagen K, Denmark.

Laura Liva, Università G. D'Annunzio – School of Advanced Studies, Via dei Vestini 31, 66013 Chieti Scalo, Italy.

Jae-myeong Pyo, Department of Philosophy, Korea University, 145, Anam-ro, Seongbuk-gu, Seoul 136–701, Korea.

Yusuke Suzuki, Saitama Prefectural University, Sannomiya 820, Koshigaya-shi, Saitama-ken, 343–8540, Japan.

Hungarian

Judit Bartha and István Czakó

I. Hungarian Translations of Kierkegaard's Works

Isten változatlansága [*The Changelessness of God*], trans. by Lajos Zsigmond Szeberényi, Békéscsaba: Evangélikus Egyházi Könyvkereskedés 1929 (*Protestáns Kultúrkönyvtár*, vol. 3) (2nd ed., Budapest: Új Mandátum 1993).

Önvizsgálat. Ajánlva a kortársaknak [*For Self-Examination: Recommended to the Present Age*], trans. by Lajos Zsigmond Szeberényi, Békéscsaba: Evangélikus Egyházi Könyvkereskedés 1929 (*Protestáns Kultúrkönyvtár*, vol. 2) (2nd ed., Budapest: Új Mandátum 1993).

"Sören Kierkegaard," in *Az egzisztencializmus* [*Existentialism* [selections from Kierkegaard's works]], trans. by Béla Brandenstein et al., ed. by Béla Köpeczi, Budapest: Gondolat 1965, pp. 59–116 (2nd ed. 1966; 3rd ed. 1972; 4th ed. 1984). ("Önmagáról" ["On Himself" [selection from *On My Work as an Author*]], pp. 61–9; "A szubjektívvé válás" ["Becoming Subjective" [selection from *Concluding Unscientific Postscript*]], pp. 70–5; "A szorongás fogalma" [*The Concept of Anxiety* [selection]], pp. 76–82; "A három stádium" ["The Three Stages" [selection from *Concluding Unscientific Postscript*]], p. 83; "Az esztétikai stádium" ["The Aesthetic Stage" [selection from *Either/Or*]], pp. 84–7; "Az etikai stádium" ["The Ethical Stage" [selection from *Either/Or*]], pp. 87–9; "A vallási stádium" ["The Religious Stage" [selection from *Either/Or*]], pp. 89–91; "A művészetről" ["On Art" [selection from *Either/Or*]], pp. 92–5; "Don Juan – Az érzéki zsenialitás mint csábítás" ["Don Juan: The Sensual Geniality as Seduction" [selection from *Either/Or*]], pp. 96–116.)

Sören Kierkegaard írásaiból [*From Søren Kierkegaard's Writings* [selections from *The Concept of Irony*, *Either/Or*, *Repetition*, *Fear and Trembling*, *The Concept of Anxiety*, and *Concluding Unscientific Postscript*]], trans. by Tivadar Dani et al., ed. by Béla Suki, Budapest: Gondolat 1969 (2nd ed. 1982; 3rd ed. 1994).

Mozart Don Juanja [*Mozart's Don Juan* ["The Immediate Erotic Stages or the Musical-Erotic" from *Either/Or*]], trans. by László Lontay, Budapest: Európa 1972 (2nd ed. 1993).

Vagy-vagy [*Either/Or*], trans. by Tivadar Dani, Budapest: Gondolat 1978 (2nd ed., Budapest: Osiris–Századvég 1994; 3rd ed., Budapest: Osiris 2001; 4th ed. 2005).

Félelem és reszketés [*Fear and Trembling*], trans. by Péter Rácz, Budapest: Európa 1986 (2nd ed., Budapest: Göncöl 2004; 3rd ed., Pécs: Jelenkor 2014).

"Minden javunkra van – ha szeretjük Istent" ["All Things Must Serve Us for Good – When We Love God" [from *Christian Discourses*]], trans. by Lajos Ordass, *Lelkipásztor*, nos. 7–8, 1992, pp. 219–23.

2 *Judit Bartha and István Czakó*

Kierkegaard-kabaré. "...egy még élő ember írásaiból...". Irodalmi összeállítás Sören Kierkegaard műveiből [Kierkegaard Cabaret. "... From the Papers of One Still Living...". A Literary Selection from Søren Kierkegaard's Works], selected by Wladimir Herman, trans. by Tivadar Dani, László Kúnos and László Lontay, ed. by László Kúnos, Budapest: Budapesti Kamaraszínház – Fekete Sas 1992.

A halálos betegség [The Sickness unto Death], trans. by Péter Rácz, Budapest: Göncöl 1993.

"A kereszténység elsajátítása" ["The Acquisition of Christianity" [selection from *Practice in Christianity*]], trans. by Gábor Miszoglád, *Pannonhalmi Szemle*, no. 1, 1993, pp. 35–42.

"Lesz feltámadásuk a halottaknak, mind igazaknak mind hamisaknak" ["There Will Be the Resurrection of the Dead, of the Righteous – and of the Unrighteous" [from *Christian Discourses*]], trans. by Anna Molnár, *Gond*, no. 4, 1993, pp. 3–11.

Mozart Don Juanja [Mozart's Don Juan [selection from *Either/Or*]], trans. by László Lontay, Budapest: Helikon 1972 (2nd ed., Budapest: Európa 1993).

A szorongás fogalma [The Concept of Anxiety], trans. by Péter Rácz, Budapest: Göncöl 1993.

Az ismétlés [Repetition], trans. by Zoltán Gyenge, Budapest: Ictus 1993 (2nd revised ed. by Anita Soós and Zoltán Gyenge, Budapest: L'Harmattan 2008).

Építő keresztény beszédek [Upbuilding Christian Discourses [selection from *Christian Discourses*]], trans. by Zoltán Bohács et al., ed. by Éva Kocziszky, Budapest: Hermeneutikai Kutatóközpont 1995.

Filozófiai morzsák [Philosophical Fragments], trans. by Zoltán Hidas, Budapest: Göncöl 1997.

A keresztény hit iskolája [Practice in Christianity], trans. by Zoltán Hidas, Budapest: Atlantisz 1998.

"Szerzői tevékenységemről" [*On My Work as an Author*], trans. by Zoltán Hidas, *Pannonhalmi Szemle*, no. 2, 1998, pp. 50–60 (2nd ed., Debrecen: Latin betűk 2000).

"'Őrizd meg lábadat, mikor az Úr házához mégy!' Részletek az *Építő keresztény beszédek* című könyvből" ["'Watch Your Step When You Go to the House of the Lord.' Excerpts form *Christian Discourses*"], trans. by Zoltán Bohács, *Sola Scriptura*, no. 2, 1999, pp. 29–31.

"Kérés a Kalózhoz" ["A Request to the *Corsair*" [selection from Kierkegaard's journals and papers]], trans. by Gábor Gulyás, *Vulgo*, nos. 3–5, 2000, p. 279.

"Ki a szerzője a *Vagy-vagy*nak" ["Who Is the Author of *Either/Or*?" [Kierkegaard's article in *Fædrelandet*]], trans. by Gábor Gulyás, *Vulgo*, nos. 3–5, 2000, pp. 274–6.

"Magyarázat és egy kicsit több" ["An Explanation and a Little More" [Kierkegaard's article in *Fædrelandet*]], trans. by Gábor Gulyás, *Vulgo*, nos. 3–5, 2000, pp. 277–8.

"Egy még élő ember papírjaiból. Előszó." [*From the Papers of One Still Living. Preface*], trans. by Anita Soós, *Pro Philosophia Füzetek*, no. 23, 2000, pp. 49–51.

Berlini töredék. Jegyzetek Schelling 1841/42 előadásairól [Berlin Fragments: Notes to Schelling's Lectures of 1841–42], trans. by Zoltán Gyenge, Budapest: Osiris-Gond-Cura Alapívány 2001.

"Egy sírnál" ["At a Graveside" [from *Three Discourses on Imagined Occasions*]], trans. by Dezső Csejtei, in his *Filozófiai etűdök a végességre. Schopenhauer, Kierkegaard és Nietzsche a halálról* [Philosophical Studies on Finitude: Schopenhauer, Kierkegaard and Nietzsche on Death], Veszprém: Veszprémi Humán Tudományokért Alapítvány 2001, pp. 269–307; republished in his *A halál filozófiai megszólításai. Søren Kierkegaard, Max Scheler, Georg Simmel, Miguel de Unamuno írásai a halálról* [Philosophical Approaches to Death: Writings on Death by Søren Kierkegaard, Max Scheler, Georg Simmel and Miguel de Unamuno], Budapest, L'Harmattan 2011, pp. 15–45.

A csábító naplója. Mesék az emberi szívről [*The Seducer's Diary: Tales from the Human Heart* ["The Seducer's Diary" from *Either/Or*]], trans. by Irini Angelisz, Szada: Kassák 2004.

Egy még élő ember írásaiból. Az irónia fogalmáról [*From the Papers of One Still Living/The Concept of Irony*], trans. by Gábor Miszoglád and Anita Soós, Pécs: Jelenkor 2004 (*Søren Kierkegaard Művei*, vol. 1).

"Futó megjegyzés a *Don Juan* egy részletéről" ["A Cursory Remark on a Passage from *Don Juan*" [Kierkegaard's article in *Fædrelandet*]], trans. by Ágnes Bogdán, *Café Bábel*, no. 51, 2005, pp. 9–14.

Naplójegyzetek AA-DD [*Journals AA-DD*], trans. by Anita Soós, Pécs: Jelenkor 2006 (*Søren Kierkegaard Művei*, vol. 2).

"Imák" ["Prayers"], trans. by Mónika Kerekes and Erika Sáli, *Pannonhalmi Szemle*, no. 1, 2008, pp. 3–6.

Stádiumok az élet útján [*Stages on Life's Way*], trans. by Anita Soós, Pécs: Jelenkor 2009 (*Søren Kierkegaard Művei*, vol. 3).

Épületes beszédek [*Upbuilding Discourses 1843–1844*], trans. by Anita Soós, Pécs: Jelenkor 2011 (*Søren Kierkegaard Művei*, vol. 4).

Imák [Prayers], trans. by Mónika Kerekes, Cluj-Napoca: Koinónia 2011.

Az ismétlés. Félelem és reszketés. Filozófiai morzsák. A szorongás fogalma. Előszó [*Repetition, Fear and Trembling, Philosophical Fragments, The Concept of Anxiety, Prefaces*], trans. by Anita Soós (*Repetition* in cooperation with Zoltán Gyenge), Pécs: Jelenkor 2014 (*Søren Kierkegaard Művei*, vol. 5).

A jelenkor kritikája [*Criticism of the Present Age* [selection from *A Literary Review*]], trans. by Csaba Szabó, Budapest: L'Harmattan 2015, pp. 5–56.

II. Secondary Literature on Kierkegaard in Hungarian

Almási, Miklós, "A kétségbeesés eszkalációja. Søren Kierkegaard: *Vagy-vagy*" [The Escalation of Despair. Søren Kierkegaard: *Either/Or*], *Világosság*, no. 10, 1978, pp. 639–43.

Antal, Éva, "Az irónia mestere – Kierkegaard contra/versus Hegel?" [The Master of Irony: Kierkegaard contra/versus Hegel?], *Pro Philosophia Füzetek*, no. 30, 2002, pp. 43–63; republished in her *Túl az irónián* [Beyond Irony], Budapest: Kijárat 2007, pp. 63–94.

— "Szókratész halott – és élvezi. A szókratészi irónia bestialitásáról" [Socrates Is Dead – And Enjoying It: On the Bestiality of Socratic Irony], *Vulgo*, nos. 3–5, 2000, pp. 206–11.

— *Túl az irónián* [Beyond Irony], Budapest: Kijárat Kiadó 2007.

Bacsó, Béla, "Ismételhető-e az ismétlés?" [Can Repetition Be Repeated?], *Gond*, no. 4, 1993, pp. 21–5.

— *Határpontok. Hermeneutikai esszék* [Border Lines: Hermenutical Essays] Budapest: Twins 1994, pp. 64–70.

— "A szorongás mint egzisztens kategória" [Anxiety as an Existence Category], in his *Írni és felejteni. Filozófiai és művészetelméleti írások* [Writing and Forgetting: Writings on Philosophy and Theory of Art], Budapest: Kijárat 2001, pp. 26–38.

— "Hit és egzisztencia (Kierkegaard és Heidegger)" [Faith and Existence: Kierkegaard and Heidegger], *Alföld*, no. 11, 2013, pp. 76–81.

Balassa, Péter, "Utószó Ábrahám hallgatásához" [Afterword to Abraham's Silence], in Søren Kierkegaard, *Félelem és reszketés* [*Fear and Trembling*], trans. by Péter Rácz, Budapest: Európa 1986, pp. 221–73; republished in his *Majdnem és talán* [*Almost and Perhaps*], Budapest: T-Twins, Lukács Archívum 1995, pp. 63–89.

— "Kierkegaard – Bergman – Pilinszky," *Beszélő*, no. 50, 1992, pp. 39–41; republished in his *Majdnem és talán* [*Almost and Perhaps*], Budapest: T-Twins, Lukács Archívum 1995, pp. 90–7.

— "Kierkegaard és Bergman" [Kierkegaard and Bergman], *Pannonhalmi Szemle*, vol. 1, no. 1, 1993, pp. 45–53.

Bali, Brigitta, "Az 'épületes gondolat' maszk mögötti arca Kierkegaard *Vagy-vagy*-ának álarcosbálján" [The Face behind the Mask of the "Upbuilding Thought" in the Carnival of Kierkegaard's *Either/Or*], *Filozófiai Figyelő*, no. 3, 1988, pp. 147–51.

Bárdos, József, "Ádám álma (Kierkegaard-hatás *Az ember tragédiájá*ban)" [Adam's Dream (Kierkegaard's Influence on *The Tragedy of Man*)], *Módszertani Lapok, Magyar*, no. 1, 2003, pp. 5–14; no. 2, 2003, pp. 4–10.

Bartha, Judit, "Az esztétikai inkognitó pluralitása. Kierkegaard korai pszeudonim műveiről" [The Plurality of the Aesthetic Incognito: On Kierkegaard's Early Pseudonymous Writings], *Gond*, nos. 27–28, 2001, pp. 133–52.

— "A progresszív transzcendentálpoézis ideája Kierkegaard Schlegel-kritikájában" [The Idea of the Progressive Transcendental Poesy in Kierkegaard's Critique of Schlegel], *Pro Philosophia Füzetek*, no. 44, 2005, pp. 37–45.

— *A szerző árnyképe. Romantikus költőmítosz Kierkegaard és E.T.A. Hoffmann alkotásesztétikájában* [The Shadow of the Author: The Myth of the Romantic Poet in the Aesthetics of Kierkegaard and E.T.A. Hoffmann], Budapest: L'Harmattan 2008. (Reviews: Somhegyi, Zoltán, review in *Élet és Irodalom*, vol. 29, 2009, p. 25; Végh, Attila, review in *Magyar Hírlap*, vol. 11, 2009, p. 12.)

Bazsányi, Sándor, "'Hiszen nem ti vagytok, akik beszéltek.' A retorika kommunikációs modelljének esztétikai fordulata Søren Kierkegaard 'Ha Istent szeretjük, minden a javunkra kell, hogy váljon' című épületes keresztény beszédben" ["For It Is not You Who Speaks, but the Holy Spirit": Aesthetical Alteration of the Communicative Model of Rhetoric in Kierkegaard's *Christian Discourse* "All Things Must Serve Us for Good – *When* We Love God"], *Vulgo*, nos. 3–5, 2000, pp. 259–72.

Belohorszky, Pál, "Madách és Kierkegaard" [Madách and Kierkegaard], *Irodalomtörténet*, no. 4, 1971, pp. 886–96.

Hungarian 5

— "Dosztojevszkij és Kierkegaard" [Dostoevsky and Kierkegaard], *Új Írás*, vol. 21, no. 6, 1981, pp. 73–86.

Bölcskey, Gusztáv, "Kierkegaard egyház- és kereszténységkritikája" [Kierkegaard's Criticism of Church and Christianity], *Debreceni Református Akadémia Theologia Évkönyve*, Debrecen 1992–93, pp. 67–85.

Brachfeld, Olivér, "Søren Kierkegaard, a 'szellem határőre'" [Søren Kierkegaard, the "Border Guard" of Spirit], *Debreceni Szemle*, no. 9, 1932, pp. 347–53.

Brandenstein, Béla, *Kierkegaard. Tanulmány* [Kierkegaard: A Study], Budapest: Franklin Társulat 1934 (2nd ed., Budapest: Kairosz 2004). (Reviews: Nagy, András, "Our Long Way From *Enten-Eller* to *Vagy-vagy*: The History of the Reception of *Either/Or* in Hungary," *Kierkegaard Studies Yearbook*, 2008, pp. 440–69; see pp. 446–47; Somogyi, József, review in *Atheneum*, vol. 20, nos. 1–3, 1934, pp. 84–5; Varga, Sándor, review in *Potestáns Szemle*, vol. 43, 1934, pp. 454–55; Veres, Ildikó, "Kierkegaard, a 'magánkeresztény'" [Kierkegaard: The "Private Christian"] in Béla Brandenstein, *Kierkegaard. Tanulmány* [Kierkegaard: A Study], Budapest: Kairosz 2005, pp. 5–25.)

— "Kierkegaard," *Budapesti Szemle*, vol. 62, no. 674, 1934, pp. 73–92; vol. 62, no. 675, 1934, pp. 180–209; vol. 62, no. 676, 1934, pp. 300–37.

Czakó, István, "Søren Kierkegaard hitkoncepciója a fundamentálteológia tükrében" [Søren Kierkegaard's Conception of Faith as Reflected in the Fundamental Theology], *Pannonhalmi szemle*, vol. 8, no. 1, 2000, pp. 17–26.

— *Hit és egzisztencia. Tanulmány Søren Kierkegaard hitfelfogásáról* [Faith and Existence: A Study on Søren Kierkegaard's Conception of Faith], Budapest: L'Harmattan 2001. (Review: Horváth, Pál, review in *Könyvjelzö*, 2001 (online journal).)

— "Kierkegaard Feuerbach-recepciójának alapvonalai a filozófiai forráskutatás és a szöveganalízis tükrében" [Outlines of Kierkegaard's Reception of Feuerbach in the Light of Philosophical *Quellenforschung* and Textual Analysis], *Pro Philosophia Füzetek*, no. 25, 2001, pp. 85–99.

— "Bibliai elbeszélés és filozófiai interpretáció: A Ter 22,1–19 'lírai-dialektikus' olvasata Søren Kierkegaard *Félelem és reszketés* című művében" [Biblical Narration and Philosophical Interpretation: The "Lyric-Dialectic" Reading of Gen 22:1–19 in Søren Kierkegaard's *Fear and Trembling*], *Tanítvány*, vol. 9, no. 1, 2003, pp. 3–21.

— "Élet és elmélet az egzisztencia évszázadában" [Life and Theory in the Century of Existence], *Pro Philosophia Füzetek*, no. 32, 2003, pp. 131–6.

— "Az ártatlanság dialektikája: Kierkegaard és Hegel a bűnbeesésről" [The Dialectic of Innocence: Kierkegaard and Hegel on the Original Sin], in *Lábjegyzetek Platónhoz: A bűn* [Footnotes to Plato, vols. 2–3: Sin], ed. by András Dékány and Sándor Laczkó, Szeged: Pro Philosophia Szegediensi Alapítvány: Librarius 2004, pp. 169–79.

— "A szabad Ismeretlen: A természetes istenismeret problematikája Karl Rahner és Søren Kierkegaard valláskoncepciójában" [The Free Unknown: The Problem of Natural Knowledge of God in the Conception of Religion of Karl Rahner and

Søren Kierkegaard], in *In memoriam Karl Rahner*, ed. by László Lukács, Budapest: Vigilia 2006, pp. 112–29.

— "A választás választása: Søren Kierkegaard szabadságértelmezésének alapvonalai" [Choosing the Choice: Outlines of Søren Kierkegaard's Conception of Freedom], *Vigilia*, vol. 71, no. 5, 2006, pp. 331–41.

— "Apokalipszis most. Kierkegaard kordiagnózisának alapvonalai" [Apocalypse Now: The Basic Lines of Kierkegaard's Diagnosis of His Age], *Pro Philosophia Füzetek*, no. 49, 2007, pp. 115–29.

— "A vallási akozmizmus problémája Karl Jaspers Kierkegaard-recepciójában" [The Problem of Religious Acosmism in Karl Jaspers' Reception of Kierkegaard], *Magyar Filozófiai Szemle*, vol. 57, no. 3, 2013, pp. 89–105.

— "*Sacrificium intellectus*: hit és ész viszonya Søren Kierkegaard gondolkodásában" [*Sacrificium intellectus*: The Relation Between Faith and Reason in the Thought of Søren Kierkegaard], in *Hit és ész. Teológiai és filozófiai közelítések* [Faith and Reason. Theological and Philosophical Approaches], ed. by Gergely Bakos et al., Budapest: L'Harmattan – Sapientia Szerzetesi Hittudományi Főiskola 2013, pp. 258–87.

Csejtei, Dezső, "Kierkegaard halálfelfogása" [Kierkegaard's Conception of Death], in his *Filozófiai etűdök a végességre. Schopenhauer, Kierkegaard és Nietzsche a halálról* [Philosophical Etudes on Finitude: Schopenhauer, Kierkegaard and Nietzsche on Death], Veszprém: Veszprémi Humán Tudományokért Alapítvány 2001.

— "Az egzisztenciálfilozófiák halálfelfogása (Søren Kierkegaard)" [Conceptions of Death in Existential Philosophies (Søren Kierkegaard)], in his *Filozófiai metszetek a halálról. A halál metamorfózisai a 19–20. századi élet- és egzisztenciálfilozófiákban* [Philosophical Sketches about Death: Metamorphoses of Death in the Philosophies of Life and Existence in the 19th–20th Centuries], Gödöllő: Attraktor 2002, pp. 147–92.

— "A hit lovagja spanyol földön. Kierkegaard-Unamuno párhuzamok" [The Knight of Faith on Spanish Land: Kierkegaard and Unamuno], *Magyar Filozófiai Szemle*, nos. 1–2, 2003, pp. 81–99.

Cseri, Kinga, "A szorongás fogalmának jelentősége és az igazság megragadásának lehetősége Kierkegaard és Heidegger filozófiájában" [The Significance of the Concept Anxiety and the Possibility of Grasping the Truth in the Philosophies of Kierkegaard and Heidegger], *Publicationes Universitatis Miskolciensis*, no. 1, 2002, pp. 27–32.

— "Kierkegaard-i stádiumok hermeneutikai elemzése" [Hermeneutical Analysis of Kierkegaard's Stages], in *Az erkölcs szépsége: a kaposvári Erkölcs-, Művészetfilozófiai és Nevelési Konferencia előadásai, 2003. augusztus 27–29* [The Beauty of Ethics: Proceedings of the Conference on Ethics, Philosophy, Aesthetics and Education, Kaposvár, August 27–29, 2003], ed. by József Czirják et al., Kaposvár: Kaposvári Egyetem Csokonai Vitéz Mihály Pedagógiai Kar 2005, pp. 93–103.

Csige, Ilona, "A szabadság dilemmái Kierkegaard *Vagy-vagy* című művében" [The Dilemmas of Freedom in Kierkegaard's *Either/Or*], *Stúdium*, no. 14, 1983, pp. 77–100.

Darida, Veronika, "Kierkegaard, a rejtőzködő" [The Hidden Kierkegaard], in her *Filozófiai vallomások. Szent Ágostontól Derridáig* [Philosophical Confessions: From St. Augustine to Derrida], Budapest: Kijárat 2011, pp. 107–27.

Dévény, István, "A költő és a filozófus. Pilinszky és Kierkegaard" [The Poet and the Philosopher: Pilinszky and Kierkegaard], *Jelenkor*, no. 9, 1994, pp. 788–96; no. 4, 1995, pp. 345–55.

— *Sören Kierkegaard*, Máriabesenyő-Gödöllő: Attraktor 2003.

Erős, Vilmos, "Hegel és Kierkegaard között: Denis de Rougemont és a történelem" [Between Hegel and Kierkegaard: Denis de Rougemont and History], *Világosság*, no. 5, 2008, pp. 81–8.

Farkas, Szilárd, "Søren Kierkegaard és Lukács György szerelemfelfogásának kapcsolódási pontjai" [Connections between Søren Kierkegaard's and Georg Lukács' Conceptions of Love], *Fordulat*, no. 10, 2010, pp. 21–131.

— "Søren Kierkegaard helye a 19. századi európai irodalomban" [The Place of Søren Kierkegaard in the European Literature of the 19th Century], in *IX. Országos Interdiszciplináris Grastyán Konferencia Kötet* [Proceedings of the 9th National Interdisciplinary Grastyán Conference], ed. by Melinda Szappanyos, Pécs: PTE—Grastyán Endre Szakkollégium 2011, pp. 91–2.

— "Kierkegaard, a látnok" [Kierkegaard, the Visionary], in *XIV. Apáczai-Napok Nemzetközi Tudományos Konferencia. Tanulmánykötet* [Proceedings of the XIVth International Apáczai-Days Conference], ed. by Ildikó Lőrincz, Győr: Nyugat-magyarországi Egyetem Kiadó 2011, pp. 578–83 (online publication).

— "Határhelyzetben – Tavaszy Sándor Kierkegaard-képe" [In a Borderline Situation: Sándor Tavaszy's Picture of Kierkegaard], *Létünk*, no. 1, 2013, pp. 16–37.

— "Válságból válságba – kierkegaard-i lábnyomok Hamvas Béla életművében" [From Crisis to Crisis: Kierkegaardian Traces in the Works of Béla Hamvas], *Létünk*, no. 1, 2014, pp. 40–67.

Gáspár, Csaba László, "Vallás, filozófia, technika. Kierkegaard olvasása közben" [Religion, Philosophy, Technology: While Reading Kierkegaard], *Budapesti Könyvszemle*, no. 3, 1999, pp. 296–302.

Gerlóczi, Ferenc, "A szorongás költője. Az új Kierkegaard-divat" [The Poet of Anxiety: The New Kierkegaard Fashion], *Heti Világgazdaság*, no. 20, 1998, pp. 83–4.

Gintly, Tibor, "Ady és Kierkegaard" [Ady and Kierkegaard], *Iskolakultúra*, no. 9, 1998, pp. 37–47.

Gulyás, Gábor, "Kierkegaard poszt. (Søren Kierkegaard: *Az ismétlés*) [Kierkegaard Post. (Søren Kierkegaard: *Repetition*)]," *Műhely*, no. 1, 1995, pp. 58–9.

— "Kierkegaard teste" [Kierkegaard's Body], *Gond*, nos. 18–19, 1999, pp. 199–232.

— "Kísértetek testedzése. Haláltánc" [Ghosts' Exercise: Dance of Death], *Vulgo*, nos. 3–5, 2000, pp. 212–18.

Gyenge, Zoltán, "Megjegyzések a *Félelem és reszketés* magyar kiadásához" [Some Remarks on the Hungarian Edition of *Fear and Trembling*], *Filozófiai Figyelő*, no. 3, 1988, pp. 152–7.

— "A megértett idő" [Comprehended Time], *Existentia*, nos. 1–4, 1992, pp. 417–33.

— "Előszó a *Filozófiai töredékek*hez és *A halálos betegség*hez" [Preface to *Philosophical Fragments* and *The Sickness unto Death*], in *Ész, élet, egzisztencia* [*Reason, Life, Existence*], ed. by Dezső Csejtei, András Dékány, Ferenc Simon, and Sándor Laczkó, Szeged: Szegedi Tudományegyetem 1992, pp. 74–5.

— "Hit és egzisztencia. Gondolatok a kierkegaard-i egzisztencia-fogalom kapcsán" [Faith and Existence: On Kierkegaard's Concept of Existence], *Gond*, no. 4, 1993, pp. 12–20.

— "Az örökké élő egzisztencia" [The Forever Existing Existence], *Eszterházy Károly Tanárképző Főiskola tudományos közleményei. Tanulmányok a filozófia köréből* [Scientific Proceedings of Eszterházy Károly College: Studies in Philosophy], vol. 22, 1995, pp. 47–80.

— "Hegel és Kierkegaard" [Hegel and Kierkegaard], in *Majdnem nem lehet másként. Tanulmányok Vajda Mihály 60. születésnapjára* [It Almost Cannot Be Otherwise: Studies on Occasion of Mihály Vajda's 60th Birthday], ed. by Ferenc Fehér, András Kardos, and Sándor Radnóti, Budapest: Cserépfalvi 1995, pp. 190–8.

— *Kierkegaard és a német idealizmus* [Kierkegaard and German Idealism], Szeged: Ictus 1996. (Review: Gulyás, Gábor, "A filozófia ritka pillanatai" [The Rare Moments of Philosophy], *Vulgo*, vol. 3, no. 1, 2002, pp. 245–52.)

— "Az irónia fogalma" [The Concept of Irony], *Gond*, no. 17, 1998, pp. 202–12.

— "A legszerencsésebbről – lelkesült peroráció egy felvonásban" [The Happiest One: Enthusiastic Peroration in One Act], *Pro Philosophia Füzetek*, nos. 17–18, 1999, pp. 217–21.

— "Az egzisztencia golgotája" [The Golgotha of Existence], in *Diotima. Heller Ágnes 70. születésnapjára* [Diotima: On Occasion of Ágnes Heller's 70th Birthday], ed. by András Kardos et al., Budapest: Osiris-Gond 1999, pp. 186–91.

— "Az inkognitó" [The Incognito], *Gond*, nos. 18–19, 1999, pp. 13–19.

— "A személytelen személyesség. A hegeli rendszerfilozófia hatása Kierkegaard filozófiájára" [The Impersonal Personality: The Influence of Hegel's Systematic Philosophy on Kierkegaard's Philosophy], *Pro Philosophia Füzetek*, no. 23, 2000, pp. 31–6.

— *Az egzisztencia évszázada* [The Century of Existence], Veszprém: Veszprémi HTA 2001. (Reviews: Czakó, István, "Élet és elmélet az egzisztencia évszázadában" [Life and Theory in the Century of Existence], *Pro Philosophia Füzetek*, no. 32, 2003, pp. 131–6; Vető, Miklós, "Le siècle de l'existentialisme," *Revue Philosophique de Louvain*, vol. 100, no. 4, 2002, pp. 830–1; Weiss, János, review in *Élet és irodalom*, vol. 45, no. 32, 2001, p. 29.)

— "Filozófia és valóság" [Philosophy and Reality], in *"Párbeszédben a világ sorsával." Filozófia a globalizáció világában* ["In Dialogue with the Fate of the World": Philosophy in the Age of Globalization], ed. by János Loboczky, Eger: Eszterházi Károly Főiskola – Líceum 2001, pp. 81–8.

— "Az egzisztencia valósága. Kierkegaard létanalízise" [The Reality of Existence: Kierkegaard's Analysis of Being], *Magyar Filozófiai Szemle*, nos. 1–2, 2003, pp. 201–16.

— "A beszéd művészete – avagy Zarathusztra és Constantin Constantius vitája" [The Art of Speech, Or the Debate between Zarathustra and Constantin Constantius], *Világosság*, nos. 11–12, 2003, pp. 259–66.

— "Az ironikus és elbeszélő érvelés – különös tekintettel Kierkegaard Szókratész-értelmezésére" [Ironic and Narrative Argumentation: With a Special Reference to Kierkegaard's Interpretation of Socrates], *Világosság*, nos. 5–6, 2003, pp. 237–44.

— "Bevezetés a vulgológiába" [Introduction to Vulgology], *Pro Philosophia Füzetek*, no. 34, 2003, pp. 147–52.

— "A bűn heteronómiája – Richard, Agamemnón vagy Ábrahám" [Heteronomy of Sin: Richard, Agamemnon or Abraham], in *Lábjegyzetek Platónhoz. A bűn* [Footnotes to Plato, vols. 2–3: Sin], ed. by András Dékány and Sándor Laczkó, Szeged and Kecskemét: Pro Philosophia Szegediensi Alapítvány and Librarius 2004, pp. 50–9.

— "A közvetett és a közvetlen közlés. Kierkegaard és a nyelv" [Direct and Indirect Communication: Kierkegaard and Language], in *Minden filozófia "nyelvkritika"* [Every Philosophy is "Critique of Language"], vols. 1–2, ed. by Katalin Neumer, vol. 1, *Nyelvfilozófia Locke-tól Kierkegaard-ig* [Philosophy of Language from Locke to Kierkegaard], Budapest: Gondolat 2004, pp. 157–73.

— "Kereszténység és nihilizmus: Kierkegaard és Nietzsche valláskritikája" [Christianity and Nihilism: Kierkegaard's and Nietzsche's Critique of Religion], *Acta Academiae Paedagogicae Agriensis Sectio Philosophica*, no. 32, 2005, pp. 99–110.

— "Lukács Kierkegaard-felfogása a *Lélek és formák*ban és *Az ész trónfosztásá*ban" [Lukács' View of Kierkegaard in his *Soul and Forms* and *The Destruction of Reason*], in *Ész, trónfosztás, demokrácia. Tanulmányok Lukács György Az ész trónfosztása c. művéről* [Reason, Destruction, Democracy: Studies on György Lukács' *The Destruction of Reason*], ed. by János Boros, Pécs: Brambauer 2005, pp. 33–47.

— "Az osztrák és a magyar századelő kapcsolata a Kierkegaard-recepció szempontjából" [The Connection between the Austrian and the Hungarian Reception of Kierkegaard in the Early Twentieth Century], *Világosság*, no. 5, 2006, pp. 95–102.

— *Zarathusztra és Viktor Eremita. Esszék és tanulmányok* [Zarathustra and Victor Eremita: Essays and Studies], Veszprém: Veszprémi Humán Tudományokért Alapítvány 2006.

— *Kierkegaard élete és filozófiája. A Kierkegaard-könyvtár teljes katalógusával* [Kierkegaard's Life and Philosophy: Along with the Whole Catalogue of Kierkegaard's Library], Máriabesnyő-Gödöllő: Attraktor 2007. (Reviews: Csejtei, Dezső, "Habemus Kierkegaard," *Élet és irodalom*, vol. 51, no. 43, 2007, p. 26; Izsó, Tímea, "Életbe zárt filozófia" [Philosophy Enclosed in Life], *Különbség*, vol. 10, no. 1, 2010, pp. 157–9.)

— "A hit lovagja, avagy a vallási egzisztencia" [The Knight of Faith, or the Religious Existence], in *Pro Philosophia Évkönyv – 2009* [Pro Philosophia Yearbook – 2009], ed. by Imre Garaczi and Zoltán Kalmár, Veszprém: Veszprémi Humán Tudományokért Alapítvány 2009, pp. 7–21.

— "A közlés formái és lehetőségei Nietzsche és Kierkegaard filozófiájában" [Forms and Possibilities of Communication in the Philosophies of Nietzsche and Kierkegaard], in *Idealizmus és hermeneutika* [Idealism and Hermeneutics], ed.

by Csaba Olay, Budapest: L'Harmattan 2010, pp. 48–59. (Review: Sár, Eszter, "Idealizmus és hermeneutika" [Idealism and Hermeneutics], *Magyar Filozófiai Szemle*, vol. 56, no. 1, pp. 177–9.)

— "Kierkegaard magiszter és Nietzsche professzor esete az egyetemmel" [The University Affairs of Magister Kierkegaard and Professor Nietzsche], in *Az egyetem eszméje az európai filozófiai tradícióban* [The Idea of the University in the European Philosophical Tradition], ed. by János Loboczky, Eger: Eszterházy Károly Főiskola – Líceum 2011, pp. 85–92.

— "Lukács és az 'irracionalista' Kierkegaard" [Lukács and the "Irrationalist" Kierkegaard], in *Közlemények* [Publications], ed. by Gábor Boros, Csaba Olay, and Reitz Timan, Budapest: Német-Magyar Filozófiai Társaság 2012, pp. 119–33.

— [Pszeudo Kierkegaard], *A megfordult világ. Ismeretlen Kierkegaard-kézirat. Közreadja Gyenge Zoltán* [The Inverted World: An Unknown Manuscript of Kierkegaard. Submitted by Zoltán Gyenge], Bratislava: Kalligram 2012. (Reviews: Antal, Éva, "Ismétlődések könyve" [The Book of Repetitions], *Élet és irodalom*, vol. 56, no. 38, 2012, p. 20; Bartha, Judit, "Nyomozás egy kézirat ürügyén" [Investigation Apropos a Manuscript], *Holmi*, vol. 25, no. 1, 2013, pp. 128–31; Kovács, Attila, "Egy érett filozófus vajon milyen könyvet ír?" [What Kind of Book Does a Mature Philosopher Write?], *Hapax*, October 6, 2012 (online journal); Szabó, István Zoltán, "Egy (ki)talált kézirat" [A Found/ Invented Manuscript], *Tiszatajonline.hu*, January 17, 2013 (online journal); Takács, Viktória, "Templomkert vagy Kierkegaard" [Churchyard or Kierkegaard], *Kultúra és Kritika*, May 24, 2013 (online journal); Vajda, Mihály, review in *Kalligram*, vol. 12, no. 5, 2013, pp. 90–1.)

— "Két szerelem margójára: Lukács – Seidler versus Kierkegaard – Regine" [On the Margin of Two Loves: Lukács – Seidler versus Kierkegaard – Regine], in *Lábjegyzetek Platónhoz 11: A szerelem* [Footnotes to Plato, vol. 11: Love], ed. by Sándor Laczkó, Szeged: Pro Philosophia Szegediensi Alapítvány – Magyar Filozófiai Társaság 2013, pp. 189–96.

— "Kierkegaard-t olvasva – 1813–2013" [While Reading Kierkegaard: 1813–2013], *Magyar Tudomány*, no. 6, 2013, pp. 719–26.

— "Jelenkorunk kritikája. Esszé egy esszéhez" [Criticism of Our Present Age: An Essay to an Essay], in *A jelenkor kritikája* [Criticism of Our Present Age], ed. by Zoltán Gyenge, Budapest: L'Harmattan 2015, pp. 59–88.

— (ed.) *Søren Kierkegaard 1813–2013*, Budapest: L'Harmattan 2014. (Zoltán Gyenge, "Bevezető gondolatok" [Introductory Reflections], pp. 9–10; Zoltán Gyenge, "Személybe zárt élet – egy bio-gráfia" [A Life Enclosed in a Person: A Bio-graphy], pp. 11–23; Ágnes Heller, "Emlékezés és ismétlés Constantin Constantius gondolkodásában" [Recollection and Repetition in the Thinking of Constantin Constantius], pp. 27–32; Ottó Hévizi, "Kierkegaard definiálhatatlan etikája" [Kierkegaard's Undefinable Ethics], pp. 33–44; Éva Kocziszky, "Agnete és a tritón. A szerelem és a hit paradoxonja a *Félelem és reszketés*ben" [Agnete and the Triton: The Paradox of Love and Faith in *Fear and Trembling*], pp. 45–54; Zoltán Gyenge, "Nyomozás egy halál ügyében" [Investigation into a Death Case], pp. 57–66; István Szalay, "Søren Kierkegaard halála orvosi szempontból. Appendix a nyomozáshoz"

[Søren Kierkegaard's Death from a Medical Point of View: Appendix to the Investigation], pp. 67–70; Judit Bartha, "A kétségbeesés humoristája. Gondolatok a kierkegaard-i nevetésről" [The Humorist of Despair: Thoughts on the Kierkegaardian Laughter], pp. 73–80; Anita Soós, "Előszót írni, óh! Paratextusból szöveg" [Writing a Preface, oh! Text from a Paratext], pp. 81–7; János Weiss, "A házasság etikai és esztétikai érvénye" [The Ethical and Aesthetic Validity of Marriage], pp. 88–100; Krisztina Soóky, "A kierkegaard-i esztétika körvonalai" [Outlines of Kierkegaard's Aesthetics], pp. 101–10; Ákos Szilágyi, "A szerző feltámasztása. Kórus és incognito: Bahtyin és Kierkegaard" [Resurrecting the Author. Choir and Incognito: Bakhtin and Kierkegaard], pp. 113–47; András Czeglédi, "Kierkegaard és Nietzsche: ukronikus találkozások" [Kierkegaard and Nietzsche: Uchronic Encounters], pp. 148–57; Sándor Bazsányi, "A viszonylagosság poétikái: Kierkegaard és Esti Kornél" [Poetics of Relativeness: Kierkegaard and Esti Kornél], pp. 158–65; Gábor Balázs, "A judaizált Kierkegaard, avagy dán kultúrhérosz az izraeli filozófiában" [The Judaized Kierkegaard or a Danish Cultural Hero in the Israeli Philosophy], pp. 166–83; István Czakó, "*Sacrificium intellectus*: Hit és ész viszonya Kierkegaard gondolkodásában" [*Sacrificium intellectus*: Faith and Reason in Kierkegaard's Thinking], pp. 187–211; Tibor Sutyák, "Kierkegaard és a paradoxon" [Kierkegaard and the Paradox], pp. 212–20; Tamás Hankovszky, "'Ugyanazt mondjuk.' Kierkegaard és Szókratész" ["We Say the Same Things": Kierkegaard and Socrates], pp. 221–9; Éva Antal, "Sub specie ironiae", pp. 230–41; Judit Bartha, "Søren Kierkegaard. Magyar nyelvű bibliográfia" [Søren Kierkegaard: Hungarian Bibliography], pp. 243–60; Zoltán Gyenge, "Kierkegaard könyvtárának teljes katalógusa" [The Complete Catalogue of Kierkegaard's Library], pp. 261–322.) (Review: Valastyán, Tamás, "In hoc tempore," *Élet és irodalom*, vol. 58, no. 35, 2014, p. 35.)

Hamvas, Béla, "Kierkegaard Szicíliában" [Kierkegaard in Sicily], in *Esszépanoráma* [Essay Panorama], vols. 1–3, ed. by Zoltán Kenyeres, Budapest: Szépirodalmi 1978, vol. 3, pp. 92–104.

Harkai Vass, Éva, "Tolsztoj és Kierkegaard Berlinben" [Tolstoy and Kierkegaard in Berlin], in her *Tolsztoj és Kierkegaard Berlinben. Bírálatok, szövegértelmezések* [Tolstoy and Kierkegaard in Berlin: Reviews and Textual Analyses], Novi Sad: Forum 2007, pp. 121–6.

Hegyi, Gyula, "Ikonosztáz. Kierkegaard szobránál" [Iconostas: By the Statue of Kierkegaard], *Mozgó Világ*, no. 10, 1985, p. 73.

Heller, Ágnes, "A kierkegaardi esztétika és a zene" [Kierkegaard's Aesthetics and Music], *Magyar Filozófiai Szemle*, vol. 9, no. 1, 1965, pp. 48–74.

— "Kierkegaard és a modern zene" [Kierkegaard and Modern Music], in her *Érték és történelem* [Value and History], Budapest: Magvető 1969, pp. 321–65.

— "A szerencsétlen tudat fenomenológiája" [The Phenomenology of the Unhappy Consciousness], *Magyar Filozófiai Szemle*, nos. 3–4, 1971, pp. 364–94 (reprinted in Søren Kierkegaard, *Vagy-vagy* [*Either/Or*], trans. by Tivadar Dani, Budapest: Gondolat 1978, pp. 1017–79 (2nd ed. Budapest: Osiris–Századvég 1994, pp. 623–58).

— *Személyiségetika* [An Ethics of Personality], Budapest: Osiris 1999.

Hermann, István, "Szorongás és tragikum. Sören Kierkegaard tragikumelmélete" [Anxiety and Tragedy: Søren Kierkegaard's Theory of Tragedy], *Világosság*, no. 5, 1972, pp. 293–8.

Hidas, Zoltán, "Az egyes és az őhozzá intézett kérdés. Kierkegaard és Buber" [The Single Individual and the Question You Want to Ask this Person: Kierkegaard and Buber], *Pannonhalmi Szemle*, no. 3, 1996, pp. 41–7.

Hodják, Gergely, "Vallás és költészet a XIX. század derekán. Madách és Kierkegaard" [Religion and Poetry in the Middle of the Nineteenth Century: Madách and Kierkegaard], in *"Vidimus enim stellam eius..." Konferenciakötet* ["Vidimus enim stellam eius..." Conference Papers], ed. by László Szávay, Budapest: Károli Gáspár Református Egyetem – L'Harmattan 2011, pp. 176–182.

Horváth, Orsolya, "Kierkegaard egyházkritikája" [Kierkegaard's Criticism of the Church], *Sola Scriptura*, nos. 3–4, 2000, pp. 42–5.

Horváth, Lajos and Katalin Balázs, "Szorongás és énhasadás. A kierkegaard-i bűn és szorongás modern lélektani interpretációi" [Anxiety and the Splitting of the Ego: Modern Psychological Interpretations of Kierkegaard's Concepts of Sin and Anxiety], *Magyar Filozófiai Szemle*, vol. 57, no. 3, pp. 106–26.

Imre, László, "Kierkegaard és az orosz szimbolizmus" [Kierkegaard and Russian Symbolism], *Studium*, vol. 2, 1971, pp. 117–21.

Joób, Máté, "'Az egyház mint Lucifer.' Kierkegaard egyházkritikájának teológiai alapjai *A halálos betegség* és *A keresztény hit iskolája* című művének tükrében" ["The Church as Lucifer": The Theological Foundations of Kierkegaard's Criticism of the Church in the Light of *The Sickness unto Death* and *Practice in Christianity*], *Lelkipásztor*, no. 2, 2000, pp. 51–6.

Joós, Ernő, *Isten és lét: körséta Heidegger, Kierkegaard, Nietzsche és más filozófusok társaságában* [God and Existence: Walking about with Heidegger, Kierkegaard, Nietzsche and Other Philosophers], Sárvár: Sylvester János Könyvtár 1994.

Kardos, András, "A metafizika tragédiája, avagy miért nem írt drámát Sören Kierkegaard?" [The Tragedy of Metaphysics, Or Why Kierkegaard Did not Write a Tragedy], *Gond*, no. 4, 1993, pp. 26–32.

Kardos Daróczi, Gábor, "Az önmagát értelmező mű mint az interpretáció kierkegaard-i alternatívája" [The Self-Interpreting Work as a Kierkegaardian Alternative to Interpretation], *Holmi*, no. 1, 1994, pp. 89–105.

Kállay, Géza, "'Vén ember mit cselekszel?' – a 'halálos betegség' szorongató öröme: Scrooge, Lear és Kierkegaard" ["What Wilt Thou Do, Old Man?"—The Anxious Happiness of "The Sickness unto Death": Scrooge, Lear and Kierkegaard], *Liget*, no. 3, 2010, pp. 37–54.

— "'Ó, természetnek roncsolt mesterműve': Kierkegaard és Lear király" ["O Ruined Piece of Nature!": Kierkegaard and King Lear], *Liget*, no. 8, 2013, pp. 39–57.

Kárpáti, Gábor, "Az irónia fogalmáról állandó tekintettel Kierkegaard-ra" [On the Concept of Irony with Continual Reference to Kierkegaard], *Pro Philosophia Füzetek*, no. 39, 2004, pp. 95–114.

Király, Béla, "A tény korrelatívumai a kierkegaard-i szubjektivizmus szemszögéből" [The Correlatives of Fact from the Point of View of Kierkegaardian Subjectivism], *Korunk*, no. 2, pp. 127–8.

Kisbali, László, "Kierkegaard *Filozófiai morzsák* című könyvéről" [On Kierkegaard's *Philosophical Fragments*], in his *Sapere aude! Esztétikai és művelődéstörténeti írások* [Sapere aude! Writings in Aesthetics and the History of Culture], ed. by Endre Szécsényi, Budapest: L'Harmattan 2009, pp. 53–9.

Kiss, Pál, "Az idő, örökkévalóság és történelem problémája Kierkegaard és Barth alapján" [The Problems of Time, Eternity and History in Kierkegaard and Barth], *Sárospataki Füzetek*, no. 1, 1997, pp. 60–6.

Kocziszky, Éva, "Don Juan. Vázlat az érzéki csábításról" [Don Juan: A Sketch of the Sensuous Seduction], *Világosság*, no. 1, 1989, pp. 34–42.

— "Mit tanulhatunk a madaraktól és a liliomoktól?" [What Can We Learn from the Birds and the Lilies?], *Gond*, no. 4, 1993, pp. 37–51.

— "Mi a halálos betegség? 200 éve született Søren Kierkegaard (1813–1855)" [What is the Sickness unto Death? The 200th Anniversary of Søren Kierkegaard's Birth (1813–1855)], *Sola Scriptura*, no. 3, 2013, pp. 2–5.

Koncz, Sándor, *Kierkegaard és a világháború utáni teológia* [Kierkegaard and Post-War Theology], Miskolc: Fekete P. 1938. (Reviews: Püsök, Sarolta, "Kierkegaard-hatások a 20. századi teológiában" [The Strands of Reception of Kierkegaard in the Theology of the 20th Century], *Református Szemle*, no. 5, 2003, pp. 494–507; Trombitás, Dezső, review in *Theologiai Szemle*, no. 1, 1942, pp. 49–50.)

Köpeczi, Béla (ed.), *Az egzisztencializmus* [Existentialism], Budapest: Gondolat 1965, pp. 59–60 (2nd ed. 1966).

Lázár, Ervin Járkáló, "150 éve halt meg a dán filozófus, teológus, író Søren Kierkegaard" [The Danish Philosopher, Theologian and Writer Søren Kierkegaard Died 150 Years Ago], *Magyar Liget*, no. 4, 2005, pp. 10–11.

Lőrinczné Thiel, Katalin, "A kierkegaard-i hatás néhány vonatkozása Hamvas Bélánál" [Some Aspects of Kierkegaard's Influence on Béla Hamvas], *Eszterházy Károly Tanárképző Főiskola Tudományos Közleménye. Tanulmányok a társadalomelmélet köréből* [Scientific Proceedings of Eszterházy Károly College: Studies in Social Theory], vol. 20, 1991, pp. 31–8.

— "A hit problematikája egy egzisztencia-filozófiai megközelítésben" [The Problem of Faith from the Perspective of the Philosophy of Existence], *Jelen-lét*, no. 2, 1993, pp. 12–17.

— *Maszkjáték. Hamvas Béla Kierkegaard és Nietzsche tükrében* [Playing with Masks: Béla Hamvas in the Light of Kierkegaard and Nietzsche], Veszprém: Veszprémi Humán Tudományokért Alapítvány 2002. (Review: Novák, Zoltán, "Hamvas a fősodorban" [Hamvas in the Mainstream], *Vulgo*, no. 2, 2003, pp. 179–85.)

Lukács, György, "Forma az élet zátonyán. Søren Kierkegaard és Regine Olsen" [The Foundering of Form against Life: Søren Kierkegaard and Regine Olsen], in his *A lélek és a formák. Kísérletek* [Soul and Forms: Experiments], Budapest: Franklin 1910, pp. 129–150.

— *Az ész trónfosztása. Az irracionalista filozófia kritikája* [The Destruction of Reason: A Criticism of Irrationalist Philosophy], Budapest: Magvető 1954, pp. 227–78.

Magyar Filozófiai Szemle, vol. 47, nos. 1–2, 2003. (Béla Bacsó, "A 'Kierkegaard gondolkodásának válaszútjai' című konferencia nyitóbeszéde" [Opening Words to the Conference "Crossroads of Kierkegaard's Thinking"], pp. 1–4; Ágnes Heller, "Két epizód Shakespeare és Kierkegaard szellemi kapcsolatából" [Two Episodes from the Hegel/Kierkegaard Relationship], pp. 5–18; George Pattison, "A szeretet ábrázolása: a költészettől a vértanúságig" [Representing Love: From Poetry to Martyrdom], pp. 19–35; Joakim Garff, "Az írástudó. Az esztétikus Kierkegaard" [A Man of Letters: The Aesthetic Kierkegaard], pp. 37–52; Begonya Saez Tajafuerce, "Kierkegaard önéletrajza. Az 'én' irodalmi reflexiójáról" [Kierkegaard's Autobiography: On the Literary Reflection of the Self], pp. 53–69; Dario González, "Az 'esztétikai' mint a gondolkodás konstruktív dimenziója" [The Aesthetic as the Constructive Dimension of Thinking], pp. 69–80; Dezső Csejtei, "A Hit Lovagja spanyol földön. Kierkegaard – Unamuno párhuzamok" [The Knight of Faith in Spain: Kierkegaard and Unamuno], pp. 81–99; Gordon Marino, "Láthatóvá tenni a sötétséget: A kétségbeesés és a depresszió különbsége Kierkegaard *Naplói*ban" [Making the Darkness Visible: On the Distinction between Despair and Depression in Kierkegaard's *Journals*], 101–12; Richard Purkarthofer, "Megjegyzések az indirekt közléssel kapcsolatosan Søren Kierkegaard írásaiban" [On the Indirect Communication in Søren Kierkegaard's Work], pp. 113–24; Anita Soós, "Narráció – csábítás – értelmezés. Søren Kierkegaard *A csábító naplója, Az ismétlés* és a *Bűnös?—Nem bűnös?* című műveinek egybevetése" [Narration – Seduction – Interpretation: A Comparison between *The Seducer's Diary, Repetition* and *Guilty? Not Guilty?*], pp. 125–36; K. Brian Söderquist, "Az esztétika és az örök *Az irónia fogalmá*ban" [Aesthetics and the Eternal in *The Concept of Irony*], pp. 137–46; Tibor Pintér, "Kierkegaard és Mozart Don Giovannija: Egy mítosz mítosza" [Kierkegaard's Relation to Mozart's *Don Giovanni*: The Myth of a Myth], pp. 147–52; Gábor Kardos, "Ki lehet gondolkodó?" [Who Can be a Thinker?], pp. 153–72; Béla Bacsó, "A szorongás mint egzisztens kategória" [Anxiety as an Existence Category], pp. 173–84; Pia Søltoft, "Etika Sartre-nál és Kierkegaard-nál" [Ethics in Sartre and Kierkegaard], pp. 185–200; Zoltán Gyenge, "Az egzisztencia valósága" [The Reality of Existence], pp. 201–16; Jon Stewart, "Hegel, Kierkegaard és a közvetítés a *Filozófiai morzsák*ban" [Hegel, Kierkegaard and Mediation in the *Philosophical Fragments*], pp. 217–32). Two additional articles were published later in *Magyar Filozófiai Szemle*, vol. 47, no. 3, 2003 (István Czakó, "Hit és történelem viszonya Kierkegaard és Karl Jaspers gondolkodásában" [Kierkegaard and Jaspers on Faith and History], pp. 359–71) and in *Magyar Filozófiai Szemle*, vol. 48, no. 1–2, 2004 (András Nagy, "Kierkegaard és az esztétika angyala" [Kierkegaard and the Angel of Aesthetics], pp. 9–25).

Matkó, László, "Örökkévalóság pillanata. Sören Kierkegaard hatása Erdélyben és Magyarországon" [The Moment of Eternity: Søren Kierkegaard's Influence in Transylvania and Hungary], *M. híd,* no. 2, 1991, p. 19; no. 3, 1991, pp. 10–11.

Márkus, György and Zádor Tordai, *Irányzatok a mai polgári filozófiában* [Trends in Contemporary Bourgeois Philosophy], Budapest: Gondolat 1964, pp. 31–45.

Mátrai, László, *Haladás és fejlődés. Filozófiai tanulmányok* [Progress and Development: Philosophical Studies], Budapest: Irodalmi és művészeti Intézet 1947, pp. 47–51.

Mesterházy, Balázs, "A szétcsúszás alakzatai két 19. századi szövegben" [The Formations of the Sliding Apart in Two Texts from the Nineteenth Century], *Literatúra*, no. 3, 1998, pp. 241–63.

Mezei, Balázs, "A filozófia átalakulása. Töprengések Kierkegaard és Jaspers kapcsán" [The Transformation of Philosophy: Reflections on Kierkegaard and Jaspers], *Vigilia*, no. 7, 2013, pp. 491–500.

Miszoglád, Gábor, "Rendszer – refrén – aforizmák. A diapszalmata szerepe Kierkegaard műveiben" [System – Refrain – Aphorism: The Role of the Diapsalmata in Kierkegaard's Works], *Pannonhalmi Szemle*, no. 3, 1996, pp. 63–7.

Nagy, András, "A csábító naplója. Kierkegaard Budapesten" [The Seducer's Diary: Kierkegaard in Budapest], *168 óra*, no. 49, 1992, pp. 24–5.

— *Főbenjárás. Kierkegaard, Mahler, Lukács. Esszék* [Parapethetics: Kierkegaard, Mahler, Lukács. Essays], Budapest: Fekete Sas 1998, pp. 11–151. (Reviews: Havasréti, József, "Séták – metafizikából morálba, morálból politikába" [Walks: From Metaphysics to Moral, From Moral to Politics], *Jelenkor*, vol. 42, no. 9, 1999, p. 954; Zsoldos, Sándor, review in *Könyvhét*, August 12, 1999, p. 16.)

— *Kis angyaltan. Kísérlet a leíró angelológiában* [Little Angel-Encyclopaedia: An Attempt at Descriptive Angelology], Budapest: Liget 2003, pp. 201–77.

— "Vagy Hegel – vagy dialektika. J.L. Heiberg, a dán aranykor különös színházi embere" [Either Hegel – Or Dialectics: J.L. Heiberg, a Strange Man of Theater in the Danish Golden Age], *Holmi*, no. 5, 2009, pp. 638–63.

— "'Egy élmény története.' Lukács újraolvassa Kierkegaard-t" [History of an Experience: Lukács Re-reads Kierkegaard], in *"A feledés árja alól új földeket hódítok vissza." Írások Tímár Árpád tiszteletére* ["I Reconquer New Lands from the Torrent of Forgetting": Papers in Honor of Árpád Tímár], ed. by István Bardoly, László Jurecskó, and György Sümegi, Budapest: MTA Művészettörténeti Kutatóintézet – Mission Art Galéria 2009, pp. 81–95.

— "A magyar Kierkegaard" [The Hungarian Kierkegaard], *Jelenkor*, no. 10, 2010, pp. 1102–1121.

— *Az árnyjátékos. Søren Kierkegaard. Irodalomtörténet, eszmetörténet és hatástörténet metszéspontján* [The Shadowplayer: Søren Kierkegaard: At the Cross-roads of History of Literature, History of Ideas and History of Reception], Budapest: L'Harmattan 2011. (Reviews: Farkas, Szilárd, "Fényt ide!" [Light Here!], *Pannon Tükör*, April, 2012, pp. 57–60; Gyenge, Zoltán, "Amikor az árnyjátékos a fénybe lép" [When the Shadowplayer Moves into the Light], *Holmi*, vol. 25, no. 1, 2013, pp. 125–8.)

— "Kierkegaard és Grundtvig" [Kierkegaard and Grundtvig], *Partium*, no. 4, 2011, pp. 80–7.

— "Megbízhatatlan számok. A matematikában való bizalomvesztés Kierkegaard kései naplóiban" [Unreliable Numbers: The Loss of Confidence in Mathematics in Kierkegaard's Late Journals], *2000*, no. 6, 2011, pp. 61–72.

— (ed.) *Kierkegaard Budapesten* [Kierkegaard in Budapest], Budapest: Fekete Sas 1994. (András Nagy, "Előszó" [Preface], pp. 7–17; György Vikár, "A Don Juan-tanulmány mint egy élettörténeti válság megoldási kísérlete" [The Don Juan Essay as an Attempt to Solve an Existential Crisis], pp. 21–32; Antal Bókay, "Az ismétlés: a lélek titkos törvénye" [Repetition as the Soul's

Secret Law], pp. 33–51; Niels Thomassen, "Kierkegaard a boldogságról" [Kierkegaard on Happiness], pp. 52–69; Ildikó Erdélyi, "A csábítás lélektana" [The Psychology of Seduction], pp. 69–84; Béla Bacsó, "Ismételhető-e az ismétlés?" [Can Repetition Be Repeated?], pp. 87–96; Sándor Radnóti, "Kierkegaard és Schlegel" [Kierkegaard and Schlegel], pp. 97–102; Poul Erik Tøjner, "Kierkegaard Hegel-kritikájának és politika-bírálatának aspektusai" [The Aspects of Kierkegaard's Criticism of Hegel and Politics], pp. 103–17; Konrad Liessmann, "Kierkegaard és Don Juan" [Kierkegaard and Don Juan], 118–26; Joakim Garff, "Kierkegaard – egy bio-gráfia" [Kierkegaard: A Biography], pp. 127–48; András Kardos, "A metafizika tragédiája, avagy miért nem írt drámát Sören Kierkegaard?" [The Tragedy of Metaphysics, Or Why Did Kierkegaard not Write a Tragedy?], pp. 149–62; Alastair McKinnon, "Kierkegaard munkássága: az első nyolc dimenzió" [Kierkegaard's Authorship: the First Eight Dimensions], pp. 163–90; Gábor Kardos, "Az önmagát értelmező mű mint az interpretáció kierkegaard-i alternatívája" [The Self-Interpreting Work as a Kierkegaardian Alternative to Interpretation], pp. 191–223; Henri-Bernard Vergote, "A hit tüzetes vizsgálata" [A Thorough Inquiry of Faith], pp. 227–54; Julia Watkin, "Kierkegaard 'Én'-felfogásának relevanciája korunkban" [The Relevance of Kierkegaard's Conception of Self in Our Time], pp. 254–72; Gábor Iványi, "Menj el!" [Go Away!], pp. 273–5; László Donáth, " 'Hite által még holta után is beszél' " ["He Died, But Through His Faith He Still Speaks"], pp. 276–87; Helmuth Vetter, "A véges szellem ámene" [The Amen of the Finite Spirit], pp. 288–303; Ferenc Szűcs, "A XX. századi teológia kezdetei és Kierkegaard. Kierkegaard és Barth Károly" [The Beginning of Twentieth-Century Theology and Kierkegaard: Kierkegaard and Karl Barth], pp. 304–10; Gusztáv Bölcskey, "Kierkegaard egyház- és kereszténységkritikája" [Kierkegaard's Criticism of Church and Christianity], pp. 311–20; Kálmán Micskey, "Kierkegaard teológiájához" [On Kierkegaard's Theology], pp. 321–7; András Masát, "Kierkegaard Ibsen drámáiban" [Kierkegaard in Ibsen's Dramas], pp. 331–46; Endre Török, "Dosztojevszkij és Kierkegaard. 'Istennel szemben soha sincs igazunk' " [Dostoevsky and Kierkegaard: "In Relation to God We Are Always in the Wrong"], pp. 347–51; Péter Balassa, "Kierkegaard – Bergman – Pilinszky," pp. 352–61; Béla Németh G., "Kierkegaard utóhatása – vallásos újjászületés?" [Kierkegaard's Aftermath: A Religious Revival?], pp. 362–71; Mihály Vajda, "Kétségbeesés és gond. Késői kora-Heideggeriánus széljegyzetek Kierkegaard *Die Krankheit zum Tode* című könyvéhez" [Despair and Anxiety: Late Notes in the Spirit of the Early Heidegger to Kierkegaard's *The Sickness unto Death*], pp. 372–89; Svend Aage Madsen, "Hogyan (nem) tudjuk Kierkegaard hatását elkerülni?" [How Can We (not) Avoid Kierkegaard's Impact?], pp. 390–400; Jörgen Dehls, "Megjegyzések Søren Kierkegaard irodalomelméletéről" [Remarks on Søren Kierkegaard's Theory of Literature], pp. 401–18; George Pattison, "Kierkegaard és/vagy posztmodernizmus?" [Kierkegaard and/or Postmodernism?], pp. 419–42.)

Nagy, Péter Miklós, "Tett vagy tétlenség. Vallásfelfogás- és gyakorlat a XIX. századi vallásos irodalomban Kierkegaard és Bhaktivinóda művei alapján" [Action or Inaction: The Concept of Religion and Religious Practice in the Religious

Literature of Nineteenth Century as Reflected in the Works of Kierkegaard and Bhaktivinóda], *Tattwa*, no. 1, 2001, pp. 17–46.

Neumer, Katalin, "Nyelv és választás. Kierkegaard írásainak nyelv-és irodalomelméleti vonatkozásairól" [Language and Choice: Kierkegaard's Writings with Reference to the Theory of Literature and Language], *Magyar Filozófiai Szemle*, no. 3 1986, pp. 407–17.

— (ed.), *Nyelvfilozófia Locke-tól Kierkegaard-ig* [Philosophy of Language from Locke to Kierkegaard], Budapest: Gondolat 2004.

Noszlopi, László, "A modern társadalom embere Kierkegaard szemléletében" [The Man of Modern Society in Kierkegaard's Thinking], *Társadalomtudomány*, vol. 13, no. 1, 1933, pp. 89–93.

— "Kierkegaard a változó korszellem tükrében" [Kierkegaard in the Light of the Changing Spirit of the Age], *Magyar Kultúra*, vol. 1, 1932, pp. 445–9.

Pálfalusi, Zsolt, "A bolond és a bűn. Kierkegaard a komolyságról" [The Idiot and the Crime: Kierkegaard on Earnestness], *Gond*, nos. 8–9, 1994–95, pp. 55–84.

Pasqualetti, Zsófia, *A démon hallgatása. Gondolatok Kierkegaard rajzaihoz / The Demon's Silence: Some Ideas about Kierkegaard's Drawings*, Budapest: Fekete Sas 1993.

Pólik, József, "Kísérlet egy utazó portréjának rekonstrukciójára" [An Attempt at the Reconstruction of the Portrait of a Traveller], *Gond*, nos. 15–16, 1998, pp. 302–26.

— "Mission Impossible avagy egy 'besúgó' mártíriuma" [Mission Impossible or a "Whistleblower's" Martyrdom], *Vulgo*, nos. 3–5, 2000, pp. 508–16.

Popovics, Zoltán, "'Hemiplegia.' Maurice Blanchot Kierkegaard-ról és a szorongásról" ["Hemiplegia": Maurice Blanchot on Kierkegaard and Anxiety], *Pro Philosophia Füzetek*, no. 32, 2003, pp. 1–17.

Pro Philosophia Füzetek, no. 28, 2001. (Ágnes Heller, "A stádiumok között" [Between the Stages], pp. 1–14; Zoltán Gyenge, "A 19. század új mitológiája. A mese szerepe Søren Kierkegaard filozófiájában" [The New Mythology of the Nineteenth Century: The Role of the Fairy Tale in Kierkegaard's Philosophy], pp. 15–27; Gábor Miszoglád, "Milyen nyelven beszél hozzánk Kierkegaard?" [In Which Language Does Kierkegaard Talk to Us?], pp. 29–32; Tamás Valastyán, "Az inkognitó, a griff és a töredék. Az aforisztikus és metaforikus beszédmódokról és azok koraromantikus vonatkozásairól – Kierkegaard, Derrida, F. Schlegel" [Incognito, Apprehension and Fragment: The Aphoristic and the Metaphorical Ways of Speaking and their Connections to the Early Romanticism – Kierkegaard, Derrida, F. Schlegel], pp. 33–44; Anita Soós, "'Maszkodról ismerlek fel.' A kierkegaard-i irónia az álneves írásokban" ["I Recognize You from Your Mask": Kierkegaardian Irony in the Pseudonymous Writings], pp. 45–59; Judit Bartha, "Alteregó-centrumok polifóniája. Megjegyzések E.T.A. Hoffmann 'Az ördög bájitala' című regényének olvasásához" [Polyphony of Alterego Centers: Notes to the Reading of E.T.A. Hoffmann's "The Devil's Elixir"], pp. 61–70; Márton Kaposi, "Az álnév elrejtő és feltáró szerepe Kierkegaard munkásságában" [The Hiding and Revealing Role of the Pseudonyms in Kierkegaard's Works], pp. 71–9; Zoltán Kalmár, "Egy tintahal monogramjai" [The Monograms of a Cuttlefish], pp. 81–7; János Weiss, "Kierkegaard, a bohóc és Ludwig Tieck" [Kierkegaard, the Clown and Ludwig Tieck], pp. 89–96; László V. Szabó, "Kierkegaard és Hermann Hesse" [Kierkegaard and Hermann Hesse], pp. 98–110; János Loboczky, "A zene és a zenei Kierkegaard-nál" [Music and the Musical in Kierkegaard], pp. 112–8; András Bohár, "Kierkegaard és az avantgárd lehetséges kapcsolatai" [Possible Connections between Kierkegaard and the Avant-garde], pp. 120–132; István Czakó, "Reflexiók Friedrich Schleiermacher valláskoncepciójára Søren Kierkegard feljegyzéseiben" [Reflections on Friedrich Schleiermacher's Concept of Religion in Kierkegaard's Notebooks and Journals], pp. 133–42; Katalin Thiel, "A hit lovagja és a 'várakozó.' Kierkegaard hatása Hamvas Bélára" [The Knight of Faith and "Someone Waiting": Kierkegaard's Influence on Béla Hamvas], pp. 143–51; Imre Garaczi, "Élet és filozófia Kierkegaard-nál" [Life and Philosophy in Kierkegaard], pp. 153–8; Ágnes Bogdán, "Csak abból táplálkozz, ami egészséges benned. A 19. sz. második felének halálos betegsége" [Nourish Yourself Only from Your Healthy Parts: The Sickness unto Death of the Second Part of the Nineteenth Century], pp. 159–74.)

Püsök, Sarolta, *Kierkegaard teológiájának súlypontjai* [Focuses of Kierkegaard's Theology], Cluj-Napoca: Bolyai Társaság – Egyetemi Műhely 2010. (Review: Avram, Laura, "Egy hiteles Kierkegaard-kép" [An Authentic Picture of Kierkegaard], *Erdélyi Múzeum Évkönyve*, 2011, pp. 201–3.)

Rácz, Péter, "A csábító naplót vezet – Kierkegaard reggeltől estig" [The Seducer Writes a Diary: Kierkegaard from Morning till Night], *Magyar Napló*, no. 1, 1993, pp. 37–9.

— "Belépés a kapcsolatba. Kierkegaard Budapesten, avagy filozófiájának hatása Martin Buberre" [Entering into Relationship: Kierkegaard in Budapest or the Influence of his Philosophy on Martin Buber], *Liget*, no. 1, 1995, pp. 10–15.

Rózsa, Erzsébet, "A csábítás metamorfózisai: A hegelizmus nyomai Kierkegaard *Vagy-vagy* című művében" [The Metamorphoses of Seduction: The Traces of Hegelianism in Kierkegaard's *Either/Or*], in *Majdnem nem lehet másként. Tanulmányok Vajda Mihály 60. születésnapjára* [It Almost Cannot Be Otherwise: Studies on Occasion of Mihály Vajda's 60th Birthday], ed. by Ferenc Fehér, András Kardos, and Sándor Radnóti, Budapest: Cserépfalvi 1995, pp. 318–29.

Rozsnyai, Ervin, "Søren Kierkegaard – létezni vagy gondolkodni" [Søren Kierkegaard: To Exist or to Think], in his *Filozófiai arcképek. Descartes, Vico, Kierkegaard* [Philosophical Portraits: Descartes, Vico, Kierkegaard], Budapest: Magvető 1970. pp. 305–450.

Rugási, Gyula, "A pillanat foglya. Kierkegaard megváltásfilozófiájáról" [The Prisoner of the Moment: Kierkegaard's Philosophy of Redemption], *Vulgo*, nos. 3–5, 2000, pp. 228–52.

— *A pillanat foglya* [The Prisoner of the Moment], Budapest: Gond – Cura – Palatinus 2002.

Sarkadi Nagy, Pál, "Az időszerű Kierkegaard" [The Current Kierkegaard], *Theológiai Szemle*, nos. 11–12, 1963, pp. 350–4.

Siklósi, István, "Az Én és a szabadság problémája Kierkegaard filozófiájában" [The Problems of Self and Freedom in Kierkegaard's Philosophy], *Elpis*, no. 1, 2007, pp. 79–112.

Soós, Anita, "A narráció mint a csábítás eszköze Søren Kierkegaard *Az ismétlés* című művében" [Narration as a Device of Seduction in Søren Kierkegaard's *Repetition*], *Pro Philosophia Füzetek*, no. 23, 2000, pp. 37–48.

— "*Ha egy arcot sokáig és figyelmesen szemlélünk...*" ["If We Watch a Face Long and Carefully Enough..."] Budapest: HASS 2002. (Review: Gyenge, Zoltán, review in *Pro Philosophia Füzetek*, no. 4, 2002, pp. 123–9.)

Suki, Béla, "Isten nélküli vallásosság avagy a paradox kereszténység. Gondolatok Sören Kierkegaard nézeteiről" [Religiosity without God or the Paradox of Christianity: Thoughts about Kierkegaard's Views], *Világosság*, no. 6, 1965, pp. 328–33.

— "Bevezetés" [Preface], in *Sören Kierkegaard írásaiból* [From Søren Kierkegaard's Writings], trans. by Tivadar Dani et al., Budapest: Gondolat 1969, pp. 5–74.

Szeberényi, Lajos Zsigmond, *Kierkegaard élete és munkái* [Kierkegaard's Life and Works], Békéscsaba: Evangélikus Egyházi könyvkereskedés 1937. (Review: Kemény, Gábor, review in *Korunk*, vol. 1, 1983, pp. 80–3.)

Széles, László, *Kierkegaard gondolkozásának alapvonalai* [The Basic Lines of Kierkegaard's Thought], Budapest: Sárkány 1933.

Szennay, András, "Sören Kierkegaard és a kereszténység" [Søren Kierkegaard and Christianity], *Vigília*, no. 5, 1963, pp. 299–302.

Szigeti, József, *Útban a valóság felé. Tanulmányok* [On the Way to Reality: Essays], Budapest: Hungária 1948.

Szilágyi, Ákos "A *Vagy – Vagy* szerelemfilozófiája" [The Philosophy of Love of *Either/Or*], *Valóság*, no. 12, 1978, pp. 14–22.

Szűcs, Ferenc, "A XX. századi teológia kezdetei és Kierkegaard. Kierkegaard és Barth Károly" [The Beginnings of the Twentieth-Century Theology and Kierkegaard: Kierkegaard and Karl Barth], *Gond*, no. 4, 1993, pp. 33–6.

Tatár, György, "A híd túl messze van" [A Bridge Too Far], *2000*, nos. 4–5, 1999, pp. 95–8.

Tavaszy, Sándor: *Kierkegaard személyisége és gondolkodása* [Kierkegaard's Personality and Thought], Cluj: Erdélyi Múzeum-Egyesület 1930.

— *A lét és valóság. Az exisztenciálizmus filozófiájának alapproblémái* [Existence and Reality: The Fundamental Problems of the Philosophy of Existence], Cluj: Erdélyi Muzeum-Egyesület 1933.

— *Kierkegaard gondolkozásának alapvonalai* [The Basic Lines of Kierkegaard's Thought], Budapest: Sárkány 1934.

Tóta, Benedek, "Ismétlés: Kísérlet Kierkegaard nyomán" [Repetition: An Attempt in the Footsteps of Kierkegaard], *Pannonhalmi Szemle*, vol. 1, no. 1, 1993, pp. 54–9.

Török, Endre, "Dosztojevszkij és Kierkegaard. 'Istennel szemben soha sincs igazunk'" [Dostoevsky and Kierkegaard: "In Relation to God We Are Always in the Wrong"], *Pannonhalmi Szemle*, vol. 1, no. 1, 1993, pp. 43–5.

Vajda, Mihály, "Kétségbeesés és gond. Késői kora-Heideggeriánus széljegyzetek Kierkegaard *Die Krankheit zum Tode* című könyvéhez" [Despair and Anxiety: Late Notes in the Spirit of the Early Heidegger to Kierkegaard's *The Sickness unto Death*], *Hiány*, no. 3, 1993, pp. 24–8.

— "Filozófia mint elbeszélés. Emlékezet és ismétlés" [Philosophy as Narration: Recollection and Repetition], *Pro Philosophia Füzetek*, no. 23, 2000, pp. 19–29.

Vajta, Vilmos, *Hit és élet összecsengése: Kierkegard* [sic!] *Ordass Lajos tolmácsolásában* [The Harmony of Life and Faith: Kierkegaard in Lajos Ordass' Interpretation], Keszthely: Ordass Baráti kör 1990.

Veres, Ildikó, "Kierkegaard, a 'magánkeresztény'" [Kierkegaard, the "Private Christian"], in Béla Brandenstein, *Kierkegaard. Tanulmány* [Kierkegaard: A Study], Budapest: Kairosz 2005, pp. 5–25; republished in her *Hiány, filozófia, kritika: válogatott tanulmányok a magyar filozófia történetéből* [Lack, Philosophy, Critique: Selected Papers from the History of Hungarian Philosophy], Cluj-Napoca and Szeged: Pro Philosophia, SZTE Társadalomtudományi Gyűjtemény 2011, pp. 185–97.

Vitéz, Ferenc, "Kierkegaard 200. Esztétika, etika és vallás" [Kierkegaard 200: Aesthetics, Ethics and Religion], *Néző.Pont*, nos. 8–9, 2013, pp. 314–23.

— "Válság és váltság: Kierkegaard és a világháború utáni teológia. 'Az értelmes hit és a cselekvő erkölcs egysége': avagy: Koncz Sándor Kierkegaard-, és református teológia-interpretációi" [Crisis and Redemption: Kierkegaard and Post-War Theology: "The Unity of Rational Faith and Active Moral," or Sándor Koncz's Interpretations of Kierkegaard and Reformed Theology], *Néző.Pont*, nos. 8–9, 2013, pp. 324–32.

Weiss, János, "A *Vagy-vagy* kerete (avagy hogyan olvassuk Kierkegaard fő művét?) [The Framework of *Either/Or* (Or How to Read Kierkegaard's Principal Work?)]," *Magyar Filozófiai Szemle*, vol. 57, no. 3, 2013, pp. 75–88.

III. Translated Secondary Literature on Kierkegaard in Hungarian

Adorno, Theodor W., "A bensőségesség szerkezete" [Konstitution der Innerlichkeit], trans. by János Weiss, *Pro Philosophia Füzetek*, no. 34, 2003, pp. 15–44.

Agacinski, Sylviane, "Értekezés egy tézisről" [On a Thesis], trans. by Éva Antal, *Vulgo*, vol. 2, nos. 3–5, 2000, pp. 181–205.

Andersen, Benny, "Kierkegaard biciklin" [Kierkegaard on a Bicycle], trans. by Gábor Miszoglád, *Forrás*, vol. 39, no. 1, 2007, pp. 8–9.

Baeumler, Alfred, "Hegel és Kierkegaard" [Hegel und Kierkegaard], trans. by Károly V. Horváth, *Jelenkor*, no. 10, 2010, pp. 1124–1133.

Bjerck-Amundsen, Petter, *Kierkegaard kezdőknek. Avagy hogyan is taníthatjuk Kierkegaardot* (sic!) *középiskolás fokon. Egy dán irodalomtanár ajánlata* [Kierkegaard for Beginners, Or How Can We Teach Kierkegaard in the Secondary School: Suggestions by a Danish Teacher of Literature], trans. by Ervin Járkáló Lázár, Budapest: Ághegy Könyvek – Közdok 2010.

Troelsen, Bjarne (ed.), "Kortársak visszaemlékezései Søren Kierkegaard-ra" [Contemporary Memories of Søren Kierkegaard [selections from *Søren Kierkegaard: A Police Agent of Ideas*]], trans. by Anita Kövi, *Jelenkor*, no. 10, 2010, pp. 1122–1123.

Caputo, John D., "Pillanatok, titkok és szingularitások. A halál adománya Kierkegaard-nál és Derridánál" [Instants, Secrets, and Singularities: Dealing

Death in Kierkegaard and Derrida], trans. by György Kalmár and Kata Simon, *Vulgo*, vol. 2, nos. 3–5, 2000, pp. 161–80.

Cavell, Stanley, "Kierkegaard az autoritásról és a megvilágosodásról" [Kierkegaard on Authority and Revelation], trans. by Éva Antal, *Vulgo*, vol. 2, nos. 3–5, 2000, pp. 131–43.

Derrida, Jacques, "A halál adománya" [Donner la mort], trans. by László Szabó, Vulgo, vol. 2, nos. 3–5, 2000, pp. 144–60.

Fehér M., István, "Schelling, Kierkegaard, Heidegger – rendszer, szabadság, gondolkodás. A poszthegelianus filozófia néhány közös motívuma és filozófiai témája" [Schelling, Kierkegaard, Heidegger hinsichtlich System, Freiheit und Denken. Gemeinsame Motive und Philosopheme der nachhegelschen Philosophie], trans. by László Vásárhelyi Szabó, *Pro Philosophia Füzetek*, nos. 11–12, 1997, pp. 3–20.

Fryszman, Alex, "Kierkegaard és Dosztojevszkij Bahtyin prizmáján át" [Kierkegaard and Dostoevsky through the Prism of Bakhtin], trans. by Adrienn Gálosi, *Pro Philosophia Füzetek*, no. 32, 2003, pp. 19–43.

Garff, Joakim, *SAK*, trans. by Ágnes Bogdán and Anita Soós, Pécs: Jelenkor 2004.

Kirmmse, Bruce H. (ed.), "Kierkegaard-anekdoták" [Anecdotes on Kierkegaard [selections from *Encounters with Kierkegaard*]], trans. by András Nagy, *2000*, no. 6, 2011, pp. 62–7.

Lévinas, Emmanuel, "Kierkegaard. Egzisztencia és etika" [Existence et éthique], trans. by László Tarnay, *Vulgo*, vol. 2, nos. 3–5, pp. 253–9.

Møller, Peter Ludwig, "A nagy filozófus" [The Great Philosopher], trans. by Gábor Gulyás, Vulgo, vol. 2, nos. 3–5, 2000, pp. 284–6.

— "Az új bolygó" [The New Planet], trans. by István Magyar, *Vulgo*, vol. 2, nos. 3–5, 2000, pp. 280–3.

Nigg, Walter, *Søren Kierkegaard. A költő, vezeklő és gondolkodó* [Sören Kierkegaard: Dichter, Büßer und Denker], trans. by Gabriella Lehr, Budapest: Kairosz 2007.

Nun, Katalin, "Színpad és nemzeti kultúra. A Dán Királyi Színház a 19. század első felében és a Heiberg család" [The Theater in Copenhagen During the Golden Age and the Heibergs], *Tekintet*, no. 1, 2000, pp. 59–75.

— "Korszakok. A 19. század első felének Dániája a kortárs szemével– Thomasine Gyllembourg és Kierkegaard" [Thomasine Gyllembourg's "Two Ages" and her Portrayal of Everyday Life], *Tekintet*, no. 6, 2003, pp. 89–110.

Pattison, George, "Ha Kierkegaard-nak igaza van az olvasással kapcsolatban, miért olvassunk Kierkegaard-t?" [If Kierkegaard Is Right about Reading, Why Read Kierkegaard?], trans. by Judit Bartha, *Pro Philosophia Füzetek*, no. 34, 2003, pp. 91–111.

— "Kierkegaard – esztétika és 'az esztétikai'" [Kierkegaard: Aesthetics and "the Aesthetic"], trans. by Judit Bartha, *Pro Philosophia Füzetek*, no. 35, 2003, pp. 103–19.

Prondoe, Grigore, "Az esztétikai idő Kierkegaard filozófiájában" [The Aesthetic Time in Kierkegaard's Philosophy], trans. by Béla Komáromi, *Korunk*, no. 1, 1983, pp. 50–3.

Ricoeur, Paul, "Kierkegaard és a rossz" [Kierkegaard et le mal], trans. by László Orosz, *Vulgo*, vol. 2, nos. 3–5, pp. 219–27.

Šajda, Peter, "Søren Kierkegaard módszertani hozzájárulása a vallásközi párbeszédhez" [Søren Kierkegaard's Methodological Contribution to Inter-religious Dialogue], trans. by Szabolcs Nagypál, in *A vallásközi párbeszéd a vallások szemszögéből* [Interreligious Dialogue from the Point of View of the Religions], ed. by Szabolcs Nagypál, Budapest and Pannonhalma: L'Harmattan and BGÖI 2011, pp. 154–66.

Sawyer, Frank, "Søren Kierkegaard (1813–1855): egzisztencialista lépések az életben" [Søren Kierkegaard (1813–1855): Existentialist Steps in Life], trans. by Gabriella Rácsok, in *Deus providebit: Tanulmányok dr. Mészáros István tiszteletére 70. születésnapja alkalmából* [Deus providebit: Studies in Honor of dr. István Mészáros on Occasion of his 70th Birthday], ed. by György Benke and Dénes Dienes, Sárospatak, Sárospataki Református Teológiai Akadémia 1999, pp. 173–86.

— "Kierkegaard: zászló a változás szelében" [Kierkegaard: A Flag in the Wind of Changes], trans. by Pálma Füsti-Molnár, in *"Krisztusért járva követségben…": teológia, igehirdetés, egyházkormányzás: tanulmánykötet a 60 éves Bölcskey Gusztáv születésnapjára* ["Now Then We Are Ambassadors for Christ": Theology, Preaching, Church Governing: Studies on Occasion of Gusztáv Bölcskey's 60th Birthday], ed. by Sándor Fazekas and Árpád Ferencz, Debrecen: DRHE 2012, pp. 255–68.

Shestov, Leo, "Kierkegaard, a vallásfilozófus" [Sören Kierkegaard. Philosophe Religieux], trans. by Éva Patkós, *Filozófiai Figyelő*, no. 3, 1988, pp. 75–94.

Icelandic

Kristian Guttesen

I. Icelandic Translations of Kierkegaard's Works

"Brotabrot úr ritum Sörens Kierkegaards" ["Fragments from the Works of Søren Kierkegaard" [from "Diapsalmata" from *Either/Or* and *The Moment*]], trans. by Guðjón Baldvinsson, *Eimreiðin*, vol. 17, no. 1, 1911, pp. 49–51; pp. 51–2.

"Liljur vallarins og fuglar himinsins" [*Lilies of the Fields and the Birds of the Air* [selection from *The Lily in the Field and the Bird of the Air*]], trans. by Gunnar Árnason, *Kirkjuritið*, vol. 22, no. 10, 1956, pp. 482–4.

"Draumur Salómons" ["Solomon's Dream" [from *Stages on Life's Way*]], trans. by Gunnar Árnason, *Kirkjuritið*, vol. 29, no. 5, 1963, pp. 222–4.

"Úr Diapsalmata" ["Selection from 'Diapsalmata'" [from *Either/Or*]], trans. by Gunnar Árnason, *Kirkjuritið*, vol. 29, no. 5, 1963, p. 224.

Endurtekningin [*Repetition*], trans. by Þorsteinn Gylfason, Reykjavik: Helgafell 1966.

"Úr *Synspunktet for min Forfatter-Virksomhed*" ["Selection from *The Point of View for My Work as an Author*"], trans. by Vilhjálmur Árnason and used as a motto of his book *Siðfræði lífs og dauða. Erfiðar ákvarðanir í heilbrigðistþjónustu* [Ethics of Life and Death: Difficult Decisions in Health Care], Reykjavik: The Centre for Ethics and the University of Iceland Press 1993 (2nd ed. 2003), p. 5.

"Ómar af strengleikum: úrval úr 'Diapsalmata. Ad se Ipsum' í *Enten-eller*" ["Sounds from Stringed Instruments: Selections from the 'Diapsalmata. Ad se Ipsum' in *Either/Or*"], trans. by Þorsteinn Gylfason, *Jón á Bægisá*, vol. 1, 1994, pp. 74–7.

Endurtekningin [*Repetition*], trans. by Þorsteinn Gylfason, Reykjavik: Hið íslenzka bókmenntafélag 2000 (*Theoretical Classics Series*).

Uggur og ótti [*Fear and Trembling*], trans. by Jóhanna Þráinsdóttir, Reykjavik: Hið íslenzka bókmenntafélag 2000 (*Theoretical Classics Series*).

"Úr *Andránni (Øieblikket)*" ["Selections from *The Moment*"], trans. by Kristján Árnason, *Tímarit Máls og menningar*, vol. 61, no. 4, 2000, pp. 15–16, pp. 33–4, p. 46.

"Úr *Sóttinni banvænu (Sygdommen Til Døden)*" ["Selections from *The Sickness unto Death*"], trans. by Kristian Guttesen, *Hugur*, vol. 23, 2011, pp. 105–9.

II. Secondary Literature on Kierkegaard in Icelandic

Ágústsdóttir, María, "Hyggið að liljum vallarins…" [Consider the Lilies of the Field…], in *Náttúrusýn* [Visions of Nature], ed. by Róbert H. Haraldsson and Þorvarður Árnason, Reykjavik: The Centre for Ethics and the University of Iceland Press 1994, pp. 59–68.

24 *Kristian Guttesen*

Albertsson, Eiríkur, *Magnús Eiríksson. Guðfræði hans og trúarlíf* [Magnús Eiríksson: His Theology and Religious Life], Reykjavik: Ísafoldarprentsmiðja 1938. (Reviews: Bjarnason, Ágúst H., review in *Skírnir*, vol. 113, 1939, pp. 302–6. Jóhannesson, Þorkell, "Magnús Eiríksson," *Tíminn*, December 29, 1938, p. 2, p. 3; Sigurðsson, Árni, "Fyrsta doktorsritgerð í guðfræði við Háskóla Íslands" [The First Doctoral Thesis in Theology at the University of Iceland], *Kirkjuritið*, vol. 5, no. 2, 1939, pp. 88–90; Sigurðsson, Haraldur, "Magnús Eiríksson. Eftir síra Eirík Albertsson" [Magnús Eiríksson. By Reverend Eiríkur Albertsson], *Þjóðviljinn*, October 12, 1938, p. 2, p. 4. Þórðarson, Skúli, "Fyrsta doktorsritgerð í guðfræði við Háskóla Íslands. Ritgerð séra Eiríks Albertssonar um Magnús Eiríksson, guðfræði hans og trúarlíf" [The First Doctoral Thesis in Theology at the University of Iceland. Reverend Eiríkur Albertsson's Treatise on Magnús Eiríksson, His Theology and Religious Life], *Alþýðublaðið*, October 14, 1938, p. 3.)

Árnason, Kristján, "Arfur Hegels" [Hegel's Heritage], *Skírnir*, vol. 161, 1987, pp. 211–17.

— "Sjálfsþekking og sjálfsval" [Knowing Oneself and Choosing Oneself], *Tímarit Máls og menningar*, vol. 61, no. 4, 2000, pp. 6–14.

— *Hið fagra er satt* [Beauty is Truth], Reykjavik: The Institute for Literature and the University of Iceland Press 2004.

Árnason, Vilhjálmur, *Broddflugur* [Gadflies], Reykjavik: The Centre for Ethics and the University of Iceland Press 1997.

— "Að velja sjálfan sig. Tilraunir Kierkegaards um mannlífið" [Choosing Oneself: Kierkegaard's Experiments with Being Human], *Tímarit Máls og menningar*, vol. 61, no. 4, 2000, pp. 17–32.

— "Tilvistargreining Kierkegaards" [Kierkegaard's Existential Analysis], in his *Farsælt líf, réttlátt samfélag – kenningar í siðfræði* [Good Life, Just Society: Theories of Ethics], Reykjavik: Heimskringla 2008, pp. 161–75.

Bjarnadóttir, Birna, "Hvers vegna er dauðinn besta gjöfin, Kierkegaard?" [Why is Death the Best Gift, Kierkegaard?], *Tímarit Máls og menningar*, vol. 61, no. 4, 2000, pp. 47–62.

— *Holdið hemur andann. Um fagurfræði í skáldskap Guðbergs Bergssonar* [The Flesh Tames the Spirit: On Aesthetics in the Fiction of Guðbergur Bergsson], Reykjavik: The University of Iceland Press 2003.

Dal, Gunnar, "Kierkegaard," in his *Existentialismi* [Existentialism], Reykjavik: Víkurútgáfan 1978, pp. 17–20.

— "Danir eru gáfuð þjóð—Sören Kierkegaard frægastur norrænna heimspekinga" [The Danes are a Gifted Nation: Søren Kierkegaard the Most Famous of Nordic Philosophers], in his *Að elska er að lifa* [To Love is to Live], Reykjavik: HKÁ 1994, pp. 99–101.

Jónsson, Bjarni, "Sören Kierkegaard," *Kirkjuritið*, vol. 21, no. 10, 1955, pp. 463–80.

Nordal, Sigurður, *Einlyndi og marglyndi* [To Will One Thing or Many], Reykjavik: Hið íslenzka bókmenntafélag 1986, see pp. 166–76. (Review: Björnsson, Sigurjón, "Lífsleiknislist og lítið eitt fleira" [The Art of Life Skills Education and a Little Bit More], *Andvari*, vol. 112, 1987, see p. 132.)

Ólafsson, Arnljótur, "Fréttir" [News], *Skírnir*, vol. 30, 1856, pp. 30–1.

Óskarsson, Þórir. "Í silkisloprokk með tyrkneskan turban á höfði" [Dressed in a Silk Robe and a Turkish Turban], *Andvari*, vol. 132, 2007, p. 136, p. 138.

Pétursson, Hannes, "Lítið eitt um Grím" [A Few Remarks on Grímur Thomsen], *Lesbók Morgunblaðsins*, November 23, 1996, p. 4.

Pétursson, Ólafur Jens, *Hugmyndasaga* [History of Ideas], Reykjavik: Mál og menning 1985, pp. 240–1.

Skúlason, Páll, "Tilvistarstefnan og Sigurður Nordal" [Existentialism and Sigurður Nordal], *Skírnir*, vol. 161, 1987, pp. 309–36.

Þorbjörnsson, Guðmundur Björn, "Samfélagsrýni og gamlar hættur. Um Kierkegaard og vangaveltusamfélagið" [The Modern Self and the Dangers of Old: Kierkegaard and the Present Age], *Hugur*, vol. 24, 2012, pp. 115–33.

— "Að elska eða láta hneykslast. Um kærleikann og hið geigvænlega verkefni að verða kristinn í guðfræði Kierkegaards" [To Love or to be Offended: On Love and the Difficult Task of Becoming a Christian in Kierkegaard's Theology], *Ritröð Guðfræðistofnunnar/Studia Theologica Islandica*, vol. 37, 2013, pp. 90–113.

Þorleifsson, Páll, "Existentíalisminn, eða tilvistarstefnan" [Existentialism], *Eimreiðin*, vol. 72, no. 1, 1966, pp. 22–4.

Þráinsdóttir, Jóhanna, "Sögulegt baksvið *Uggs og ótta*" [Historical Background of *Fear and Trembling*], in Søren Kierkegaard, *Uggur og ótti* [*Fear and Trembling*], trans. by Jóhanna Þráinsdóttir, Reykjavik: Hið íslenzka bókmenntafélag 2000, pp. 231–45 (*Theoretical Classics Series*).

— "Er trúin þverstæða? Gagnrýni Magnúsar Eiríkssonar á trúarskoðunum Kierkegaards í *Ugg og ótta*" [Is Faith a Paradox? Magnús Eiríksson's Critique of Kierkegaard's Theological Position in *Fear and Trembling*], *Tímarit Máls og menningar*, vol. 61, no. 4, 2000, pp. 35–45.

III. Translated Secondary Literature on Kierkegaard in Icelandic

Schreiber, Gerhard, "Magnús Eiríksson. Vanræktur samtímamaður Sørens Kierke-gaard" [Magnús Eiríksson: A Neglected Contemporary of Søren Kierkegaard], trans. by Aðalsteinn Garðarsson, *Skírnir*, vol. 188, 2014, pp. 116–43.

Søe, Niels H., "Kierkegaard og existentíalisminn" [Kierkegaard and existentialism], no translator given, *Lesbók Morgunblaðsins*, May 19, 1963, p. 1, p. 12.

Italian

Laura Liva

I. Italian Translations of Kierkegaard's Works

Il più infelice ["The Unhappiest One" [from *Either/Or*]], trans. by Knud Ferlov, *Leonardo*, vol. 5, no. 3, 1907, pp. 246–77.

Il diario del seduttore ["The Seducer's Diary" [from *Either/Or*]], trans. by Luigi Redaelli, Turin: Fratelli Bocca 1910 (2nd ed. 1921; 3rd ed. 1942; 4th ed. 1946; 5th ed. Milan: Fratelli Melina 1990).

In vino veritas, con l'aggiunta del più infelice e diapsalmata ["In Vino Veritas" [from *Stages on Life's Way*], "The Unhappiest One" and "Diapsalmata" [from *Either/Or*]], trans. by Knud Ferlov, Lanciano: R. Carabba 1910 (2nd ed. 1913; 3rd ed. 1919; 4th ed. 1922; 5th ed. 1943; 6th ed. 2003; 7th ed. 2008; La Spezia: Fratelli Melita 1990).

Il valore estetico del matrimonio ["The Esthetic Validity of Marriage" [from *Either/Or*]], trans. and ed. by Gualtiero Petrucci, Naples: F. Perrella e C. 1912.

L'erotico nella musica ["The Immediate Erotic Stages" [from *Either/Or*]], trans. by Gualtiero Petrucci, Genova: A. F. Formiggini 1913.

L'Ora. Atti d'accusa al cristianesimo del Regno di Danimarca [*The Moment. Acts of Accusation of Christendom in the Kingdom of Denmark*], vols. 1–2, trans. by Antonio Banfi, Milan and Rome: Doxa 1931 (2nd ed. in one volume, Milan: Bocca 1951).

"Appendice: Kierkegaard su Kierkegaard. Testimonianze e frammenti" ["Appendix: Kierkegaard on Kierkegaard: Testimonies and Fragments" [selections from journals and papers]], in *Kierkegaard. Con una scelta di passi nuovamente tradotti* [*Kierkegaard: With a New Translation of a Series of Passages*], trans. by Franco Lombardi, Florence: La Nuova Italia 1936, pp. 255–322 (2nd enlarged ed., entitled *Søren Kierkegaard. Con una antologia dagli scritti e una bibliografia sistematica* [*Søren Kierkegaard: With an Antology and a Systematic Bibliography*], Florence: Sansoni 1967.

"L'angoscia e il peccato. L'angoscia e l'istante" ["Anxiety and Sin. Anxiety and the Moment" [selections from *The Concept of Anxiety*]], trans. by Armando Carlini, in *Il mito del realismo* [*The Myth of Realism*], Florence: Sansoni 1936, pp. 59–67.

Il concetto dell'angoscia [*The Concept of Anxiety*], trans. by Michele Federico Sciacca, Milan: Fratelli Bocca 1940 (2nd ed. 1944; 3rd revised ed. 1950).

I would like to thank Ingrid Basso for her generous bibliographical help.

Il concetto dell'angoscia. Una semplice ricerca psicologica sul problema del peccato originale [*The Concept of Anxiety: A Simple Psychologically Orienting Deliberation on the Dogmatic Issue of Hereditary Sin*], trans. by Meta Corssen, Florence: Sansoni 1942.

"Il valore dell'angoscia morale; la fede come salvezza dall'angoscia" ["The Value of Moral Anxiety; Faith as Salvation from Anxiety" [selections from *The Concept of Anxiety*]], in Nicola Abbagnano, *Pagine di scrittori morali moderni* [*Pages by Modern Moral Writers*], Turin: Paravia 1943, pp. 257–69.

Aut-aut. Estetica ed etica nella formazione della personalità [*Either/Or: The Balance between the Esthetic and the Ethical in the Development of the Personality*], trans. by Kirsten Montanari Guldbrandsen and Remo Cantoni, Milan: M.A. Denti 1944 (Milan: Mondadori 1956; 2nd ed. 1975; 3rd ed. 1976; 4th ed. 1977; 5th ed. 1979; 6th ed. 1981; 7th ed. 1986; 8th ed. 1988; 9th ed. 1989; 10th ed. 1990; 11th ed. 1992; 12th ed. 1993; 13th ed. 1998; 14th ed. 2006; Milan: CDE 1990; 2nd ed. 1995; 3rd ed. 1996).

Don Giovanni. La musica di Mozart e l'Eros [*Don Giovanni. Mozart's Music and the Erotic* ["The Immediate Erotic Stages, Or the Musical-Erotic" from *Either/ Or*]], trans. by Kirsten Montanari Guldbrandsen and Remo Cantoni, Milan: M.A. Denti 1944 (Milan: Mondadori 1976; 2nd ed. 1981; 3rd ed. 1988; 4th ed. 1991; 5th ed. 1994; 6th ed. 1997).

Gli uccelli dell'aria e i gigli del campo [*The Birds of the Air and the Lilies of the Field*], trans. and introduction by G.D.M. (Nazzareno Padellaro), Rome: La Bussola 1945.

I gigli dei campi e gli uccelli del cielo [*The Lilies of the Field and the Birds of the Air*], trans. by Eugenio Augusto Rossi, Milan: Fratelli Bocca 1945.

La ripetizione. Saggio d'esperienza psicologica [*Repetition: A Venture in Experimenting Psychology*], trans. by Enrichetta Valenziani, Milan: Fratelli Bocca 1945.

La malattia mortale. Svolgimento psicologico cristiano di Anti Climacus [*The Sickness unto Death: A Christian Psychological Exposition for Edification and Awakening*], trans. by Meta Corssen, Preface by Paolo Brezzi, Milan: Ed. Di Comunità 1947 (2nd ed. 1952; 3rd revised edition 1965 contains selections from journals and papers (1849) ("Climacus e Anticlimacus" ["Climacus and Anticlimacus"]; "Lettera Al Professor Rasmus Nielsen e Riguardo a lui. (Da una brutta copia di una lettera datata 4 agosto 1849 a R.N.)" ["A Letter to Professor Rasmus Nielsen and about Him (from a rough copy of a letter to R.N. dated August 4th 1849)"]; "Nota dell'Editore alla *Malattia mortale*" ["A Note on *The Sickness unto Death* by the Editor]"); 4th ed. Rome: Newton Compton 1976; 5th ed. Milan: Mondadori 1991; 6th ed. 1998; 7th ed. 2007).

Lo specchio della parola [*The Mirror of the Word* [*For Self-Examination: Recommended to the Present Age*]], trans. by Enrichetta Valenziani and Cornelio Fabro, Florence: F. Fussi 1948.

Timore e tremore. Lirica dialettica [*Fear and Trembling: Dialectical Lyric*], trans. by Franco Fortini and Kirsten Montanari Guldbrandsen, Milan: Ed. Di Comunità 1948 (2nd ed. 1952; 3rd ed. 1962; Milan: SE 1990; 2nd ed. 1999; Milan: Mondadori 1991; 2nd ed. 1997; 3rd ed. 2003; Rome: Newton Compton 1976).

Diario [*Diary*], trans. by Cornelio Fabro, vols. 1–3, Brescia: Morcelliana 1948–51 (2nd revised ed., vols. 1–2, 1962–63; 3rd revised and enlarged ed., vols. 1–12, 1980–83).

"Pagine di Kierkegaard dal 'Diario' della maturità" ["Pages from Kierkegaard's Late Journals"], trans. by Cornelio Fabro, *Humanitas*, no. 5, 1950, pp. 1–11.

Scuola di cristianesimo [*Practice in Christianity*], trans. by Agostino Miggiano and Kirsten Montanari Guldbrandsen, Milan: Ed. Di Comunità 1950 (2nd ed. 1960; Rome: Newton Compton 1977).

Preghiere [*Prayers*], trans. and ed. by Cornelio Fabro, Brescia: Morcelliana 1951 (2nd ed. 1953; 3rd ed. 1963; 4th ed. 1979).

Antologia kierkegaardiana [*Kierkegaard Anthology* [selections from the journals and papers]], trans. and ed. by Cornelio Fabro, Turin: S.E.I. 1952 (2nd ed. 1967).

Ritratto della malinconia [*Portrait of Melancholy* [selections from Kierkegaard's writings]], trans. and ed. by Romana Guarnieri, Brescia: Morcelliana 1952 (2nd ed. 1954; 3rd ed. 1990).

Il concetto dell'angoscia. La malattia mortale [*The Concept of Anxiety/The Sickness unto Death*], trans. by Cornelio Fabro, Florence: Sansoni 1953 (2nd ed. 1965; 3rd ed. 1973; 4th ed. 1991).

Il concetto dell'angoscia [*The Concept of Anxiety*], trans. and ed. by Enzo Paci, Turin: Paravia 1954.

La ripresa. Tentativo di psicologia sperimentale di Constantin Constantius [*Repetition: A Venture in Experimenting Psychology by Constantin Constantius*], trans. by Angela Zucconi, Milan: Ed. Di Comunità 1954 (2nd ed. 1963; Milan: SE 2013).

Diario del seduttore ["The Seducer's Diary" [from *Either/Or*]], trans. by Attilio Veraldi, Milan: Rizzoli 1955 (2nd ed. 1973; 3rd ed. 1978; 4th ed. 1980; 5th ed. 1983; 6th ed. 1990; 7th ed. 1993; 8th ed. 1994; 9th ed. 1996; 10th ed. 1998; 11th ed. 1999; 12th ed. 2002; 13th ed. 2004; 14th ed. 2005; Milan: Opportunity Book 1996; Milan: Fabbri 1996; 2nd ed. 1998; 3rd ed. 2001; 4th ed. 2004; Milan: SE 2013).

"La dialettica della comunicazione etica ed etico-religiosa" ["The Dialectic of Ethical and Ethical-Religious Communication" [selection from Kierkegaard's papers]], trans. and ed. by Cornelio Fabro, in *Studi kierkegaardiani* [*Kierkegaard Studies*], Brescia: Morcelliana 1957, pp. 359–414.

L'esistenzialismo. Una antologia dagli scritti di Kierkegaard, Heidegger, Jaspers, Marcel, Sartre, Abbagnano [*Existentialism: An Anthology of the Writings by Kierkegaard, Heidegger, Jaspers, Marcel, Sartre, Abbagnano*], ed. by Pietro Chiodi, Turin: Loescher 1957 (2nd ed. 1958; 3rd ed. 1964; 4th ed. 1965; 5th ed. 1968; 6th ed. 1969; 7th ed. 1970; 8th ed. 1972; 9th ed. 1973; 10th ed. 1974; 11th ed. 1975; 12th ed. 1977; 13th ed. 1979; 14th ed. 1981; 15th ed. 1987; 16th ed. 1990).

Breviario [*Breviary* [selections from Kierkegaard]], trans. and ed. by Domenico Tarizzo and Pucci Panzieri, Milan: Il Saggiatore 1959 (2nd ed. 1961).

"Il giglio e l'uccello" ["The Bird and the Lily" [*The Lily in the Field and the Bird of the Air: Three Devotional Discourses*]], in Pius Aimone Reggio, *La gioia* [*The Joy*], trans. by Luciana Bulgheroni Spallino, Milan: Ediz. Corsia dei Servi 1960.

La sinistra hegeliana [*The Left Hegelians*], trans. by Claudio Cesa, Bari: Laterza 1960 (selections from journals and papers, pp. 449–50; "Un manifesto letterario" ["A Literary Manifest"], pp. 451–9; "Gli scritti su se stesso" ["Writings on Himself"], pp. 460–8; "L'unica cosa che è necessaria" ["The Only Necessary Thing"], pp. 469–78.)

Briciole di filosofia ovvero una filosofia in briciole; Postilla conclusiva non scientifica alle "Briciole di filosofia" [*Philosophical Fragments or a Fragment of Philosophy/ Concluding Unscientific Postscript to Philosophical Fragments*], vols. 1–2, trans. and ed. by Cornelio Fabro, Bologna: Zanichelli 1962.

Discorsi cristiani [*Christian Discourses*], trans. and ed. by Dino T. Donadoni, Turin: Borla 1963.

"Risoluzione e frammento sui quattro stadi della vita (II A 118–121; I C 226)" ["Resolution and Fragment on the Four Stages of Life (II A 118–121; I C 226)"], trans. by Alessandro Cortese, *Filosofia e Vita*, vol. 7, no. 22, 1965, pp. 46–9.

La difficoltà di essere cristiani [*On the Difficulties of Being a Christian* [selection of Kierkegaard's texts], trans. and ed. by Jacques Colette, Alba: Paoline 1967 (2nd ed. 1970).

La lotta tra il vecchio e il nuovo negozio del sapone [*The Battle between the Old and the New Soap-Cellars*], trans. and ed. by Alessandro Cortese, Padua: Liviana 1967.

L'inquietudine della fede [*The Anxiety of Faith* [selections from *Fear and Trembling*, *The Sickness unto Death*, *The Concept of Anxiety* and the journals]], trans. and ed. by Massimo Tosco, Turin: Gribaudi 1968.

La comunicazione della singolarità [*The Communication of Singularity* [*The Dialectic of Ethical and Religious Communication*]], ed. by Mauro La Spisa, Naples: Istituto Editoriale del Mezzogiorno 1969 (2nd revised ed., Palermo: Herbita 1982).

È magnifico essere uomini [*It Is Wonderful to Be Human* [*What We Learn from the Lilies of the Field and the Birds of the Air*]], trans. by Luigi Rosadoni, Turin: Gribaudi Turin 1971 (2nd ed. 1990).

Esercizio del cristianesimo [*Practice in Christianity*], trans. and ed. by Cornelio Fabro, Rome: Editrice Studium 1971.

"La 'neutralità armata,' ossia la mia posizione come scrittore cristiano nella cristianità" [*Armed Neutrality: Or My Position as a Christian Author in Christendom*], trans. by Cornelio Fabro, in *Esercizio del cristianesimo* [*Practice in Christianity*], trans. and ed. by Cornelio Fabro, Rome: Editrice Studium 1971, pp. 327–41.

Vangelo delle sofferenze ["The Gospel of Sufferings" [from *Upbuilding Discourses in Various Spirits*]], trans. by Cornelio Fabro, Fossano: Esperienze 1971.

"Che cosa giudica Cristo del cristianesimo ufficiale" [*What Christ Judges of Official Christianity*], trans. by Alessandro Cortese, *Contributi dell'Istituto di filosofia dell'Università Cattolica del S. Cuore di Milano*, vol. 2, 1972, pp. 57–64.

"È vero che il vescovo Mynster fu un 'Sandhedsvidne' ['testimone della verità'], uno 'de rette Sandhedsvidner' ['gli autentici testimoni della verità']?" ["Was Bishop Mynster a 'Truth-Witness,' One of 'the Authentic Truth-Witnesses'— Is This the Truth?"], trans. by Alessandro Cortese, *Contributi dell'Istituto di filosofia dell'Università Cattolica del S. Cuore di Milano*, vol. 2, 1972, pp. 52–6.

La neutralità armata e il piccolo intervento [*Armed Neutrality and the Little Intervention*], ed. by Mariano Cristaldi and Gregor Malantschuk, trans. by Nicola De Domenio and Pina Zaccarin-Lauritzen, Messina: A.M. Sortino 1972.

Opere [*Works* [selections from *Either/Or*; *Fear and Trembling*; *The Concept of Anxiety*; *Philosophical Fragments*; *Concluding Unscientific Postscript*; *The Sickness unto Death*; *Practice in Christianity*; "Gospel of Sufferings" [from *Upbuilding Discourses in Various Spirits*]; *For Self-Examination*; *The Changelessness of God*]], trans. and ed. by Cornelio Fabro, Florence: Sansoni 1972; republished as *Le grandi opere filosofiche e teologiche* [*Philosophical and Theological Works*], Milan: Bompiani 2013.

Puoi soffrire con gioia [*You Can Suffer with Joy* [selections from *Christian Discourses*]], trans. and ed. by Luigi Rosadoni, Turin: Gribaudi 1972.

Peccato, perdono, misericordia [*Sin, Forgiveness, and Mercy* [selections from *Christian Discourses*]], trans. by Laura Vagliasindi, Turin: Gribaudi 1973.

Diario [*Diary*], trans. and ed. by Cornelio Fabro, Milan: Biblioteca Universale Rizzoli 1975 (2nd ed. 1979; 3rd ed. 1983; 4th ed. 1988; 5th ed. 1992; 6th ed. 1996; 7th ed. 2000; 8th ed. 2004).

Dell'autorità e della rivelazione. Libro su Adler [*On Authority and Revelation: The Book on Adler*], trans. and ed. by Cornelio Fabro, Padua: Gregoriana 1976.

Enten-Eller: un frammento di vita [*Either/Or: A Fragment of Life*], vols. 1–5, trans. by Alessandro Cortese, Milan: Adelphi 1976–89.

"Pure una difesa delle alte qualità della donna" ["Another Defense of Woman's Great Abilities"], trans. by Salvatore Spera, in his *Il pensiero del giovane Kierkegaard. Indagini critiche sulla filosofia della religione e studi sugli aspetti inediti del pensiero kierkegaardiano* [*The Thought of the Young Kierkegaard: Critical Investigations on Philosophy of Religion and Studies on Some Unknown Aspects of Kierkegaard's Thought*], Padua: CEDAM 1977, pp. 150–3.

Il problema della fede [*The Problem of Faith* [selections from Kierkegaard's writings]], trans. and ed. by Cornelio Fabro, Brescia: La Scuola 1978.

"La nostra letteratura giornalistica" ["Our Journalistic Literature"], trans. by Salvatore Spera in his *Kierkegaard politico* [*Kierkegaard Politician*], Rome: Istituto di Studi Filosofici 1978, pp. 98–119.

"Lettere a Regine" ["Letters to Regine"], trans. by Vanina Sechi, *Comunità*, no. 179, 1978, pp. 379–405.

Scritti sulla comunicazione [*Writings on Communication*], trans. and ed. by Cornelio Fabro, vols. 1–2, Rome: Logos 1979–82. (vol. 1: "La dialettica della comunicazione etica ed etico-religiosa" ["The Dialectic of Ethical and Ethical-Religious Communication"]; "Sulla mia attività letteraria" [*On My Work as a Writer*]; "Il punto di vista della mia attività letteraria" [*The Point of View for My Work as an Author*]; vol. 2: "Due piccole dissertazioni etico-religiose" [*Two Ethical-Religious Essays*]; "La neutralità armata" [*Armed Neutrality*]; "La risposta al 'pastore di campagna'" ["The Answer to the Country Pastor"]; "Testi complementari sulla comunicazione" ["Complementary Texts on Communication"].)

In vino veritas: un ricordo riferito da William Afham ["In Vino veritas. A Recollection Related by William Afham" [from *Stages on Life's Way*]], ed. by Domenico Pertusati, Rapallo: Ipotesi 1982.

Pensieri che feriscono alle spalle e altri discorsi edificanti [*Thoughts that Wound from Behind – For Upbuilding and Other Edifying Discourses*], trans. and ed. by Cornelio Fabro, Padua: EMP 1982 ("Il pungolo nella carne" ["The Thorn in the Flesh"]; "Tre discorsi per la comunione del venerdì" [*Three Discourses at the Communion on Fridays*]; "Due discorsi per la comunione del venerdì" [*Two Discourses at the Communion on Fridays*]; "Un discorso edificante: 'La peccatrice'" [*An Upbuilding Discourse*: "The Woman Who Was a Sinner"].)

Gli atti dell'amore [*Works of Love*], trans. and ed. by Cornelio Fabro, Milan: Rusconi 1983 (2nd ed., Milan: Bompiani 2003).

In vino veritas ["In Vino Veritas" [from *Stages on Life's Way*]], trans. and ed. by Icilio Vecchiotti, Rome-Bari: Universale Laterza 1983 (2nd ed. 1993; 3rd ed. 1997; 4th ed. 2001; 5th ed. 2005; 6th ed. 2007).

"Indirizzo 'al benevolo lettore'" ["Lectori Benevolo" [from *Stages on Life's Way*]], trans. by Alessandro Cortese, in *Kierkegaard oggi. Atti del Convegno dell'11 novembre 1982* [*Kierkegaard Today. Proceedings of the Congress November 11th, 1982*], Milan: Vita e Pensiero 1986, pp. 145–50.

"*L'Istante*, n. 1, 24 maggio 1855" [*The Moment*, no. 1, May 24th, 1855], trans. by Alessandro Cortese, in *Kierkegaard oggi. Atti del Convegno dell'11 novembre 1982* [Kierkegaard Today. Proceedings of the Congress November 11th, 1982], Milan: Vita e Pensiero 1986, pp. 152–71.

Briciole filosofiche [*Philosophical Fragments*], trans. by Salvatore Spera, Brescia: Queriniana 1987 (2nd ed. 1992; 3rd ed. 2001; 4th ed. 2003; 5th ed. 2012).

"Johannes Climacus ovvero 'De omnibus dubitandum est.' Un racconto" [*Johannes Climacus, or De Omnibus Dubitandum Est: A Narrative*], trans. and ed. by Cornelio Fabro, in *Nuovi Studi Kierkegaardiani* [*New Kierkegaard Studies*], ed. by Giuseppe Mario Pizzuti, Potenza: Centro Italiano di Studi Kierkegaardiani 1989, pp. 165–211.

Sul concetto di ironia in riferimento costante a Socrate [*The Concept of Irony with Continual Reference to Socrates*], trans. by Dario Borso, Milan: Guerini e Associati 1989 (2nd ed., Milan: Biblioteca Universale Rizzoli 1995).

"La crisi e una crisi nella vita di un'attrice" [*The Crisis and a Crisis in the Life of an Actress*], trans. and ed. by Inge Lise Rasmussen Pin, in *Maschere Kierkegaardiane* [*Kierkegaardian Masks*], ed. by Leonardo Amoroso, Turin: Rosemberg & Sellier 1990, pp. 201–32.

Prefazioni. Lettura ricreativa per determinati ceti a seconda dell'ora e della circostanza [*Prefaces: Light Reading for Certain Classes as the Occasion May Require*], trans. by Dario Borso, Milan: Guerini e Associati 1990 (2nd ed., Milan: Biblioteca Universale Rizzoli 1996).

La ripetizione [*Repetition*], trans. by Dario Borso, Milan: Guerini e Associati 1991 (2nd ed. 1996; 3rd ed. 2008).

Filosofia e paradosso [*Philosophy and Paradox* [selections from Kierkegaard's writings]], ed. by Anna Giannatiempo Quinzio, Turin: SEI 1993.

Per provare sé stesso. Giudica da te! [*For Self-Examination/Judge For Yourself!*], trans. by Knud Ferlov and Maria Laura Sulpizi, Florence: Ponte alle Grazie 1993.

Stadi sul cammino della vita [*Stages on Life's Way*], ed. by Ludovica Koch, trans. by Anna Maria Segala and Anna Grazia Calabrese, Milan: Rizzoli 1993 (2nd ed., Milan: Biblioteca Universale Rizzoli 2001).

Due epoche [*Two Ages* [selections]], trans. by Dario Borso, Viterbo: Stampa Alternativa 1994.

Il concetto dell'angoscia [*The Concept of Anxiety*], ed. by Bruno Segre, Milan: E. Opportunity Book 1994.

Il mio punto di vista [*The Point of View for My Work as an Author*], trans. by Lidia Mirabelli, Vimercate: La Spiga 1994.

Aforismi e pensieri [*Aphorisms and Thoughts*], trans. by Silvia Giulietti, ed. by Massimo Baldini, Rome: Tascabili economici Newton 1995.

Diario di un seduttore ["The Seducer's Diary" [from *Either/Or*]], trans. and ed. by Alessandro Quattrone, Bussolengo: Demetra 1995.

Johannes Climacus o De omnibus dubitandum est. Un racconto [*Johannes Climacus, or De Omnibus Dubitandum Est. A Narrative*], trans. by Simonella Davini, Pisa: ETS 1995.

Opere [Works], vols. 1–3, trans. and ed. by Cornelio Fabro, Casale Monferrato: Piemme 1995 (vol. 1: *Sulla mia attività di scrittore* [*On My Work as an Author*]; *Il punto di vista sulla mia attività di scrittore* [*The Point of View for My Work as an Author*]; *Aut-Aut* ("Diapsalmata" e "Il riflesso del tragico antico nel tragico moderno") [*Either/Or* ("Diapsalmata" and "The Tragic in Ancient Drama Reflected in the Tragic in Modern Drama")]; *Timore e tremore* [*Fear and Trembling*]; *Il concetto dell'angoscia* [*The Concept of Anxiety*]; vol. 2: *Briciole di filosofia* [*Philosophical Fragments*]; *Postilla conclusiva non scientifica alle "Briciole di filosofia"* [*Concluding Unscientific Postscript to "Philosophical Fragments"*]; vol. 3: *La malattia mortale* [*The Sickness unto Death*]; *Esercizio del cristianesimo* [*Practice in Christianity*]; *Vangelo delle sofferenze* ["The Gospel of Sufferings" [from *Upbuilding Discourses in Various Spirits*]]; *Per l'esame di se stessi raccomandato ai contemporanei* [*For Self-Examination: Recommended to the Present Age*]; *L'immutabilità di Dio* [*The Changelessness of God*].)

Una recensione letteraria [*A Literary Review*], trans. by Dario Borso, Milan: Guerini & Associati 1995.

Diapsalmata ["Diapsalmata" [from *Either/Or*]], ed. by Bruno Segre, Milan: Opportunity Book 1996.

In vino veritas ["In Vino Veritas" [from *Stages on Life's Way*]], ed. by Dario Borso and Simonella Davini, Milan: G. Tranchida 1996.

Breviario [*Breviary* [selections from Kierkegaard's works and journals]], trans. by Cornelio Fabro, ed. by Dario Antiseri, Milan: Rusconi 1997.

" 'Guardate gli uccelli del cielo' (da *Il giglio nel campo e l'uccello nel cielo. Tre discorsi religiosi*)" ["Look at the Birds of the Air" [from *The Lily of the Field and the Bird of the Air. Three Religious Discourses*]], trans. by Ettore Rocca, in *Micromega*, no. 1997, pp. 175–90.

L'attrice. Opera pseudonima di Kierkegaard (1848), Inter et Inter [*The Actress. A Pseudonymous Work by Kierkegaard (1848), Inter et Inter* [*The Crisis and a Crisis in the Life of an Actress*]], ed. by Alessandro Cortese, Treviso: Antilia 1997.

"Una fugace osservazione su un particolare nel Don Giovanni" ["A Cursory Observation Concerning a Detail in Don Giovanni"], trans. by Marcello Gallucci and U. Hammer Mikkelsen, in *Musicus discologus – Musiche e scritti per il 70° anno di Carlo Marinelli* [*Musicus discologus – Tunes and Writings for Carlo*

Marinelli's 70th Birthday], ed. by Giuliano Macchi, Marcello Gallucci and Carlo Scimone, Vibo Valentia: Monteleone 1997, pp. 203–19.

Discorsi edificanti 1843, (*Due discorsi edificanti, Tre discorsi edificanti; Quattro discorsi edificanti*) [*Upbuilding Discourses 1843 (Two Upbuilding Discourses; Three Upbuilding Discourses; Four Upbuilding Discourses)*], trans. and ed. by Dario Borso, Casale Monferrato: Piemme 1998.

Il giglio nel campo e l'uccello nel cielo. Discorsi 1849–1851 ("Il sommo sacerdote"— "Il pubblicano"—"La peccatrice." Tre discorsi per la comunione del venerdì; Un discorso edificante; Due discorsi per la comunione del venerdì) [*The Lily in the Field and the Bird of the Air. Discourses 1849–1851 ("The High Priest"; "The Tax Collector"; "The Woman Who Was a Sinner"; Three Discourses at the Communion on Fridays; One Edifying Discourse; Two Discourses at the Communion on Fridays)*], trans. and ed. by Ettore Rocca, Rome: Donzelli 1998.

Mozart. L'erotico nella musica. Dalle "Nozze di Figaro" al "Don Giovanni" [*Mozart. The Musical-Erotic. From "Nozze di Figaro" to "Don Giovanni"* ["The Immediate Erotic Stages, Or the Musical-Erotic" from *Either/Or*]], trans. by Gualtiero Petrucci, Foggia: Bastogi Editrice Italiana 1998.

Accanto a una tomba ["At a Graveside" [from *Three Discourses on Imagined Occasions*]], trans. and ed. by Roberto Garaventa, Genoa: Il Melangolo 1999.

Dalle carte di uno ancora in vita [*From the Papers of One Still Living*], trans. by Dario Borso, Brescia: Morcelliana 1999.

La malattia per la morte [*The Sickness unto Death*], trans. and ed. by Ettore Rocca, Rome: Donzelli 1999 (2nd ed. 2011).

Esercizio di cristianesimo [*Practice in Christianity*], trans. by Cornelio Fabro, ed. by Salvatore Spera, Casale Monferrato: Piemme 2000.

"Esercizi di cristianesimo (Due sermoni inediti per la comunione del venerdì: 18 giugno 1847 e 27 agosto 1847, Vor Frue Kirke)" ["Practice in Christianity. Two Discourses at the Communion on Fridays: June 18th, 1847 and August 27th, 1847, Vor Frue Kirke" [selections from "Discourses at the Communion on Fridays" from *Christian Discourses*]], trans. and ed. by Ettore Rocca, *Micromega*, no. 2, 2000, pp. 97–108.

"L'arte di raccontare storie ai bambini" ["The Art of Telling Stories to the Children" [selection from *Journal BB*]], trans. and ed. by Ettore Rocca, *Micromega*, no. 5, 2000, pp. 236–45.

"S. Kierkegaard, Post-Scriptum a *Enten-Eller*" ["S. Kierkegaard: Post-Script to *Either/Or*" [*Pap.* IV B 51]], trans. by Andrea Scaramuccia, *NotaBene. Quaderni di Studi Kierkegaardiani*, vol. 1, *Leggere oggi Kierkegaard* [*Reading Kierkegaard Today*], 2000, pp. 191–210.

"Preghiere di Soren Kierkegaard" ["Søren Kierkegaard's Prayers"], in Mario Carrera, *Un'alba di luce. Via Crucis per condividere il dramma della sofferenza* [*A Dawn of Light. Via Crucis to Share the Tragedy of Suffering*], Milan: Paoline 2001.

"L'attrice di Inter e Inter (1848); Due discorsi edificanti del maggio 1843" ["The Actress by Inter and Inter (1848)" [*The Crisis and a Crisis in the Life of an Actress*]; "Two Upbuilding Discourses – May 1843"], in *Carte personali e opere pubbliche di S. Kierkegaard* [*Søren Kierkegaard's Personal Papers and Public Works*], ed. by Alessandro Cortese, Genoa: Marietti 2002.

"La sapienza segreta (Predica dimissoria 1844)" ["The Secret Wisdom. Dimissory Sermon 1844"], trans. by Simonella Davini, *"Seconda navigazione"* Annuario *di filosofia*, 2002, pp. 217–254.

L'istante [*The Moment*], trans. and ed. by Alberto Gallas, Genova: Marietti 2002.

"Antologia dal Diario" ["Anthology from Kierkegaard's Diary"], in *Il mistero della Passione* [*The Mystery of Passion*], ed. by Tito Di Stefano, Padua: Messaggero 2003.

"Il mito di Faust. Appunti e annotazioni dei *Papirer* (vols. 1 e 12)" ["The Myth of Faust. Notes and Annotations from *Papirer* (vols. 1 and 12)"], trans. by Carola Scanavino, *NotaBene. Quaderni di Studi Kierkegaardiani*, vol. 3, *L'arte dello sguardo: Kierkegaard e il cinema* [*The Art of Looking: Kierkegaard and the Cinema*], 2003, pp. 183–207.

Sulla mia attività di scrittore [*On My Work as an Author*], trans. by Andrea Scaramuccia, Pisa: ETS 2006.

Il concetto dell'angoscia [*The Concept of Anxiety*], trans. by Cornelio Fabro, Milan: SE 2007.

"Il Sig. Phister nel ruolo di Capitan Scipione (nell'opera comica *Ludovic*). Un ricordo e per il ricordo" [*Phister as Captain Scipio (in the Comic Opera* Ludovic*): A Recollection and for Recollection*], trans. by S. Davini, *Notabene. Quaderni di studi kierkegaardiani*, vol. 6, *La profondità della scena. Il teatro visitato da Kierkegaard, Kierkegaard visitato dal teatro* [*The Depth of the Scene: The Theater Seen by Kierkegaard, Kierkegaard Seen by the Theater*], 2008, pp. 227–38.

Gli atti dell'amore [*Works of Love*], trans. by Umberto Regina, Brescia: Morcelliana 2009; partially republished as "Tu devi amare *il prossimo*" ["You shall love *your* neighbor"], *Notabene. Quaderni di studi kierkegaardiani*, vol. 7, *Kierkegaard e la condizione desiderante. La seduzione dell'estetico* [*Kierkegaard and the Desiring Condition: The Seduction of the Aesthetic*], 2009, pp. 155–67.

Appunti sulle lezioni berlinesi di Schelling sulla "Filosofia della rivelazione", 1841– 1842 [*Notes on Schelling's Berlin Lectures on the "Philosophy of Revelation," 1841–1842*], trans. by Ingrid Basso, Milan: Bompiani 2008.

In vino veritas ["In Vino Veritas" [from *Stages on Life's Way*]], trans. by Laura Liva, Turin: Ananke 2010.

Briciole filosofiche, ovvero un poco di filosofia [*Philosophical Fragments, or A Fragment of Philosophy*], trans. by Umberto Regina, Brescia: Morcelliana 2012.

Il riflesso del tragico antico nel tragico moderno. Un esperimento di ricerca frammentaria ["The Tragic in Ancient Drama Reflected in the Tragic in Modern Drama" [from *Either/Or*]], trans. by Laura Liva, Genoa: Il Melangolo 2012.

II. Secondary Literature on Kierkegaard in Italian

Abbagnano, Nicola, "Kierkegaard," in his *Storia della Filosofia* [History of Philosophy], Turin: UTET 1946–1950, vol. 2, part 2 ("Il Romanticismo" [Romanticism]), pp. 179–93 (in the 3rd edition of 1963, vol. 3, Chapter 8, pp. 181–99).

— "Filosofia della possibilità. Kant e Kierkegaard" [The Philosophy of Possibility: Kant and Kierkegaard], in his *Esistenzialismo positivo* [Positive Existentialism], Turin: Taylor 1948, pp. 31–3.

Accardi, Giuseppe Fulvio, "'Døbte Hedninge' / 'Pagani battezzati'. Approcci pascaliani nel pensiero di Søren Kierkegaard" ["Baptized Pagans": Pascalian Approaches in Søren Kierkegaard's Thought], *NotaBene. Quaderni di studi Kierkegaardiani*, vol. 9, *Kierkegaard duecento anni dopo* [Kierkegaard Two Hundred Years Later], 2014, pp. 289–302.

Acone, Giuseppe, "L'opposizione kierkegaardiana a Hegel" [Kierkegaard's Opposition to Hegel], *Rivista di Studi Salernitani*, no. 1, 1968, pp. 189–205.

Adinolfi, Isabella, *Poeta o testimone? Il problema della comunicazione del cristianesimo in Søren Aabye Kierkegaard* [Poet or Witness? The Problem of the Communication of Christianity in Søren Aabye Kierkegaard], Genova: Marietti 1991.

— "Oltre l'etica: il rapporto tra morale e sovramorale in Søren Kierkegaard" [Beyond Ethics: The Relation between Moral and Supra-Moral in Søren Kierkegaard], in *L'etica e il suo Altro* [Ethics and its Other], ed. by Carmelo Vigna, Milan: F. Angeli 1994, pp. 150–88.

— "Kierkegaard: libertà e ragione" [Kierkegaard: Freedom and Reason], in *La libertà del bene* [The Freedom of the Good], ed. by Carmelo Vigna, Milan: Vita e Pensiero 1998, pp. 319–50.

— *Il cerchio spezzato: linee di antropologia in Pascal e Kierkegaard* [The Broken Circle: Anthropological Outlines in Pascal and Kierkegaard], Rome: Città nuova 2000.

— "Søren Kierkegaard e Woody Allen: l'umorismo come comunicazione indiretta della 'contraddizione priva di dolore,'" [Søren Kierkegaard and Woody Allen: Humor as Indirect Communication of the "Painless Contradiction"], *NotaBene. Quaderni di Studi Kierkegaardiani*, vol. 1, *Leggere oggi Kierkegaard* [Reading Kierkegaard Today], 2000, pp. 147–62.

— "'Djävlens öga': variazioni bergmaniane su temi kierkegaardiani" [Djävlens öga: Bergmanian Variations on Kierkegaardian Themes], *NotaBene. Quaderni di Studi Kierkegaardiani*, vol. 3, *L'arte dello sguardo: Kierkegaard e il cinema* [The Art of Looking: Kierkegaard and the Cinema], 2003, pp. 43–57.

— "Introduzione: L'edificante in Kierkegaard" [Introduction: The Edifying in Kierkegaard], *NotaBene. Quaderni di studi kierkegaardiani*, vol. 4, *L'edificante in Kierkegaard* [The Edifying in Kierkegaard], 2005, pp. 9–20.

— "Verità storiche contingenti e verità eterne di ragione in Pascal e Kierkegaard" [Contingent Historical Truths and the Eternal Truths of Reason in Pascal e Kierkegaard], *NotaBene. Quaderni di studi kierkegaardiani*, vol. 4, *L'edificante in Kierkegaard* [The Edifying in Kierkegaard], 2005, pp. 197–224.

—"Introduzione: 'L'esperto dell'anima.' Centralità della psicologia nell'opera di Kierkegaard" [Introduction: "The Soul Expert." The Importance of Psychology in Kierkegaard's Authorship], *Notabene. Quaderni di studi kierkegaardiani*, vol. 5, *Le malattie dell'anima. Kierkegaard e la psicologia* [The Sicknesses of the Soul: Kierkegaard and Psychology], 2007, pp. 7–20.

— "Colpa o malattia? Riflessioni sulla concezione kierkegaardiana della melanconia suscitate dalla lettura di un romanzo di Henrik Stangerup" [Guilt or Sickness? Reflections on Kierkegaard's Concept of Melancholy After Reading a Novel by Henrik Stangerup], *Notabene. Quaderni di studi kierkegaardiani*,

vol. 5, *Le malattie dell'anima. Kierkegaard e la psicologia* [The Sicknesses of the Soul: Kierkegaard and Psychology], 2007, pp. 65–110.
— "Metamorfosi filosofiche di Antigone. Lettura hegeliana e kierkegaardiana della tragedia di Sofocle" [Philosophical Metamorphoses of Antigone: Hegelian and Kierkegaardian Readings of Sophocles' Tragedy], *Notabene. Quaderni di studi kierkegaardiani*, vol. 6, *La profondità della scena. Il teatro visitato da Kierkegaard, Kierkegaard visitato dal teatro* [The Depth of the Scene: The Theater Seen by Kierkegaard, Kierkegaard Seen by the Theater], 2008, pp. 39–68.
— "A partire da Rashômon: Riflessioni filosofiche sulla credenza in Pascal e Kierkegaard" [Starting from *Rashômon*: Philosophical Reflections on Faith in Pascal and Kierkegaard], *Revista Portuguesa de Filosofia*, vol. 64, no. 2, 2008, pp. 1067–1098.
— *Le ragioni della virtù. Il carattere etico-religioso nella letteratura e nella filosofia* [The Reasons of Virtue: The Ethical-Religious Character in Literature and Philosophy], Genoa: Il Melangolo 2008.
— "Kierkegaard, Rosenzweig e la 'parola vivente'" [Kierkegaard, Rosenzweig and the "Living Word"], *Notabene. Quaderni di studi kierkegaardiani*, vol. 7, *Kierkegaard e la condizione desiderante. La seduzione dell'estetico* [Kierkegaard and the Desiring Condition: The Seduction of the Aesthetic], 2009, pp. 139–48.
— "Insegnare il cristianesimo nel Novecento. La ricezione di Kierkegaard in Italia" [Teaching Christianity in the Twentieth Century: The Reception of Kierkegaard in Italy], *Notabene. Quaderni di studi kierkegaardiani*, vol. 8, *Insegnare il Cristianesimo nel Novecento. La ricezione di Kierkegaard e Rosmini* [Teaching Christianity in the Twentieth Century: The Reception of Kierkegaard and Rosmini], 2011, pp. 143–64.
— *Studi sull'interpretazione kierkegaardiana del cristianesimo* [Essays on Kierkegaard's Interpretation of Christianity], Genoa: Il Melangolo 2012.
— "La dialettica tra mondo esterno e interno secondo Johannes de Silentio" [The Dialectics Between Inner World and Outer World According to Johannes de Silentio], *NotaBene. Quaderni di studi Kierkegaardiani*, vol. 9, *Kierkegaard duecento anni dopo* [Kierkegaard Two Hundred Years Later], 2014, pp. 273–287.
— (ed.), *Il religioso in Kierkegaard. Atti del convegno di studi organizzato dalla Società Italiana per gli Studi Kierkegaardiani tenutosi dal 14 al 16 dicembre 2000 a Venezia* [The Religious in Kierkegaard: Proceedings of the Congress Organized by The Italian Society for Kierkegaard Sudies in Venice, December 14th-16th, 2000], Brescia: Morcelliana 2002. (Tito Perlini, "Kierkegaard in Šestov" [Kierkegaard in Shestov], pp. 39–69; Vittorio Possenti, "Kierkegaard e Dostoevskij. Nella filosofia futura" [Kierkegaard and Dostoevsky: In the Philosophy of the Future], pp. 71–100; Giorgio Penzo, "Kierkegaard: il divino cristiano e il negativo" [Kierkegaard: The Christian Divine and the Negative], pp. 101–7; Virgilio Melchiorre, "Una circolarità ermeneutica. Tra fede cristiana e filosofia" [A Hermeneutical Circularity: Between Christian Faith and Philosophy], pp. 109–33; Joakim Garff, "Il poeta del martirio – il martirio del poeta" [The Poet of Martyrdom: The Martyrdom of the Poet], trans. by Andrea Scaramuccia, pp. 135–148; George Pattison, "La testimonianza socratica dell'amore" [The Socratic Witness to Love], trans. by Isabella Strano and Birgit Wunder,

pp. 149–163; Pierangelo Sequeri, "Fede e sapere in Kierkegaard" [Faith and Knowledge in Kierkegaard], pp. 165–183; Ivan Z. Sørensen, "Il doppio movimento della fede in *Timore e tremore*" [The Double Movement of Faith in "Fear and Trembling"], pp. 185–197; Anna Giannatiempo Quinzio, "Il malinteso tra speculazione e cristianesimo. Critica delle prove tradizionali dell'esistenza di Dio" [The Misunderstanding between Speculation and Christianity: The Criticism of the Traditional Proofs of God's Existence], pp. 199–218; Giuseppe Goisis, " 'L'istante.' Kierkegaard e l'attacco alla 'cristianità costituita'" ["The Moment." Kierkegaard and the Attack Against the Established Christianity], pp. 219–43; Jørgen Bonde Jensen, "La contemporaneità è l'essenziale. La religiosità di Søren Kierkegaard e le sue conseguenze" [Contemporaneity is What is Decisive: On Søren Kierkegaard's Religiosity and its Consequences], trans. by Andrea Scaramuccia, pp. 245–258; Marco Fortunato, "Irragione, dolore e protesta in Kierkegaard" [Irrationality, Suffering and Kierkegaard's Protest], pp. 259–70; Massimo Iiritano, "La lacerazione dell'io tra disperazione e fede" [The Tearing of the Self between Despair and Faith], pp. 271–82; Bettina Faber, "L'inattualità del religioso in Kierkegaard" [The Untimeliness of the Religious in Kierkegaard], pp. 283–303; Umberto Regina, "Dal padre nei cieli prende nome ogni paternità" [After the Father in Heaven is Named Every Paternity], pp. 305–17; Giuseppe Modica, "*Ordet* di Dreyer. Percorsi kierkegaardiani" [*The Word* by Dreyer: Kierkegaard's Routes], pp. 319–47; Inge Lise Rasmussen, "L'aspetto demoniaco della penitenza. Rilettura di *Romersholm* di Henrik Ibsen in chiave kierkegaardiana" [The Demonic Aspect of Penance: A Kierkegaardian Reading of Henrik Ibsen's *Romersholm*], pp. 349–60; Franco Macchi, "Con Kierkegaard oltre Kierkegaard" [With Kierkegaard, Beyond Kierkegaard], pp. 361–76; Luciano Sesta, "Onnipotenza divina, creazione dal nulla e libertà umana in Søren Kierkegaard" [Divine Omnipotence, Creation ex nihilo and Human Freedom in Søren Kierkegaard], pp. 379–92; Giacomo Bonagiuso, "Dalla morte: il silenzio e la parola. Kierkegaard e Rosenzweig" [From Death: Silence and the Word. Kierkegaard and Rosenzweig], pp. 393–409; Massimiliano Dal Vecchio, "L'amore di Dio secondo Kierkegaard" [God's Love in Kierkegaard], pp. 411–20; Giulio Goggi, "Il 'Non-io' di Fiche e l' 'ignoto' di Kierkegaard. Analogie" [Fichte's "Not-I" and Kierkegaard's "Unknown": Analogies], pp. 421–35; Marco Tuono, "La metafora della rinascita in una teologia capovolta. Suggestioni antropologiche del pensiero di Kierkegaard nella "Metamorfosi" di Kafka" [The Metaphor of Rebirth in an Overturned Theology: Anthropological Suggestions of Kierkegaard's Thought in Kafka's *Metamorphosis*], pp. 437–45).

Aliotta, Antonio, *Critica dell'esistenziaismo* [Critique of Existentialism], Rome: Cremonese 1951 (2nd ed. 1957).

Amato, Luigi, "Amleto, Kierkegaard e lo 'Strano Anello' (Studio di un meccanismo)" [Hamlet, Kierkegaard and the "Strange Ring" (A Study on a Mechanism)], *Notabene. Quaderni di studi kierkegaardiani*, vol. 7, *Kierkegaard e la condizione desiderante. La seduzione dell'estetico* [Kierkegaard and the Desiring Condition: The Seduction of the Aesthetic], 2009, pp. 77–91.

Amoroso, Leonardo, "L'esistenza sorniona e il suo discorso. L'arte della comunicazione in Søren Kierkegaard" [The Sly Existence and Its Discourse: The Art of

Communication in Søren Kierkegaard], *Studi Filosofici e Pedagogici*, no. 2, 1977, pp. 101–36.

— *Maschere kierkegaardiane* [Kierkegaardian Masks], Turin: Rosemberg and Sellier 1990.

— "Kierkegaard, Schiller e l'estetico. A partire da uno spunto di Heidegger" [Kierkegaard, Schiller and the Aesthetics. Starting from Heidegger], *NotaBene. Quaderni di studi Kierkegaardiani*, vol. 9, *Kierkegaard duecento anni dopo* [Kierkegaard Two Hundred Years Later], 2014, pp. 31–9.

Antiseri, Dario, *Come leggere Kierkegaard* [How to Read Kierkegaard], Milan: Bompiani 2005.

Armellini, Rina Anna, *Genesi ed evoluzione dell'angoscia esistenzialista* [Genesis and Development of Existentialistic Anxiety], Rovigo: Centro di cultura Aldo Masieri, Tip. Ster, Soc. Tip. Ed. Rodigina 1951.

— "L'arte della comunicazione di Kierkegaard e il Platone di Schleiermacher" [The Art of Communication in Kierkegaard and Schleiermacher's Plato], *Rivista di Filosofia Neo-Scolastica*, vols. 3–4, 2013, pp. 463–76.

Armetta, Francesco, *Storia e idealità in Kierkegaard* [History and Ideality in Kierkegaard], n.p.: Dialogo 1972.

Armieri, Salvatore, *Søren Kierkegaard e il cristianesimo* [Søren Kierkegaard and Christianity], Lugano: Edizioni del Cenobio 1956.

Bach, Giovanni, "Note sulla cultura scandinava" [Notes on Scandinavian Culture], *Archivio di storia della filosofia*, no. 1, 1932, pp. 61–72.

Balbino, Giulian, "Søren Kierkegaard," in his *Il cammino del pensiero* [The Way of Thought], Florence: Le Monnier 1962, pp. 626–8.

Banfi, Antonio, "Il problema dell'esistenza" [The Problem of Existence], *Studi Filosofici*, 1941, pp. 170–92.

— "Filosofia e teologia della crisi. I. Kierkegaard" [Philosophy and Theology of Crisis: I. Kierkegaard], in *Filosofi contemporanei* [Contemporary Philosophers], ed. by Remo Cantoni, Milan and Florence: Parenti 1961, pp. 255–62.

Basso, Ingrid, "Cento anni di studi kierkegaardiani in Italia: 1904–2004" [One Hundred Years of Kierkegaard Studies in Italy: 1904–2004], *NotaBene. Quaderni di studi kierkegaardiani*, vol. 4, *L'edificante in Kierkegaard* [The Edifying in Kierkegaard], 2005, pp. 305–26.

— *Kierkegaard uditore di Schelling: tracce della filosofia schellinghiana nell'opera di Søren Kierkegaard* [Kierkegaard Auditor of Schelling: Traces of Schelling's Philosophy in Søren Kierkegaard's Works], Milan: Mimesis 2007. (Review: Cavazzini, Andrea, review in *Freiburger Zeitschrift für Philosophie und Theologie*, vol. 56, 2009, pp. 294–7.)

— "'Il riflesso del tragico antico' nel *Brand* di Ibsen. Una lettura kierkegaardiana del dramma poetico" ["Ancient Tragedy's Reflection" in Ibsen's *Brand*: A Kierkegaardian Reading of the Poetic Drama], *Notabene. Quaderni di studi kierkegaardiani*, vol. 6, *La profondità della scena. Il teatro visitato da Kierkegaard, Kierkegaard visitato dal teatro* [The Depth of the Scene: The Theater Seen by Kierkegaard, Kierkegaard Seen by the Theater], 2008, pp. 161–85.

— "Kierkegaard e Schelling: Il rapporto tra coscienza e rivelazione in *Briciole di Filosofia* e *Filosofia della Rivelazione*" [Kierkegaard and Schelling: The

Relationship between Consciousness and Revelation in *Philosophical Fragments* and the *Philosophy of Revelation*], *Revista Portuguesa de Filosofia*, vol. 64, no. 2, 2008, pp. 1099–1111.

— "La riflessione di Kierkegaard sulla prima triade della Logica hegeliana alla luce della "meontologia" di Schelling" [Kierkegaard's Reflections on the First Triad of the Hegelian Logic in Light of Schelling's "Meontology"], *NotaBene. Quaderni di studi Kierkegaardiani*, vol. 9, *Kierkegaard duecento anni dopo* [Kierkegaard Two Hundred Years Later], 2014, pp. 41–55.

Battaglia, Felice, "Kierkegaard fra il singolo e Dio" [Kierkegaard between the Single Individual and God], in his *Il problema della morale nell'esistenzialismo* [The Moral Problem in Existentialism], Bologna: Zuffi 1946, pp. 9–81.

Bausola, Adriano, "Sul rapporto Schelling-Kierkegaard" [On the Relation Schelling-Kierkegaard], in F.W.J. Schelling, *Filosofia della Rivelazione* [Philosophy of Revelation], trans. by Adriano Bausola, Milan: Rusconi 1997, pp. LXXIX-LXXXIII.

Bazzi, Tullio, and Renato Giorda, "L'angoscia: ambiguità del termine (comunicazione e angoscia)" [Anxiety: The Ambiguity of the Word (Communication and Anxiety)], *Rassegna di Pedagogia*, vol. 41, nos. 2–3, 1983, pp. 122–9.

Bellezza, Vito Antonio, "Nota sull'esistenzialismo italiano" (analisi critica degli scritti di Cornelio Fabro) [Note on Italian Existentialism (Critical Analysis of Cornelio Fabro's Writings)], *Archivio di Filosofia*, vol. 15, nos. 1–2, 1946, pp. 143–62.

— "La lotta al teocentrismo nell'esistenzialismo kierkegaardiano" [The Fight against the Theocentrism in Kierkegaard's Existentialism], *Archivo di Filosofia*, no. 18, 1949, pp. 49–59.

— "Lo specchio della parola di Kierkegaard" [The Mirror of Kierkegaard's Word], *Archivio di filosofia*, no. 18, 1949, pp. 120–3.

— "Recenti critiche dell'esistenzialismo" [Recent Criticism of Existentialism], *Rassegna di filosofia*, vol. 2, no. 1, 1952, pp. 119–39.

— "Il singolo e la comunità nel pensiero di Kierkegaard" [The Individual and the Community in Kierkegaard's Thought], *Archivio di filosofia* (*Kierkegaard e Nietzsche*), 1953, pp. 133–89.

Bellisario, Vincenzo, "Il dramma di Kierkegaard" [The Drama of Kierkegaard], *Rivista di Filosofia Neo-Scolastica*, no. 34, 1942, pp. 127–36.

Benzo, Massimo, "Kierkegaard e la denuncia del dramma della filosofia hegeliana nel *Libro su Adler*" [Kierkegaard and the Denunciation of the Drama of Hegelian Philosophy in *The Book on Adler*], *Per la Filosofia*, no. 35, 1995, pp. 88–95.

— "S. Kierkegaard e il *Libro su Adler*: Ambiguità o coerenza?" [S. Kierkegaard and *The Book on Adler*: Ambiguity or Consistency?], *NotaBene. Quaderni di studi kierkegaardiani*, vol. 4, *L'edificante in Kierkegaard* [The Edifying in Kierkegaard], 2005, pp. 157–84.

Berardini, Sergio Fabio, "Oltre il nichilismo. Kierkegaard e Nietzsche" [Beyond Nihilism: Kierkegaard and Nietzsche], *NotaBene. Quaderni di studi kierkegaardiani*, vol. 4, *L'edificante in Kierkegaard* [The Edifying in Kierkegaard], 2005, pp. 241–57.

— "La malattia mortale: Dio, l'uomo, il mondo" [The Sickness unto Death: God, World, Man], *Notabene. Quaderni di studi kierkegaardiani*, vol. 5, *Le malattie dell'anima. Kierkegaard e la psicologia* [The Sicknesses of the Soul: Kierkegaard and Psychology], 2007, pp. 153–67.

— "Lo spirito sognante: innocenza e angoscia nel *Pinocchio* di Carmelo Bene" [The Dreaming Spirit: Innocence and Anxiety in Carmelo Bene's *Pinocchio*], *Notabene. Quaderni di studi kierkegaardiani*, vol. 6, *La profondità della scena. Il teatro visitato da Kierkegaard, Kierkegaard visitato dal teatro* [The Depth of the Scene: The Theater Seen by Kierkegaard, Kierkegaard Seen by the Theater], 2008, pp. 207–18.

— "Il poeta e la soglia. Etica ed estetica tra Kierkegaard, Heidegger e Pound" [The Poet and the Threshold: Ethics and Aesthetics between Kierkegaard, Heidegger, and Pound], *Notabene. Quaderni di studi kierkegaardiani*, vol. 7, *Kierkegaard e la condizione desiderante. La seduzione dell'estetico* [Kierkegaard and the Desiring Condition: The Seduction of the Aesthetic], 2009, pp. 93–109.

— *La malattia per la morte di Kierkegaard. Introduzione e commento* [Kierkegaard's *The Sickness unto Death*: Introducion and Commentary], Rome: Aracne 2010.

— "La realtà della possibilità. Decisione, disperazione e fede nella *Malattia per la morte* di Kierkegaard" [The Actuality of Possibility. Decision, Despair, and Faith in Kierkegaard's *Sickness Unto Death*], *NotaBene. Quaderni di studi Kierkegaardiani*, vol. 9, *Kierkegaard duecento anni dopo* [Kierkegaard Two Hundred Years Later], 2014, pp. 261–272.

Bertin, Giovanni M., "Comico, ironia e umorismo nel pensiero di Kierkegaard" [The Comic, Irony and Humor in Kierkegaard's Thought], in *Pedagogia tra tradizione e innovazione. Studi in onore di A. Agazzi* [Pedagogy between Tradition and Innovation: Studies in Honour of A. Agazzi], Milan: Vita e Pensiero 1979, pp. 361–82.

Bettiolo, Paolo, "Interpretazioni dell'Eden e aporie del Regno. Variazioni su motivi kierkegaardiani" [Interpretations of Eden and the Aporias of the Kingdom: Variations on Kierkegaardian Themes], *Notabene. Quaderni di studi kierkegaardiani*, vol. 7, *Kierkegaard e la condizione desiderante. La seduzione dell'estetico* [Kierkegaard and the Desiring Condition: The Seduction of the Aesthetic], 2009, pp. 121–38.

Bianchi, Cirillo, "Cristo scandalo della ragione e oggetto della fede secondo Kierkegaard" [Christ as Scandal of Reason and Object of Faith in Kierkegaard], *Rivista Rosminiana*, no. 68, 1974, pp. 316–21.

Bignone, Ettore, "Søren Kierkegaard," *Le Cronache Letterarie*, no. 4, 1910, p. 1.

— "Søren Kierkegaard. II. La filosofia dello stadio estetico" [Søren Kierkegaard: The Philosophy of the Aesthetic Stage], *Le Cronache Letterarie*, no. 9, 1910, p. 3.

Bobbio, Norberto, "Kierkegaard e noi" [Kierkegaard and Us], *Comunità*, no. 4, 1950, pp. 54–5.

Bochi, Giulia, *Pecato e fede. Motivi pietistici nel pensiero di Kierkegaard* [Sin and Faith: Pietistic Motifs in Kierkegaard's Thought], Faenza: Tipografia Lega 1957.

Bonagiuso, Giacomo, "La donna che camminava con Dio. Una lettura filosofica per 'Breaking the Waves' di Lars von Trier" [The Woman Who Walked with God: A Philosophical Reading of Lars von Trier's *Breaking the Waves*],

NotaBene. Quaderni di Studi Kierkegaardiani, vol. 3, *L'arte dello sguardo: Kierkegaard e il cinema* [The Art of Looking: Kierkegaard and the Cinema], 2003, pp. 81–99.

Borgese, Giuseppe Antonio, "Don Giovanni in Danimarca" [Don Juan in Denmark], in his *La vita e il libro. Saggi di letteratura e cultura contemporanea* [The Life and the Book: Essays on Literature and Contemporary Culture], vols. 1–3, Turin: Bocca 1910–13, vol. 2, pp. 231–41.

Borgia, Salvatore, "Il riscatto del singolo nella dialettica qualitativa di Kierkegaard" [The Redemption of the Single Individual in Kierkegaard's Qualitative Dialectics], in *Sapere assoluto e verità soggettiva* [Absolute Knowledge and Subjective Truth], Galatina: Editrice Salentina 1971, pp. 45–254.

Borso, Dario, "Due note kierkegaardiane" [Two Kierkegaardian Notes], *Rivista di Storia della Filosofia*, vol. 49, no. 3, 1994, pp. 547–58.

Bortolasi, Giovanni, "Interiorità ed esistenza. *La postilla non scientifica* di Soeren Kierkegaard" [Inwardness and Existence: Søren Kierkegaard's *Unscientific Postscript*], *Civiltà cattolica*, vol. 114, 1963, pp. 132–40.

— "Storia e cristianesimo. Le *Briciole di filosofia* di Soeren Kierkegaard" [History and Christianity: Søren Kierkegaard's *Philosophical Fragments*], *Civiltà cattolica*, vol. 114, 1963, pp. 455–63.

Bottani, Livio, "Noia, acedia ed epoché" [Boredom, *acedia* and *epoché*], *Sapienza*, no. 44, 1991, pp. 113–91.

— "Malinconia e nichilismo. I. Dalla ferita mortale alla ricomposizione dell'infranto" [Melancholy and Nihilism: I. From the Mortal Wound to the Recomposition of the Broken], *Filosofia*, vol. 43, no. 2, 1992, pp. 269–93.

Brancatisano, Fortunato, "Angoscia e inquietudine in Kierkegaard" [Anxiety and Worry in Kierkegaard], *Noesis*, no. 1, 1946, pp. 291–316.

Brandalise, Adone, "Stato d'animo. Sguardo e cinematografia a proposito di Kierkegaard" [Mood: Look and Cinematography about Kierkegaard], *NotaBene. Quaderni di Studi Kierkegaardiani*, vol. 3, *L'arte dello sguardo: Kierkegaard e il cinema* [The Art of Looking: Kierkegaard and the Cinema], 2003, pp. 115–20.

Brianese, Giorgio, "Kierkegaard e Schopenhauer: un dialogo impossibile?" [Kierkegaard and Schopenhauer: An Impossible Dialogue?], *NotaBene. Quaderni di studi Kierkegaardiani*, vol. 9, *Kierkegaard duecento anni dopo* [Kierkegaard Two Hundred Years Later], 2014, pp. 133–157.

Bubbio, Paolo Diego, "Ira, demoniaco e sacrificio in Kierkegaard" [Wrath, the Demonic and Sacrifice in Kierkegaard], in *Ira e sacrificio. Negazione del divino e dell'umano?* [Wrath and Sacrifice: Denial of the Divine and the Human], ed. by Maurizio Marin and Mauro Mantovani, Rome: LAS 2003, pp. 359–81 (*Biblioteca di scienze religiose*, vol. 185).

— "L'Abramo impossibile. Il concetto di sacrificio nel pensiero di Kierkegaard" [The Impossible Abraham: The Concept of Sacrifice in Kierkegaard's Thought], *NotaBene. Quaderni di studi kierkegaardiani*, vol. 4, *L'edificante in Kierkegaard* [The Edifying in Kierkegaard], 2005, pp. 225–39.

Bucceri, Stefania, "Kierkegaard e Dostoevskij di fronte al problema del male nel mondo" [Kierkegaard and Dostoevsky Confronted by the Problem of the Evil of the World], in *Atti del Congresso Internazionale di Filosofia 1946* [Proceedings of the International Congress of Philosophy 1946], Milan and Rome: Castellani 1947, vol. 2 (*L'esistenzialismo*).

Buonaiuti, Ernesto, "Ancora Kierkegaard" [Kierkegaard Again], *Religio*, no. 13, 1937, pp. 366–7.

— "Carlo Barth e la teologia della crisi" [Karl Barth and the Theology of Crisis], *La Nuova Europa*, vol. 2, no. 1, 1945, p. 11.

Burghi, Giancarlo, "Conversazione con Cornelio Fabro" [Conversation with Cornelio Fabro], *Aquinas*, vol. 39, no. 3, 1996, pp. 459–74.

Caccia, Gabriele, *La fede ed il suo oggetto nell'"Esercizio del cristianesimo" di Søren Kierkegaard* [Faith and Its Object in Søren Kierkegaard's *Practice in Christianity*], Rome: Tipografia poliglotta della Pontificia Università Gregoriana 1992.

Calamita, Nicolò, "Il silenzio in Kierkegaard. Specchiarsi nella parola. L'esempio della donna" [Silence in Kierkegaard: Reflecting Oneself in the Word. The Example of the Woman], in *Tra linguaggi e silenzi: riflessioni filosofiche* [Between Languages and Silences: Philosophical Reflections], ed. by Ferruccio De Natale, Bari: Adriatica Editrice 2004, pp. 81–105.

Calò, Giovanni, "La diffusione dell'idealismo Romantico nei paesi scandinavi: Søren Aabye Kierkegaard" [The Diffusion of Romantic Idealism in the Scandinavian Countries: Søren Aabye Kierkegaard], in his "L'individualismo etico nel secolo XIX" [Ethical Individualism in the 19th Century], *Atti della Reale Accademia di Scienze Morali e Politiche di Napoli*, vol. 37, 1906, pp. 156–70.

Calogero, Giuseppe, "Frammenti pedagogici di Søren Kierkegaard" [Pedagogical Fragments by Søren Kierkegaard], *I Problemi della Pedagogia*, vol. 23, no. 17, 1971, pp. 10–23.

Calvi, Guido, *Il singolo e la comunità in Søren Kierkegaard* [The Individual and the Community in Søren Kierkegaard], Rome: ITAL, edizioni italiane 1983.

Cannistra, Saverio, "Storia e fede nell'*Interludio* delle *Briciole filosofiche* di S. Kierkegaard" [History and Faith in the *Interlude* of S. Kierkegaard's *Philosophical Fragments*], *Teresianum*, vol. 43, no. 1, 1992, pp. 241–50.

Cantillo, Giuseppe, "Troeltsch e Kierkegaard tra teologia e filosofia" [Troeltsch and Kierkegaard between Theology and Philosophy], *NotaBene. Quaderni di studi Kierkegaardiani*, vol. 9, *Kierkegaard duecento anni dopo* [Kierkegaard Two Hundred Years Later], 2014, pp. 159–174.

Cantoni, Remo, *Crisi dell'uomo. Il pensiero di Dostoevskij* [The Crisis of the Human Being: Dostoevsky's Thought], Milan: Mondadori 1948.

— *La coscienza inquieta. Søren Kierkegaard* [The Anxious Consciousness: Søren Kierkegaard], Milan: Mondadori 1949 (2nd revised ed., Milan: Il Saggiatore 1976). (Reviews: Caruso, Emanuele, review in *Giornale di Metafisica*, vol. 5, no. 2, 1950, pp. 241–2; Castagnino, Franca, *Gli studi italiani su Kierkegaard 1906–1966*, Rome: Edizioni dell'Ateneo 1972, pp. 190–7; Fabro, Cornelio, review in *Meddelelser fra Søren Kierkegaard Selskabet*, vol. 3, no. 4, 1952, pp. 134–5; Frieiro, Eduardo, review in *Kriterion* (Minas Gerais), vol. 5, nos. 19–20, 1952, 267–8; Leger, Guy, review in *Revue des Sciences Philosophiques et Théologiques*, vol. 35, no. 4, 1951, p. 714.)

— "Umanesimo vecchio e nuovo" [Old and New Humanism], *Il Pensiero Critico*, no. 1, 1950, pp. 1–19.

— "La figura del *Freigeist* in Nietzsche" [The Figure of the *Freigeist* in Nietzsche], *Archivio di filosofia* (*Kierkegaard e Nietzsche*), 1953, pp. 209–240.

— "Kierkegaard Søren Aabye. Polemica antihegeliana" [Kierkegaard Søren Aabye: Anti-Hegelian Polemics], in his *Filosofia della storia e senso della vita* [The Philosophy of History and the Meaning of Life], Milan: La goliardica 1965.

Cantoro, Umberto, *Variazioni sull'angoscia di Kierkegaard* [Variations on Kierkegaard's Anxiety], Padua: Liviana 1948.

Capecci, Giorgio, "Aspettando un temporale, ovvero 'Niels Lyhne' e 'La Ripetizione'" [Waiting for a Storm or *Niels Lyhne* and *Repetition*], *Studi Nordici*, vol. 11, 2004, pp. 11–21.

Capone Braga, Gaetano, "Il valore dell'argomento ontologico secondo il Kierkegaard" [The Value of the Ontological Argument in Kierkegaard], *Sophia*, no. 22, 1954, pp. 148–51.

Cappuccio, Sofia, "Le dimensioni dello spirito umano nell'esistenzialismo di Kierkegaard e di G. Marcel" [The Dimensions of the Human Spirit in Kierkegaard and G. Marcel's Existentialism], in *Storia e Valori. Convegno di Napoli (16–17 ottobre 1990)* [History and Values: Proceedings of the Congress in Naples (October 16th-17th, 1990)], Naples: Loffredo 1992, pp. 157–63.

Capucci, Flavio, "La rilettura di un filosofo religioso: interpretazione di Kierkegaard" [The Rereading of a Religious Philosopher: Interpretation of Kierkegaard], *Studi Cattolici*, no. 136, 1972, pp. 411–19.

Caputo, Annalisa, "Esistenza. Categorie filosofiche del novecento" [Existence: Philosophical Categories of the Twentieth Century], *Paradigmi*, vol. 20, no. 59, 2002, pp. 291–302.

Carlini, Armando, "Il problema dell'interiorità nel Kierkegaard e nello Heidegger. Kierkegaard: I. L'angoscia e il peccato. II. L'angoscia e l'istante" [The Problem of Inwardness in Kierkegaard and Heidegger: I. Anxiety and Sin. II: Anxiety and Moment], in his *Il mito del realismo* [The Myth of Realism], Florence: Sansoni 1936, pp. 57–67.

Carrano, Antonio, "Tempo erotico e limite del tempo in Kierkegaard" [Erotic Time and Limit of Time in Kierkegaard], *Il Cannocchiale*, nos. 1–3, 1981, pp. 167–79.

— "Verità e scrittura in Søren Kierkegaard" [Truth and Writing in Kierkegaard], *Il Cannocchiale*, nos. 1–2, 1987, pp. 91–116.

Casellato, Sante, *Di alcune considerazioni intorno alla verità e all'errore* [Some Considerations on Truth and Error], Padua: CEDAM 1958.

Casini, Leonardo, "Il Diario di Søren Kierkegaard" [Søren Kierkegaard's Diary], *Humanitas*, vol. 39, no. 6, 1984, pp. 937–40.

— "Singolo, genere umano e storia universale. Un confronto tra Feuerbach e Kierkegaard" [Singular Individual, Humankind and Universal History: A Comparison of Feuerbach and Kierkegaard], *Filosofia e Teologia*, vol. 4, no. 2, 1990, pp. 317–28.

Castagnino, Franca, *Gli studi italiani su Kierkegaard 1906–1966* [Italian Studies on Kierkegaard 1906–1966], Rome: Edizioni dell'Ateneo 1972. (Review:

Garin, Eugenio, review in *Rivista critica di storia della filosofia*, vol. 28, 1973, pp. 452–56.)

— *Ricerche non scientifiche su Søren Kierkegaard* [Unscientific Research on Søren Kierkegaard], Rome: Cadmo 1977.

Castellana, Wanda, "La crisi del modello hegeliano in Søren Kierkegaard" [The Crisis of the Hegelian Model in Søren Kierkegaard], in *Saggi e ricerche di filosofia* [Philosophical Essays and Research], ed. by Ada Lamacchia, Lecce: Milella 1973, pp. 41–57.

Castelli, Enrico, *Esistenzialismo teologico* [Theological Existentialism], Rome: Abete 1966.

— "Søren Kierkegaard suscitatore di realtà eterne e invisibili" [Søren Kierkegaard Evoker of Eternal and Invisible Realities], *La Civiltà Cattolica*, vol. 127, no. 2, 1976, pp. 456–63.

Castoro, Eliseo, *Esistenza in preghiera sulle orme di Kierkegaard* [Praying Existence in Kierkegaard's Footsteps], Casale Monferrato: Piemme 2001.

— *Infanzia nello spirito: Teresa di Lisieux, Kierkegaard: cristiani e geni della modernità* [Childhood in the Spirit: Thérèse of Lisieux, Kierkegaard: Christian Geniuses of Modernity], Trapani: Il Pozzo di Giacobbe 2007.

Casuscelli, Paolo, "Musica e linguaggio? Kierkegaard e Don Giovanni" [Music and Language? Kierkegaard and Don Juan], *Rivista di Estetica*, vol. 26, no. 23, 1986, pp. 51–62.

Cenacchi, Giuseppe, "Kierkegaard: fenomenologia del peccato e filosofia esistenziale in *Il concetto dell'angoscia*" [Kierkegaard: Phenomenology of Sin and Existential Philosophy in *The Concept of Anxiety*], in *Nuovi Studi Kierkegaardiani. Bollettino del Centro Italiano di Studi Kierkegaardiani* [New Kierkegaard Studies: Bulletin of the Italian Center for Kierkegaard Studies], ed. by Giuseppe Mario Pizzuti, vol. 1, 1993, pp. 25–40.

Cerasi, Enrico, "Singolo o comunità? Per un confronto tra Kierkegaard e Barth" [Singular Individual or Community? For a Comparison between Kierkegaard and Barth], *NotaBene. Quaderni di Studi Kierkegaardiani*, vol. 3, *L'arte dello sguardo: Kierkegaard e il cinema* [The Art of Looking: Kierkegaard and the Cinema], 2003, pp. 143–58.

— "'Con gli occhi chiusi'. Note sull'edificante in Kierkegaard" ["With the Eyes Closed": Remarks on the Edifying in Kierkegaard], *NotaBene. Quaderni di studi kierkegaardiani*, vol. 4, *L'edificante in Kierkegaard* [The Edifying in Kierkegaard], 2005, pp. 115–36.

— "Per un'ermeneutica della sequela. Kierkegaard e Bonhoeffer" [For an Hermeneutic of Imitation: Kierkegaard and Bonhoeffer], *Notabene. Quaderni di studi kierkegaardiani*, vol. 5, *Le malattie dell'anima. Kierkegaard e la psicologia* [The Sicknesses of the Soul: Kierkegaard and Psychology], 2007, pp. 243–64.

— "La realtà della maschera. Su Kierkegaard e Pirandello" [The Truth of the Mask: On Kierkegaard and Pirandello], *Notabene. Quaderni di studi kierkegaardiani*, vol. 6, *La profondità della scena. Il teatro visitato da Kierkegaard, Kierkegaard visitato dal teatro* [The Depth of the Scene: The Theater Seen by Kierkegaard, Kierkegaard Seen by the Theater], 2008, pp. 187–205.

Cerrigone, Mario Enrico, "Il demoniaco in Kierkegaard" [The Demonic in Kierkegaard], *Divus Thomas*, vol. 105, no. 2, 2002, pp. 59–87.

Chiesa, Mario, "Cinque esistenzialisti. (Kierkegaard, Dostoevskij, Barth, Marcel, Berdiaeff)" [Five Existentialists. (Kierkegaard, Dostoevsky, Barth, Marcel, Berdyaev)], *Rivista Rosminiana di filosofia e cultura*, no. 44, 1950, pp. 67–74.

Chiuchiù, Lorenzo, "Una nota su Camus lettore di Kierkegaard" [A Note on Camus as a Reader of Kierkegaard], *Notabene. Quaderni di studi kierkegaardiani*, vol. 5, *Le malattie dell'anima. Kierkegaard e la psicologia* [The Sicknesses of the Soul: Kierkegaard and Psychology], 2007, pp. 283–8.

Ciaravolo, Pietro, "Insorgenza e ambiguità del concetto di singolo in S. Kierkegaard" [Emergence and Ambiguity of the Concept of the Singular Individual in S. Kierkegaard], *Contributo*, no. 1, 1981, pp. 21–36.

Collenea Isernia, Gino, "La difficile rivoluzione di Søren Kierkegaard" [The Hard Revolution of Søren Kierkegaard], *Città Vita*, no. 1, 1972, pp. 91–100.

Colombo, Giuseppe, "Il Cristianesimo di Kierkegaard e la modernità" [Kierkegaard's Christianity and Modernity], *Per la Filosofia*, no. 38, 1996, pp. 50–7.

— "La salvezza nell'essere che è parola e azione. Riflessioni *sull'Esercizio del Cristianesimo* di S. Kierkegaard" [The Salvation in Being which is Word and Action: Reflections on Kierkegaard's *Practice in Christianity*], *Per la Filosofia*, no. 40, 1997, pp. 61–9.

Colombo, Yoseph, "Il dramma di Abramo nel tormentato pensiero di Kierkegaard" [Abraham's Drama in Kierkegaard's Tormented Thought], *Annuario di Studi Ebraici*, 1969, pp. 89–108.

— "Il dramma di Abramo visto da Søren Kierkegaard" [Abraham's Drama Seen by Kierkegaard], *La Rassegna Mensile d'Israele*, no. 3, 1970, pp. 122–39.

Colosio, Innocenzo P., "Il Cristianesimo radicale di Kierkegaard nella sua ultima polemica contro la chiesa costituita" [Kierkegaard's Radical Christianity in his Late Polemics against the Established Church], *Rivista di Ascetica e Mistica*, no. 5, 1968, pp. 517–27.

— "Il Cristianesimo come antiborghesia nell'ultima polemica di Kierkegaard contro la chiesa di stato" [Christianity as Anti-Bourgeoisie in Kierkegaard's Late Polemics against the State Church], in *La borghesia e la sua crisi nella cultura contemporanea italiana e tedesca nel quadro dell'unità culturale europea. Atti del VIII Convegno Internazionale di studi italo-tedeschi, Merano 1971* [The Bourgeoisie and Its Crisis in Italian and German Contemporary Culture, within the Frame of the European Cultural Unity. Proceedings of the VIIIth International Congress of Italian-German Studies, Meran 1967], Bolzano: La Bodoniana 1971, pp. 445–53.

Contri, Giacomo B., "Kierkegaard. Il Vangelo della sofferenza. Dolor diabolicus" [Kierkegaard: The Gospel of Suffering. Dolor diabolicus], *Il Nuovo Areopago*, no. 2, 1995, pp. 59–70.

Corsano, Antonio, "Dimensioni del fatto religioso" [The Dimension of the Religious Fact], *Giornale Critico della Filosofia Italiana*, no. 51, no. 4, 1972, pp. 516–24.

Cortella, Lucio, "Da Hegel a Kierkegaard (e ritorno)" [From Hegel to Kierkegaard (and Back)], *NotaBene. Quaderni di studi Kierkegaardiani*, vol. 9, *Kierkegaard duecento anni dopo* [Kierkegaard Two Hundred Years Later], 2014, pp. 247–59.

Cortese, Alessandro, "Una nuova bibliografia kierkegaardiana (Complète la S.K. International Bibliografi par una Integrazione alle edizioni italiane e agli studi in lingua italiana et un Supplemento pour 1956 – août 1962)" [A New Kierkegaard Bibliography (Completing the Søren Kierkegaard International Bibliography with the Integration of the Italian Editions and Italian Secondary Literature, and a Supplement for the Years 1956-August 1962], *Rivista di Filosofia Neo-Scolastica*, vol. 55, 1963, pp. 98–108.

— "In margine all'estetica di Kierkegaard" [Marginal Notes on Kierkegaard's Aesthetics], *Nuova Presenza*, no. 17, 1965, pp. 10–22.

— "Kierkegaard-Sartre: appunti di metodologia" [Kierkegaard-Sartre: Methodological Notes], *Filosofia e Vita*, no. 6, 1965, pp. 31–49.

— "L'Organico culturale: paragrafi Kierkegaardiani" [The Cultural Structure: Kierkegaardian Paragraphs], *Vita e Pensiero*, vol. 48, no. 2, 1965, pp. 132–44.

— "Søren Aabye Kierkegaard. Abbozzo sulla sua vita" [Søren Aabye Kierkegaard: A Sketch of His Life], *Vita e Pensiero*, vol. 48, no. 1, 1965, pp. 38–54.

— "Filosofia, pena e tempo. La coscienza della pena in Kierkegaard" [Philosophy, Pain and Time: The Awareness of Pain in Kierkegaard], in *Archivio di Filosofia (Il mito della Pena)*, Padua: CEDAM 1967 (*Atti del Colloquio internazionale Rome 7–12 gennaio 1967* [Proceedings of the International Congress in Rome January 7th-12th, 1967]), pp. 469–81.

— "Il pastore Adler: Della libertà religiosa in Kierkegaard" [Pastor Adler: On Religious Freedom in Kierkegaard], *Archivio di Filosofia*, 1968, pp. 630–46; republished in his *Il pastore A. P. Adler o della libertà religiosa in Kierkegaard* [Pastor A.P. Adler or On Religious Freedom in Kierkegaard], Milan: Vita e Pensiero 1969 (*Contributi dell'Istituto di Filosofia*, vol. 1), pp. 81–113.

— "La domanda su Kierkegaard (*La lotta tra il vecchio ed il nuovo negozio del sapone*)" [The Question on Kierkegaard (The Battle between the Old and the New Soap-Cellars)], *Archivio di Filosofia*, no. 1, 1968, pp. 143–58.

— "Del nome di Dio come l'edificante in Søren Kierkegaard" [The Name of God as the Edifying in Søren Kierkegaard], *Archivio di Filosofia* (*L'analisi del linguaggio teologico. Il nome di Dio*), nos. 2–3, 1969, pp. 539–50.

— "Dell'Infallibilità come Messaggio di Cristo in Søren Kierkegaard" [On Infallibility as Message of Christ in Søren Kierkegaard], *Archivio di Filosofia*, nos. 2–3, 1970, pp. 603–13; republished in *L'infallibilità: l'aspetto filosofico e teologico. Atti del Convegno internazionale tenuto a Roma nel 1970* [Infallibility: The Philosophical and the Theological Aspect. Proceedings of the International Congress in Rome 1970], ed. by Enrico Castelli, Milan: Vita & Pensiero 1972 (*Contributi dell'Istituto di Filosofia*, vol. 2), pp. 30–64.

— "Kierkegaard oggi: tra nichilismo e rinascita della filosofia" [Kierkegaard Today: Between Nihilism and the Rebirth of Philosophy], *Itinerari*, no. 3, 1980, pp. 45–88.

48 *Laura Liva*

—"Kierkegaard oggi" [Kierkegaard Today], *Rivista di Filosofia Neo-Scolastica*, vol. 75, no. 3, 1983, pp. 500–10.

— *Per il concetto di ironia* [For the Concept of Irony], Genoa: Marietti 2004.

Costa, Filippo, "Intra-soggetto ed inter-soggetto in Kierkegaard" [Intra-Subject and Inter-Subject in Kierkegaard], *Giornale di Metafisica*, vol. 25, no. 1, 2003, pp. 9–28.

— *Ermeneutica ed esistenza. Saggio su Kierkegaard* [Hermeneutics and Existence: An Essay on Kierkegaard], Pisa: ETS 2003.

Costa, Giuseppe, "Personalità religiose moderne" [Modern Religious Personalities], *Bilychnis*, nos. 8–9, 1930, pp. 117–19.

Costantini, A., "Concetto di peccato in Kierkegaard" [The Concept of Sin in Kierkegaard], *Rivista di Teologia Morale*, vol. 14, no. 56, 1982, pp. 553–68.

Costantino, Salvatore, "Il linguaggio della fede e del paradosso. S.A. Kierkegaard" [The Language of Faith and Paradox: S.A. Kierkegaard], in his *Il linguaggio dei filosofi. Dalla menzogna alla verità* [The Language of the Philosophers: From Falsehood to Truth], Rome: Gangemi 1988, pp. 27–70.

Cristaldi, Giuseppe, *Il senso della fede in Kierkegaard* [The Meaning of Faith in Kierkegaard], Milan: Servizio librario dell'ISU dell'Università Cattolica del Sacro Cuore 1983.

Cristaldi, Mariano, "Materialismo storico ed esistenzialismo: Kierkegaard e Marx" [Historical Materialism and Existentialism: Kierkegaard and Marx], *Humanitas*, no. 4, 1949, pp. 1043–1046.

— "Kierkegaard, Feuerbach, Marx e la dialettica" [Kierkegaard, Feuerbach, Marx and Dialectics] and "Struttura del paradosso kierkegaardiano" [The Structure of the Kierkegaardian Paradox], in his *Filosofia e Metafisica: studi sull'antimetafisicismo contemporaneo* [Philosophy and Metaphysics: Studies on Contemporary Anti-Metaphysics], Catania: Tip. Etna 1957, pp. 61–104 and pp. 105–127; republished as an appendix to his *Problemi di storiografia kierkegaardiana* [Problems of Kierkegaardian Historiography], Catania: Giannotta 1973, pp. 137–96.

—*Problemi di storiografia kierkegaardiana* [Problems of Kierkegaardian Historiography], Catania: Giannotta 1973.

Cristaldi, Rosario Vittorio, "Kierkegaard o della testimonianza impossibile" [Kierkegaard or the Impossible Testimony], *Teoresi*, vol. 32, 1977, pp. 233–46.

Cristellon, Luca, "Silenzio e comunicazione nel pensiero di Kierkegaard" [Silence and Communication in Kierkegaard's Thought], in *Nuovi Studi Kierkegaardiani. Bollettino del Centro Italiano di Studi Kierkegaardiani* [New Kierkegaard Studies: Bulletin of the Italian Center for Kierkegaard Studies], ed. by Giuseppe Mario Pizzuti, vol. 1, 1993, pp. 41–56.

Curi, Umberto, *Filosofia del Don Giovanni: alle origini di un mito moderno* [The Philosophy of Don Juan: On the Origins of a Modern Myth], Milan: B. Mondadori 2002.

Czakó, István, "Abramo come paradigma del credente nel libro 'Timore e tremore' di Søren Kierkegaard" [Abraham as a Paradigm of the Believer from the Book *Fear and Trembling* by Søren Kierkegaard], *Folia theologica*, vol. 8, 1997, pp. 199–226.

D'Agostino, Francesco, "La fenomenologia dell'uomo giusto: un parallelo tra Kierkegaard e Platone" [The Phenomenology of the Just Man: A Comparison between Kierkegaard and Plato], *Rivista Internazionale di Filosofia del Diritto*, vol. 49, no. 2, 1972, pp. 153–72.

— "Considerazioni sul problema del divenire in Søren Kierkegaard" [A Consideration of the Problem of Becoming in Søren Kierkegaard], *La Cultura*, no. 16, 1978, pp. 409–43.

Dalledonne, Andrea, "*L'Esercizio del Cristianesimo* nel *Diario* di S. Kierkegaard" [*Practice in Christianity* in Kierkegaard's Diary], *Renovatio*, no. 4, 1985, pp. 407–28.

— "La dottrina kierkegaardiana del Singolo come critica cristiana del collettivismo giudaico" [Kierkegaard's Doctrine of the Singular Individual as Christian Criticism of Jewish Collectivism], in *Nuovi Studi Kierkegaardiani. Bollettino del Centro Italiano di Studi Kierkegaardiani* [New Kierkegaard Studies: Bulletin of the Italian Center for Kierkegaard Studies], ed. by Giuseppe Mario Pizzuti, vol. 1, March 1993, pp. 57–74.

D'Angelo, Antonello, "Considerazioni sul problema del divenire in Søren Kierkegaard" [Considerations on the Problem of Becoming in Søren Kierkegaard], *La Cultura*, vol. 16, 1978, pp. 409–43.

— "La dialettica della ripresa in Søren Kierkegaard" [The Dialectics of Repetition in Søren Kierkegaard], *La Cultura*, vol. 20, 1982, pp. 110–55.

Davini, Simonella, *Il circolo del salto. Kierkegaard e la ripetizione* [The Circle of the Leap: Kierkegaard and Repetition], Pisa: Edizioni ETS 1996.

— "Sapere, passione, verità nell'interpretazione kierkegaardiana dello scetticismo antico" [Knowledge, Passion, Truth in Kierkegaard's Interpretation of Ancient Scepticism], *NotaBene. Quaderni di Studi Kierkegaardiani*, vol. 1, *Leggere oggi Kierkegaard* [Reading Kierkegaard Today], 2000, pp. 61–78.

— *Arte e critica nell'estetica di Kierkegaard* [Art and Criticism in Kierkegaard's Aesthetics], Palermo: Centro Internazionale Studi di Estetica 2003.

— "Il corpo dello scrittore. Kierkegaard e il problema dell'autore" [The Body of the Writer: Kierkegaard and the Problem of the Author], *NotaBene. Quaderni di studi Kierkegaardiani*, vol. 9, *Kierkegaard duecento anni dopo* [Kierkegaard Two Hundred Years Later], 2014, pp. 83–95.

De Feo, Nicola Massimo, "La dialettica dell'inversione" [The Dialectics of the Inversion], in his *L'ontologia fondamentale. Kierkegaard, Nietzsche, Heidegger* [Fundamental Ontology: Kierkegaard, Nietzsche, Heidegger], Milan: Silva 1964, pp. 19–38.

— "L'uomo-dio nel cristianesimo di Kierkegaard" [The Man-God in Kierkegaard's Christianity], in *Giornale Critico della Filosofia Italiana*, vol. 44, 1965, pp. 369–85.

Della Volpe, Galvano, *Appunti sulla filosofia contemporanea. I. (Banfi, Bariè, Carabellese, Kierkegaard)* [Notes on Contemporary Philosophy. I. (Banfi, Bariè, Carabellese, Kierkegaard)], Rocca di San Casciano: Tipografia Cappelli 1937, pp. 61–76.

De Luca, Erri, "Avventura del nome" [The Adventure of the Name], *NotaBene. Quaderni di Studi Kierkegaardiani*, vol. 2, *Kierkegaard e la letteratura* [Kierkegaard and Literature], 2002, pp. 11–12.

De Natale, Ferruccio, *Esistenza, filosofia, angoscia: tra Kierkegaard e Heidegger* [Existence, Philosophy and Anxiety: Between Kierkegaard and Heidegger], Bari: Adriatica Editrice 1995.

De Paz, Alfredo, *Europa Romantica: fondamenti e paradigmi della sensibilità moderna* [Romantic Europe: Grounds and Paradigms of the Modern Sensibility], Naples: Liguori 1994.

De Rosa, Gabriele, "Il vescovo luterano Mynster, S. Alfonso de' Liguori e Kierkegaard" [The Lutheran Bishop Mynster, S. Alfonso de' Liguori and Kierkegaard"], in *Veritatem in caritate. Studi in onore di Cornelio Fabro* [*Veritatem in caritate*. Studies in Honor of Cornelio Fabro], ed. by Giuseppe Mario Pizzuti, Potenza: Ermes 1991, pp. 275–89; republished in *Ricerche di storia sociale e religiosa*, vol. 21, no. 41, 1992, pp. 7–21.

— "Cornelio Fabro fra S. Tommaso, Kierkegaard e la morte a Pompei" [Cornelio Fabro between St. Thomas, Kierkegaard and Death in Pompei], *Ricerche di Storia Sociale e Religiosa*, no. 48, 1995, pp. 165–70.

De Ruggiero, Guido, "La filosofia dell'esistenza" [The Philosophy of Existence], *Rivista di Filosofia*, no. 33, 1942, pp. 4–42.

Diddi, Roul, "Il momento etico nel pensiero di Kierkegaard" [The Ethical Moment in Kierkegaard's Thought], *Pagine Nuove*, vol. 2, no. 6, 1948, pp. 248–51.

Di Giamberardino, Oscar, "Kierkegaard iniziatore dell'esistenzialismo" [Kierkegaard Founder of Existentialism], in his *Dall'esistenzialismo alla filosofia della sensibilità* [From Existentialism to Philosophy of Sensibility], Padua: CEDAM 1951, pp. 7–28.

Di Monte, Italo, "Kierkegaard tra idealità e realtà. La dialettica della fede contro i falsi fideismi. Noterelle polemiche" [Kierkegaard between Ideality and Reality: The Dialectic of Faith Against the False Fideisms: Short Polemical Notes], in *Nuovi Studi Kierkegaardiani* [New Kierkegaard Studies], ed. by Giuseppe Mario Pizzuti, Potenza: Centro Italiano di Studi Kierkegaardiani 1988, pp. 101–15.

Di Stefano, Tito, "La sofferenza di Cristo nella teologia della croce di S. Kierkegaard" [The Suffering of Christ in Kierkegaard's Theology of the Cross], in *La sapienza della Croce oggi: atti del Congresso internazionale, Rome 13–18 ottobre 1975* [The Wisdom of the Cross Today: Proceedings of the International Congress in Rome, October 13th-18th, 1975], Turin: Leumann, Elle Di Ci 1976, vol. 3, pp. 68–75.

— *Il paradigma della verità esistenziale secondo S. Kierkegaard* [The Paradigm of Existential Truth in Kierkegaard], Perugia: Galeno 1985.

— *La libertà rischio della verità. Il problema di Lessing. La soluzione di Kierkegaard* [Freedom as Risk of the Truth: The Problem of Lessing. Kierkegaard's Solution], Città di Castello: Galeno 1985.

— *Søren Kierkegaard: dalla situazione dell'angoscia al rischio della fede* [Søren Kierkegaard: from the Situation of the Anxiety to the Risk of Faith], Assisi: Cittadella 1986.

— "Il ruolo dell'etica nella struttura dell'esistenza secondo S. Kierkegaard" [The Role of Ethics in the Structure of Existence in S. Kierkegaard], *Antonianum*, vol. 71, no. 1, 1996, pp. 105–13.

Dietz, Walter, "La rinascita kierkegaardiana e la teologia dialettica" [The Kierkegaard Renaissance and Dialectical Theology], in *Storia della filosofia*, vol. 6: *Il novecento*, I. [The History of Philosophy, vol. 6, the 19th Century], ed. by Pietro Rossi and Carlo A. Viano, Bari: Editori Laterza 1999, pp. 443–68 (*Enciclopedia del sapere*).

Dottori, Riccardo, "La testimonianza di Kierkegaard" [Kierkegaard's Testimony], *Archivio di Filosofia* (*Informazione e testimonianza*), no. 3, 1972, pp. 55–66.

Dottorini, Daniele, "Il pensiero dello spettro. Note sul rapporto tra Kierkegaard e il cinema" [The Thought of the Spectre: Notes on the Relation between Kierkegaard and the Cinema], *NotaBene. Quaderni di Studi Kierkegaardiani*, vol. 3, *L'arte dello sguardo: Kierkegaard e il cinema* [The Art of Looking: Kierkegaard and the Cinema], 2003, pp. 101–13.

Ducci, Edda, *La maieutica kierkegaardiana* [Kierkegaardian Maieutics], Turin: Società Editrice Internazionale 1967.

Duval, Raymond, "L'unicita dell'individuo e la solitudine del divenire" [The Uniqueness of the Individual and the Loneliness of Becoming], *Concilium*, vol. 5, 1981, pp. 49–61.

Fabbri, Maurizio, *Nel cuore della scelta: Kierkegaard, l'etica senza fondamenti e l'angoscia della formazione* [In the Heart of Choice: Kierkegaard, Ethics without Foundations and the Anxiety of Education], Milan: UNICOPLI 2005.

Faber, Bettina, *La contraddizione sofferente: la teoria del tragico in Søren Kierkegaard* [The Suffering Contradiction: The Theory of the Tragic in Søren Kierkegaard], Padua: Il poligrafo 1998. (Review: Fortunato, Marco, review in *Studi Nordici*, vol. 6, 1999, pp. 147–50.)

Fabris, Adriano "La filosofia, la malattia, la morte. A proposito della *Malattia per la morte* di Søren Kierkegaard" [Philosophy, Sickness, Death: About Kierkegaard's *Sickness unto Death*], *NotaBene. Quaderni di Studi Kierkegaardiani*, vol. 3, *L'arte dello sguardo: Kierkegaard e il cinema* [The Art of Looking: Kierkegaard and the Cinema], 2003, pp. 137–42.

Fabro, Cornelio, *Introduzione all'esistenzialismo* [Introduction to Existentialism], Milan: Vita e Pensiero 1943, pp. 24–44.

— "Centenari kierkegaardiani" [Kierkegaard's Centenaries], *Osservatore Romano*, June 18, 1944, p. 3.

— "Kierkegaard e Marx" [Kierkegaard and Marx], in *Atti del congresso internazionale di filosofia 1946* [Proceedings of the International Congress of Philosophy 1946], Milan and Rome: Castellani 1947, vol. 1 (*Il materialismo storico* [Historical Materialism]), pp. 3–16; republished in his *Tra Kierkegaard e Marx. Per una definizione dell'esistenza* [Between Kierkegaard and Marx: For a Definition of the Existence], Florence: Vallecchi 1952, pp. 9–39.

— "Kierkegaard in inglese" [Kierkegaard in English], *Euntes Docete*, no. 1, 1948, pp. 163–6.

— "Kierkegaard poeta-teologo dell'Annunciazione" [Kierkegaard as Poet-Theologian of Annunciation], *Humanitas*, no. 3, 1948, pp. 1025–1034.

— "La religiosità di Kierkegaard nel suo *Diario*" [Kierkegaard's Religiousness in his Diary], *Humanitas*, no. 3, 1948, pp. 209–16.

—"Critica di Kierkegaard all'Ottocento" [Kierkegaard's Criticism of the Nineteenth Century], in *Atti del XV Congresso Nazionale di Filosofia 1948*

[Proceedings of the XVth National Congress of Philosophy 1948], Messina: G. D.'Anna 1949, pp. 375–85.

— "Esistenzialismo teologico" [Theological Existentialism], in *L'esistenzialismo* [Existentialism], Florence: Città di Vita 1950, pp. 15–40; republished in his *Tra Kierkegaard e Marx. Per una definizione dell'esistenza* [Between Kierkegaard and Marx: For a Definition of Existence], Florence: Vallecchi 1952, pp. 9–39.

— "Rassegna dell'esistenzialismo" [A Review of Existentialism], *Divus Thomas*, no. 27, 1950, pp. 265–73.

— "L'Assoluto nel tomismo e nell'esistenzialismo" [The Absolute in Thomism and in Existentialism], *Salesianum*, no. 13, 1951, pp. 185–201; republished in his *L'Assoluto nell'esistenzialismo* [The Absolute in Existentialism], Catania: Miano 1954, pp. 67–104.

— "Recenti studi danesi su Kierkegaard" [Recent Danish Studies on Kierkegaard], *Rassegna di Filosofia*, no. 1, 1952, pp. 347–54; republished in his "Note di bibliografia kierkegaardiana" [Notes of Kierkegaardian Bibliography], in *Studi kierkegaardiani* [Kierkegaard Studies], ed. by Cornelio Fabro, Brescia: Morcelliana 1957, pp. 417–38.

— "La dialettica della libertà e l'Assoluto. Per un confronto tra Kierkegaard ed Hegel" [The Dialectics of Freedom and the Absolute: A Comparison of Kierkegaard and Hegel], *Archivio di Filosofia* (*Kierkegaard e Nietzsche*), 1953, pp. 45–69.

— "L'esistenzialismo kierkegaardiano" [Kierkegaard's Existentialism], in *Storia della filosofia* [History of Philosophy], ed. by Cornelio Fabro, Rome: Colletti 1954, pp. 773–856 (2nd ed., vols. 1–2, 1959 as "L'esistenzialismo kierkegaardiano" [Kierkegaard's Existentialism] and "La Kierkegaard renaissance" [The Kierkegaard-Renaissance], vol. 2, pp. 839–918).

— "Attualità e ambiguità nell'opera kierkegaardiana" [Actuality and Ambiguity in Kierkegaard's Work], *Orbis Litterarum*, no. 10, 1955, pp. 66–74; republished as "L'ambiguità del cristianesimo kierkegaardiano" [The Ambiguity of Kierkegaard's Christianity] in his *Dall'essere all'esistente* [From Being to the Existent], Brescia: Morcelliana 1957, pp. 277–333.

— "La dialettica della fede nell'idealismo trascendentale" [The Dialectics of Faith in Transcendental Idealism], *Archivio di Filosofia*, no. 2, 1955, pp. 116–23.

— "Kierkegaard," in *Vite di pensatori* [Lives of Thinkers], Milan and Rome: RAI 1956, pp. 34–5.

— "Kierkegaard e il cattolicesimo" [Kierkegaard and Catholicism], *Divus Thomas*, no. 59, 1956, pp. 67–70.

— "Kierkegaard e San Tommaso" [Kierkegaard and St. Thomas], *Sapienza*, no. 9, 1956, pp. 292–308.

—"Sant'Agostino e l'esistenzialismo" [St. Augustine and Existentialism], in *Sant'Agostino e le grandi correnti della filosofia contemporanea. Atti del congresso italiano di filosofia agostiniana. Roma 20–23 ottobre 1954* [St. Augustine and the Great Currents of the Contemporary Philosophy: Proceedings of the Italian Congress of Augustinian Philosophy. Rome, October 20th-23th, 1954], Rome: Tolentino 1956, pp. 141–66.

—"Estetica mozartiana nell'opera di Kierkegaard" [Mozart's Aesthetics in Kierkegaard's Work], in *Atti del III congresso internazionale di estetica. Venezia 3–5 settembre 1956* [Proceedings of the Third International Congress of Aesthetics. Venice, September 3rd-5th, 1956], Turin: Istituto di estetica dell'Università di Torino, Ed. della Rivista di Estetica 1957, pp. 706–10.

—"Kierkegaard," in *Enciclopedia filosofica* [Encyclopaedia of Philosophy], vols. 1–4, Florence: Sansoni 1957, vol. 2 (ER-LE), columns 1699–1713.

— "La 'comunicazione della verità' nel pensiero di Kierkegaard" [The "Communication of the Truth" in Kierkegaard's Thought], in *Studi Kierkegaardiani* [Kierkegaard Studies], ed. by Cornelio Fabro, Brescia: Morcelliana 1957, pp. 125–63.

— "La fenomenologia della fede. Ambiguità della fede in Søren Kierkegaard" [The Phenomenology of Faith: Ambiguity of Faith in Søren Kierkegaard], *Archivio di Filosofia*, nos. 1–2, 1957, pp. 187–97.

— "Kierkegaard e Karl Barth" [Kierkegaard and Karl Barth], *Studi Francescani*, no. 55, 1958, pp. 155–8.

— "Il problema del peccato nell'esistenzialismo" [The Problem of Sin in Existentialism], in *Il peccato* [The Sin], ed. by Salvatore Canals and Pietro Palazzini, Rome: Ares 1959, pp. 712–25.

— "Influssi cattolici sulla spiritualità kierkegaardiana" [Catholic Influences on Kierkegaardian Spirituality], *Humanitas*, no. 7, 1962, pp. 501–7.

— "Le prove dell'esistenza di Dio in Kierkegaard" [The Proof of the Existence of God in Kierkegaard], *Humanitas*, no. 17, 1962, pp. 97–110.

— "Kierkegaard e la donna" [Kierkegaard and the Woman], *Mater Ecclesiae*, no. 2, 1967, pp. 240–4.

— "Kierkegaard e San Tommaso" [Kierkegaard and St. Thomas], *Mater Ecclesiae*, no. 1, 1967, pp. 152–60.

— "Il Cristianesimo come contemporaneità e impegno essenziale" [Christianity as Contemporaneity and Essential Engagement], in *Il Cristianesimo nella società di domani* [Christianity in the Future Society], ed. by Pietro Prini, Rome: Edizioni Abete 1968, pp. 49–80.

— "Kierkegaard e la teologia dialettica" [Kierkegaard and Dialectical Theology], in his *L'uomo e il rischio di Dio* [The Human Being and the Risk of God], Rome: Editrice Studium 1969, pp. 446–8.

— "La missione di Kierkegaard" [The Mission of Kierkegaard], *Ethica*, no. 8, 1969, pp. 169–80.

— "I caratteri dell'amore cristiano secondo Kierkegaard" [The Characteristics of Christian Love in Kierkegaard], *Ecclesia Mater*, no. 1, 1970, pp. 50–5.

— "Inediti kierkegaardiani" [Kierkegaard's Unpublished Works], *Humanitas*, no. 7, 1970, pp. 707–11.

— "Kierkegaard critico di Hegel" [Kierkegaard as Critic of Hegel], in *Incidenza di Hegel. Studi raccolti in occasione del II centenario della nascita del filosofo* [The Influence of Hegel: Studies Collected on the Occasion of the Second Centenary of Hegel's Birth], ed. by Fulvio Tessitore, Naples: Morano 1970, pp. 499–563.

— "Kierkegaard e la Madonna" [Kierkegaard and the Virgin Mary], *Ecclesia Mater*, no. 2, 1971, pp. 132–44.
— "Il conforto del Paradiso in Søren Kierkegaard" [The Consolation of Heaven in Kierkegaard], *Ecclesia Mater*, no. 3, 1971, pp. 226–34.
—"La libertà umana e l'eternità dell'inferno in Søren Kierkegaard" [Human Freedom and the Eternity of the Hell in Søren Kierkegaard], *Ecclesia Mater*, no. 2, 1971, pp. 143–6.
—"Pensieri sulla morte in Søren Kierkegaard" [Thoughts on Death in Søren Kierkegaard], *Ecclesia Mater*, no. 1, 1971, pp. 43–7.
— "Cristologia kierkegaardiana" [Kierkegaardian Christology], *Divinitas*, vol. 16, no. 1, 1972, pp. 130–5.
— "La sofferenza di Cristo nella teologia di Søren Kierkegaard" [The Suffering of Christ in Kierkegaard's Theology], *Tabor*, nos. 11–12, 1972, pp. 330–2.
—"Sull'essenza della testimonianza cristiana" [On the Essence of Christian Testimony], *Archivio di Filosofia (Informazione e testimonianza)*, no. 3, 1972, pp. 39–54.
— "L'attività oratoria, dottrinale e pastorale di un vescovo luterano dell'Ottocento: J.P. Mynster" [The Oratorical, Doctrinal and Pastoral Activity of a Lutheran Bishop in the Nineteenth Century: J.P. Mynster], *Ricerche di Storia Sociale e Religiosa*, no. 1, 1973, pp. 41–108.
— "Spunti cattolici nel pensiero di Søren Kierkegaard" [Catholic Ideas in Søren Kierkegaard's Thought], *Doctor Communis*, no. 4, 1973, pp. 251–80.
— "La dialettica della situazione nell'etica di Søren Kierkegaard" [The Dialectics of the Situation in Søren Kierkegaard's Ethics], in *L'etica della situazione* [The Ethics of Situation], ed. by Pietro Piovani, Naples: Guida 1974, pp. 73–96.
— "La *pistis* aristotelica nell'opera di Søren Kierkegaard" [The Aristotelian *Pistis* in Søren Kierkegaard's Work], *Proteus*, no. 5, 1974, pp. 3–24.
— "Kierkegaard e la dissoluzione idealistica della libertà" [Kierkegaard and the Idealistic Dissolution of Freedom], in *Problemi religiosi e filosofia* [Religious Problems and Philosophy], ed. by Albino Babolin, Padua: Editrice La garangola 1975, pp. 99–122; republished in *Scritti di filosofia in onore di Cleto Carbonara* [Philosophical Writings in Honor of Cleto Carbonara], ed. by Università dgli Studi di Napoli, Facoltà di Lettere e Filosofia, Naples: Giannini Editore 1976, pp. 304–22.
—"La fondazione metafisica della libertà di scelta in S. Kierkegaard" [The Metaphysical Foundation of Choice in S. Kierkegaard], in *Studi di filosofia in onore di Gustavo Bontadini* [Philosophical Studies in Honor of Gustavo Bontadini], vols. 1–2, ed. by F. Carlomagno, Milan: Vita e Pensiero 1975, vol. 2, pp. 86–116.
— "Kierkegaard. Cristianesimo tragico o drammatico?" [Kierkegaard: Tragic or Dramatic Christianity?], *Humanitas*, no. 7, 1976, pp. 532–7.
—"Egli imparò l'obbedienza da ciò che soffrì" [He Learned Obedience by Suffering], *Ecclesia Mater*, no. 1, 1977, pp. 11–13.
— "La dialettica d'intelligenza e volontà nella costituzione dell'atto libero" [The Dialectics of the Intelligence and the Will in the Constitution of the Free Act], *Doctor Communis*, no. 2, 1977, pp. 163–91.

— "La dialettica qualitativa di Søren Kierkegaard" [The Qualitative Dialectics of Søren Kierkegaard], in *Dialettica e religione. Atti del 2° Convegno di Studi di Filosofia della Religione* [Dialectics and Religion. Proceedings of the 2nd Congress of Studies in Philosophy of Religion], ed. by Albino Babolina, Perugia: Benucci 1977, pp. 1–50.

— "Sorpresa e attesa cristiana della morte in Kierkegaard" [The Christian Surprise and the Wait for Death in Kierkegaard], *Nuova Rivista di Ascetica e Mistica*, no. 3, 1977, pp. 297–310.

— "Il problema della chiesa in Newman e Kierkegaard" [The Problem of the Church in Newman and Kierkegaard], *Newman Studien*, no. 10, 1978, pp. 120–39.

— "La critica di Kierkegaard alla dialettica hegeliana nel *Libro su Adler*" [Kierkegaard's Criticism of the Hegelian Dialectic in *The Book on Adler*], *Giornale Critico della Filosofia Italiana*, no. 9, 1978, pp. 1–32.

— "Preghiera e dialettica dell'esistenza in Kierkegaard" [Prayer and the Dialectics of the Existence in Kierkegaard], in his *La preghiera nel pensiero moderno* [Prayer in Modern Thought], Rome: Edizioni di Storia e Letteratura 1979, pp. 363–96.

— "Dialettica della libertà e necessità nella storia in Kierkegaard e Tolstoj" [The Dialectics of Freedom and the Necessity of History in Kierkegaard and Tolstoy], in *Tolstoj oggi* [Tolstoy Today], ed. by Sante Graciotti and Vittorio Strada, Florence: Quaderni di S. Giorgio 1980, pp. 111–28.

— "Circa l'ispirazione cristiana dell'opera di Kierkegaard. In margine ad una nota di Franco Lombardi" [About the Christian Inspiration of Kierkegaard's Work: Marginal Notes to a Note by Franco Lombardi], in *Scritti in onore di Nicola Petruzzellis* [Writings in Honor of Nicola Petruzzellis], ed. by Università dgli Studi di Napoli, Facoltà di Lettere e Filosofia, Naples: Giannini 1981, pp. 105–12.

—"La dialettica della prima e seconda immediatezza nella soluzione-dissoluzione dell'Assoluto hegeliano" [The Dialectic of the First and the Second Immediacy in the Solution-Dissolution of the Hegelian Absolute], *Aquinas*, vol. 24, nos. 2–3, 1981, pp. 245–78.

— "La negazione assurda" [Absurd Negation], *Quadrivium*, no. 4, 1981, pp. 434–88.

—"Convergenze tomistiche nell'opera di Søren Kierkegaard nel centenario dell'Enciclica *Aeterni Patris*" [Thomistic Convergences in Søren Kierkegaard's Work in the Centenary of the Encyclical *Aeterni Patris*], in *Atti dell'VIII Congresso Tomistico Internazionale* [Proceedings of the VIIIth International Thomistic Congress], vol. 8: *S. Tommaso nella storia del pensiero* [St. Thomas in the History of Thought], Vatican: Pontificia Accademia di S. Tommaso e di Religione Cattolica 1982, pp. 191–208.

—"L'angoscia esistenziale come tensione di essere-nulla, uomo-mondo nella prospettiva di Heidegger e Kierkegaard" [Existential Anxiety as Tension between Being and Nothing, Human Being and World in Kierkegaard's and Heidegger's Perspective], *Le Panarie*, no. 55, 1982, pp. 79–94.

—"Negatività e dialettica nell'opera di Søren Kierkegaard e di Karl Barth" [Negativity and Dialectics in the Work of Søren Kierkegaard and Karl Barth], *Annali del Liceo Gian Giacomo Adria*, 1982, pp. 1–42.

—"Dall'ammirazione alla riprovazione della linea di Spinoza-Lessing nell' evoluzione del pensiero di S. Kierkegaard" [From Admiration to Criticism of the Spinoza-Lessing Line in the Development of S. Kierkegaard's Thought], *Studi Urbinati*, 1983, pp. 9–39.

— "La comunicazione nella dialettica esistenziale di S. Kierkegaard" [Communication in the Existential Dialectics of S. Kierkegaard], in *Conoscenza e comunicazione nella filosofia moderna e contemporanea* [Knowledge and Communication in Modern and Contemporary Philosophy], ed. by Edda Ducci and Mario Sina, Rome: Studium 1983 (*Quaderni dell'Istituto Universitario pareggito di Magistero "Maria FF. Assunta,"* vol. 1), pp. 33–46.

— "La sicurezza del numero come oppio del popolo nell'ultimo Kierkegaard" [The Certainty of Number as the Opium of the People in the Late Kierkegaard], *Humanitas*, vol. 38, no. 2, 1983, pp. 214–26.

— *Riflessioni sulla libertà* [Reflections on Freedom], Rimini: Maggioli 1983.

—"Kierkegaard e Lutero: incontro-scontro" [Kierkegaard and Luther: An Encounter], *Humanitas*, vol. 39, no. 1, 1984, pp. 5–12.

— "Kierkegaard e la Chiesa di Danimarca" [Kierkegaard and the Church of Denmark], in *Nuovi Studi Kierkegaardiani* [New Kierkegaard Studies], ed. by Giuseppe Mario Pizzuti, Potenza: Centro Italiano di Studi Kierkegaardiani 1988, pp. 117–23.

— "Ragione e fede in Rasmus Nielsen" [Reason and Faith in Rasmus Nielsen], in *Nuovi Studi Kierkegaardiani. Bollettino del Centro Italiano di Studi Kierkegaardiani* [New Kierkegaard Studies: Bulletin of the Italian Center for Kierkegaard Studies], ed. by Giuseppe Mario Pizzuti, vol. 1, 1993, pp. 11–24.

— "Il pentimento cristiano nella dialettica esistenziale di S. Kierkegaard" [Christian Repentance in Kierkegaard's Existential Dialectics], *NotaBene. Quaderni di Studi Kierkegaardiani*, vol. 1, *Leggere oggi Kierkegaard* [Reading Kierkegaard Today], 2000, pp. 167–77.

— (ed.), *Studi kierkegaardiani* [Kierkegaard Studies], Brescia: Morcelliana 1957. (Nicola Abbagnano, "Kierkegaard e il sentiero della possibilità" [Kierkegaard and the Path of Possibility], pp. 9–28; Felice Battaglia, "Etica e religione nel 'Diario' di Kierkegaard" [Ethics and Religion in Kierkegaard's "Diary"], pp. 29–65; F.J. Billeskov Jansen, "I grandi romanzi filosofici di Kierkegaard" [The Great Philosophical Novels of Kierkegaard], pp. 67–92; Remo Cantoni, "L'eredità spirituale di Soeren Kierkegaard" [The Spiritual Heir of Søren Kierkegaard], pp. 93–104; James Collins, "Fede e riflessione in Kierkegaard" [Faith and Reflection in Kierkegaard], pp. 105–23; Cornelio Fabro, "La 'comunicazione della verità' nel pensiero di Kierkegaard" [The "Communication of Truth" in the Thought of Kierkegaard], pp. 125–63; Régis Jolivet, "La libertà e l'omnipotenza secondo Kierkegaard" [Freedom and Omnipotence according to Kierkegaard], pp. 165–79; Karl Löwith, "Kierkegaard: 'quel singolo'" [Kierkegaard: "that individual"], pp. 181–201; Giuseppe Masi, "Il significato cristiano dell'amore in Kierkegaard" [The Meaning of Love in Kierkegaard], pp. 203–42; Virgilio Melchiorre, "Kierkegaard ed Hegel. La polemica sul 'punto di partenza'" [Kierkegaard and Hegel: The Polemics about the Point of Departure], pp. 243–66; Pierre Mesnard, "Spigolame filosofico al Congresso kierkegaardiano di Copenaghen" [Philosophical "Gleaning" at the Kierkegaard Congress in Copenhagen], pp. 267–82; Carlo Perris, "Psicopatologia ed esistenzialismo. Il problema della vita di Kierkegaard e la valutazione critica dei rapporti tra psicopatologia clinica e filosofia esistenziale" [Psychopathology and Existentialism: The Problem of Life in Kierkegaard and the Critical Judgment of the Relations between Clinical Psychopathology and Existential Philosophy], pp. 283–322; Niels Thulstrup, "Incontro di Kierkegaard e Hamann" [Kierkegaard's Encounter with Hamann], pp. 323–57; Kierkegaard, "La dialettica della comunicazione etica ed etico-religiosa" [The Dialectic of Ethical and Ethical-Religious Communication], pp. 359–413; Cornelio Fabro, "Note di bibliografia kierkegaardiana" [Notes for a Kierkegaard Bibliography], pp. 415–33.) (Reviews: Brunello, B., review in *Humanitas*, 1959, pp. 243–4; Gives, G., review in *Italia Scrive*, 1957, p. 195; Garulli, E., review in *Giornale critico della filosofia italiana*, 1958, pp. 571–74.)

Faggi, Vico, *Kierkegaard: due radiodrammi* [Kierkegaard: Two Radio Plays], Savona: Sabatelli 1984.

Faggin, Stefano, "Kierkegaard e Kafka. Materiali per un'ermeneutica esistenziale" [Kierkegaard and Kafka: Materials for an Existential Hermeneutics], *NotaBene. Quaderni di Studi Kierkegaardiani*, vol. 2, *Kierkegaard e la letteratura* [Kierkegaard and Literature], 2002, pp. 139–42.

Farias, Domenico, "La cultura tra invidia e comunione: Kierkegaard e Dante" [Culture between Envy and Communion: Kierkegaard and Dante], *Rivista di Filosofia Neo-Scolastica*, no. 55, 1963, pp. 317–42.

Farina, Marcello, "Più profonda è l'angoscia, più grande è l'uomo: considerazioni sulla sofferenza nella lettura del *Diario* di S. Kierkegaard" [Deeper is Anxiety, Greater is the Man: Considerations on Suffering in S. Kierkegaard's Diary], *Per la Filosofia*, no. 36, 1996, pp. 62–9.

Fazio, Mariano, "Il singolo kierkegaardiano: una sintesi in divenire" [The Kierkegaardian Single Individual: A Becoming Synthesis], *Acta Philosophica*, vol. 5, no. 2, 1996, pp. 221–49.

— *Un sentiero nel bosco: guida al pensiero di Kierkegaard* [A Path in the Wood: A Guide to Kierkegaard's Thought], Rome: Armando 2000.

Fimiani, Antonella, "Femminilità, alterità e desiderio in Søren Kierkegaard. Un'analisi del ruolo e dell'importanza del femminile nella dialettica degli stadi" [Femininity, Otherness and Desire in Søren Kierkegaard: An Analysis of the Role and Importance of Women in the Dialectic of the Stages], *Rivista di Filosofia Neo-Scolastica*, vol. 99, 2007, pp. 655–80.

— *Sentieri del desiderio: femminile e alterità in Søren Kierkegaard* [Paths of Desire: Feminine and Alterity in Kierkegaard], Soveria Mannelli: Rubbettino 2010.

Fioravanti, Andrea, "L'indicibile come paradosso: il volto di Bergman attraverso l'analisi di Gilles Deleuze" [The Unspeakable as Paradox: Bergman's Face through Gilles Deleuze's Analysis], *NotaBene. Quaderni di Studi Kierkegaardiani*, vol. 3, *L'arte dello sguardo: Kierkegaard e il cinema* [The Art of Looking: Kierkegaard and the Cinema], 2003, pp. 59–70.

Forte, Bruno, *Fare teologia dopo Kierkegaard* [Doing Theology after Kierkegaard], Brescia: Morcelliana 1997.

— "Pensare l'interruzione: Kierkegaard ai teologi" [Thinking the Interruption: Kierkegaard to the Theologians], *NotaBene. Quaderni di Studi Kierkegaardiani*, vol. 1, *Leggere oggi Kierkegaard* [Reading Kierkegaard Today], 2000, pp. 135–45.

— "'Il settimo sigillo' di Ingmar Bergman. Nota teologica" ["The Seventh Seal" by Ingmar Bergman: A Theological Note], *NotaBene. Quaderni di Studi Kierkegaardiani*, vol. 3, *L'arte dello sguardo: Kierkegaard e il cinema* [The Art of Looking: Kierkegaard and the Cinema], 2003, pp. 39–41.

Fortunato, Marco, *Il mondo giudicato: l'immediato e la distanza nel pensiero di Rensi e di Kierkegaard* [The Judged World: Immediacy and Distance in Kierkegaard's and Rensi's Thought], Milan: Mimesis 1998.

— "Kierkegaard 'contro' il cinema e alcuni argomenti in difesa dell'arte cinematografica" [Kierkegaard "Against" Cinema and Some Arguments in Defense of Cinematographic Art], *NotaBene. Quaderni di Studi Kierkegaardiani*, vol. 3, *L'arte dello sguardo: Kierkegaard e il cinema* [The Art of Looking: Kierkegaard and the Cinema], 2003, pp. 121–33.

— "Percorsi dell'obbedienza" [Paths of Obedience], *Notabene. Quaderni di studi kierkegaardiani*, vol. 5, *Le malattie dell'anima. Kierkegaard e la psicologia* [The Sicknesses of the Soul: Kierkegaard and Psychology], 2007, pp. 135–52.

— "Credere possibile l'impossibile. La critica di Šestov a Kierkegaard" [Believing Possible the Impossible: Shestov's Critique of Kierkegaard], *NotaBene. Quaderni di studi Kierkegaardiani*, vol. 9, *Kierkegaard duecento anni dopo* [Kierkegaard Two Hundred Years Later], 2014, pp. 185–221.

Franchi, Alfredo, "La tradizione filosofica moderna d'ispirazione immanentistica: analisi di alcuni brani" [The Immanentist-Inspired Tradition of Modern Philosophy: Analysis of Some Passages], *Sapienza*, no. 38, 1985, pp. 63–72.

— "Kierkegaard irrazionalista? Filosofi e filosofie nella interpretazione del filosofo danese" [Kierkegaard Irrationalist? Philosophers and Philosophies in the Interpretation of the Danish Philosopher], *Sapienza*, no. 43, 1990, pp. 271–91.

— "Tra malinconia e riso. La crisi dell'uomo contemporaneo" [Between Melancholy and Laughter: The Crisis of Contemporary Man], *Sapienza*, vol. 46, no. 3, 1993, pp. 263–86.

— "La crisi dell'uomo contemporaneo. Osservazioni sulla figura dell'esteta tra Ottocento e Novecento" [The Crisis of Contemporary Man: Remarks on the Figure of the Esthete in the Nineteenth and Twentieth-Century], *Sapienza*, vol. 52, no. 3, 1999, pp. 281–315.

Francia, Ennio, "Il significato di Søren Kierkegaard" [The Meaning of Søren Kierkegaard], *Studium. Rivista Universitaria*, vol. 31, 1935, pp. 334–41.

— "Preludio su Kierkegaard" [Prelude to Kierkegaard], *Frontespizio*, no. 3, 1938, pp. 188–99.

Franco, Vittoria, *Etiche possibili: il paradosso della morale dopo la morte di Dio* [Possible Ethics: The Paradox of Morality after the Death of God], Rome: Donzelli 1996.

Franzini, Elio, "Kierkegaard e il senso del tragico" [Kierkegaard and the Sense of the Tragic], in *Tragico e modernità. Studi sulla teoria del tragico da Kleist ad Adorno* [The Tragic and Modernity: Studies on the Theory of the Tragic from

Kleist to Adorno], ed. by Fuvio Carmagnola, Milan: Franco Angeli Editore 1985, pp. 68–85.

Fruscione, Salvatore, "Kierkegaard di fronte all'esistenza di Dio" [Kierkegaard on the Existence of God], *La Civiltà Cattolica*, no. 102, 1951, pp. 618–31.

Gabetti, Giuseppe, "Søren Aabye Kierkegaard," in *Enciclopedia italiana* [Italian Encyclopaedia], Rome: Istituto della Enciclopedia Italiana, Treccani 1933, vol. 20, pp. 193–4.

Gaeta, Giancarlo, "Kierkegaard: cristianità come *ordine stabilito* e la contemporaneità con Cristo" [Kierkegaard: Christianity as *Established Order* and Contemporaneity with Christ], *Il Cristianesimo nella Storia*, vol. 5, no. 3, 1984, pp. 563–76.

Gaiani, Alberto, "Kierkegaard e il pensiero ebraico del novecento. Per un'analisi critica dei fondamenti della riflessione kierkegaardiana" [Kierkegaard and Twentieth-Century Jewish Thought: For a Critical Analysis of the Foundations of Kierkegaard's Thought], *Notabene. Quaderni di studi kierkegaardiani*, vol. 5, *Le malattie dell'anima. Kierkegaard e la psicologia* [The Sicknesses of the Soul: Kierkegaard and Psychology], 2007, pp. 265–82.

Galanti Grollo, Sebastiano, "L'alterità tra etica e religione: Kierkegaard e Levinas" [The Alterity Between Ethics and Religion: Kierkegaard and Levinas], *NotaBene. Quaderni di studi Kierkegaardiani*, vol. 9, *Kierkegaard duecento anni dopo* [Kierkegaard Two Hundred Years Later], 2014, pp. 303–313.

Gallas, Alberto, "Contemporaneità e critica della cristianità stabilita in Søren Kierkegaard" [Contemporaneity and Criticism of the Established Christianity in Søren Kierkegaard], in *La cattura della fine: variazioni dell'escatologia in regime di cristianità* [Capturing the End: Variations on the Eschatology within Christianity], ed. by Giuseppe Ruggieri, Genoa: Marietti 1992, pp. 225–70.

— "È Lutero un dialettico? L'evoluzione del giudizio di Kierkegaard sul Reformatore di Wittenberg" [Is Luther a Dialectician? The Evolution of the Judgment of Kierkegaard on Reformer of Wittenberg], in *Lutero e i linguaggi dell'Occidente. Atti del convegno tenuto a Trento dal 29 al 31 maggio 2000* [Luther and the Languages of the West: Proceedings of the Conference held in Trento from May 29th to 31st, 2000], ed. by Giuseppe Beschin, et al., Brescia: Morcelliana 2002, pp. 387–409.

— " 'Ma io posso edificare me stesso col pensiero che sono un cittadino del cielo'. Osservazioni su ubbidienza religiosa e ubbidienza politica in Søren Kierkegaard" ["But I Am Permitted to Be Built Up Religiously by the Thought That Essentially I Am a Citizen of Heaven": Remarks on Religious Obedience and Political Obedience in Søren Kierkegaard], *NotaBene. Quaderni di studi kierkegaardiani*, vol. 4, *L'edificante in Kierkegaard* [The Edifying in Kierkegaard], 2005, pp. 23–44.

Gallino, Guglielmo, "Kierkegaard e l'ironia socratica" [Kierkegaard and Socratic Irony], *Filosofia*, vol. 45, no. 2, 1994, pp. 143–61.

— "Kierkegaard. La Seduzione, l'Interiorità, l'Ironia" [Kierkegaard: Seduction, Inwardness, Irony], *Filosofia*, vol. 45, no. 3, 1994, pp. 291–328.

Gallucci, Marcello, "Una fugace osservazione su un particolare nel *Don Giovanni*, di Søren Kierkegaard. Con una Nota su Kierkegaard recensore" [A Cursory

Observation Concerning a Detail in Don Giovanni, by Søren Kierkegaard. With
a Note on Kierkegaard as a Reviewer], in *Musicus discologus. Musiche e scritti
per il 70o anno di Carlo Marinelli* [Musicus discologus. Music and Texts for
the 70th Birthday of Carlo Marinelli], ed. by Giuliano Macchi, et al., Valentia:
Monteleone 1997, pp. 203–19.

Garaventa, Roberto, "Preoccupazione e angoscia nei 'Discorsi edificanti'"
[Preoccupation and Anxiety in the "Edifying Discourses"], *NotaBene. Quaderni
di studi kierkegaardiani*, vol. 4, *L'edificante in Kierkegaard* [The Edifying in
Kierkegaard], 2005, pp. 59–97.

— "Søren Kierkegaard: una fenomenologia dell'angoscia" [Søren Kierkegaard:
A Phenomenology of Anxiety], in his *Angoscia* [Anxiety], Naples: Guida 2006,
pp. 16–34.

— *Angoscia e peccato in Søren Kierkegaard* [Anxiety and Sin in Søren Kierkegaard],
Rome: Aracne 2007.

— "Angoscia del bene, della libertà, dell'Eterno. Su alcuni tratti demoniaci della
società moderna" [Anxiety for the Good, for Freedom, for the Eternal: On
Some Demonic Traits of the Modern Society], *Notabene. Quaderni di studi
kierkegaardiani*, vol. 5, *Le malattie dell'anima. Kierkegaard e la psicologia* [The
Sicknesses of the Soul: Kierkegaard and Psychology], 2007, pp. 23–48.

— "La ricezione di Kierkegaard nel mondo di lingua tedesca: Christoph Schrempf
e Theodor Haecker" [The Reception of Kierkegaard in the Germanophone
World: Christoph Schrempf e Theodor Haecker], *Notabene. Quaderni di studi
kierkegaardiani*, vol. 8, *Insegnare il Cristianesimo nel Novecento. La ricezione
di Kierkegaard e Rosmini* [Teaching Christianity in the Twentieth Century: The
Reception of Kierkegaard and Rosmini], 2011, pp. 117–41.

— "Il paradosso in Kierkegaard" [The Paradox in Kierkegaard], *NotaBene. Quaderni
di studi Kierkegaardiani*, vol. 9, *Kierkegaard duecento anni dopo* [Kierkegaard
Two Hundred Years Later], 2014, pp. 13–30.

— *Rileggere Kierkegaard* [Rereading Kierkegaard], Naples: Orthotes 2014.

Garaventa, Roberto, and Diego Giordano (eds.), *Il discepolo di seconda mano: saggi su
Søren Kierkegaard* [The Disciple at Second Hand: Essays on Søren Kierkegaard],
Naples: Orthotes 2011. (Laura Liva, "Lo strano caso dell'etica secondo Vigilius
Haufniensis. Uno sguardo all'Introduzione di *Begrebet Angest*" [The Strange
Case of Ethics According to Vigilius Haufniensis: A Glance at the Introduction
of *Begrebet Angest*], pp. 13–28; Alessandra Granito, "La fenomenologia della
disperazione come critica della società. *La malattia per la morte* nella prospettiva
ermeneutica di Bruce H. Kirmmse" [The Phenomenology of Despair as a Critique
of Society: Bruce H. Kirmmse's Interpretation of *The Sickness unto Death*],
pp. 29–71; Antonella Fimiani, "Nella carne dell'esistere. Sessualità, alterità e
desiderio in Kierkegaard" [In the Flesh of Existence: Sensuousness, Otherness
and Desire in Kierkegaard], pp. 73–86; Federica Scorolli, "La soggettività come
compito. Il passaggio dall'estetico all'etico in Søren Kierkegaard" [Subjectivity
as a Task: From the Aesthetic to the Ethical in Søren Kierkegaard], pp. 87–98;
Gordon D. Marino, "Il ruolo della ragione nell'etica di Kierkegaard" [The
Place of Reason in Kierkegaard's Ethics], trans. by Laura Liva, pp. 101–18;
Umberto Regina, "La 'Scienza nuova' di Søren Kierkegaard. *Gli atti dell'amore*"

[Søren Kierkegaard's 'New Science'. *Works of Love*], pp. 119–42; Jon Stewart, "Hegel e Kierkegaard su fede e sapere" [Kierkegaard and Hegel on Faith and Knowledge], trans. by Diego Giordano and Alessandra Granito, pp. 143–68; Anna Valentinetti, "*Vitam impendere vero.* Kierkegaard a confronto con Schopenhauer" [*Vitam Impendere Vero*: A Comparison Between Kierkegaard and Schopenhauer], pp. 169–211).

Gardini, Michele, "L'uomo è un rapporto: l'antropologia di Kierkegaard in margine a un giudizio Heideggeriano" [The Human Being is a Relation: Kierkegaard's Anthropology Compared to a Heideggerian Judgment], *Discipline filosofiche*, vol. 12, no. 1, 2002, pp. 351–82.

Gargano, Monica, "Cristianesimo tragico, cristianesimo ludico: i due volti della fedeltà al Dio dialettico" [Tragic Christianity, Playful Christianity: The Two Faces of the Fidelity to the Dialectical God], *Du*, vol. 42, no. 1, 1991, pp. 61–83.

Garin, Eugenio, *Cronache di filosofia italiana (1900–1943)* [Accounts of Italian Philosophy (1900–1943)], Bari: Laterza 1955, p. 24; p. 26; p. 512; pp. 515–19.

— "Kierkegaard in Italia," *Rivista Critica di Storia della Filosofia*, vol. 28, 1973, pp. 452–6.

Garrera, Gianni, "Musicalità dell'intelligenza demoniaca" [The Musical Essence of the Demonic Intelligence], *NotaBene. Quaderni di Studi Kierkegaardiani*, vol. 1, *Leggere oggi Kierkegaard* [Reading Kierkegaard Today], 2000, pp. 87–100.

Gavazzeni, Gianandrea, "Kierkegaard, il Don Giovanni e la musica" [Kierkegaard, Don Juan and Music], *Rassegna d'Italia*, vol. 2, no. 2, 1947, pp. 54–6.

Gherardini, Brunero, "La teologia della croce di Kierkegaard" [The Theology of the Cross in Kierkegaard], *Studi Cattolici*, nos. 198–199, 1977, pp. 496–501.

Giampiccoli, Guglielmo, "Kierkegaard e Leopardi" [Kierkegaard and Leopardi], *Gioventù Cristiana*, nos. 2–3, 1940, pp. 80–3.

Giannatiempo Quinzio, Anna, *Il "cominciamento" in Hegel* [The "Starting Point" in Hegel], Rome: Storia e Letteratura 1983.

— *L'estetico in Kierkegaard* [Aesthetics in Kierkegaard], Naples: Liguori 1992.

— "Notabene cristiano: il fatto storico che Dio è esistito" [Christian Notabene: the Fact that God Has Existed], *NotaBene. Quaderni di Studi Kierkegaardiani*, vol. 1, *Leggere oggi Kierkegaard* [Reading Kierkegaard Today], ed. by Isabella Adinolfi, Rome: Città nuova 2000, pp. 101–14.

Giannini, Florio, "Pregare il Padre celeste con Kierkegaard" [Praying to the Heavenly Father with Kierkegaard], Massarosa: Il Dialogo 2003.

Gigante, Mario, "Il messaggio esistenziale di Kierkegaard e la filosofia hegeliana" [The Existential Message of Kierkegaard and Hegelian Philosophy], *Asprenas*, no. 17, 1970, pp. 392–412.

— *Religiosità di Kierkegaard* [Religiousness in Kierkegaard], Naples: Morano 1972.

— *Il matrimonio nel giovane Kierkegaard* [Marriage in the Young Kierkegaard], Salerno: Istituto Superiore di Scienze Religiose 1982.

Giordano, Diego, "Kierkegaard e il divenire della libertà. Relazione a sé, relazione a Dio" [Kierkegaard and the Evolution of Freedom: Relation to Oneself, Relation to God], in *La libertà in discussione* [Freedom in Question], ed. by Sergio Sorrentino, Rome: Aracne 2007 (*Quaestiones disputatae*, vol. 2), pp. 67–78.

— "Kierkegaard e il Paradosso: Oscillazioni tra Fede e Ragione" [Kierkegaard and Paradox: Oscillations between Faith and Reason], *Revista Portuguesa de Filosofia*, vol. 64, no. 2, 2008, pp.1057–1066.

— "Alla fine dell'amore. Osservazioni sulla *ripetizione*" [At the End of Love: Remarks on the *Repetition*], *Notabene. Quaderni di studi kierkegaardiani*, vol. 7, *Kierkegaard e la condizione desiderante. La seduzione dell'estetico* [Kierkegaard and the Desiring Condition: The Seduction of the Aesthetic], 2009, pp. 111–17.

— "La presenza di Schopenhauer nell'opera di Kierkegaard" [The Presence of Schopenhauer in Kierkegaard's Works], in *Tebe dalle cento porte. Saggi su Arthur Schopenhauer* [Thebes of the 1000 Gates: Essays on Arthur Schopenhauer], ed. by Roberto Garaventa, Rome: Aracne 2010, pp. 75–97.

— "Verità e paradosso. Tra Kierkegaard e la filosofia analitica" [Truth and Paradox: Between Kierkegaard and Analytic Philosophy], in *L'Era di Antigone*, vol. 4: *L'etica dell'equità, l'equità dell'etica* [The Age of Antigone, vol. 4, The Ethics of Fairness, the Fairness of Ethics], ed. by Giuseppe Limone, Milan: Franco Angeli 2010, pp. 315–328.

— *Verità e paradosso in Søren Kierkegaard: una lettura analitica* [Truth and Paradox in Søren Kierkegaard: An Analytic Reading], Naples: Orthotes 2011.

Giovanni, Biagio de, "Kierkegaard ed Hegel. (Riflessione in margine ad una recente traduzione italiana)" [Kierkegaard and Hegel. (Reflection on the Sidelines of a recent Italian Translation)], *Atti dell'Accademia Nazionale di Scienze Morali e Politiche di Napoli*, vol. 75, 1964, pp. 1–43.

Givone, Sergio, "Aut Hegel Aut Kierkegaard," in *Cristo nel pensiero contemporaneo* [Christ in Contemporary Thought], ed. by Gino Ciolini et al., Palermo: Augustinus 1988, pp. 43–51.

— "A partire da Kierkegaard" [Starting from Kierkegaard], *NotaBene. Quaderni di Studi Kierkegaardiani*, vol. 1, *Leggere oggi Kierkegaard* [Reading Kierkegaard Today], 2000, pp. 79–86.

Glässer, Gustav, "L'irrazionalismo religioso di Søren Kierkegaard. La dottrina del salto qualitativo" [The Religious Irrationalism of Søren Kierkegaard: The Doctrine of the Qualitative Leap], *Bilychnis*, no. 15, 1926, pp. 99–112.

Gneo, Corrado, "L'opzione radicale come fondamento dell'essere e Duns Scoto" [The Radical Option as Ground of Being in Duns Scotus"], *Aquinas*, no. 14, 1971, pp. 125–32.

Gozzini, Mario, "La tragedia dell'io in Søren Kierkegaard" [The Tragedy of the Self in Søren Kierkegaard], *L'Ultima*, no. 35, 1948, pp. 9–23; nos. 37–38, 1949, pp. 27–45.

Granito, Alessandra, *Eugen Drewermann interprete di Kierkegaard. Le quattro forme kierkegaardiane della disperazione rilette alla luce della psicoanalisi* [Eugen Drewermann Reading Kierkegaard: The Four Kierkegaardian Forms of Despair Reinterpreted in the Light of Psychoanalysis], Naples: Orthotes 2013.

— "Kierkegaard contemporaneo. Sull'attualità di *Una recensione letteraria* a partire dalla ricezione haeckeriana" [Contemporary Kierkegaard: On the Modernity of *A Literary Review*, Starting from Haecker's Reception], *NotaBene. Quaderni di studi Kierkegaardiani*, vol. 9, *Kierkegaard duecento anni dopo* [Kierkegaard Two Hundred Years Later], 2014, pp. 97–131.

Guanti, Giovanni, "La musica come metafora teologica in Agostino e in Kierkegaard" [Music as Theological Metaphor in Augustine and Kierkegaard], *Rivista di Estetica*, nos. 26–27, 1987, pp. 153–69.

— "Tempo musicale e tempo storico in Agostino e in Kierkegaard" [Musical Time and Historical Time in Augustine and Kierkegaard], *Rivista di estetica*, vol. 30, no. 36, 1990, pp. 95–141

Guzzo, Augusto, *Gli Entretiens di Copenhagen su Kierkegaard* [Copenhagen "Entretiens" on Kierkegaard], Turin: Edizioni di Filosofia 1967.

Henrici, Peter, "Per una filosofia cristiana della prassi" [For a Christian Philosophy of Praxis], *Gregorianum*, vol. 53, 1972, pp. 717–30.

— "Maurice Blondel di fronte alla filosofia tedesca" [Maurice Blondel in Front of German Philosophy], *Gregorianum*, vol. 56, no. 4, 1975, pp. 615–38.

Heschel, Abraham Joshua, "Il chassidismo e Kierkegaard" [Chassidism and Kierkegaard], *Conoscenza Religiosa*, no. 3, 1971, pp. 337–53.

Humanitas. Rivista Bimestrale di Cultura, vol. 42, vol. 4, 2007, *Søren Kierkegaard. Filosofia ed esistenza* [Søren Kierkegaard. Philosophy and Existence]. (Giorgio Penzo, "Kierkegaard tra nichilismo e secolarizzazione" [Kierkegaard between Nihilism and Secularization], pp. 632–41; Marcello Farina, "La critica a Hegel nelle pagine del Diario di Kierkegaard" [The Critique of Hegel in the Pages of the Diary of Kierkegaard], pp. 642–52; Silvano Zucal, "Si soffre una volta sola, ma il trionfo è eterno. Kierkegaard e il problema del dolore" [One Only Suffers Once but Triumphs Eternally: Kierkegaard and the Problem of Pain], pp. 653–65; Michele Nicoletti, "Kierkegaard e il moderno" [Kierkegaard and the Modern], pp. 666–78; Nestore Pirillo, "Kierkegaard – Sartre. Il Novecento, la filosofia e le radici cristiane" [Kierkegaard – Sartre: The Twentieth Century, Philosophy and the Radical Christian], pp. 679–94; Maria Luisa Martini, "Gadamer e Kierkegaard" [Gadamer and Kierkegaard], pp. 695–704; Carlo Brentari, "La riflessione su Kierkegaard e il superamento dell'idealismo nello sviluppo della filosofia di Arnold Gehlen" [Reflection on Kierkegaard and the Overcoming of Idealism in the Development of the Philosophy of Arnold Gehlen], pp. 705–10; Massimo Giuliani, "Kierkegaard nella teologia ebraica del Novecento" [Kierkegaard in Jewish Theology of the Twentieth Century], pp. 711–22; Elena Alessiato, "Søren Kierkegaard critico della modernità. Una recensione letteraria" [Søren Kierkegaard Critic of Modernity: *A Literary Review*], pp. 723–67; Karl Barth, "Kierkegaard e i teologi" [Kierkegaard and Theologians], pp. 768–71.)

Iiritano, Massimo, "Il paradosso kierkegaardiano come 'emergenza' storica ed esistenziale" [The Kierkegaardian Paradox as Historical and Existential "Emergence"], *Aquinas*, vol. 40, no. 3, 1997, pp. 499–507.

— *Disperazione e fede in Søren Kierkegaard: una lotta di confine* [Despair and Faith in Søren Kierkegaard: A Border Struggle], Soveria Mannelli: Rubbettino 1999. (Review: Baldini, Franca, review in *Studi Nordici*, vol. 6, 1999, pp. 143–47.)

— "La 'sesta parte del mondo': la disperazione del moderno tra estetico e religioso in Kierkegaard [The "Sixth Part of the World": Kierkegaard and the Despair of Modernity between the Aesthetical and the Religious], *NotaBene*.

64   *Laura Liva*

Quaderni di Studi Kierkegaardiani, vol. 1, *Leggere oggi Kierkegaard* [Reading Kierkegaard Today], 2000, pp. 45–60.
— "Amore e paradosso. Una lettura kierkegaardiana del 'Gertrud' di Dreyer" [Love and Paradox: A Kierkegaardian Reading of *Gertrud* by Dreyer], *NotaBene. Quaderni di Studi Kierkegaardiani*, vol. 3, *L'arte dello sguardo: Kierkegaard e il cinema* [The Art of Looking: Kierkegaard and the Cinema], 2003, pp. 15–38.
Impara, Paolo, *Kierkegaard interprete dell'ironia socratica* [Kierkegaard as Commentator of Socratic Irony], Rome: Armando 2000.
Innamorati, Marco, *Il concetto di Io in Kierkegaard* [The Concept of the Self in Kierkegaard], Rome: Edizioni dell'Ateneo 1991.
Jaworski, Marian, "Dio e l'esistenza umana" [God and Human Existence], *Acta Philosophica*, vol. 5, no. 1, 1996, pp. 95–101.
Jesi, Furio, *Kierkegaard*, Fossano: Esperienze 1972 (2nd ed., ed. by Andrea Cavalletti, Turin: Bollati Boringhieri 2001).
Kierkegaard. Esistenzialismo e dramma della persona. Atti del convegno di Assisi (29 nov.-1 dic. 1984) [Existentialism and the Situation of the Individual. Proceedings of Congress in Assisi, November 29th-December 1st, 1984], no editor given, Brescia: Morcelliana 1985. (Pietro Prini, "Kierkegaard e la filosofia come giornale intimo" [Kierkegaard and Philosophy as Intimate Journal], pp. 13–21; Alessandro Klein, "La critica di Kierkegaard a Hegel" [Kierkegaard's Criticism of Hegel], pp. 23–37; Paolo Ricca, "Lutero e Kierkegaard" [Luther and Kierkegaard], pp. 39–65; Salvatore Spera, "Ambiguità e inconclusività della politica nel pensiero di Kierkegaard" [Ambiguity and Inconclusiveness of Politics in Kierkegaard], pp. 67–91; Antonio Pieretti, "Per una semantica dell'angoscia" [About a Semantics of Anxiety], pp. 93–104; Mariano Cristaldi, "Søren Kierkegaard: la rivelazione sofferente" [Søren Kierkegaard: The Suffering Revelation], pp. 105–28; Emilio Baccarini, "Esistenza ed etica. Letture ebraiche di Kierkegaard" [Ethics and Existence: Hebraic Readings of Kierkegaard], pp. 131–46; Leonardo Casini, "Kierkegaard e il cristianesimo contemporaneo" [Kierkegaard and Contemporary Christianity], pp. 147–60; Paolo Nepi, "Dallo stadi etico al paradosso" [From the Ethical Stage to the Paradox], pp. 161–8; Michele Nicoletti, "Kierkegaard e la 'teologia politica'" [Kierkegaard and "Political Theology"], pp. 169–81; Giuseppe Mario Pizzuti, "Inattualità di Kierkegaard" [Kierkegaard's Untimeliness], pp. 183–202; Maurizio Schoepflin, "Dall'ammirazione all'imitazione di Cristo" [From Admiration to the Imitation of Christ], pp. 203–11; Aurelio Rizzacasa, "Søren Kierkegaard: la dinamica del rapporto esistenza-storia nelle riflessioni del 'Diario'" [Søren Kierkegaard: The Dynamic of the Relationship between Existence and History in the "Diary"], pp. 213–24; Bruno Belletti, "Appunti su Peter Wust lettore di Kierkegaard" [Notes on Peter Wust as Reader of Kierkegaard], pp. 225–33.) (Review: Belletti, Bruno, review in *Humanitas*, vol. 41, 1986, pp. 72–9.)
Klein, Alessandro, *Antirazionalismo di Kierkegaard* [Kierkegaard's Antirationalism], Milan: Mursia 1979. (Reviews: Colette, Jacques, review in *Les Études Philosophiques*, no. 1, 1981, pp. 91–5; Lacoste, Jean-Yves, review in *Revue Philosophique de Louvain*, vol. 78, no. 40, 1980, p. 600.)
Koch, Ludovica, "Gli 'stadi sul cammino della vita'" [The Stages on Life's Way], in her *Al di qua o al di là dell'umano. Studi e esperienze di letteratura* [On this Side

or beyond the Human: Studies and Experiences of Literature], Rome: Donzelli 1997, pp. 201–38.

La Spisa, Mauro, *Fede e scandalo nei diari di S.A. Kierkegaard* [Faith and Offense in the Diaries of S.A. Kierkegaard], Florence: G&G 1970; Palermo: Herbita 1983.

Lamanna, Eustachio Paolo, "L'anti-idealismo nei paesi germanici e nordici. 8: La filosofia della "personalità" nei paesi nordici: Kierkegaard" [The Anti-Idealism in the German and Nordic Countries. 8: The Philosophy of "Personality" in the Nordic Countries: Kierkegaard], in *Storia della filosofia* [History of Philosophy], vols. 1–2, Florence: Le Monnier 1936, vol. 2, pp. 530–1.

Lancellotti, Marco, "Ritorno di Kierkegaard" [The Return of Kierkegaard], *Il Veltro. Rivista della Civiltà Italiana*, vol. 21, 1977, pp. 290–96.

— "Kierkegaard: tragico e dialettica" [Kierkegaard: The Tragic and Dialectics], *Il Veltro*, no. 22, 1978, pp. 525–32.

— "Kierkegaard 1843: morfologia dell'arte e dialettica" [Kierkegaard 1843: Morphology of Art and Dialectics], in his *Filosofie sintetiche del linguaggio: Kierkegaard, Croce, Cassirer, Heidegger* [Synthetic Philosophies of Language: Kierkegaard, Croce, Cassirer, Heidegger], Rome: Bulzoni 1982, pp. 11–62.

Lazzarini, Renato, "Logica esistenzialistica e logica agonistica in Kierkegaard" [Existential Logic and Agonistic Logic in Kierkegaard], in *Atti del Congresso Internazionale di Filosofia 1946* [Proceedings of the International Congress of Philosophy 1946], ed. by Enrico Castelli, Milan and Rome: Castellani & C., 1948, vol. 2 (*L'esistenzialismo*), pp. 313–19.

Licciardello, P. Nicola, "Itinerari dell'esistenzialismo Romantico: Søren Kierkegaard" [Itineraries in Romantic Existentialism: Søren Kierkegaard], *Teoresi*, no. 15, 1960, pp. 25–42.

Limentani, Ludovico, "Søren Kierkegaard. Polemica antihegeliana" [Søren Kierkegaard. Anti-Hegelian Polemics], in his *Il pensiero moderno. Storia della filosofia da R. Descartes a H. Spencer* [Modern Thought: The History of Philosophy from R. Descartes to H. Spencer], Milan: Società Editrice Anonima Dante Alighieri 1930, pp. 542–9.

Liotta, Rosario, "L'educazione della possibilità in Søren Kierkegaard" [The Education of the Possibility in Søren Kierkegaard], *Prospettive Pedagogiche*, no. 3, 1968, pp. 204–13.

Lisi, Leonardo, "Kierkegaard in una casa di bambola" [Kierkegaard in a Doll's House], *Notabene. Quaderni di studi kierkegaardiani*, vol. 6, *La profondità della scena. Il teatro visitato da Kierkegaard, Kierkegaard visitato dal teatro* [The Depth of the Scene: The Theater Seen by Kierkegaard, Kierkegaard Seen by the Theater], 2008, pp. 143–160.

Liva, Laura, "*Quasi Solo un Poeta* – Melanconia e Genialità Poetica" [*Almost a Poet* – Melancholy and Poetic Genius], *Notabene. Quaderni di studi kierkegaardiani*, vol. 5, *Le malattie dell'anima. Kierkegaard e la psicologia* [The Sicknesses of the Soul: Kierkegaard and Psychology], 2007, pp. 121–34.

— "Tra continuità e rottura. La teoria kierkegaardiana della comunicazione del cristianesimo e l'attacco alla cristianità stabilita nella Danimarca del XX secolo" [Between Continuity and Rupture: Kierkegaard's Theory of Christian Communication and His Attack on Christendom in Denmark in the Twentieth Century],

Notabene. Quaderni di studi kierkegaardiani, vol. 8, *Insegnare il Cristianesimo nel Novecento. La ricezione di Kierkegaard e Rosmini* [Teaching Christianity in the Twentieth Century: The Reception of Kierkegaard and Rosmini], 2011, pp. 97–116.

— "L'angoscia del bene e l'ermetismo demoniaco: tra psicologia e analisi esistenziale" [Anxiety for the Good and Demonic Hermetism: Between Psychology and Existential Analysis], *NotaBene. Quaderni di studi Kierkegaardiani*, vol. 9, *Kierkegaard duecento anni dopo* [Kierkegaard Two Hundred Years Later], 2014, pp. 175–184.

— *Il demoniaco nella scrittura. Kierkegaard e lo specchio della pseudonimia* [The Demonic in Writing: Kierkegaard and the Mirror of Pseudonymity], Genoa: Il melangolo 2015.

Llevadot, Laura, "Il tempo della ripetizione: l'istante" [The Time of Repetition: The Moment], *La Società degli Individui*, no. 19, 2004, pp. 23–35.

Lodovici, Umberto, "Il bacio di Giuda. La ricezione di Kierkegaard e Peterson" [The Kiss of Judas: The Reception of Kierkegaard and Peterson], *NotaBene. Quaderni di studi Kierkegaardiani*, vol. 9, *Kierkegaard duecento anni dopo* [Kierkegaard Two Hundred Years Later], 2014, pp. 315–327.

Lombardi, Franco, *Kierkegaard*, Florence: La Nuova Italia 1936 (2nd revised and enlarged ed., Florence: Sansoni 1967). (Review: Quattrocchi, Ludovico, review in *Bollettino filosofico*, 1969, pp. 64–6.)

— "Alcune riflessioni su Kierkegaard ed altre poche cose" [Some Considerations on Kierkegaard and a Few Other Things], *Archivio di Filosofia* (*Kierkegaard e Nietzsche*), 1953, pp. 105–13.

— "Kierkegaard oggi" [Kierkegaard Today], *Il Cannocchiale*, no. 1, 1968, pp. 47–65.

Lombardi, Riccardo, "Il momento religioso nel pensiero kierkegaardiano" [The Religious Moment in Kierkegaard's Thought], *La Civiltà Cattolica*, no. 2258, 1944, pp. 87–98.

— "Søren Kierkegaard un pensatore triste" [Søren Kierkegaard: An Unhappy Philosopher], *La Civiltà Cattolica*, no. 2254, 1944, pp. 247–55.

— "Søren Kierkegaard precursore dell'esistenzialismo" [Søren Kierkegaard, Forerunner of Existentialism], *La Civiltà Cattolica*, no. 2256, 1944, p. 366–76.

Longo, Giulia, *Kierkegaard, Nietzsche: eternità dell'istante, istantaneità dell'eterno* [Kierkegaard, Nietzsche: The Eternity of the Moment, the Instantaneousness of the Eternal], Milan: Mimesis 2007.

— "Kierkegaard in Italia. La scoperta napoletana" [Kierkegaard in Italy: The Neapolitan Discovery], *Archivio di storia della cultura*, vol. 21, 2008, pp. 253–61.

Luisi, Giuseppe M., "Etica, ontologia, antropologia" [Ethics, Ontology, Anthropology], *Giornale Critico della Filosofia Italiana*, no. 48, 1969, pp. 561–82.

Lunardi, Lorenzo, *La dialettica in Kierkegaard* [Dialectics in Kierkegaard], Padua: Liviana 1982.

Magnino, Bianca, "Enrico Ibsen e Søren Kierkegaard" [Henrik Ibsen and Søren Kierkegaard], *Nuova Antologia*, vol. 7, no. 336, 1928, pp. 298–311.

— "Il problema religioso di Søren Kierkegaard" [The Religious Problem of Søren Kierkegaard], *Giornale Critico della Filosofia Italiana*, no. 11, 1938, pp. 215–39.

Maiorani, Arianna, "Blixen e Kierkegaard: dialogo sul seduttore" [Blixen and Kierkegaard: Dialogue on the Seducer], *Intersezioni*, vol. 20, no. 1, 2000, p. 43–57.

Majoli, Bruno, "La critica ad Hegel in Schelling e Kierkegaard" [The Criticism of Hegel in Schelling and Kierkegaard], *Rivista di Filosofia Neo-Scolastica*, no. 46, 1954, pp. 222–63.

Mancinelli, Paola, "Homo absconditus homo revelatus: su alcune tracce kierkegaardiane in René Girard" [Homo absconditus homo revelatus: On Some Kierkegaardian Traces in René Girard], *NotaBene. Quaderni di Studi Kierkegaardiani*, vol. 2, *Kierkegaard e la letteratura* [Kierkegaard and Literature], 2002, pp. 127–37.

Mancini, Italo, *Filosofi esistenzialisti* [Existentialist Philosophers], Urbino: Argalia Editore 1964 (*Pubblicazioni dell'Università di Urbino. Serie di Lettere e Filosofia*, vol. 18).

Mancini, Pompeo Fabio, *Il singolare universale: esitenza, libertà e assoluto tra Kierkegaard e Sartre* [The Singular Universal: Existence, Freedom and Absolute Between Kierkegaard and Sartre], Bari: Laterza 2010.

Mangiagalli, Maurizio, "Il tempo dell'autenticità" [The Time of Authenticity], *Sapienza*, vol. 53, no. 1, 2000, pp. 69–86.

— "L'angoscia quale cifra patetica dell'ermeneutica kierkegaardiana" [Anxiety as a Pathetic Figure of Kierkegaard's Hermeneutics], *Sapienza. Rivista di Filosofia e di Teologia*, vol. 61, 2008, pp. 425–43.

Manzia, Carlo, "Il problema della fede in Kierkegaard" [The Problem of Faith in Kierkegaard], *Analecta Gregoriana*, vol. 68, 1954, pp. 123–32.

Marchesi, Angelo, "Due scelte di fronte a Cristo: Kierkegaard e Nietzsche" [Two Choices in Front of Christ: Kierkegaard and Nietzsche], in *Il Cristo dei filosofi, Atti del XXX Convegno di Gallarate 1975* [The Christ of the Philosophers, Proceedings of the 30th Congress of Gallarate 1975], Brescia: Morcelliana 1976, pp. 149–66.

— *L'uomo contemporaneo: smarrimenti e recupero* [Contemporary Man: Disorientations and Rehabilitation], Milan: Vita e Pensiero 1977.

Mariani, Eliodoro, *Analisi esistenziale e pre-comprensione della fede: da Kierkegaard ad Heidegger e Bultmann, le premesse filosofiche della demitizzazione* [Existential Analysis and Pre-Comprehension of Faith: From Kierkegaard to Heidegger and Bultmann, the Philosophical Premises of Demythologization], Rome: Istituto Pedagogico Pontificio Ateneo Antonianum 1980.

Mariani, Emanuele, *Kierkegaard e Nietzsche, il Cristo e l'anticristo* [Kierkegaard and Nietzsche, the Christ and the Antichrist], Milan: Mimesis 2009.

Marini, Sergio, "Soggettività ed educazione in Kierkegaard" [Subjectivity and Education in Kierkegaard], in *Il problema dell'antropologia. Atti del 24° Convegno di assistenti universitari di filosofia, Padova 1979* [The Problem of Anthropology. Proceedings of the 24th Congress of the University Assistants, Padua 1979], Padua: Gregoriana 1980, pp. 81–95.

— "Il 'divenire' e il 'possibile' nelle 'Briciole di filosofia' di Søren Kierkegaard ["Becoming" and "Possibility" in Søren Kierkegaard's "Philosophical Fragments"], *Humanitas*, vol. 36, 1981, pp. 325–44.

— "Il 're dei ladri.' Appunti su una figura del 'Diario' di Kierkegaard [The "King of Thieves": Notes on a Figure of Kierkegaard's Diary], *Humanitas*, vol. 36, 1981, pp. 826–35.

— "Il rifiuto kierkegaardiano dell'argomento ontologico" [The Kierkegaardian Refutation of the Ontological Argument], *Humanitas*, vol. 38, no. 3, 1983, pp. 343–57.

— "La presenza di Kierkegaard nel pensiero di Wittgenstein" [The Presence of Kierkegaard in the Thought of Wittgenstein], *Rivista di Filosofia Neo-Scolastica*, no. 2, 1986, pp. 211–26.

— "Socrate 'quel Singolo.' A proposito di alcune annotazioni del 'Diario' kierkegaardiano" [Socrates "that Individual": About Some Notes from Kierkegaard's "Diary"], in *Nuovi Studi Kierkegaardiani. Bollettino del Centro Italiano di Studi Kierkegaardiani* [New Kierkegaard Studies: Bulletin of the Italian Center for Kierkegaard Studies], ed. by Giuseppe Mario Pizzuti, vol. 1, March 1993, pp. 75–85.

Masi, Giuseppe, *La determinazione della possibilità dell'esistenza in Kierkegaard* [The Definition of the Possibility of the Existence in Kierkegaard], Bologna: C. Zuffi Editore 1949.

— "Storicità e cristianesimo in Kierkegaard" [Historicity and Christianity in Kierkegaard], *Archivio di Filosofia (Kierkegaard e Nietzsche)*, no. 2, 1953, pp. 115–32.

— *Disperazione e speranza. Saggio sulle categorie kierkegaardiane* [Despair and Hope: Essay on Kierkegaard's Categories], Padua: Gregoriana 1971.

Matassi, Elio, "La figura impossibile: Kierkegaard, Mozart e l' 'assolutamente musicale'" [The Impossible Figure: Kierkegaard, Mozart, and the "Absolutely Musical"], *Notabene. Quaderni di studi kierkegaardiani*, vol. 7, *Kierkegaard e la condizione desiderante. La seduzione dell'estetico* [Kierkegaard and the Desiring Condition: The Seduction of the Aesthetic], 2009, pp. 29–37.

— "Kierkegaard, il Don Giovanni di Mozart e le malattie dell'anima" [Kierkegaard, Don Giovanni, and the Sicknesses of the Soul], in *Derive. Figure della soggettività* [Drifting: Figures of Subjectivity], ed. by Isabella Adinolfi and Mario Galzigna, Milan: Mimesis 2010, pp. 135–46.

Matteo, Armando, "Riflessi kierkegaardiani nella teologia contemporanea" [Kierkegaardian Variations in Contemporary Theology], *Notabene. Quaderni di studi kierkegaardiani*, vol. 5, *Le malattie dell'anima. Kierkegaard e la psicologia* [The Sicknesses of the Soul: Kierkegaard and Psychology], 2007, pp. 217–29.

Maugeri, Luca S., "Dal concetto teosofico di angosica al *Begrebet Angest* kierkegaardiano – Un abbozzo di percorso storico-concettuale [From the Theosophical Concept of Dread to Kierkegaard's *Begrebet Angest*: Outline of a Historical-Conceptual Route], *Søren Kierkegaard Newsletter*, no. 55, 2009, pp. 19–25.

— *Il dono di un segno: mistica, ascesi ed edificazione in Søren Kierkegaard* [The Gift of a Sign: Mysticism, Asceticism, and Edification in Søren Kierkegaard], Bologna: Pardes 2012.

Mazzatosta, Teresa Maria, "Educazione e seduzione in Kierkegaard" [Education and Seduction in Kierkegaard], *Problemi di Pedagogia*, vol. 29, nos. 1–2, 1983, pp. 1–8.

Mazzù, Domenica, "Il tema kierkegaardiano dell'identità e la polemica antihegeliana" [The Kierkegaardian Theme of Identity and the Anti-Hegelian Polemics], *Incontri Culturali*, no. 7, 1974, pp. 257–67.

Melchiorre, Virgilio, "Kierkegaard e il fideismo" [Kierkegaard and Fideism], *Rivista di Filosofia Neo-Scolastica*, no. 45, 1953, pp. 143–76.

— "Il principio di analogia come categoria metafisica nella filosofia di Kierkegaard" [The Principle of the Analogy as Metaphysical Category in Kierkegaard's Philosophy], *Giornale Critico della Filosofia Italiana*, no. 34, 1955, pp. 56–66.

— "Metafisica e storia in Søren Kierkegaard" [Metaphysics and History in Søren Kierkegaard], *Sapienza*, no. 8, 1955, pp. 203–21.

— "Possibilità e realtà nell'estetica di Kierkegaard" [Possibility and Actuality in Kierkegaard's Aesthetics], in his *Arte ed esistenza* [Art and Existence], Florence: Philosophia 1956, pp. 203–21.

— "La dialettica della 'ripresa' in Søren Kierkegaard [The Dialectic of "Repetition" in Søren Kierkegaard], in *Kierkegaard oggi. Atti del Convegno dell'11 novembre 1982, Università Cattolica del Sacro Cuore, Milan* [Kierkegaard Today: Proceedings of the Congress of November 11th, 1982, Università Cattolica del Sacro Cuore, Milan], ed. by Alessandro Cortese, Milan: Vita e pensiero 1986, pp. 88–118.

— *Saggi su Kierkegaard* [Essays on Kierkegaard], Genova Marietti 1987 (2nd revised and enlarged ed., 1998). (Review: Kjøller Ritzu, Merete, review in *Nordica*, vol. 5, 1988, pp. 185–87.)

— *Figure del sapere* [Figures of Knowing], Naples: Vitale 1994.

— "Esperienza religiosa e filosofia in Kierkegaard" [Religious Experience and Philosophy in Kierkegaard], in *Filosofia ed esperienza religiosa: a partire da Luigi Pareyson. VI colloquio su filosofia e religione (Macerata, 7–9 ottobre 1993)* [Philosophy and Religious Experience: Starting with Luigi Pareyson. Sixth Congress on Philosophy and Religion (Macerata, October 7th-9th, 1993)], ed. by Giovanni Ferretti, Macerata: Giardini 1995, pp. 97–140.

— *Gli stadi di vita in Søren Kierkegaard. Schemi e materiali di lavoro* [The Stages of Life in Søren Kierkegaard: Schemes and Work Materials], Milan: ISU Università Cattolica 2000.

— "Il cristianesimo in Kierkegaard" [Christianity in Kierkegaard], *NotaBene. Quaderni di Studi Kierkegaardiani*, vol. 1, *Leggere oggi Kierkegaard* [Reading Kierkegaard Today], 2000, pp. 27–44.

—"Pentimento e ripresa in Kierkegaard. Dal Qohelet ai gigli del campo" [Repentance and Repetition in Kierkegaard: From the Qohelet to the Lilies in the Field], *NotaBene. Quaderni di studi kierkegaardiani*, vol. 4, *L'edificante in Kierkegaard* [The Edifying in Kierkegaard], 2005, pp. 45–57.

— "L'io diviso. Ripresa e variazioni da un testo di Kierkegaard" [The Divided Self: Repetition and Variations on a Kierkegaardian Text] in *Derive. Figure della soggettività* [Drifting: Figures of Subjectivity], ed. by Isabella Adinolfi and Mario Galzigna, Milan: Mimesis 2010, pp. 83–98.

— "Due itinerari critici sulla cristianità. Considerazioni introduttive" [Two Critical Views on Christendom: Introductory Remarks], *Notabene. Quaderni di studi kierkegaardiani*, vol. 8, *Insegnare il Cristianesimo nel Novecento. La ricezione di*

Kierkegaard e Rosmini [Teaching Christianity in the Twentieth Century: The Reception of Kierkegaard and Rosmini], 2011, pp. 11–17.

— "Il Diario del seduttore. Un percorso dialettico nell'opera di Kierkegaard" [The Seducer's Diary: A Dialectic Path in Kierkegaard's Authorship], *NotaBene. Quaderni di studi Kierkegaardiani*, vol. 9, *Kierkegaard duecento anni dopo* [Kierkegaard Two Hundred Years Later], 2014, pp. 57–70.

Mennini, Sandra M., "La vera fede soprannaturale, virtù indispensabile alla formazione del missionario: il concetto di scandalo in S.A. Kierkegaard" [The Real Supernatural Faith, Essential Virtue in the Education of the Missionary], in *La Formazione del Missionario oggi: atti del Simposio internazionale di missiologia, 24–28 ottobre 1977* [The Education of the Missionary Today: Proceedings of the International Symposium, October 24th-28th, 1977], Brescia: Paideia Editrice 1978, pp. 245–58.

Miano, Vincenzo, "Filosofi cristiani di fronte all'ateismo" [Christian Philosophers in the Face of Atheism], in *L'ateismo contemporaneo* [Contemporary Atheism], ed. by Facoltà Filosofica della Pontificia Università Salesiana di Rome, Turin: S.E.I. 1969, vol. 3, pp. 127–35.

Micheletti, Mario, "Wittgenstein, Kierkegaard e il 'problema di Lessing'" [Wittgenstein, Kierkegaard and the "Problem of Lessing"], *NotaBene. Quaderni di Studi Kierkegaardiani*, vol. 2, *Kierkegaard e la letteratura* [Kierkegaard and Literature], 2002, pp. 143–54.

Miegge, Giovanni, "Kierkegaard e la Chiesa" [Kierkegaard and the Church], *Gioventù Cristiana*, no. 10, 1931, pp. 75–7.

— "Diritto e società in Kierkegaard e Dostoevskij" [Law and Society in Kierkegaard and Dostoevsky], *Rivista Internazionale di Filosofia del Diritto*, no. 38, 1961, pp. 474–90.

Miegge, Mario, "Il divorzio tra la riflessione e la storia (dalla polemica di Kierkegaard alla evasioni nella 'storicità')" [The Divorce between Reflection and History (from the controversy of the evasion in Kierkegaard "Historicity"], *Protestantesimo*, vol. 19, 1964, pp. 23–32; republished in his *Il protestante nella storia* [The Protestant in History], Turin: Claudiana 1970, see pp. 137–54.

Migliorini, Giulio, "Diritto e società in Kierkegaard e in Dostojevskij" [Law and Society in Kierkegaard and Dostoevsky], *Rivista internazionale di Filosofia del Diritto*, vol. 38, 1961, pp. 474–90.

Milan, Andrea, "Il 'divenire di Dio' in Hegel, Kierkegaard e San Tommaso d'Aquino" [The "Becoming of God" in Hegel, Kierkegaard and St. Thomas Aquinas], in *San Tommaso e il pensiero moderno: saggi* [St. Thomas and Modern Thought: Essays], ed. by Pontificia Accademia Romana di S. Tommaso d'Aquino, Rome: Città nuova 1974, pp. 284–94.

— "Deus immutabilis: l'infinita differenza qualitativa e l'immutabilita di Dio in Kierkegaard" [Deus immutabilis: The Infinite Qualitative Difference and the Changelessness of God in Kierkegaard], in *Parola e spirito: studi in onore di Settimio Cipriani* [Word and Spirit: Studies in Honor of Settimio Cipriani], ed. by Cesare Casale Marcheselli, Brescia: Paideia Editrice 1982, vol. 2, pp. 1451–1477.

Modica, Giuseppe, *Fede, libertà, peccato: figure ed esiti della "prova" in Kierkegaard* [Faith, Freedom, Sin: Figures and Results of the "Proof" in Kierkegaard], Palermo:

Palumbo 1992. (Review: Davini, Simonella, review in *Kierkegaardiana*, vol. 17, 1994, pp. 197–9.)

— "Kierkegaard e l'estetica del Don Giovanni. Postille" [Kierkegaard and the Aesthetics of Don Juan: Marginal Notes], *Giornale di Metafisica*, vol. 17, no. 3, 1995, pp. 379–92.

— "Alterità e paradosso in Kierkegaard" [Alterity and Paradox in Kierkegaard], *Giornale di Metafisica*, vol. 20, nos. 1–2, 1998, pp. 61–86.

— "*Ordet* di Dreyer. Percorsi kierkegaardiani" [*The Word* by Dreyer: Kierkegaard's Routes], *Giornale di Metafisica*, vol. 23, no. 1, 2001, pp. 5–34; republished in *Il religioso in Kierkegaard. Atti del convegno di studi organizzato dalla Società Italiana per gli Studi Kierkegaardiani tenutosi dal 14 al 16 dicembre 2000 a Venezia* [The Religious in Kierkegaard: Proceedings of the Congress Organized by The Italian Society for Kierkegaard Sudies in Venice, December 14th-16th, 2000], ed. by Isabella Adinolfi, Brescia: Morcelliana 2002, pp. 320–47.

— *Una verità per me: itinerari kierkegaardiani* [A Truth for Myself: Kierkegaardian Paths], Milan: Vita e Pensiero 2007. (Reviews: Bonagiuso, Giacomo, review in *Giornale di Metafisica*, vol. 2, 2007, pp. 611–15; Sesta, Luciano, review in *Bioethos*, vol. 4, 2008, pp. 98–9.)

Modica, Giuseppe and Marco Ravera, "Søren Aabye Kierkegaard (1813–1855)," in *Il peccato originale nel pensiero moderno* [The Original Sin in Modern Thought], ed. by Giuseppe Riconda, et al., Brescia: Morcelliana 2009, pp. 649–62.

Mollo, Gaetano, "Fede e ragione: un raffronto tra san Bonaventura e Søren Kierkegaard" [Faith and Reason: a Comparison of St. Bonaventure and Søren Kierkegaard], *Miscellanea Francescana*, vol. 75, no. 1, 1975, pp. 721–32.

— "La passione della croce come culmine dialettico della fede in Søren Kierkegaard" [The Passion of the Cross as the Dialectical Acme of Faith in Søren Kierkegaard], in *La sapienza della Croce oggi: atti del Congresso internazionale, Roma, 13–18 ottobre 1975* [The Wisdom of the Cross Today: Proceedings of the International Congress, Rome, October 13th-18th, 1975], vols. 1–3, Turin: Leumann, Elle Di Ci 1976, vol. 3, pp. 144–56.

— "Mondo della cultura e carattere. Un confronto tra Hegel e Kierkegaard" [The World of the Culture and Character: A Comparison of Hegel and Kierkegaard], in *Il problema della cultura. Atti del 21. Convegno di assistenti universitari di filosofia Padova 1976* [The Problem of Culture. Proceedings of the 21st Congress of the University Philosophy Assistants in Padua, 1976], Padua: Gregoriana 1977, pp. 65–76.

— "Soggettività ed educazione in Kierkegaard" [Subjectivity and Education in Kierkegaard], *Il problema dell'antropologia. Atti del 24. Convegno di Assistenti Universitari di Filosofia* [The Problem of the Anthropology. Proceedings of the 24th Congress of University Philosophy Assistants in Padua], Padua: Gregoriana 1980, pp. 81–95.

— *Al di là dell'angoscia, l'educazione etico-religiosa in S. Kierkegaard* [Beyond Anxiety, the Ethical-Religious Education in S. Kierkegaard], S. Assisi: Maria degli Angeli, Porziuncola 1988.

— "Estetica ed etica in Kierkegaard" [Aesthetics and Ethics in Kierkegaard], *Per la Filosofia*, no. 24, 1992, pp. 52–61.

72 *Laura Liva*

— "L'educazione etico-religiosa in S. Kierkegaard" [The Ethical-Religious Education in S. Kierkegaard], *Pedagogia e Vita*, no. 4, 1997, pp. 36–54.

Mondin, Battista, "La teologia esistenziale di S. Kierkegaard" [The Existential Theology of S. Kierkegaard], *Sapienza*, vol. 49, no. 4, 1996, pp. 397–416.

Montanari, Primo, "Intorno alle *Briciole di filosofia* e *Postilla non scientifica* di Kierkegaard" [On Kierkegaard's *Philosophical Fragments* and *Postscript*], *Studia Patavina*, no. 12, 1965, pp. 143–5.

Morandi, Franco, "Rileggendo Kierkegaard un secolo dopo" [Reading Kierkegaard after one Century], in *Nuovi Studi Kierkegaardiani. Bollettino del Centro Italiano di Studi Kierkegaardiani* [New Kierkegaard Studies: Bulletin of the Italian Center for Kierkegaard Studies], ed. by Giuseppe Mario Pizzuti, vol. 1, March 1993, pp. 101–7.

Morando, Dante, "Kierkegaard padre dell'esistenzialismo" [Kierkegaard as the Father of Existentialism], *Rivista Rosminiana*, no. 2, 1942, pp. 50–7.

— "Søren Kierkegaard padre dell'esistenzialismo" [Søren Kierkegaard as the Father of Existentialism], in his *Saggi sull'esistenzialismo teologico* [Essays on Theological Existentialism], Brescia: Morcelliana 1949, pp. 17–41.

— "I maestri dell'esistenzialismo" [The Masters of Existentialism], in *L'esistenzialismo* [The Existentialism], Florence: Città di Vita 1950, pp. 99–116.

Moretti, Giancarlo, "Delitto, peccato e punizione nel *Don Giovanni* di Mozart e Da Ponte (Kierkegaard)" [Crime, Sin and Punishment in Mozart and Da Ponte's *Don Juan* (Kierkegaard)], *Filosofia Oggi*, vol. 14, no. 4, 1991, pp. 521–30.

— "L'attimo (Augenblick) in Søren Kierkegaard e in Friedrich Schleiermacher" [The Moment (Augenblick) in Søren Kierkegaard and Friedrich Schleiermacher], *Humanitas. Rivista Bimestrale di Cultura*, vol. 61, 2006, pp. 904–18.

Morigi, Silvio, "Nervature kierkegaardiane nel pensiero francese del Novecento: da Gabriel Marcel a Denis de Rougemont e René Girard" [Kierkegaardian Nuances in Twentieth-Century French Thought: From Gabriel Marcel to Denis de Rougemont and René Girard], *NotaBene. Quaderni di Studi Kierkegaardiani*, vol. 2, *Kierkegaard e la letteratura* [Kierkegaard and Literature], 2002, pp. 101–25.

Morra, Gianfranco, "La sospensione della morale secondo S.A. Kierkegaard" [The Suspension of Ethics in S.A. Kierkegaard], *Ethica*, no. 1, 1962, pp. 121–37.

— "Chi sono gli pseudonimi di Kierkegaard" [Who are Kierkegaard's Pseudonyms?], *Ethica*, no. 11, 1972, pp. 41–50.

Muccio, Antimo, *Cenni dell'esistenzialismo del Kierkegaard e la persona umana* [An Outline of Kierkegaard's Existentialism and the Human Being], Aversa: Arti grafiche fratelli Macchione 1968.

Mura, Gaspare, *Angoscia ed esistenza: da Kierkegaard a Moltmann, Giobbe e la sofferenza di Dio* [Anxiety and Existence: From Kierkegaard to Moltmann, Job and the Suffering of God], Rome: Città Nuova 1982.

Nardi, Lorenzo, *Kierkegaard e il cristianesimo tragico* [Kierkegaard and Tragic Christianity], Rome: Cremonese 1976.

Navarria, Salvatore, *Søren Kierkegaard e l'irrazionalismo di Karl Barth* [Søren Kierkegaard and the Irrationalism of Karl Barth], Palermo: Palumbo 1943.

Ndreca, Adrian, *Meditazione o paradosso? Kierkegaard contra Hegel* [Meditation or Paradox? Kierkegaard against Hegel], Pavia: Bonomi 2000.

— *La soggettività in Kierkegaard* [Subjectivity in Kierkegaard], Vatican City: Urbaniana University Press 2005.

Negri, Antimo, "Il lavoro nella filosofia moderna: Kierkegaard" [Work in Modern Philosophy: Kierkegaard], *Cultura e Scuola*, vol. 113, 1990, pp. 80–6.

Nepi, Paolo, *L'"Esercizio del cristianesimo" di Kierkegaard e il Cristo dei filosofi* [Kierkegaard's *Practice in Christianity* and the Christ of the Philosophers], Turin: Paravia 1992.

Nicoletti, Michele, "Un frutto dall'albero di Kierkegaard" [A Fruit from Kierkegaard's Tree], *Nottola*, no. 4, 1982, pp. 77–9.

— *La dialettica dell'Incarnazione: soggettività e storia nel pensiero di Søren Kierkegaard* [The Dialectics of the Incarnation: Subjectivity and History in Søren Kierkegaard's Thought], Bologna: Dehoniane 1983 (2nd ed., Trento: Istituto di Scienze Religiose 1984).

— "Søren Aabye Kierkegaard. Il Cristo: mediatore, paradosso e modello" [Søren Aabye Kierkegaard. Christ: Mediator, Paradox and Model], in *La figura di Cristo nella filosofia contemporanea* [The Figure of Christ in Contemporary Philosophy], ed. by Silvano Zucal, Milan: Cinisello Balsamo 1993, pp. 161–95.

— and Giorgio Penzo (eds.), *Kierkegaard: filosofia e teologia del paradosso, Atti del Convegno tenuto a Trento il 4–6 dicembre 1996* [Kierkegaard: Philosophy and Theology of Paradox. Proceeding of the Congress of Trento December 4th-6th, 1996], Brescia: Morcelliana 1999. (Giorgio Penzo, "Il paradosso come verità esistenziale in Kierkegaard" [The Paradox as Existential Truth in Kierkegaard], pp. 13–30; Bruno Forte, "Fare teologia dopo Kierkegaard" [Doing Theology after Kierkegaard], pp. 31–52; Michele Nicoletti, "Genialità, scacco del pensiero e terapia. Il paradosso kierkegaardiano tra dimensioni teoretiche e aspetti pratici" [Brilliance, Setback of Thought and Therapy: The Kierkegaardian Paradox between Theoretical Dimensions and Practical Aspects], pp. 53–68; Virgilio Melchiorre, "Il paradosso come passione del pensiero. Saggio su Kierkegaard" [The Paradox as Passion of Thought: Essay on Kierkegaard], pp. 69–90; Poul Lübcke, "Paradosso e scandalo in Kierkegaard" [Paradox and Scandal in Kierkegaard], pp. 91–103; Hermann Fischer, "La cristologia di Kierkegaard come paradigma del pensiero del paradosso" [Christology in Kierkegaard as a Paradigm of the Paradox], pp. 105–17; Xavier Tilliette, "La cristologia di Kierkegaard nelle *Briciole filosofiche*" [Kierkegaard's Christology in *Philosophical Fragments*], pp. 119–26; Anna Giannatiempo Quinzio, "Il paradosso categoria dell'assurdo e oggetto della fede" [The Paradox as Category of the Absurd and Object of Faith], pp. 127–137; Joachim Ringleben, "Paradosso e dialettica" [Paradox and Dialectics], pp. 139–53; Franco Ferrarotti, "Riflessioni preliminari sul concetto di *singulus* in Søren Kierkegaard" [Preliminary Reflections on the Concept of "Singulus" in Søren Kierkegaard], pp. 155–62; Giuseppe Modica, "Alterità e paradosso in Kierkegaard" [Alterity and Paradox in Kierkegaard], pp. 163–84; Salvatore Spera, "Paradosso cristiano e scandalo della cristianità" [Christian Paradox and the Scandal of Christianity], pp. 185–202; Rainer Thurner, "Sul concetto di ripetizione in Kierkegaard" [On the Concept of Repetition in Kierkegaard], pp. 203–20; Isabella Adinolfi, "La dialettica della fede in Pascal e Kierkegaard" [The Dialectic of Faith in Pascal and

Kierkegaard], pp. 223–50; Francesco Tomasoni, "La morte come paradosso tra Feuerbach e Kierkegaard" [Death as Paradox in Feuerbach and Kierkegaard], pp. 251–64; Giuseppe Cantillo, "Kierkegaard e la filosofia dell'esistenza di Karl Jaspers" [Kierkegaard and the Philosophy of Existence of Karl Jaspers], pp. 265–78; Umberto Regina, "La finitudine dell'uomo, l'onnipotenza di Dio e il senso dell'essere. Da Kierkegaard a Heidegger" [The Finitude of the Human Being, the Omnipotence of God and the Sense of Being: From Kierkegaard to Heidegger], pp. 279–91; Henning Schröer, "Il paradosso nel pensiero teologico del XX secolo. La contrapposizione tra Barth e Tillich sul paradosso positivo e sulle sue conseguenze" [The Paradox in the 20th Century Theological Thought: The Contraposition between Barth and Tillich on the Positive Paradox and Its Consequences], pp. 293–300; Luca Cristellon, "L'interpretazione del paradosso kierkegaardiano in Theodor Haecker" [The Interpretation of the Kierkegaardian Paradox in Theodor Haecker], pp. 301–26.)

Nielsen, Jens Viggo, "'Sulla lettura di Brandes,' la società, l'individuo e la storia universale. Brandes visto attraverso il suo rapporto con Nietzsche e Kierkegaard" ["On the Reading of Brandes," Society, Individual, and Universal History: Brandes Seen Through His Relationship with Nietzsche and Kierkegaard], in *Georg Brandes e l'Europa* [Brandes and Europe], vols. 1–2, ed. by Jørgen Stender Clausen, Pisa/Rome, 2004, vol. 2, pp. 113–21 (*Studi Nordici*, vols. 9–10, 2002–2003).

Nobile Ventura, Attilio, "Kierkegaard. L'angoscia come apertura alla fede" [Kierkegaard: Anxiety as an Opening to Faith], *Idea*, no. 12, 1974, pp. 47–8.

NotaBene. Quaderni di Studi Kierkegaardiani, vol. 1, *Leggere oggi Kierkegaard* [Reading Kierkegaard Today], ed. by Isabella Adinolfi, Rome: Città nuova 2000.

NotaBene. Quaderni di Studi Kierkegaardiani, vol. 2, *Kierkegaard e la letteratura* [Kierkegaard and Literature], ed. by Massimo Iritano and Inge Lise Rasmussen, Rome: Città Nuova 2002.

NotaBene. Quaderni di Studi Kierkegaardiani, vol. 3, *L'arte dello sguardo: Kierkegaard e il cinema* [The Art of Looking: Kierkegaard and the Cinema], ed. by Isabella Adinolfi, Rome: Città nuova 2003.

NotaBene. Quaderni di studi kierkegaardiani, vol. 4, *L'edificante in Kierkegaard* [The Edifying in Kierkegaard], ed. by Isabella Adinolfi and Virgilio Melchiorre, Genoa: Il Melangolo 2005.

Notabene. Quaderni di studi kierkegaardiani, vol. 5, *Le malattie dell'anima. Kierkegaard e la psicologia* [The Sicknesses of the Soul: Kierkegaard and Psychology], ed. by Isabella Adinolfi and Roberto Garaventa, Genoa: Il Melangolo 2007.

Notabene. Quaderni di studi kierkegaardiani, vol. 6, *La profondità della scena. Il teatro visitato da Kierkegaard, Kierkegaard visitato dal teatro* [The Depth of the Scene: The Theater Seen by Kierkegaard, Kierkegaard Seen by the Theater], ed. by Isabella Adinolfi and Inge Lise Rasmussen, Genoa: Il Melangolo 2008.

Notabene. Quaderni di studi kierkegaardiani, vol. 7, *Kierkegaard e la condizione desiderante. La seduzione dell'estetico* [Kierkegaard and the Desiring Condition: The Seduction of the Aesthetic], ed. by Isabella Adinolfi, Marco Fortunato and Elio Matassi, Genoa: Il Melangolo 2009.

Notabene. Quaderni di studi kierkegaardiani, vol. 8, *Insegnare il Cristianesimo nel Novecento. La ricezione di Kierkegaard e Rosmini* [Teaching Christianity in the Twentieth Century: The Reception of Kierkegaard and Rosmini], ed. by Isabella Adinolfi, and Giuseppe Goisis, Genoa: Il Melangolo 2011.

Notabene. Quaderni di studi kierkegaardiani, vol. 9, *Kierkegaard duecento anni dopo* [Kierkegaard Two Hundred Years Later], ed. by Isabella Adinolfi, Roberto Garaventa, Laura Liva and Ettore Rocca, Genoa: Il Melangolo 2014.

Oggioni, Emilio, *L'esistenzialismo* [Existentialism], Bologna: Patron 1956.

Olesen, Søren Gosvig, "Kierkegaard nel sistema o il sistema in Kierkegaard. Note per una lettura" [Kierkegaard in the System or the System in Kierkegaard: Notes for a Reading], *Rivista di Estetica*, vol. 47, 2007, pp. 199–208.

Orlando, Pasquale, "L'immutabilità di Dio. Il pensiero di S. Tommaso di fronte ad Hegel e a Kierkegaard" [The Changelessness of God: St. Thomas' Thought compared to Hegel and Kierkegaard], *Doctor Communis*, vol. 40, no. 3, 1987, pp. 278–84.

Ottonello, Pier Paolo, "Misticismo e Ascesi in Kierkegaard" [Mysticism and Ascesis in Kierkegaard], *Rivista di Ascetica e Mistica*, vol. 33, 1964, pp. 62–77 and pp. 173–84.

— "Gli studi kierkegaardiani in Italia nell'ultimo ventennio" [Kierkegaard Studies in Italy in the Last Two Decades], *Cultura e scuola*, vol. 28, 1968, pp. 127–38.

— "Søren Kierkegaard," in *Grande Antologia Filosofica* [Great Philosophical Anthology], Milan: Marzorati 1971, vol. 18, pp. 1169–1188.

— *Kierkegaard e il problema del tempo* [Kierkegaard and the Problem of Time], Genova: Tilgher 1972.

— *Struttura e forma del nichilismo europeo* [The Structure and Form of European Nihilism], vol. 2: *Da Lutero a Kierkegaard* [From Luther to Kierkegaard], L'Aquila-Rome: Japadre 1988.

Paci, Enzo, "Studi su Kierkegaard" [Studies on Kierkegaard], *Studi Filosofici*, vol. 1, nos. 2–3, 1940, pp. 279–91; republished as "Personalità ed esistenza nel pensiero di Kierkegaard" [Personality and Existence in Kierkegaard's Thought] in his *Pensiero, esistenza e valore* [Thought, Existence, Value], Milan and Messina: Principato 1940, pp. 77–97.

— *L'esistenzialismo* [Existentialism], Padua: CEDAM 1943.

— *Kierkegaard e Nietzsche* [Kierkegaard and Nietzsche], Milan: Fratelli Bocca Editore 1953.

— "Il cammino della vita" [Life's Way], *Aut-Aut*, no. 20, 1954, pp. 111–26.

— "Ironia, demoniaco ed eros in Kierkegaard" [Irony, the Demonic and Eros in Kierkegaard], in *Archivio di Filosofia* (*Kierkegaard e Nietzsche*), 1953, pp. 71–113; republished in his *Relazioni e significati. II. Kierkegaard and Thomas Mann* [Relations and Meanings: II. Kierkegaard and Thomas Mann], Milan: Lampugnani Nigri, and Vicenza: C. Stocchero 1965, pp. 8–45.

— "Kierkegaard e la dialettica della fede" [Kierkegaard and the Dialectic of Faith], *Archivio di Filosofia* (*Kierkegaard e Nietzsche*), 1953, pp. 9–44; republished as "La dialettica della fede" [The Dialectic of Faith] in his *Relazioni e significati. II. Kierkegaard and Thomas Mann* [Relations and Meanings: II. Kierkegaard and

Thomas Mann], Milan: Lampugnani Nigri, and Vicenza: C. Stocchero 1965, pp. 80–119.

— *L'esistenzialismo* [Existentialism], Turin: Edizioni Radio Italiana 1953, pp. 87–180.

— "Angoscia e fenomenologia dell'eros" [Anxiety and Phenomenology of Eros], *Aut-Aut*, no. 24, 1954, pp. 468–85; republished in his *Relazioni e significati. II. Kierkegaard e Thomas Mann* [Relations and Meanings: II. Kierkegaard and Thomas Mann], Milan: Lampugnani Nigri, and Vicenza: C. Stocchero 1965, pp. 197–213.

— "Angoscia e relazione in Kierkegaard" [Anxiety and Relation in Kierkegaard], *Aut-Aut*, no. 23, 1954, pp. 363–76; republished in his *Relazioni e significati. II. Kierkegaard and Thomas Mann* [Relations and Meanings: II. Kierkegaard and Thomas Mann], Milan: Lampugnani Nigri, and Vicenza: C. Stocchero 1965, pp. 184–196.

— "Il significato dell'Introduzione kierkegaardiana al *Concetto dell'angoscia* [The Meaning of Kierkegaard's Introduction to *The Concept of Anxiety*], *Rivista di Filosofia*, no. 45, 1954, pp. 392–98; republished as "La psicologia e il problema dell'angoscia" [The Psychology and the Problem of Anxiety] in his *Relazioni e significati. II. Kierkegaard and Thomas Mann* [Relations and Meanings: II. Kierkegaard and Thomas Mann], Milan: Lampugnani Nigri, and Vicenza: C. Stocchero 1965, pp. 176–183.

— "Kierkegaard contro Kierkegaard" [Kierkegaard against Kierkegaard], *Aut-Aut*, no. 22, 1954, pp. 269–301; republished as "Estetica ed etica" [*Aesthetics and Ethics*] in his *Relazioni e significati. II. Kierkegaard and Thomas Mann* [Relations and Meanings: II. Kierkegaard and Thomas Mann], Milan: Lampugnani Nigri, and Vicenza: C. Stocchero 1965, pp. 47–79.

— "Ripetizione, ripresa e rinascita in Kierkegaard" [Repetition, Resumption and Rebirth in Kierkegaard], *Giornale Critico della Filosofia Italiana*, no. 33, 1954, pp. 313–40; republished as "Ripetizione e ripresa: il teatro e la sua funzione catartica" [Repetition and Resumption: The Theatre and its Cathartic Function] in his *Relazioni e significati. II. Kierkegaard and Thomas Mann* [Relations and Meanings: II. Kierkegaard and Thomas Mann], Milan: Lampugnani Nigri, and Vicenza: C. Stocchero 1965, pp. 120–50.

— "Storia ed apocalisse in Kierkegaard" [History and Apocalypse in Kierkegaard], *Archivio di Filosofia* (*Apocalisse e insecuritas*), 1954, pp. 141–62; republished as "Storia ed apocalisse" [History and Apocalypse] in his *Relazioni e significati. II. Kierkegaard and Thomas Mann* [Relations and Meanings: II. Kierkegaard and Thomas Mann], Milan: Lampugnani Nigri, and Vicenza: C. Stocchero 1965, pp. 151–175.

— "Su due significati del concetto dell'angoscia in Kierkegaard" [On the Twofold Meaning of *The Concept of Anxiety* in Kierkegaard], *Orbis litterarum*, no. 10, 1955, pp. 196–207; republished as "L'intenzionalità e l'amore" [Intentionality and Love] in his *Relazioni e significati. II. Kierkegaard and Thomas Mann* [Relations and Meanings: II. Kierkegaard and Thomas Mann], Milan: Lampugnani Nigri, and Vicenza: C. Stocchero 1965, pp. 214–28.

— *Kierkegaard e Thomas Mann 4.* [Kierkegaard and Thomas Mann 4.], Milan: Bompiani, Dipartimento di filosofia dell'Università degli studi 1991.

Palermo, Sandra, "La scena e il prisma. Teatro e cinema come immagini concettuali in Kierkegaard e Benjamin" [The Scene and the Prism: Theatre and Cinema as Conceptual Images in Kierkegaard and Benjamin], *NotaBene. Quaderni di Studi Kierkegaardiani*, vol. 2, *Kierkegaard e la letteratura* [Kierkegaard and Literature], 2002, pp. 83–99.

Papuzza, Carlo, "Angoscia e trascendenza in Kierkegaard" [Anxiety and Transcendence in Kierkegaard], *Il Dialogo*, no. 1, 1970, pp. 41–6.

Parente, Pietro, "Il vero volto di Kierkegaard" [The Real Face of Kierkegaard], *L'Osservatore Romano*, vol. 11, no. 3, 1952, p. 3.

Paresce, Enrico, "Hume, Hamann, Kierkegaard e la filosofia della credenza" [Hume, Hamann, Kierkegaard and the Philosophy of Belief], *Rivista Internazionale di Filosofia del Diritto*, vol. 26, series 3, no. 4, 1949, pp. 357–75.

Pareyson, Luigi, "Note sulla filosofia dell'esistenza" [Notes on the Philosophy of Existence], *Giornale Critico della Filosofia Italiana*, no. 19, 1938, pp. 407–38.

— "Nota Kierkegaardiana" [A Kierkegaardian Note], *Annali della R. Scuola Normale Superiore di Pisa*, no. 8, 1939, pp. 53–68.

— *La filosofia dell'esistenza e Carlo Jaspers* [The Philosophy of Existence and Karl Jaspers], Naples: Loffredo 1940.

— "La dissoluzione dello hegelismo e l'esistenzialismo" [The Dissolution of Hegelianism and Existentialism] and "Søren Kierkegaard e l'esistenzialismo" [Søren Kierkegaard and Existentialism] in his *Studi sull'esistenzialismo* [Studies on Existentialism], Florence: Sansoni 1943, pp. 69–78; pp. 79–110.

— "Due possibilità: Kierkegaard e Feuerbach" [Two Possibilities: Kierkegaard and Feuerbach] and "Esistenzialismo ed umanesimo" [Existentialism and Humanism] in his *Esistenza e persona* [Existence and Person], Turin: Taylor 1950, pp. 11–46, pp. 69–78.

— "Kierkegaard e la poesia d'occasione" [Kierkegaard and Occasional Poems], *Rivista di Estetica*, no. 10, 1965, pp. 248–55.

— *L'etica di Kierkegaard nella prima fase del suo pensiero* [Kierkegaard's Ethics in the First Phase of His Thought], Turin: G. Giappichelli 1965. (Reviews: Bernascone, Bianca, review in *Filosofia*, vol. 1, 1969, pp. 147–50; Castagnino, Franca, review in her *Gli studi italiani su Kierkegaard: 1906–1966*, Rome: Edizioni dell'Ateneo 1972, pp. 296–8.)

— *L'etica di Kierkegaard nella Postilla* [Kierkegaard's Ethics in the *Postscript*], Turin: G. Giappichelli 1971. (Review: Basso, Ingrid, "The Italian Reception of Kierkegaard's *Concluding Unscientific Postscript*," in *Kierkegaard Studies Yearbook* 2005, pp. 400–17, in particular, pp. 412–14.)

— *Kierkegaard e Pascal* [Kierkegaard and Pascal], ed. by Sergio Givone, in his *Opere complete* [Complete Works], vols. 1–20, Milan: Mursia 1998ff., vol. 13.

Pastore, Annibale, "Il messaggio di Søren Kierkegaard" [Søren Kierkegaard's Message], *Logos*, nos. 1–2, 1943; republished in his *La volontà dell'assurdo* [The Will of the Absurd], Milan: Bolla 1948, pp. 49–58.

— "Kierkegaard. Pensare il paradosso" [Kierkegaard. Thinking the Paradox], in *In Lotta con l'Angelo. La filosofia degli ultimi due secoli di fronte al Cristianesimo* [Fighting against the Angel: The Last Two Centuries of Philosophy in the Face of Christianity], ed. by Claudio Ciancio, Giovanni Ferretti, Annamaria Pastore, and Ugo Perone, Turin: SEI 1989, pp. 114–28.

Pellegrini, Alessandro, "Il *sistema* e gli eretici" [The *System* and the Heretics], *Archivio di Storia della Filosofia Italiana*, no. 4, 1935, pp. 159–65.

Pellegrini, Giovanni, "Kafka lettore di Kierkegaard. Analisi di una interpretazione" [Kafka as Reader of Kierkegaard: Analysis of an Interpretation], *Tempo Presente*, no. 172, 1995, pp. 52–8.

— "Colpa e peccato in Kierkegaard e Nietzsche" [Fault and Sin in Kierkegaard and Nietzsche], *Il Cannocchiale*, no. 3, 1997, pp. 101–25.

— "Abramo, l'argomentazione e l'incantesimo: Kafka interprete di Kierkegaard" [Abraham, the Argumentation and the Spell: Kafka Commentator of Kierkegaard], *Il Cannocchiale*, no. 3, 1999, pp. 69–110.

— *La legittimazione di sé: Kafka interprete di Kierkegaard* [Self-Legitimation: Kafka Commentator of Kierkegaard], Turin: Trauben 2001.

Pellegrino, Antonia, "Paradosso della fede e paradosso della modernità: Franz Overbeck e Søren Kierkegaard" [Paradox of Faith and Paradox of Modernity: Franz Overbeck and Søren Kierkegaard], *NotaBene. Quaderni di Studi Kierkegaardiani*, vol. 2, *Kierkegaard e la letteratura* [Kierkegaard and Literature], 2002, pp. 155–86.

Penelhum, Terence, "Ateismo, scetticismo e fideismo" [Atheism, Scepticism and Fideism], *Rivista di Filosofia Neo-Scolastica*, vol. 86, no. 1, 1994, pp. 134–53.

Penzo, Giorgio, *Friedrich Gogarten. Il problema di Dio tra storicismo ed esistenzialismo* [Friedrich Gogarten: The Problem of God between Historicism and Existentialism], Rome: Città Nuova 1981.

— "Un nuovo studio italiano su Kierkegaard" [A New Italian Research on Kierkegaard], in *Nuovi Studi Kierkegaardiani. Bollettino del Centro Italiano di Studi Kierkegaardiani* [New Kierkegaard Studies: Bulletin of the Italian Center for Kierkegaard Studies], ed. by Giuseppe Mario Pizzuti, vol. 1, March 1993, pp. 115–19.

— *Kierkegaard: la verità eterna che nasce nel tempo* [Kierkegaard: The Eternal Truth Which is Born in Temporality], Padua: Messaggero 2000. (Review: Spadaro, Antonio, review in *La civiltà cattolica*, vol. 1, no. 153, 2002, pp. 520–521.)

Perini, Giuseppe, "Søren Kierkegaard: il coraggio di dire *io*" [Søren Kierkegaard and the Courage to Say *I*], *Idea*, no. 1, 1970, pp. 41–8.

— "Søren Kierkegaard: ricostruire il cristiano" [Søren Kierkegaard: Rebuilding the Christian], *Idea*, no. 11, 1971, pp. 19–26.

— "Søren Kierkegaard: ricostruire l'uomo" [Søren Kierkegaard: Rebuilding Man], *Idea*, nos. 6–7, 1971, pp. 23–8.

— "Søren Kierkegaard: smaltire la sbornia dei sogni" [Søren Kierkegaard: Sobering up of Dreams], *Idea*, no. 5, 1971, pp. 13–17.

— "Il *Diario* di Kierkegaard in italiano. Nuova edizione" [Kierkegaard's *Diary* in Italian: The New Edition], *Divus Thomas*, vol. 87, nos. 1–2, 1984, pp. 87–98.

Perini, Roberto, *Soggetto e storicità. Il problema della soggettività finita tra Hegel e Kierkegaard* [The Subject and Historicity: The Problem of Finite Subjectivity in Hegel and Kierkegaard], Naples: Edizioni Scientifiche Italiane 1995, pp. 89–157.

Perlini, Tito, *Che cosa ha veramente detto Kierkegaard* [What Kierkegaard Really Said], Rome: Ubaldini 1968.

Pertici, Alessandra, "Søren Kierkegaard su Savonarola" [Søren Kierkegaard on Savonarola], *L'Ambra. Rivista di cultura scandinava*, vol. 4, no. 1, 1998, pp. 23–8.

Piazzesi, Chiara, *La verità come trasformazione di sé: terapie filosofiche in Pascal, Kierkegaard e Wittgenstein* [The Truth as Self-Transformation: Philosophical Therapies in Pascal, Kierkegaard, and Wittgenstein], Pisa: ETS 2009.

Pieretti, Antonio, "Analisi semantica del concetto di angoscia esistenziale" [Semantic Analysis of the Concept of Existential Anxiety], *Studium*, vol. 78, 1982, pp. 601–10.

Pinto, Valeria, "L'esperienza cristiana della verità. Appunti per un confronto tra Heidegger e Kierkegaard" [The Christian Experience of Truth: Some Notes for a Comparison between Heidegger and Kierkegaard], *Atti Accademia di Scienze Morali e Politiche di Napoli*, vol. 100, 1990, pp. 283–308.

Pizzorni, Reginaldo M., "Dio fondamento ultimo della morale e del diritto" [God as the First Ground of Morality and Law], *Sapienza*, vol. 49, no. 4, 1996, pp. 435–48.

Pizzuti, Giuseppe Mario, "Perché Kierkegaard lasciò Regina. Note sul rapporto tra esemplarità e dialettica nell'estetica kierkegaardiana" [Why Kierkegaard Left Regine: Notes on the Relationship between Exemplariness and Dialectics in Kierkegaard's Aesthetics], *Filosofia*, no. 33, 1982, pp. 463–71.

— "Kierkegaard e Regina. Metafisica della crisi e dialettica dell'eccezione" [Kierkegaard and Regine: Metaphysics of Crisis and Dialectics of the Exception], *Atti Accademia di Scienze Morali e Politiche di Napoli*, vol. 93, 1983, pp. 325–46.

— "Recenti studi italiani su Kierkegaard" [Recent Italian Studies on Kierkegaard], *Filosofia*, vol. 35, 1984, pp. 127–138.

— "La dialettica dell'edificante nella polemica antihegeliana di S. Kierkegaard" [The Dialectics of the Edifying in Kierkegaard's Anti-Hegelian Polemics], *Atti dell'Accademia di Scienze Morali e Politiche di Napoli*, vol. 95, 1985, pp. 1–18.

— *Tra Kierkegaard e Barth: l'ombra di Nietzsche. La crisi come odissea dello spirito* [Between Kierkegaard and Barth: The Shadow of Nietzsche. The Crisis as Odyssey of the Spirit], Venosa: Edizioni Osanna Venosa 1986.

— "Esemplarità di Abramo. Trascendenza e trascendentalità della libertà nell'opera di S. Kierkegaard e di Karl Barth" [Abraham's Exemplariness: Transcendence and Transcendentality of Freedom in Kierkegaard's Work], in *Nuovi Studi Kierkegaardiani* [New Kierkegaard Studies], ed. by Giuseppe Mario Pizzuti, Potenza: Centro Italiano di Studi Kierkegaardiani 1988, pp. 23–52.

— "Kierkegaard e Mozart. Sulle ragioni di una confessione autobiografica" [Kierkegaard and Mozart: On the Reasons of an Autobiographical Confession], in *Nuovi Studi Kierkegaardiani* [New Kierkegaard Studies], ed. by Giuseppe Mario Pizzuti, Potenza: Centro Italiano di Studi Kierkegaardiani 1988, pp. 125–34.

— "Sulle tracce del soggetto. Fenomenologia e dialettica della soggettività in Kierkegaard" [On the Subject's Trail: Phenomenology and the Dialectics of Subjectivity in Kierkegaard], *Filosofia e Teologia*, vol. 3, no. 3, 1989, pp. 533–45.

— "Morte o aurora della filosofia? Sull'u-topia del pensare dopo Kierkegaard e Nietzsche" [Death or Dawn of Philosophy? On the U-topia of Thinking after Kierkegaard and Nietzsche], *Velia*, no. 1, 1990, pp. 109–46.

— "Fede filosofica e rivelazione: trascendenza e comunicazione. Convergenza e distonie nel rapporto Jaspers-Kierkegaard" [Philosophical Faith and Revelation: Transcendence and Communication. Convergences and Dissonances in the Relationship between Kierkegaard and Jaspers], *Velia*, no. 4, 1991, pp. 45–59.

— "Gli pseudonimi di Kierkegaard" [Kierkegaard's Pseudonyms], *Annuario Filosofico*, no. 7, 1991, pp. 369–93.

— "Un filosofo inattuale. Cornelio Fabro nel suo ottantesimo genetliaco" [An Untimely Philosopher: Cornelio Fabro on His Eightieth Birthday], *Humanitas*, vol. 46, no. 5, 1991, pp. 680–93.

— "Suggestioni e referenze kierkegaardiane dell'esperienza di Dio nella biografia speculativa di Karl Barth e di Karl Jaspers" [Kierkegaard's Suggestions and References on the Experience of God in the Speculative Biography of Karl Barth and Karl Jaspers], in *Teologia razionale, filosofia della religione, linguaggio su Dio* [Rational Theology, Philosophy of Religion, Language on God], ed. by Marcello Sanchez Sorondo, Rome: Università Pontificia Lateranense and Herder 1992, pp. 299–335.

— "Genesi e fenomenologia dell'uomo-massa nell'opera di Søren Kierkegaard" [Genesis and Phenomenology of Mass-Man in Søren Kierkegaard's Work], in *Nuovi Studi Kierkegaardiani. Bollettino del Centro Italiano di Studi Kierkegaardiani* [New Kierkegaard Studies: Bulletin of the Italian Center for Kierkegaard Studies], ed. by Giuseppe Mario Pizzuti, vol. 1, March 1993, pp. 86–100.

— *Kierkegaard: una biografia intellettuale. Il discorso cifrato di uno psicologo estetizzante* [Kierkegaard: An Intellectual Biography. The Coded Discourse of a Psychologist Posing as an Esthete], Potenza: Edizioni Ermes 1993.

— "Una rivista kierkegaardiana" [A Kierkegaardian Review], in *Nuovi Studi Kierkegaardiani. Bollettino del Centro Italiano di Studi Kierkegaardiani* [New Kierkegaard Studies: Bulletin of the Italian Center for Kierkegaard Studies], ed. by Giuseppe Mario Pizzuti, vol. 1, March 1993, pp. 7–10.

— "Anti-Climacus. Dialettica e struttura dell'ultimo pseudonimo di kierkegaaard" [Anti-Climacus: Dialectics and Structure of the Last Pseudonym of Kierkegaard], *Annuario Filosofico*, no. 11, 1995, pp. 225–70.

— *Invito al pensiero di Kierkegaard* [Introduction to Kierkegaard's Thought], Milan: Mursia 1995.

— *L'eredità teo-logica del pensiero occidentale: Auschwitz* [The Theo-logic Legacy of Western Thought: Auschwitz], Soveria Mannelli: Rubbettino 1997, pp. 187–92 (*Scaffale universitario*, vol. 47).

— (ed.), *Nuovi Studi Kierkegaardiani*, Potenza: Centro Italiano di Studi Kierkegaardiani 1989, vol. 1. (Cornelio Fabro, "Nuovi Studi Kierkegaardiani" [New Kierkegaard Studies], pp. 7–21; Giuseppe Mario Pizzuti, "Esemplarità di Abramo. Trascendenza e trascendentalità della libertà nell'opera di Soeren Kierkegaard e di Karl Barth" [Exemplariness of Abraham. Transcendence and Transcendentality of Freedom in Søren Kierkegaard's Authorship], pp. 23–52; Anna Maria Sini, "L'itinerario fondamentale della libertà in Soeren Kierkegaard" [The Essential

Itinerary of Freedom in Søren Kierkegaard], pp. 53–79; Sergio Marini, "Schede di bibliografia kierkegaardiana in lingua italiana 1967–1986" [Bibliographical Reports on Kierkegaard in Italian Language 1967–1986], pp. 81–97; Italo di Monte, "Kierkegaard tra idealità e realtà. La Dialettica della Fede contro i falsi Fideismi. Noterelle polemiche" [Kierkegaard between Ideality and Actuality. The Dialectic of Faith Against False Fideism. Short Polemical Notes], pp. 101–15; Cornelio Fabro, "Kierkegaard e la Chiesa in Danimarca" [Kierkegaard and the Church of Denmark], pp. 117–23; Giuseppe Mario Pizzuti, "Kierkegaard e Mozart sulle ragione di una confessione autobiografica" [Kierkegaard and Mozart on the Reasons for an Autobiographical Confession], pp. 125–32; Mario Pizzuti, "Postilla di letteratura kierkegaardiana 1988" [Postscript on Kierkegaardian Literature 1988], pp. 133–64; "Testi kierkegaardiani" [Kierkegaardian Texts], pp. 165–211; "Documentazione," [Documents] pp. 213–39).

— (ed.), *Nuovi Studi Kierkegaardiani. Bollettino del Centro Italiano di Studi Kierkegaardiani*, Potenza: Centro Italiano di Studi Kierkegaardiani 1993. (Cornelio Fabro, "Ragione e fede in Rasmus Nielsen" [Reason and Faith in Rasmus Nielsen], pp. 11–24; Giuseppe Cenacchi, "Kierkegaard: Fenomenologia del peccato e filosofia esistenziale in 'Il concetto dell'angoscia'" [Kierkegaard: Phenomenology of Sin and Existential Philosophy in "The Concept of Anxiety"], pp. 25–40; Luca Cristellon, "Silenzio e comunicazione nel pensiero di Kierkegaard" [Silence and Communication in Kierkegaard's Thought], pp. 41–56; Andrea Dalledonne, "La dottrina kierkegaardiana del Singolo come critica cristiana del collettivismo giudaico" [The Kierkegaardian Theory of the Single Individual as Christian Critique of Jewish Collectivism], pp. 57–74; Sergio Marini, "Socrate 'quel Singolo.' A proposito di alcune annotazioni del 'Diario' kierkegaardiano" [Socrates "That Individual". About Some Notes From Kierkegaard's Diary], pp. 75–85; Giuseppe Mario Pizzuti, "Genesi e fenomenologia dell'uomo-massa nell'opera di Soeren Kierkegaard [I]" [Genesis and Phenomenology of Mass-Man in Søren Kierkegaard's Work], pp. 86–100; Franco Morandi, "Rileggendo Kierkegaard un secolo dopo" [Reading Kierkegaard after a Century], pp. 101–108; Sergio Marini, "Schede di bibliografia kierkegaardiana in lingua italiana 1987–1991" [Bibliographical Reports on Kierkegaard in Italian Language 1987–1991], pp. 109–114; Giorgio Penzo, "Un nuovo studio italiano su Kierkegaard (a proposito di: Anna Giannatiempo Quinzio, 'L'estetico in Kierkegaard' [SK 3783]" [A New Italian Research on Kierkegaard. About Anna Giannatiempo Quinzio's "Aesthetics in Kierkegaard"], pp. 115–119; "Postille di letteratura kierkegaardiana" [Postscripts on Kierkegaardian Literature], pp. 120–123.)

Polizzi, Paolo, *Kierkegaard, ovvero Della dialettica della scelta* [Kierkegaard or The Dialectics of Choice], ed. by Centro studi G. Toniolo di Palermo, Palermo: S. F. Flaccovio 1991.

Ponzio, Augusto, *Filosofia del linguaggio* [Philosophy of Language], Bari: Adriatica 1985.

Possenti, Vittorio, *La filosofia dopo il nichilismo: sguardi sulla filosofia futura* [Philosophy after Nihilism: A Look at the Future Philosophy], Soveria Mannelli: Rubettino 2001.

Preti, Giulio, "Kierkegaard, Feuerbach e Marx" [Kierkegaard, Feuerbach and Marx], *Studi Filosofici*, no. 10, 1949, pp. 187–208.

Prezzo, Rosella, "Gli stili di Kierkegaard" [Kierkegaard's Styles], *Aut-Aut*, no. 1, 1994, pp. 195–207.

Prini, Pietro, *Kierkegaard testimonio della verità sofferente è e una biografia dell'esistenzialismo Romantico* [Kierkegaard as Witness of the Suffering Truth and a Biography of the Romantic Existentialism], in his *L'esistenzialismo* [Existentialism], Rome: Studium 1953, pp. 11–30.

— "Le tre età dell'esistenzialismo" [The Three Ages of Existentialism], *Studi Francescani*, no. 55, 1958, pp. 159–75.

— "Kierkegaard e la filosofia come giornale intimo" [Kierkegaard and Philosophy as Intimate Journal], *Archivio di Filosofia*, 1959, pp. 73–90; republished in his *Esistenzialismo* [Existentialism], Rome: Studium 1971, pp. 10–53.

— "Kierkegaard, escritor autobiográfico" [Kierkegaard, Autobiographical Writer], *Psicopatología*, vol. 6, 1986, pp. 151–56.

— "La teologia sperimentale di Søren Kierkegaard" [Søren Kierkegaard's Experimental Theology], in his *Storia dell'esistenzialismo. Da Kierkegaard a oggi* [History of Existentialism: From Kierkegaard Until Today], Rome: Studium 1989, pp. 13–46.

Puccini, Gianni, Giulio Alliney and G. Agenore Magno, "Søren Kierkegaard" in *Dizionario di centouno capolavori delle letterature scandinave* [Dictionary of One Hundred and One Masterpieces of Scandinavian Literatures], ed. by Franco Moccia, Milan: Bompiani 1967, pp. 30–38.

Quinzio, Sergio, "Kierkegaard, il cristiano moderno" [Kierkegaard, the Modern Christian], *NotaBene. Quaderni di Studi Kierkegaardiani*, vol. 1, *Leggere oggi Kierkegaard* [Reading Kierkegaard Today], 2000, pp. 179–89.

Rad, Gerhard von, *Il sacrificio di Abramo* [Abraham's Sacrifice], Brescia: Morcelliana 1977 (2nd revised ed. 2009).

Rasmussen, Inge Lise, "La disperazione e il desiderio di morte. Echi di *La malattia per la morte* di Søren Kierkegaard in *Alkmene* di Karen Blixen" [Despair and the Desire of Death: Echoes of Søren Kierkegaard's *The Sickness unto Death* in Karen Blixen's *Alkmene*], *Notabene. Quaderni di studi kierkegaardiani*, vol. 5, *Le malattie dell'anima. Kierkegaard e la psicologia* [The Sicknesses of the Soul: Kierkegaard and Psychology], 2007, pp. 169–77.

— "Scene di matrimoni. Riflessioni di Kierkegaard, Ibsen e Strindberg" [Scenes from Marriages: Reflections by Kierkegaard, Ibsen, and Strindberg], *Notabene. Quaderni di studi kierkegaardiani*, vol. 6, *La profondità della scena. Il teatro visitato da Kierkegaard, Kierkegaard visitato dal teatro* [The Depth of the Scene: The Theater Seen by Kierkegaard, Kierkegaard Seen by the Theater], 2008, pp. 131–42.

Regina, Umberto, *La costruzione dell'interiorità in Kierkegaard dalla ripetizione esistenziale al salto del paradosso* [The Construction of Kierkegaard's Inwardness from the Existential Repetition to the Leap of Paradox], Venice: La Baùta 1995.

— "La visione esistenziale della natura in Kierkegaard, Nietzsche, Heidegger" [The Existential View of Nature in Kierkegaard, Nietzsche and Heidegger], in *La concezione della natura nella scienza attuale, nella poesia, nella filosofia.*

Convegno di Napoli (26–27 ottobre 1994) [The Idea of Nature in Contemporary Science, Poetry and Philosophy. Congress in Naples (October 26th-27th, 1994)], ed. by Ambrogio Giacomo Manno, Naples: Loffredo 1995, pp. 151–66.

— "Filosofia e religione nella formazione della coscienza europea" [Philosophy and Religion in the Building of the European Consciousness], *Philo-Logica*, vol. 5, no. 9, 1996, pp. 47–59.

— *La differenza Amata e il Paradosso cristiano: gli "Stadi sul cammino della vita" di Søren Kierkegaard* [The Beloved Difference and the Christian Paradox: Kierkegaard's *Stages on Life's Way*], Verona: CUSL 1997.

— "Oltre la modernità ripercorrendo la via esistenziale da Kierkegaard al secondo Heidegger" [Beyond Modernity, Going Along the Existential Path from Kierkegaard to the Second Heidegger], *Acta Philosophica*, vol. 8, no. 2, 1999, pp. 223–50.

— "L'attualità dell' 'edificante' per poter ancora sperare" [The Actuality of the "Edifying" in order to Hope Again], *NotaBene. Quaderni di Studi Kierkegaardiani*, vol. 1, *Leggere oggi Kierkegaard* [Reading Kierkegaard Today], 2000, pp. 127–34.

— "Il rafforzamento dell'uomo interiore in Søren Kierkegaard" [The Strengthening of the Inner Man in Søren Kierkegaard], *Progresso del Mezzogiorno*, vol. 25, nos. 1–2 (special issue), 2001, pp. 121–40.

— *Kierkegaard: l'arte dell'esistere* [Kierkegaard: The Art of Existence], Brescia: Morcelliana 2005.

— "Quando l'ideale insidia l'edificante" [When the Ideal Undermines the Edifying], *NotaBene. Quaderni di studi kierkegaardiani*, vol. 4, *L'edificante in Kierkegaard* [The Edifying in Kierkegaard], 2005, pp. 99–113.

— "La buona intesa con Dio. Bisogno di Dio e perfezione umana in Kierkegaard" [The Good Understanding With God: The Need of God and Human Perfection in Kierkegaard], *Notabene. Quaderni di studi kierkegaardiani*, vol. 5, *Le malattie dell'anima. Kierkegaard e la psicologia* [The Sicknesses of the Soul: Kierkegaard and Psychology], 2007, pp. 111–20.

—"La presenza di Kierkegaard in Heidegger" [The Presence of Kierkegaard in Heidegger], *Notabene. Quaderni di studi kierkegaardiani*, vol. 5, *Le malattie dell'anima. Kierkegaard e la psicologia* [The Sicknesses of the Soul: Kierkegaard and Psychology], 2007, pp. 203–15.

— "L'attualità de *Gli atti dell'amore*" [The Modernity of *Work of Love*], *Notabene. Quaderni di studi kierkegaardiani*, vol. 7, *Kierkegaard e la condizione desiderante. La seduzione dell'estetico* [Kierkegaard and the Desiring Condition: The Seduction of the Aesthetic 2009, pp. 149–53.

— "Per l'attualità filosofica del Cristianesimo. Kierkegaard e Rosmini" [On the Philosophical Modernity of Christianity: Kierkegaard and Rosmini], *Notabene. Quaderni di studi kierkegaardiani*, vol. 8, *Insegnare il Cristianesimo nel Novecento. La ricezione di Kierkegaard e Rosmini* [Teaching Christianity in the Twentieth Century: The Reception of Kierkegaard and Rosmini], 2011, pp. 19–27.

— " 'La prospettiva della fede': vittoria su ogni altra prospettiva" ["The Point of View of Faith": Victory Over Every Other Point of View], *NotaBene. Quaderni di studi Kierkegaardiani*, vol. 9, *Kierkegaard duecento anni dopo* [Kierkegaard Two Hundred Years Later], 2014, pp. 71–82.

Regina, Umberto and Ettore Rocca (eds.), *Kierkegaard contemporaneo: ripresa, pentimento, perdono* [Contemporary Kierkegaard: Repetition, Repentance, Forgiveness], Brescia: Morcelliana 2007. (Umberto Regina, "Ripresa, pentimento, perdono. 'Un mondo d'aiuto per il mondo di oggi'" [Repetition, Repentance, Forgiveness: "A World of Help for the World of Today"], pp. 11–19; Poul Lübcke, "Pentimento, perdono e assenza di generosità nelle opere di Kierkegaard" [Remorse, Forgiveness, and the Absence of Generosity in Kierkegaard's Works], trans. by Ingrid Basso, pp. 21–43; Ettore Rocca, "La percezione del peccato. Per un'estetica teologica" [The Perception of Sin: For a Theological Aesthetic], pp. 45–62; Alessandro Cortese, "Di 'Anger,' 'Pentimento,' con Kierkegaard, all'avvio dell'attività di scrittore e fino ad *Enten-Eller*" ["Repentance", with Kierkegaard, from the Beginning of his Work as an Author to *Either-Or*], pp. 63–76; Roberto Garaventa, "Angoscia, colpa, redenzione. Kierkegaard a confronto con l'antropologia e la psicoanalisi" [Anxiety, Guilt, Atonement: Kierkegaard, Anthropology, and Psychoanalysis], pp. 77–120; François Bousquet, "Il pentimento e il diventare soggetto davanti a Dio" [To Repent and to Become Subject before God], trans. by Enrica Manfredotti and Ettore Rocca, pp. 121–32; Simonella Davini, "Agnese e il Tritone. Una storia di redenzione?" [Agnes and the Merman. A Story of Redemption?], pp. 133–54; Giovanni Ferretti, "Pentimento e perdono in Scheler, Levinas e Ricoeur" [Repentance and Forgiveness in Scheler, Levinas, and Ricoeur], pp. 155–74; Umberto Curi, "Il mancato pentimento di Don Giovanni" [The Absence of Repentance in Don Giovanni], pp. 175–95; Virgilio Melchiorre, "Pentimento e ripresa in Kierkegaard. Dal Qohelet ai gigli del campo" [Repentance and Repetition in Kierkegaard. From Ecclesiastes to the Lilies in the Field], pp. 197–213; Arne Grøn, "La temporalità del pentimento – la temporalità del perdono" [Temporality of Repentance – Temporality of Forgiveness], trans. by Simonella Davini, pp. 215–28; Hugh Pyper, "Perdonare l'imperdonabile. Kierkegaard, Derrida e lo scandalo del perdono" [Forgiving the Unforgivable: Kierkegaard, Derrida and the Scandal of Forgiveness], trans. by Andrea Scaramuccia, pp. 229–46; Leonardo Amoroso, "Buber, Kierkegaard e la prova di Abramo" [Buber, Kierkegaard, and the Trial of Abraham], pp. 247–263; Niels Jørgen Cappelørn, "Sequela, peccato, perdono, sequela" [Imitation, Sin, Forgiveness, Imitation] trans. by Ettore Rocca, pp. 265–77; Giuseppe Modica, "Per un'ermeneutica dell'ironia. I presupposti socratici dell'edificazione kierke-gaardiana" [For an Hermeneutic of Irony: The Socratic Presuppositions of the Kierkegaardian Edification], pp. 279–300.)

Riconda, Giuseppe, "L'eredità di Kierkegaard e la teologia dialettica nel suo significato speculativo" [Kierkegaard's Heritage and Dialectical Theology in its Speculative Meaning], *Filosofia*, no. 25, 1974, pp. 215–32.

Rinaldi, Francesco, "Della presenza schellinghiana nella critica di Kierkegaard a Hegel" [About Schelling's Influence on Kierkegaard's Criticism to Hegel], *Studi Urbinati*, no. 43, 1969, pp. 243–62.

Rizzacasa, Aurelio, *Kierkegaard. Storia ed esistenza* [Kierkegaard: History and Existence], Rome: Studium 1984.

— *Il tema di Lessing: è possibile provare una verità eterna a partire da un fatto storico?* [The Theme of Lessing: Is it Possible to Demonstrate an Eternal Truth from a Historical Fact?], Cinisello Balsamo: San Paolo Edizioni 1996.

— "La semantica dell'*edificante* nel pensiero di Søren Kierkegaard" [The Semantics of the *Edifying* in the Thought of Søren Kierkegaard], *NotaBene. Quaderni di studi kierkegaardiani*, vol. 4, *L'edificante in Kierkegaard* [The Edifying in Kierkegaard], 2005, pp. 137–55.

Rocca, Ettore, "Kierkegaard: comunicazione diretta e indiretta. Un'analisi" [Kierkegaard: Direct and Indirect Communication], in *Senso e storia dell'estetica* [Sense and History of Aesthetics], ed. by Pietro Montanari, Parma: Pratiche 1995, pp. 389–402.

— "Kierkegaard predicatore del venerdì" [Kierkegaard, Friday Preacher], *Micromega. Almanacco di Filosofia*, no. 2, 2000, pp. 97–9.

— "La memoria, il silenzio e lo straniero: Søren Kierkegaard, Primo Levi e i campi di sterminio" [Memory, Silence and the Foreigner: Søren Kierkegaard, Primo Levi and the Death Camps], *NotaBene. Quaderni di Studi Kierkegaardiani*, vol. 1, *Leggere oggi Kierkegaard* [Reading Kierkegaard Today], 2000, pp. 115–25.

— "La seconda estetica di Kierkegaard" [Kierkegaard's Second Aesthetics], *Il Pensiero*, no. 1, 2000, pp. 85–97.

— "Quando il malato è l'uomo occidentale e il medico si chiama Kierkegaard" [When the Patient is the Western Man and the Doctor is Called Kierkegaard], *L'Arco di Giano. Rivista di Medical Humanities*, no. 24, 2000, pp. 153–65.

— "Un Kierkegaard sorprendente" [A Surprising Kierkegaard], *Micromega*, no. 5, 2000, pp. 236–8.

— "Kierkegaard" in *Dal senso comune alla filosofia. Profili* [From Common Sense to Philosophy: Profiles], vols. 1–3, ed. by Guido Boffi, Clotilde Calabi, Elisabetta Cattaneo, et al., Florence: Sansoni 2001, vol. 2, pp. 298–306.

— "L'Antigone di Kierkegaard o della morte del tragico" [Kierkegaard's Antigone or the Death of the Tragic], in *Antigone e la filosofia. Hegel, Kierkegaard, Hölderlin, Heidegger, Bultmann* [Antigone and Philosophy: Hegel, Kierkegaard, Hölderlin, Heidegger, Bultmann], ed. by Pietro Montani, Rome: Donzelli 2001, pp. 73–84.

— "La parola della fede o se Abramo è un uomo" [The Word of Faith or if Abraham is a Man], in *Strutture dell'esperienza. III. Mente, linguaggio, espressione* [The Structure of the Experience. III. Death, Language, Expression], Milan: Mimesis 2001 (*Annuario di Itinerari Filosofici*, vol. 5), pp. 141–9.

— *Tra estetica e teologia. Studi kierkegaardiani* [Between Aesthetics and Theology: Kierkegaard Studies], Pisa: ETS 2004. (Review: Basso, Ingrid, review in *Rivista di Filosofia Neo-Scolastica*, vol. 97, no. 3, 2005, pp. 537–42.)

— "Kierkegaard, Don Giovanni e la non verità" [Kierkegaard, Don Giovanni and Untruth], in *Ravenna Festival 2006. Mozart? Mozart!*, no editor given, Ravenna: Fondazione Ravenna Manifestazioni 2006, pp. 57–61.

— "Il Socrate cristiano" [The Christian Socrates], *MicroMega*, no. 1, 2006, pp. 139–42.

— *Kierkegaard*, Rome: Carocci 2012.

— "Poesia apocalittica e morte dell'arte. Heiberg, Martensen e Kierkegaard" [Apocalytic Poetry and the Death of Art: Heiberg, Martensen and Kierkegaard], _Rivista di filosofia neoscolastica_, nos. 3–4, 2013, pp. 963–977.
— "Il pittore e il filosofo. Søren Kierkegaard letto da Johan Thomas Lundbye" [The Painter and the Philosopher. Soren Kierkegaard Read by Johan Thomas Lundbye], _NotaBene. Quaderni di studi Kierkegaardiani_, vol. 9, _Kierkegaard duecento anni dopo_ [Kierkegaard Two Hundred Years Later], 2014, pp. 223–46.
— (ed.), _Søren Kierkegaard: l'essere umano come rapporto. Omaggio a Umberto Regina_, Brescia: Morcelliana 2008. (Umberto Regina, "Stato, chiesa e uguaglianza di tutti gli uomini" [State, Church and Equality of All Men], pp. 3–14; Niels Jørgen Cappelørn, "Confessione – comunione / peccato – grazia" [Confession – Communion/Sin – Grace], trans. by Ettore Rocca, pp. 15–27; Virgilio Melchiorre, "Kierkegaard: l'arte come seconda immediatezza" [Kierkegaard: Art as a Second Immediacy], pp. 29–42; Joakim Garff, "L'essere umano è un rapporto a se stesso – e a un racconto. Su narratività e formazione nell'opera letteraria di Kierkegaard" [The Human Being is a Relationship to Itself – and to a Tale: On Narrativity and Education on Kierkegaard's Literary Works], trans. by Andrea Scaramuccia, pp. 43–59; Vincenzo Vitiello, "La mediazione immediata e l'_exaíphnes_" [The Immediate Mediation and the _exaíphnes_], pp. 61–72; Poul Lübcke, "'Aver posto se stesso o essere stato posto da un altro'" ["Being Established by Itself ot Having Been Established by Another"], trans. by Ettore Rocca, pp. 73–88; Piero Coda, "Antropologia della relazione e Trinità" [Anthropology of the Relation and Trinity], pp. 89–101; Arne Grøn, "Comprensione di sé e dialettica della comunicazione" [Understanding of Itself and the Dialectics of Communication], trans. by Andrea Scaramuccia, pp. 103–118; Simonella Davini, "Da demone a potenza demoniaca: l'eros in Platone e in Kierkegaard" [From Demon to Demonic Power: Eros in Plato and in Kierkegaard], pp. 119–32; Pia Søltoft, "L'amore copre molti peccati" [Love Covers a Moltitude of Sins], trans. by Ingrid Basso, pp. 133–48; Dario González, "Umorismo e singolarità" [Humor and Singularity], pp. 149–58; Ingrid Basso, "Libertà come relazione e relazione come libertà nell'antropologia kierkegaardiana" [Freedom and Relation and Relation as Freedom in the Kierkegaardian Anthropology], pp. 159–71; René Rosfort, "L'antropologia fra teoria e prassi: una domanda kantiana a Kierkegaard" [Anthropology Between Theory and Praxis: A Kantian Question to Kierkegaard], trans. by Ingrid Basso, pp. 173–86; Ettore Rocca, "Il bisogno di Dio" [The Need of God], pp. 187–96).
Rollier, Mario Alberto, "_L'Ora_ di Søren Kierkegaard" [Søren Kierkegaard's _The Moment_], _Gioventù cristiana_, no. 10, 1931, pp. 73–5.
Romano, Bruno, _Il senso esistenziale del diritto nella prospettiva di Kierkegaard_ [The Existential Meaning of Law in Kierkegaard's Perspective], Milan: Giuffrè 1973.
Rosati, Massimo, "Poter-essere-se-stessi e essere soggetti morali. J. Habermas tra Kierkegaard e Kant" [Being-Able-to-be-Oneself and Being a Moral Subject: J. Habermas between Kierkegaard and Kant], _Rassegna Italiana di Sociologia_, vol. 44, no. 4, 2003, pp. 493–513.
Rossini, Manuel, "Introduzione a Karl Löwith, _Kierkegaard e Nietzsche (1933)_" [Introduction to Karl Löwith, _Kierkegaard and Nietzsche (1933)_], _NotaBene._

Quaderni di studi kierkegaardiani, vol. 4, *L'edificante in Kierkegaard* [The Edifying in Kierkegaard], 2005, pp. 259–63.

Rosso, Luciano, "Il pungolo della carne in Kierkegaard" [The Thorn in the Flesh in Kierkegaard], *Idea*, nos. 6–7, 1974, pp. 41–4.

Sacchi, Dario, *Le ragioni di Abramo: Kierkegaard e la paradossalità del logos* [Abraham's Reasons: Kierkegaard and the Paradox of Logos], Milan: Angeli 2011.

Salami, S., "Amore nella verità. Gli *Atti dell'Amore* di Kierkegaard" [Love within the Truth: Kierkegaard's *Works of Love*], *Pedagogia e Vita*, no. 5, 1984, pp. 523–40.

Salmona, Bruno, "La socialità nel *Diario* di Kierkegaard" [Sociality in Kierkegaard's *Diary*], *Sapienza*, no. 11, 1958, pp. 409–23.

Sanmarchi, Alessandro, "Lo stile come cifra della libertà intellettuale. Il filosofare secondo Cornelio Fabro" [Style as a Figure of Intellectual Freedom: Philosophizing according to Cornelio Fabro], *Rivista di filosofia neo-scolastica*, vol. 93, 2001, pp. 95–128.

Santucci, Antonio, *Esistenzialismo e filosofia italiana* [Existentialism and Italian Philosophy], Bologna: Il Mulino 1959.

Saraceno, Luca, *La vertigine della libertà: l'angoscia in Sören Kierkegaard* [Freedom's Vertigo: Anxiety in Søren Kierkegaard], Catania: Studio teologico S. Paolo 2007.

Scapolo, Barbara, *Leggere* Timore e Tremore *di Kierkegaard* [Reading Kierkegaard's *Fear and Trembling*], Como and Pavia: Ibis 2013.

Scaramuccia, Andrea, *L'ironista nella botte: Søren Kierkegaard e la ricezione di Enten-Eller* [The Ironist in the Barrel: Kierkegaard and the Reception of *Either/Or*], Pisa: ETS 2006.

Sciacca, Giuseppe Maria, *L'esperienza religiosa e l'io in Hegel e Kierkegaard* [The Religious Experience and the Self in Hegel and Kierkegaard], Palermo: Palumbo 1948.

— *La filosofia dell'esistenza e Søren Kierkegaard* [The Philosophy of Existence and Søren Kierkegaard], Palermo: Lilia 1949.

— "Significato dell'irrazionalismo di Kierkegaard" [The Meaning of Kierkegaard's Irrationalism], in *Atti del XV Congresso Nazionale di filosofia, Messina 24–29 settembre 1948* [Proceedings of the XVth National Congress of Philosophy, Messina, September 24–29, 1948], no editor given, Messina-Florence: D'anna 1949, pp. 643–52.

Sciacca, Michele Federico, "L'esperienza etico-religiosa di Søren Kierkegaard" [The Ethical-Religious Experience of Søren Kierkegaard], *Logos*, no. 20, 1937, pp. 121–8.

— "Søren Kierkegaard il poeta della solitudine eroica" [Søren Kierkegaard, the Poet of Heroic Solitude] in his *La filosofia oggi* [Philosophy Today], vols. 1–2, Milan and Rome: Bocca 1945, vol. 1, pp. 104–28.

— "Kierkegaard il filosofo del *salto*" [Kierkegaard, the Philosopher of the *Leap*], *Rivista dei Giovani*, no. 5, 1947, pp. 25–8.

— *L'estetismo, Kierkegaard, Pirandello* [Estheticism, Kierkegaard, Pirandello], Milan: Marzorati 1974.

Sciamannini, Raniero, "La morale esistenzialistica" [Existentialist Ethics], *Città di Vita*, no. 5, part 1, 1950, pp. 75–83.

88 *Laura Liva*

Sefanini, Luigi, "L'estetica dell'esistenzialismo" [The Esthetics of Existentialism], *Città di Vita*, no. 5, part 1, 1950, pp. 4–56.

Serra, Antonio, "Istanze pedagogiche nel pensiero di Søren Kierkegaard" [Pedagogical Issues in Søren Kierkegaard's Thought], *Rivista Rosminiana*, no. 71, 1977, pp. 133–49.

— "Eros ed estetismo nell'opera conviviale di Kierkegaard" [Eros and Aestheticism in Kierkegaard's Convivial Writing], *Giornale di Metafisica*, no. 3, 1981, pp. 327–46.

Sessa, Piero, "La persona di Cristo nel pensiero di Søren Kierkegaard" [The Person of Christ in Søren Kierkegaard's Thought], *La Scuola Cattolica*, no. 93, 1965, pp. 223–38.

Sesta, Luciano, "Fede e paradosso in Kierkegaard" [Faith and Paradox in Kierkegaard], *Giornale di Metafisica*, vol. 22, nos. 1–2, 2000, pp. 327–35

Sfriso, Maurizio, "Cristianesimo e Cristianità in S. Kierkegaard" [Christianity and Christendom in S. Kierkegaard], *Città di Vita*, vol. 52, no. 3, 1997, pp. 297–309.

— "La filosofia dell'esistenza di Kierkegaard e la crisi della soggettività" [The Philosophy of Existence of Kierkegaard and the Crisis of Subjectivity], *Rivista Rosminiana di Filosofia e di Cultura*, vol. 92, nos. 3–4, 1998, pp. 275–92.

— "Rosmini e Kierkegaard" [Rosmini and Kierkegaard], *Rivista Rosminiana di Filosofia e di Cultura*, vol. 94, nos. 3–4, 2000, pp. 239–62.

— "Hegel e Kierkegaard. Per quale realtà?" [Hegel and Kierkegaard: To Which Acuality?], *Filosofia Oggi*, vol. 26, no. 1, 2003, pp. 42–68.

— "Il christianesimo e Cristo in Hegel e Kierkegaard" [Christianity and Christ in Hegel and Kierkegaard], *Città di Vita. Bimestrale di Religione, Arte e Scienza*, vol. 59, 2004, pp. 231–48.

— "Scienza e progresso nel pensiero di Søren Kierkegaard" [Science and Progress in the Thought of Søren Kierkegaard], *Città di Vita. Bimestrale di Religione, Arte e Scienza*, vol. 60, 2005, pp. 201–12.

— "Cristianesimo e cristianità in Hegel, Kierkegaard e Nietzsche" [Christianity and Christendom in Hegel, Kierkegaard and Nietzsche], *Città di Vita. Bimestrale di Religione, Arte e Scienza*, vol. 62, 2007, pp. 13–28.

Sgalambro, Manlio, "Estetica e materialismo in Kierkegaard" [Aesthetics and Materialism in Kierkegaard], *Tempo Presente*, no. 9, 1964, pp. 69–72.

Sibilio, F. Romeno, "Il rapporto al padre: Kierkegaard" [The Relation to the Father: Kierkegaard], *Ricerche Metodologiche*, no. 1, 1969, pp. 14–24.

Siclari, Alberto, *L'Ascetica dell'uomo comune: Cristianesimo e cultura nel "Diario" di Søren Kierkegaard* [The Asceticism of the Common Man: Christianity and Culture in Søren Kierkegaard's *Diary*], Milan: ISU Università Cattolica 1989.

— "La comunicazione di Søren Kierkegaard e le sue modalità" [Søren Kierkegaard's Communication and its Modalities], *Philo-Logica*, vol. 4, no. 8, 1995, pp. 63–96.

— "Kierkegaard e i doveri della singolarità" [Kierkegaard and the Duties of Singularity], *La Società degli Individui*, no. 3, 1998, pp. 33–51.

— "Per una teologia della crisi: tempo ed eternità in Kierkegaard" [For a Theology of the Crisis: Time and Eternity in Kierkegaard], *Annali di Scienze Religiose*, no. 6, 2001, pp. 15–56.

— "Le opere e la misericordia negli *Atti dell'amore* di Kierkegaard" [Works and Mercy in Kierkegaard's *Works of Love*], *La Società degli Individui*, vol. 6, no. 18, 2003, pp. 103–18.

— "Kierkegaard e la communicazione indiretta" [Kierkegaard and Indirect Communication], *La Società degli Individui*, vol. 21, 2004, pp. 81–93.

— *L'itinerario di un cristiano nella cristianità: la testimonianza di Kierkegaard* [A Christian's Path in Christianity: Kierkegaard's Testimony], Milan: Franco Angeli 2004.

Silvestri, Filippo, "Ontologia del divenire e necessità di una scelta trascendentale. Kierkegaard e Hegel" [The Ontology of Becoming and the Necessity of a Transcendental Choice: Kierkegaard and Hegel], *Atti dell'Accademia di Scienze Morali e Politiche di Napoli*, vol. 108, no. 1, 1997, pp. 311–25.

Sini, Anna Maria, "Søren Kierkegaard," in *Grande Dizionario Enciclopedico*, Turin: UTET 1986, vol. 6.

— "L'itinerario fondamentale della libertà in Søren Kierkegaard" [The Essential Itinerary of Freedom in Søren Kierkegaard], in *Nuovi Studi Kierkegaardiani* [New Kierkegaard Studies], ed. by Giuseppe Mario Pizzuti, Potenza: Centro Italiano di Studi Kierkegaardiani 1988, pp. 53–79.

Slataper Camusso, Giulia, "Romanticismo come letterarietà: approssimazione all'estetismo kierkegaardiano" [Romanticism as Literariness: Approximation to Kierkegaard's Aestheticism], in *Atti del Congresso Internazionale di filosofia 1946* [Proceedings of the International Congress of Philosophy 1946], vols. 1–2, ed. by Enrico Castelli, Milan and Rome: Castellani 1947, vol. 2 (*L'esistenzialismo* [Existentialism]) pp. 453–5.

Sogni, Cesare, *Pensare la morte nel discorso "Vicino a una tomba" di S. Kierkegaard* [Thinking Death in Kierkegaard's Discourse "At a Graveside"], Gallarate: published by the author 2000.

Sørensen, Ivan, "'Saremmo perduti – se non ci fosse stata la scienza'. Kierkegaard e Savonarola" ["We would be lost, if it were not for science." Kierkegaard and Savonarola], *L'Ambra. Rivista di cultura scandinava*, vol. 4, no. 1, 1998, pp. 19–28.

— "Il libro d'esordio di Søren Kierkegaard 'Dalle carte di uno ancora in vita' e la tradizione italiana" [The Debut Book of Søren Kierkegaard, *From the Papers of One Still Living*, and the Italian tradition], *Studi Nordici*, vol. 6, 1999, pp. 21–30.

Sorrentino, Sergio, "Verità e salvezza. Kierkegaard e Nietzsche di fronte al Cristianesimo" [Truth and Salvation: Kierkegaard and Nietzsche in the Face of Christianity], in *Veritatem in caritate. Studi in onore di Cornelio Fabro* [*Veritatem in caritate*. Studies in Honor of Cornelio Fabro], ed. by Giuseppe Mario Pizzuti, Potenza: Ermes 1991, pp. 259–72.

Soster, Maria, "Kierkegaard in Francia nella crisi di inizio anni '30 del XX secolo. Due testimonianze e una nota di contestualizzazione" [Kierkegaard in France in the Crisis at the Beginning of the Thirties of the Twentieth Century: Two Testimonies and a Note of Contextualization], *NotaBene. Quaderni di studi kierkegaardiani*, vol. 4, *L'edificante in Kierkegaard* [The Edifying in Kierkegaard], 2005, pp. 283–8.

Spera, Salvatore, "Il mito di Faust. Aspirazioni letterarie, riflessioni filosofiche, preoccupazioni religiose del giovane Kierkegaard" [The Myth of Faust: Literary Ambitions, Philosophical Reflections], *Archivio di Filosofia*, 1974, pp. 309–340; republished in his *Il giovane Kierkegaard. Indagini critiche sulla filosofia della religione e studi sugli aspetti inediti del pensiero kierkegaardiano* [The Young Kierkegaard: Critical Investigations on the Philosophy of Religion and Studies on Unknown Aspects of Kierkegaard's Thought], Padua: CEDAM 1977.

— "Il divenire cristiano come imitazione del Cristo sofferente in Søren Kierkegaard" [Christian Becoming as Imitation of the Suffering Christ in Søren Kierkegaard], *Bollettino Stauros*, no. 2, 1976.

— "L'influsso di Schelling sulla formazione del giovane Kierkegaard" [Schelling's Influence on the Young Kierkegaard's Education], *Archivio di Filosofia*, no. 1, 1976, pp. 73–108.

— *Il pensiero del giovane Kierkegaard. Indagini critiche sulla filosofia della religione e studi sugli aspetti inediti del pensiero kierkegaardiano* [The Young Kierkegaard: Critical Investigations on the Philosophy of Religion and Studies on Unknown Aspects of Kierkegaard's Thought], Padua: CEDAM 1977.

— "Aspetti del demoniaco in una prospettiva di filosofia della religione" [Some Aspects of the Demonic from the Perspective of Philosophy of Religion], *Aquinas*, no. 21, 1978, pp. 382–99.

— *Kierkegaard politico* [The Political Kierkegaard], Rome: Istituto di studi filosofici 1978.

— "Kierkegaard e la crisi europea del 1848" [Kierkegaard and the European Crisis of 1848], *Archivio di Filosofia*, nos. 2–3, 1978, pp. 385–407.

— *Introduzione a Kierkegaard* [Introduction to Kierkegaard], Rome-Bari: Laterza 1983 (2nd ed. 1986; 3rd ed. 1992; 4th ed. 1994; 5th ed. 1996; 6th ed. 1998; 7th ed. 2000; 8th ed. 2002; 9th ed. 2005).

— "Kierkegaard e Schleiermacher" [Kierkegaard and Schleiermacher], *Archivio di Filosofia*, nos. 1–3, 1984, pp. 435–63.

— "Le carte schleiermacheriane di Kierkegaard" [Kierkegaard's Papers on Schleiermacher], *Aquinas*, no. 27, 1984, pp. 287–316.

Stanco, F.M.T., *Il tema dell'angoscia in Kierkegaard* [The Theme of Anxiety in Kierkegaard], Naples: Ferraro 1977.

Stefani, Piero, "Risonanze filosofiche del Qohelet" [Philosophical Resonances of Qohelet], *Humanitas*, vol. 50, no. 3, 1995, pp. 393–409.

Stefanini, Luigi, "L'estetica di Kierkegaard" [Kierkegaard's Aesthetics], in his *Esistenzialismo ateo ed esistenzialismo teistico* [Atheistic and Theistic Existentialism], Padua: CEDAM 1952, pp. 354–61; republished as "L'esteticità come antitesi di eternità e realtà in Søren Kierkegaard" [The Aestheticism as Antithesis of Eternity and Actuality in Søren Kierkegaard], in his *Arte e critica* [Art and Criticism], Milan: Principato 1953, pp. 75–84.

Stella, Fernando, "Kierkegaard: un uomo in presenza di Dio" [Kierkegaard: A Man in the Presence of God], *Raccolta di Studi e Ricerche*, no. 2, 1978, pp. 331–41.

Suozzo, Pietro, *Aure kierkegaardiane in Bergman* [Kierkegaardian Auras in Bergman], Recco: Le Mani Università 2011.

Svartholm, Nils, "Søren Kierkegaard e la fisica moderna" [Søren Kierkegaard and Modern Physics], *L'Umana Avventura*, no. 12, 1989, pp. 61–3.

Tavilla, Igor, *Senso tipico e profezia in Søren Kierkegaard: verso una definizione del fondamento biblico della categoria di Gjentagelse* [Typical Sense and Prophecy in Søren Kierkegaard: Towards a Definition of the Foundations of the Category of *Gjentagelse*], Milan: Mimesis 2012.

Terzi, Carlo, *Il Kierkegaard di Régis Jolivet* [Régis Jolivet's Kierkegaard], Turin: Edizioni di Filosofia 1967.

Tilliette, Xavier, "Chiose alla *Postilla* di Climacus-Kierkegaard" [Notes on Climacus-Kierkegaard's *Postscript*], *NotaBene. Quaderni di studi kierkegaardiani*, vol. 4, *L'edificante in Kierkegaard* [The Edifying in Kierkegaard], 2005, pp. 187–96.

Tomassone, Letizia, "La critica di Kierkegaard alle filosofie della storia" [Kierkegaard's Criticism of the Philosophies of History], *Protestantesimo*, vol. 41, no. 3, 1986, pp. 129–41.

Tonon, Margherita, "Wahl interprete di Kierkegaard" [Wahl's Interpretation of Kierkegaard], *NotaBene. Quaderni di studi kierkegaardiani*, vol. 4, *L'edificante in Kierkegaard* [The Edifying in Kierkegaard], 2005, pp. 179–84.

— "Il recupero dell'estetica kierkegaardiana nell'interpretazione di T.W. Adorno" [The Recuperation of the Kierkegaardian Aesthetics in the Interpretation of T.W. Adorno's], *Notabene. Quaderni di studi kierkegaardiani*, vol. 7, *Kierkegaard e la condizione desiderante. La seduzione dell'estetico* [Kierkegaard and the Desiring Condition: The Seduction of the Aesthetic], 2009, pp. 13–27.

Tortora, Giuseppe, "Kierkegaard and Schopenhauer on Hegelianism," *Metalogicon*, no. 1, 1994, pp. 69–84.

Trenti, Zelindo, "Il rinnovamento del linguaggio religioso e le sue matrici esistenziali" [The Renewal of the Religious Language and Its Existential Matrices], *Orientamenti Pedagogici*, vol. 34, no. 203, 1987, pp. 895–909.

Tricomi, Flavia, "Søren Kierkegaard e la morale kantiana" [Søren Kierkegaard and Kantian Ethics], in *A partire da Kant. L'eredità della "Critica della ragion pratica"* [Beginning from Kant: The Heritage of the *Critique of Practical Reason*], ed. by Adriano Fabris and Luca Baccelli, Milan: Franco Angeli 1989, pp. 199–201.

Tunisini Bertozzi, Rita, *La spina nella carne. Søren Kierkegaard: dramma in due atti* [The Thorn in the Flesh. Søren Kierkegaard: A Drama in Two Acts], Forlì: Forum 1975.

Ubaldo, Nicola, *Antologia illustrata di filosofia. Dalle origini all'era moderna* [Illustrated Anthology of Philosophy: From its Origins to the Modern Era], Florence: Giunti 2000, pp. 381–9.

Vaccaro, Gian Battista, "Il Kierkegaard di Adorno e la critica dell'ontologia esistenziale" [Adorno's Kierkegaard and the Criticism of Existential Theology], *Annali della Facoltà di Lettere e Filosofia, Università di Siena*, 1989, pp. 67–89.

Valenziano, Crispino, "Limiti della cristologia kierkegaardiana" [The Limits of Kierkegaard's Christology], *Giornale di Metafisica*, no. 20, 1965, pp. 20–9.

Valori, Paolo, "Husserl e Kierkegaard" [Husserl and Kierkegaard], *Archivio di Filosofia (Kierkegaard e Nietzsche)*, 1953, pp. 191–200.

Vecchi, Giovanni, "Il problema dell'arte nell'esistenzialismo di Kierkegaard" [The Problem of Art in Kierkegaard's Existentialism], *Rivista di Filosofia Neo-Scolastica*, no. 38, 1946, pp. 61–9.

Vela, Raffaele, "Kierkegaard e la verità esistenziale" [Kierkegaard and the Existential Truth], *Vita Sociale*, no. 23, 1966, pp. 231–9.

Velocci, Giovanni, *Filosofia e fede in Kierkegaard* [Philosophy and Faith in Kierkegaard], Rome: Città nuova 1976.

— "Filosofia e fede in Kierkegaard" [Philosophy and Faith in Kierkegaard], *Divinitas*, vol. 22, 1978, pp. 250–54.

— *La donna in Kierkegaard* [The Woman in Kierkegaard], L'Aquila: Japadre 1980.

Vettori Vittorio, "Giovanni Gentile tra Kierkegaard e Marx" [Giovanni Gentile between Kierkegaard and Marx], *Città di Vita*, no. 9, 1954, pp. 685–91.

Vircillo, Domenico, "Ambiguità e fede in Kierkegaard, Nietzsche e Kafka" [Ambiguity and Faith in Kierkegaard, Nietzsche and Kafka], *Sapienza*, no. 26, 1973, pp. 27–69.

Vozza, Marco, *A debita distanza: Kierkegaard, Kafka, Kleist e le loro fidanzate* [At a Safe Distance: Kierkegaard, Kafka, Kleist, and Their Fiancées], Reggio Emilia: Diabasis 2007.

Zanovello, Nevio, "La soggettività della verità in Kierkegaard" [The Subjectivity of the Truth in Kierkegaard], *Rivista Rosminiana di Filosofia e di Cultura*, no. 73, 1979, pp. 47–56.

Zarone, Giuseppe, "*Itinerarium in fidem*. Pascal-Agostino-Kierkegaard," *Filosofia e Teologia*, 1997, pp. 527–44.

Zecchi, Stefano, "Il paradosso della rinascita. Tra Kierkegaard e Husserl" [The Paradox of the Rebirth: Between Kierkegaard and Husserl], *Aut-Aut*, nos. 214–215, 1986, pp. 97–110.

Zejmo, Marek, *La categoria della possibilità nelle opere pseudonime di S. Kierkegaard* [The Category of Possibility in S. Kierkegaard's Pseudonymous Works], Rome: Pontificia Università Lateranense 1986.

Zizi, Paolo, *Ontologia della libertà. (Tra Kierkegaard-Heidegger-Fabro)* [The Ontology of Freedom. (Between Kierkegaard, Heidegger and Fabro)], Sassari: Edizioni Unidata 1987.

III. Translated Secondary Literature on Kierkegaard in Italian

Adorno, Theodor W., *Kierkegaard. La costruzione dell'estetico* [Kierkegaard: Konstruktion des Ästhetischen], trans. by A. Bürger Cori, Milan: Longanesi 1983 (2nd ed., Parma: Guanda 1993).

Corbin, Henry, "Omaggio a Kierkegaard" [Témoignage à Kierkegaard], trans. by Maria Soster, *NotaBene. Quaderni di studi kierkegaardiani*, vol. 4, *L'edificante in Kierkegaard*, 2005, pp. 289–91.

Cruysberghs, Paul, "Kierkegaard e Mozart, una storia di sensualità, desiderio e seduzione" [Kierkegaard and Mozart, a Story of Sensuousness, Desire and Seduction], trans. by Margherita Tonon, *Notabene. Quaderni di studi kierkegaardiani*, vol. 7, *Kierkegaard e la condizione desiderante. La seduzione dell'estetico* [Kierkegaard and the Desiring Condition: The Seduction of the Aesthetic], 2009, pp. 39–58.

Damgaard, Claus, "Con tutta l'interiorità della personalità. Una chiacchierata sull'esercizio della produzione letteraria di Søren Kierkegaard" [With All the Interiority of Personality: A Chat on the Exercise of Søren Kierkegaard's Literary Production], *Notabene. Quaderni di studi kierkegaardiani*, vol. 6, *La profondità della scena. Il teatro visitato da Kierkegaard, Kierkegaard visitato dal teatro* [The Depth of the Scene: The Theater Seen by Kierkegaard, Kierkegaard Seen by the Theater], 2008, pp. 17–38.

Depelsenaire, Yves, *Un'analisi con Dio. L'appuntamento di Lacan con Kierkegaard* [Une analise avec Dieu. Le rendez-vous de Lacan et de Kierkegaard], trans. by M.R. Conrado, Macerata: Quodlibet 2009.

Derrida, Jacques, "A chi dare (saper di non sapere)" [A qui donner (savoir ne pas savoir)], in his *Donare la morte* [Donner la mort], trans. by Luca Berta, Milan: Jaca Book 2002, pp. 89–113.

Dietz, Walter, "Disperazione *en masse*. Il singolo kierkegaardiano e la critica della massa" [Verzweiflung en masse. Kierkegaards Einzelner und die Kritik der Masse], trans. by Roberto Garaventa, *Notabene. Quaderni di studi kierkegaardiani*, vol. 8, *Insegnare il Cristianesimo nel Novecento. La ricezione di Kierkegaard e Rosmini* [Teaching Christianity in the Twentieth Century: The Reception of Kierkegaard and Rosmini], 2011, pp. 167–89.

Elbrønd-Bek, Bo, "Don Giovanni. L'ombra di Søren Kierkegaard" [Don Giovanni: The Shadow of Søren Kierkegaard], trans. by Ingrid Basso, *Notabene. Quaderni di studi kierkegaardiani*, vol. 6, *La profondità della scena. Il teatro visitato da Kierkegaard, Kierkegaard visitato dal teatro* [The Depth of the Scene: The Theater Seen by Kierkegaard, Kierkegaard Seen by the Theater], 2008, pp. 77–105.

Garff, Joakim, "'Lo sbuffo dello spirito' o *ab posse ad esse*. Kierkegaard: teatro, formazione e decostruzione" ["The Puff of the Spirit" or ab posse ad esse. Kierkegaard: Theater, Education and Deconstruction], trans. by Ingrid Basso, *Notabene. Quaderni di studi kierkegaardiani*, vol. 6, *La profondità della scena. Il teatro visitato da Kierkegaard, Kierkegaard visitato dal teatro* [The Depth of the Scene: The Theater Seen by Kierkegaard, Kierkegaard Seen by the Theater], 2008, pp. 107–29.

— "La seduzione del seduttore" [The Seducer's Seduction], trans. by Laura Liva, *Notabene. Quaderni di studi kierkegaardiani*, vol. 7, *Kierkegaard e la condizione desiderante. La seduzione dell'estetico* [Kierkegaard and the Desiring Condition: The Seduction of the Aesthetic], 2009, pp. 59–76.

— *SAK. Søren Aabye Kierkegaard. Una biografia* [SAK. Søren Aabye Kierkegaard. A Biography], trans. by Simonella Davini and Andrea Scaramuccia, Rome: Castelvecchi 2013.

Grimault, Marguerite, *Kierkegaard*, trans. by C. Smet, Turin: S.E.I. 1974.

Haecker, Theodor, *La nozione della verità in Søren Kierkegaard* [Der Begriff der Wahrheit bei Søren Kierkegaard], trans. by L. Meini, Milan: Rosa e Ballo 1954.

Hauberg Mortensen, Finn, "'Visione di vita'. Su Søren Kierkegaard e Hans Christian Andersen" ["Vision of life." Søren Kierkegaard and Hans Christian Andersen], *Studi Nordici*, vol. 6, 1999, pp. 31–53.

— "Kierkegaard e Holberg – con costante riguardo alle *Briciole filosofiche*" [Kierkegaard and Holberg – With Constant Reference to *Philosophical*

Fragments], trans. by Ingrid Basso, *Notabene. Quaderni di studi kierkegaardiani*, vol. 6, *La profondità della scena. Il teatro visitato da Kierkegaard, Kierkegaard visitato dal teatro* [The Depth of the Scene: The Theater Seen by Kierkegaard, Kierkegaard Seen by the Theater], 2008, pp. 69–76.

Høffding, Harald, "Un discendente di Amleto" [A Descendant of Hamlet], *Leonardo. Rivista di Idee*, vol. 4, 1906, pp. 65–79.

— *Compendio di storia della filosofia moderna* [A Brief History of Modern Philosophy], ed. by L. Limentani, Turin: Bocca 1915, pp. 219–22 (2nd ed. 1923; 3rd ed. Milan 1946).

Jaspers, Karl, "Chi è Kierkegaard?" [Who is Kierkegaard?], trans. by Maurizio Malaguti, *Ethica*, vol. 8, 1969, pp. 81–90

Jézéquel, Roger, "Commento al *Traité du désespoir* di Kierkegaard" [Commentaire en marge du *Traité du désespoir* de Kierkegaard], trans. by M. Soster, *NotaBene. Quaderni di studi kierkegaardiani*, vol. 4, *L'edificante in Kierkegaard* [The Edifying in Kierkegaard], 2005, pp. 293–304.

Jolivet, Régis, *Kierkegaard: alle fonti dell'esistenzialismo cristiano* [Aux sources de l'existentialisme chrétien: Kierkegaard], trans. by Ines Andreini Rossi, Rome: Paoline 1960.

Koch, Carl, "Søren Kierkegaard," trans. by R. Lund, *Il Rinascimento 2*, vol. 3, 1908, no. 1, pp. 27–42.

Levinas, Emmanuel, "Esistenza ed etica" [Existence et éthique], in his *Nomi propri* [Noms propres], trans. by F.P. Ciglia, Casale Monferrato: Marietti 1984, pp. 81–9.

— "A proposito di '*Kierkegaard vivant*,'" [A propos de "Kierkegaard vivant"], in his *Nomi propri* [Noms propes], trans. by F.P. Ciglia, Casale Monferrato: Marietti 1984, pp. 90–3.

— *Kierkegaard*, trans. by C. Armeni, Rome: Castelvecchi 2013.

Lowrie, Walter, "Søren Kierkegaard," *Religio 11*, no. 1, January, 1935, pp. 1–15.

— [under pseudonym of Peder Pedersen], "Un panegirico (sullo Kierkegaard)" [A Panegyric (on Kierkegaard)], *Religio 14*, no. 2, 1938, pp. 81–5.

Löwith, Karl, "La conclusione della filosofia classica con Hegel e la sua dissoluzione in Marx e Kierkegaard" [L'achèvement de la philosophie classique par Hegel et sa dissolution chez Marx et Kierkegaard], *Giornale critico della filosofia italiana*, nos. 4–5, 1935, pp. 343–71.

— *Da Hegel a Nietzsche* [Von Hegel zu Nietzsche], trans. by G. Colli, Turin: Einaudi 1949 (2nd ed. 1959).

— "Kierkegaard e Nietzsche" [Kierkegaard und Nietzsche], trans. by M. Rossini, *NotaBene. Quaderni di studi kierkegaardiani*, vol. 4, *L'edificante in Kierkegaard* [The Edifying in Kierkegaard], 2005, pp. 265–81.

Lukács, György, "Quando la forma si frange sugli scogli dell'esistenza: Søren Kierkegaard e Regine Olsen" [Das Zerschellen der Form am Leben: Sören Kierkegaard und Regine Olsen], in his *L'anima e le forme* [Die Seele und die Formen], trans. by S. Bologna, Milan: SE 2002, pp. 53–72.

Lübcke, Poul, "Il demoniaco" [The Demonic], trans. by Roberto Garaventa, *Notabene. Quaderni di studi kierkegaardiani*, vol. 5, *Le malattie dell'anima. Kierkegaard e la psicologia* [The Sicknesses of the Soul: Kierkegaard and Psychology], 2007, pp. 49–64.

Malantschuk, Gregor, "Il concette di 'sacro' in Sören Kierkegaard" [The Concept of the "Sacred" in Søren Kierkegaard], *Archivio di Filosofia*, vol. 1, 1975, pp. 225–34.

Nyman, Alf, "La vita di Soeren Kierkegaard alla luce della moderna ricerca" [The Life of Søren Kierkegaard in the Light of Modern Research], in *Scritti di sociologia e politica in onore di Luigi Sturzo*, Bologna: Zanichelli 1953, vol. 2, pp. 581–600.

O'Hara, Shelley, *Kierkegaard alla portata di tutti: un primo passo per comprendere Kierkegaard* [Kierkegaard Within Your Grasp: The First Step to Understanding Kierkegaard], trans. by Giovanni Stelli, Rome: Armando 2007.

Otani, Masaru, "Un possibile contatto ideale tra il buddhismo shin e la nozione kierkegaardiana di Dio" [On the Possibility of Ideal Contact between the Japanese Shin-Buddhism and Kierkegaard's Concept of God], *Liber Academiæ Kierkegaardiensis Annuarius*, vols. 2–4, *1979–81*, 1982, pp. 94–104.

Ricoeur, Paul, *Kierkegaard: la filosofia e l'eccezione* [Kierkegaard et le mal], Brescia: Morcelliana 1995 (2nd ed. 1996).

Rohde, Peter P., *Søren Kierkegaard*, trans. by Johanne Mengel and Teresa Nardi, Copenhagen: Ufficio Stampa ed Informazioni del Ministero Reale degli Affari Esteri 1963.

Schillinger-Kind, Asa A., *Enten-Eller (Aut-Aut) di Søren Kierkegaard. Guida e commento* [Kierkegaard für Anfänger: Entweder-Oder], trans. by Tomaso Cavallo, Milan: Garzanti 1999.

Shestov, Leo, *Kierkegaard e la filosofia esistenziale* [Kierkegaard et la philosophie existentielle], trans. by Enrico Macchetti, ed. by Glauco Tiengo and Enrico Macchetti, Milan: Bompiani 2009.

Thulstrup, Niels, "Presenza e funzione dei concetti kierkegaardiani nella teologia contemporanea scandinava e germanica" [The Presence and Function of Kierkegaardian Concepts in Contemporary Scandinavian and German Theology], *Liber Academiae Kierkegaardiensis*, vol. 1, 1980, pp. 29–40.

Wahl, Jean, "Kierkegaard: l'angoscia e l'istante" [Kierkegaard: l'angoisse et l'instant], trans. by M. Tonon, *NotaBene. Quaderni di studi kierkegaardiani*, vol. 4, *L'edificante in Kierkegaard* [The Edifying in Kierkegaard], 2005, pp. 185–97.

Japanese

Yusuke Suzuki

I. Japanese Translations of Kierkegaard's Works

『反復』 [*Repetition*], trans. by Keizaburo Masuda, Tokyo: Iwanami-shoten 1925 (2nd ed. 1983) (岩波文庫 [*Iwanami Library*]).

『憂愁の哲理』 [*Either/Or* [selections]], trans. by Koichiro Miyahara, Tokyo: Shunju-sha 1930 (世界大思想全集 [*Works of the World's Great Thinkers*], vol. 36).

「使徒と天才の相違に就いて」 ["The Difference between a Genius and an Apostle" [from *Two Ethical-Religious Essays*]], trans. by Kagami Hashimoto, Tokyo: Jujikanoshingaku-sha 1931 (十字架の神学叢書 [*Library of the Cross Theology*], vol. 16).

キェルケゴール選集 [*Kierkegaard's Selected Works*], vols. 1–3, ed. by Kiyoshi Miki, Tokyo: Kaizo-sha 1935;

— vol. 1, 『不安の概念』 [*The Concept of Anxiety*], trans. by Goichi Ito; 「現代の批判」 ["The Present Age" [from *A Literary Review*]], trans. by Shigeru Miki; and 『死に至る病』 [*The Sickness unto Death*], trans. by Enkichi Kan and Haruo Omura;

— vol. 2, 『基督教に於ける訓練』 [*Practice in Christianity*], trans. by Hidenobu Kuwata; 『懼れとおののき』 [*Fear and Trembling*], trans. by Eiichi Kito; and 「誘惑者の日記」 ["The Seducer's Diary" [from *Either/Or*]], trans. by Kotaro Jinbo;

— vol. 3, 『アイロニーの概念』 [*The Concept of Irony*], trans. by Kiyoshi Miki and Keizaburo Masuda; 『反復』 [*Repetition*], trans. by Keizaburo Masuda; and 『瞬間』 [*The Moment*], trans. by Masataka Fujimoto.

『哲学的断片後書』 [*Concluding Unscientific Postscript*], trans. by Eiichi Kito, Tokyo: Mikasa-shobo 1938 (現代思想全書 [*Modern Thoughts Series*]).

『死に至る病』 [*The Sickness unto Death*], trans. by Shinji Saito, Tokyo: Iwanami-shoten 1939 (2nd ed. 1983) (岩波文庫 [*Iwanami Library*]).

『ドン＝ジュアン論』 [*Don Juan* [selections from *Either/Or*]], trans. by Munetaka Iijima, Tokyo: Hanawa-shobo 1947.

『死に至る病』 [*The Sickness unto Death*], trans. by Shinzaburo Matsunami, Tokyo: Koishikawa-shobo 1948.

『野の百合・空の鳥』 [*The Lily in the Field and the Bird of the Air*], trans. by Yasushi Kuyama, Tokyo: Koubun-do 1948 (アテネ文庫 [*Athenian Library*]) (2nd ed., Nishinomiya: Kirisutokyogakuto-kyodaidan 1963).

『哲学的断片』 [*Philosophical Fragments*], trans. by Isaku Yanaihara, Tokyo: Kadokawa-shoten 1948.

「誘惑者の日記」 ["The Seducer's Diary" [from *Either/Or*]], trans. by Munetaka Iijima, Tokyo: Kadokawa-shoten 1948 (2nd revised edition, ed. by Satoshi Nakazato, Tokyo: Michitani 2000).

『死に至る病』 [*The Sickness unto Death*], trans. by Tomio Yasunaka, Tokyo: Shigaku-sha 1948.

「追憶の哲理」 ["In Vino Veritas" [from *Stages on Life's Way*]], trans. by Kenichi Yoshida and Yoshie Hotta, Tokyo: Daichi-shobo 1948.

「使徒と天才の相違について」・「人は真理のために殺される権利をもつか」 [*Two Ethical-Religious Essays*], trans. by Kagami Hashimoto and Yoshiyuki Yokoyama, Tokyo: Shinkyo-shuppansha 1948.

「初恋」 ["The First Love" [from *Either/Or*]], trans. by Munetaka Iijima, Tokyo: Kadokawa-shoten 1948 (2nd revised ed., ed. by Satoshi Nakazato, Tokyo: Michitani 2000).

『説教集』 ["The High Priest," "The Tax Collector," "The Woman Who Was a Sinner" [from *Three Discourses at the Communion on Fridays*]], trans. by Yoshiyuki Yokoyama, Tokyo: Shinkyo-shuppansha 1948.

「愛は多くの罪を掩う」 ["Love Will Hide a Multitude of Sins" [from *Three Upbuilding Discourses*, 1843]], trans. by Yasushi Kuyama, Tokyo: Koubun-do 1948 (アテネ文庫 [*Athenian Library*]).

「イエスの招き」 [*Practice in Christianity*, Nos. I and II], trans. by Yoshio Inoue, Tokyo: Kadokawa-shoten 1948.

「快楽と絶望」 [*Either/Or* [selections]], trans. by Nobuo Sumi, Tokyo: Daichi-shobo 1948.

ゼエレン＝キェルケゴオル選集 [*Søren Kierkegaard's Selected Works*], vols. 1–13 (in 15 tomes), Kyoto: Jimbun-shoin 1948–49;

— vol. 1, 『あれかこれか』 [*Either/Or*, Part One], trans. by Mayumi Haga;

— vol. 2, 『あれかこれか』 [*Either/Or*, Part One], trans. by Mayumi Haga;

— vol. 3.1, 『あれかこれか』 [*Either/Or*, Part Two], trans. by Mayumi Haga;

— vol. 3.2, 『あれかこれか』 [*Either/Or*, Part Two], trans. by Mayumi Haga;

— vol. 4, 『恐怖と戦慄』 [*Fear and Trembling*], trans. by Shoji Ishinaka;

— vol. 5, 『人生行路の諸段階』 [*Stages on Life's Way*], trans. by Koki Nakazawa;

— vol. 6, 『人生行路の諸段階』 [*Stages on Life's Way*], trans. by Yukio Takahashi;

— vol. 7, 『不安の概念』 [*The Concept of Anxiety*], trans. by Shoji Ishinaka;

— vol. 8, 『哲学屑』 [*Philosophical Fragments*], trans. by Masaru Otani;

— vol. 9, 『愛について』 [*Works of Love*], trans. by Mayumi Haga;

— vol. 10, 『死に至る病』 [*The Sickness unto Death*], trans. by Yasuo Katayama:

— vol. 11, 『瞬間』 [*The Moment*], trans. by Shinnosuke Yamada;

— vol. 12, 『我が著作活動の視点』 [*The Point of View for my Work as an Author*], trans. by Gisaburo Tabuchi;

— vol. 13, 『日記』 [*Journals*], trans. by Masaru Otani;

— Supplementary volume, 『許嫁への手紙』 [*Letters to the Engaged*], trans. by Masaru Otani.

『わが魂の戦ひ、自己検察の為に』 [*For Self-Examination*], trans. by Shinichi Sato, Tokyo: Kadokawa-shoten 1949.

「美しき人生観」［"The Immediate Erotic Stages or The Musical-Erotic" [from *Either/Or*]], trans. by Munetaka Iijima, Tokyo: Kadokawa-shoten 1949 (2nd revised edition, ed. by Satoshi Nakazato, Tokyo: Michitani 2000).

「結婚の美的権利」［"The Esthetic Validity of Marriage" [from *Either/Or*]], trans. by Munetaka Iijima, Tokyo: Kadokawa-shoten 1949 (2nd revised edition, ed. by Satoshi Nakazato, Tokyo: Michitani 2000).

『キェルケゴールの日記』［*Journals* [selections]], trans. by Yoshinori Tamabayashi and Yasushi Kuyama, Tokyo: Kobun-do 1949.

『神の不変性』［*The Changelessness of God*], trans. by Yoshiyuki Yokoyama, Tokyo: Shinkyo-shuppansha 1949.

『聖餐式のための説話』［*Two Discourses at the Communion on Fridays*], trans. by Yoshiyuki Yokoyama, Tokyo: Shinkyo-shuppansha 1949.

「現代の批判」［"The Present Age" [from *A Literary Review*]]; 「単独者―わが著作活動に関する二つの『覚書』」［"'The Single Individual.' Two 'Notes' Concerning My Work as an Author" [from *The Point of View for My Work as an Author*]], trans. by Munetaka Iijima, Tokyo: Sogen-sha 1949.

『不安の概念』［*The Concept of Anxiety*], trans. by Kiyoshi Hirose, Tokyo: Kadokawa-shoten 1950.

『不安の概念』［*The Concept of Anxiety*], trans. by Shinji Saito, Tokyo: Iwanami-shoten 1951 (岩波文庫 [*Iwanami Library*]).

キルケゴール全集 [*Kierkegaard's Collected Works*], vols. 1–38, with a supplementary volume, trans. by Keizaburo Masuda, Tokyo: Chikuma-shobo 1952–1966 (only four volumes were published);

— vol. 2, 『あれか―これか』第 1 部下 [*Either/Or*, Part One];

— vol. 5, 『おそれとおののき』 [*Fear and Trembling*]; 『一つの教化的講話』 [*An Upbuilding Discourse*];

— vol. 6, 『反復』 [*Repetition*]; 『三つの教化的講話』 [*Three Upbuilding Discourses, 1843*];

— vol. 24, 『死にいたる病』 [*The Sickness unto Death*]; 「『大祭司』『収税人』『罪ある女』」［"The High Priest," "The Tax Collector," "The Woman Who Was a Sinner" [from *Three Discourses at the Communion on Fridays*]].

『婚約』 [*Journals* [selections]], trans. and ed. by Masaru Otani, Tokyo: Mikasa-shobo 1953 (2nd ed., Fukuoka: Sogen-sha 1972).

キルケゴール選集 [*Kierkegaard's Selected Works*], vols. 1–8, (only four volumes were published), Tokyo: Sogen-sha 1953–1954;

— vol. 1, 「誘惑者の日記」［"The Seducer's Diary" [from *Either/Or*]], trans. by Munetaka Iijima;

— vol. 3, 『哲学的断片』 [*Philosophical Fragments*], trans. by Masaru Otani;

— vol. 6, 『死にいたる病』 [*The Sickness unto Death*], trans. by Munetaka Iijima;

— vol. 8, 『わが著作活動の視点』 [*The Point of View for my Work as an Author*], trans. by Gisaburo Tabuchi; 『瞬間』 [*The Moment*], trans. by Gisaburo Tabuchi.

『死にいたる病』 [*The Sickness unto Death*], trans. by Munetaka Iijama, Tokyo: Kawade-shobo-shinsha 1954 (2nd ed., 1982) (キリスト教古典叢書 [Series of Christian Classics]).

『神への思い』 [*An Anthology of the Upbuilding Discourses*], trans. and ed. by Isao Kuramatsu, Tokyo: Shinkyo-shuppansha 1958 (2nd ed., 1996) (新教新書 [Shinkyo Paperback Edition]).

『哲学的断片への結びの学問外れな後書』 [*Concluding Unscientific Postscript*], vols. 1–2, trans. by Masaru Otani, Tokyo: Shinkyo-shuppansha 1959.

世界文学大系２１ [*Series of World Literatures*, vol. 21] (「誘惑者の日記」 ["The Seducer's Diary" [from *Either/Or*]]; 『おそれとおののき』 [*Fear and Trembling*]; 『反復』 [*Repetition*] and 『死に至る病』 [*The Sickness unto Death*]), trans. by Keizaburo Masuda, Tokyo: Chikuma-shobo 1961.

『死にいたる病』・「現代の批判」 [*The Sickness unto Death*; "The Present Age" [from *A Literary Review*]], trans. by Shinzaburo Matsunami and Munetaka Iijima, Tokyo: Hakusui-sha 1962 (2nd ed. 1975).

キルケゴール著作集 [*Kierkegaard's Selected Works*], vols. 1–22, with a supplementary volume, Tokyo: Hakusui-sha 1962–1968;

— vol. 1, 『あれか・これか』第１部上 [*Either/Or*, part 1 (1)], trans. by Masao Asai;

— vol. 2, 『あれか・これか』第１部下 [*Either/Or*, part 1 (2)], trans. by Masao Asai;

— vol. 3, 『あれか・これか』第２部上 [*Either/Or*, part 2 (1)], trans. by Masaru Asai;

— vol. 4, 『あれか・これか』第２部下 [*Either/Or*, part 2 (2)], trans. by Masao Asai;

— vol. 5, 『おそれとおののき』 [*Fear and Trembling*] trans. by Keizaburo Masuda; 『反復』 [*Repetition*], trans. by Keisaku Maeda;

— vol. 6, 『哲学的断片または一断片の哲学』 [*Philosophical Fragments*], trans. by Hidehito Otani; 『危機および一女優の生涯における一つの危機』 [*The Crisis and a Crisis in the Life of an Actress*], trans. by Hidehito Otani;

— vol. 7, 『哲学的断片への結びとしての非学問的あとがき』上 [*Concluding Unscientific Postscript*, part 1], trans. by Yoshimu Sugiyama and Keiji Ogawa;

— vol. 8, 『哲学的断片への結びとしての非学問的あとがき』中 [*Concluding Unscientific Postscript*, part 2], trans. by Yoshimu Sugiyama and Keiji Ogawa;

— vol. 9, 『哲学的断片への結びとしての非学問的あとがき』下 [*Concluding Unscientific Postscript*, part 3], trans. by Yoshimu Sugiyama and Keiji Ogawa;

— vol. 10, 『不安の概念』 [*The Concept of Anxiety*], trans. by Hidehiro Hikami; 『序文ばかり』 [*Prefaces*], trans. by Yoshinobu Kumazawa;

— vol. 11, 『死にいたる病』 [*The Sickness unto Death*], trans. by Shinzaburo Matsunami; 『現代の批判』 ["The Present Age" [from *A Literary Review*]], trans. by Munetaka Iijima;

— vol. 12, 『人生行路の諸段階』上 [*Stages on Life's Way*, part 1], trans. by Koichi Sato;

— vol. 13, 『人生行路の諸段階』中 [*Stages on Life's Way*, part 2], trans. by Koichi Sato;

— vol. 14, 『人生行路の諸段階』下 [*Stages on Life's Way*, part 3], trans. by Koichi Sato;

— vol. 15, 『愛の業』第一部 [*Works of Love*, part 1], trans. by Kazuo Muto and Takeo Ashizu;

— vol. 16, 『愛の業』第二部 [*Works of Love*, part 2], trans. by Kazuo Muto and Takeo Ashizu;

— vol. 17, 『キリスト教の修練』 [*Practice in Christianity*], trans. by Yoshimu Sugiyama;

—vol. 18, 『わが著作活動の視点』 [*The Point of View for my Work as an Author*], trans. by Gisaburo Tabuchi; 『野の百合、空の鳥』 [*The Lily in the Field and the Bird of the Air*], trans. by Yasushi Kuyama;

— vol. 19, 『瞬間』 [*The Moment*], trans. by Shinzaburo Matsunami and Harunori Izumi.

— vol. 20, 『イロニーの概念』上 [*The Concept of Irony*, part 1], trans. by Munetaka Iijima and Yasuo Fukushima;

— vol. 21, 『イロニーの概念』下 [*The Concept of Irony*, part 2], trans. by Munetaka Iijima and Yasuo Fukushima;

— Supplementary volume, キルケゴール研究 [*Kierkegaard Studies*], ed. by Munetaka Iijima and Shinzaburo Matsunami.

『死にいたる病』 [*The Sickness unto Death*], trans. by Keizaburo Masuda, Tokyo: Chikuma-shobo 1963 (2nd ed. 1996) (ちくま学芸文庫 [*Series of Literary and Artistic Achievements*]).

『不安の概念』 [*The Concept of Anxiety*]. 『序文ばかり』 [*Prefaces*], trans. by Hidehiro Hikami and Yoshinobu Kumazawa, Tokyo: Hakusui-sha 1964 (2nd ed. 1979).

キルケゴール講話・遺稿集 [*Selected Works of Kierkegaard's Discourses, Journals and Papers*], vols. 1–6, ed. by the Japanese Society of Existentialism, Tokyo: Riso-sha 1964 (only one volume was published).

— vol. 6, 『アドラーの書』 [*The Book on Adler*], trans. by Tasuku Hara; 『武装せる中立』 [*Armed Neutrality*], trans. by Hidehito Otani; 「倫理的伝達と倫理・宗教的伝達との弁証法」 ["The Dialectic of Ethical and Ethical-Religious Communication: A Little Sketch"], trans. by Hidehito Otani.

「誘惑者の日記」 ["The Seducer's Diary" [from *Either/Or*]], trans. by Masao Asai, Tokyo: Hakusui-sha 1965 (2nd ed. 1975; 3rd ed. 1998).

「誘惑者の日記」 ["The Seducer's Diary" [from *Either/Or*]], trans. by Keizaburo Masuda, Tokyo: Chikuma-shobo 1966 (2nd ed. 1998) (ちくま学芸文庫 [*Series of Literary and Artistic Attainments*]).

「現代の批判」 ["The Present Age" [from *A Literary Review*]], trans. by Keizaburo Masuda, Tokyo: Iwanami-shoten 1966 (2nd ed. 1981) (岩波文庫 [*Iwanami Library*]).

世界の大思想24 「キルケゴール」 [*Great Thoughts of the World*, vol. 24, Kierkegaard] (『おそれとおののき』 [*Fear and Trembling*], trans. by Keizaburo Masuda; 『哲学的断片』 [*Philosophical Fragments*], trans. by Isaku Yanaihara; 『不安の概念』 [*The Concept of Anxiety*], trans. by Tasuku Hara and Munetaka Iijima and 『死にいたる病』 [*The Sickness unto Death*], trans. by Shinzaburo Matsunami), Tokyo: Kawade-shobo-shinsha 1966 (2nd ed., Tokyo: Kawade-shobo-shinsha 2004).

世界の名著 ４０ 「キルケゴール」 [*World Masterpieces*, vol. 40, Kierkegaard] (『哲学的断片』 [*Philosophical Fragments*], trans. by Yoshimu Sugiyama; 『不安の概念』 [*The Concept of Anxiety*], trans. by Gisaburo Tabuchi; 「現代の批判」 ["The Present Age" [from *A Literary Review*]] and 『死にいたる病』 [*The Sickness unto Death*], trans. by Keizaburo Masuda), Tokyo: Chuokoron-sha 1966.

『キルケゴールの言葉』 [*An Anthology of Kierkegaard's Works*], trans. and ed. by Hidehito Otani, Tokyo: Yayoi-shobo 1969.

現代キリスト教思想叢書５ 「ヘーゲル・キルケゴール」 [*Series of Modern Christian Thoughts*, vol. 5, Hegel and Kierkegaard] (「苦難の福音」 ["States of Mind in the Strife of Suffering" [from *Christian Discourses*]] and 「人は真理のために打ち殺されることが許されるか？」 ["Does a Human Being Have the Right to Let Himself Be Put to Death for the Truth" [from *Two Ethical-Religious Essays*]]), trans. by Yoshimu Sugiyama, Tokyo: Hakusui-sha 1974.

「異教徒の憂い」 ["The Cares of the Pagans" [from *Christian Discourses*]], trans. by Yoshiko Shishido, Tokyo: Shinkyo-shuppansha 1976.

「背後から傷つける思想」 ["Thoughts that Wound from Behind – for Upbuilding" [from *Christian Discourses*]], trans. by Jun Hashimoto, Tokyo: Shinkyo-shuppansha 1976.

『キルケゴール』 [*Kierkegaard* [selections from Kierkegaard's writings]], trans. by Hideo Maze and Kazuhiko Ozaki, ed. by Frederik Billeskov Jansen and Fujio Makino, Tokyo: Tokaidaigaku-shuppannkai 1976 (デンマーク文学作品集 [Collected Works of Danish Literature]).

『恐れとおののき』 [*Fear and Trembling*], trans. by Hideo Akiyama, Tokyo: Shuhunotomo-sha 1977 (キリスト教文学 １３ [*Christian Literature*, vol. 13]).

キルケゴールの講話・遺稿集 [*Selected Works of Kierkegaard's Discourses, Journals and Papers*], vols. 1–9, ed. by Munetaka Iijima, Tokyo: Shinchi-shobo 1979–83;

— vol. 1, 『二つの建徳的講話』 [*Two Upbuilding Discourses* (1843)], trans. by Yasuo Fukushima; 『三つの建徳的講話』 [*Three Upbuilding Discourses* (1843)], trans. by Yasuo Fukushima; 『四つの建徳的講話』 [*Four Upbuilding Discourses* (1843)], trans. by Masatoshi Yamada; 『牧師資格取得説教』 [*Trial Sermon held in Trinitatis Church* (February 24, 1844)], trans. by Masatoshi Yamada;

— vol. 2, 『二つの建徳的講話』 [*Two Upbuilding Discourses* (1844)], trans. by Genpo Yamada; 『三つの建徳的講話』 [*Three Upbuilding Discourses* (1844)], trans. by Genpo Yamada; 『四つの建徳的講話』 [*Four Upbuilding Discourses* (1844)], trans. by Junko Hamada;

— vol. 3, 『さまざまの精神における建徳的講話』 １、 ２ [*Upbuilding Discourses in Various Spirits*, parts 1 and 2], trans. by Gisaburo Tabuchi, Keiichi Kashiwabara and Yoshiya Goto;

— vol. 4, 『さまざまの精神における建徳的講話』 ３ [*Upbuilding Discourses in Various Spirits*, part 3], trans. by Tatsuro Iwanaga; 『想定された機会における三つの講話』 [*Three Discourses on Imagined Occasions*], trans. by Junichi Toyofuku;

— vol. 5, 「単独者」["The Single Individual" [from *The Point of View for My Work as an Author*]], trans. by Munetaka Iijima; 『キリスト教的講話』1、2 [*Christian Discourses*, parts 1 and 2], trans. by Kazuhiko Nakamura;

— vol. 6, 『キリスト教的講話』3、4 [*Christian Discourses*, parts 3 and 4], trans. by Nagamitsu Miura, Norihiko Mikame and Kazuhiko Nakamura; 『野の百合と空の鳥』[*The Lily in the Field and the Bird of the Air*], trans. by Kazuhiko Ozaki;

— vol. 7, 『二つの倫理的・宗教的小論』[*Two Ethical-Religious Essays*], trans. by Shoshu Kawakami, 『大祭司・収税人・罪ある女』["The High Priest," "The Tax Collector," "The Woman Who Was a Sinner" [from *Three Discourses at the Communion on Fridays*]], trans. by Kyoichi Murakami; 『一つの建徳的講話』[*An Upbuilding Discourse*], trans. by Shigeru Kobayashi; 『金曜日の聖餐式における二つの講話』[*Two Discourses at the Communion on Fridays*], trans. by Shigeru Kobayashi; 『これは言わねばならぬ、だからここで言わせてもらう』[*This Must Be Said; So Let it Be Said*], trans. by Kyoichi Murakami and Shigeru Kobayashi; 『公認のキリスト教をキリストはいかに判断するか』[*What Christ Judges of Official Christianity*], trans. by Shigeru Kobayashi; 『神の不変性』[*The Changelessness of God*], trans. by Shoshu Kawakami;

—vol. 8, 『いまなお生ける者の手記より』[*From the Papers of One Still Living*], trans. by Hidehito Otani; 『ヨハンネス＝クリマクス、またすべてのものが疑われねばならぬ』[*Johannes Climacus, or De omnibus dubitandum est*], trans. by Katsumi Kitada; 『倫理的伝達の、また倫理―宗教的伝達の弁証法』["The Dialectic of Ethical and Ethical-Religious Communication. A Little Sketch"], trans. by Hidehito Otani; 『武装せる中立』[*Armed Neutrality*], trans. by Hidehito Otani;

— vol. 9, 『アドラーの書』[*The Book on Adler*], trans. by Tasuku Hara and Munetaka Iijima.

『セーレン＝キルケゴールの日誌』第1巻 [*Journals* [selected entries about Regine Olsen]], trans. by Jun Hashimoto, Tokyo: Mirai-sha 1985.

『不安の概念』[*The Concept of Anxiety*], ed. by Kyoichi Murakami, Tokyo: Daigaku-shorin 1985.

原典訳記念版キェルケゴール著作全集 [*Kierkegaard's Selected Works: Commemorative Original Translation Edition*], vols. 1–15, ed. by Masaru Otani, Fukuoka: Sogen-sha 1988–2011;

— vol. 1, 『これか―あれか』第1部 [*Either/Or*, part 1], trans. by Sanae Ota and Masaru Otani;

— vol. 2, 『これか―あれか』第2部 [*Either/Or*, part 2], trans. by Sanae Ota and Masaru Otani;

— vol. 3, 『畏れとおののき』[*Fear and Trembling*], trans. by Kazuhiko Ozaki; 『受取り直し』[*Repetition*], trans. by Kazuhiko Ozaki; 『不安の概念』[*The Concept of Anxiety*], trans. by Masaru Otani;

— vol. 4, 『人生行路の諸段階』前半 [*Stages on Life's Way*, part 1], trans. by Tetsyoshi Kunii and Masaru Otani;

— vol. 5, 『人生行路の諸段階』後半 [*Stages on Life's Way*, part 2], trans. by Kuniko Yamamoto and Masaru Otani;

— vol. 6, 『哲学的断片或いは一断片の哲学』 [*Philosophical Fragments*]; 『哲学的断片への結びの学問外れな後書』第一部 [*Concluding Unscientific Postscript*, part 1], trans. by Masaru Otani;

— vol. 7, 『哲学的断片への結びの学問外れな後書』第二部 [*Concluding Unscientific Postscript*, part 2], trans. by Masaru Otani;

— vol. 8, 『序言』 [*Prefaces*], trans. by Kuniko Yamamoto; 『仮想された機会での三つの談話』 [*Three Discourses on Imagined Occasions*], trans. by Masaru Otani; 『文芸批評』 [*A Literary Review*], trans. by Masaru Otani; 『或る女優の生涯における危機と或る危機』 [*The Crisis and a Crisis in the Life of an Actress*], trans. by Masaru Otani;

— vol. 9, 『種々の精神での建徳的談話』 [*Upbuilding Discourses in Various Spirits*], trans. by Masaru Otani and Shozo Fujiki;

— vol. 10, 『愛の業』 [*Works of Love*], trans. by Kazuhiko Ozaki and Koji Sato;

— vol. 11, 『キリスト教談話』 [*Christian Discourses*], trans. by Shozo Fujiki;

— vol. 12, 『野の百合と空の鳥』 [*The Lily in the Field and the Bird of the Air*], trans. by Masaru Otani; 『二つの倫理的—宗教的小＝論文』 [*Two Religious-Ethical Essays*], trans. by Masaru Otani; 『死に至る病』 [*The Sickness unto Death*], trans. by Hidetomo Yamashita (2nd ed., Fukuoka: Sogen-sha 2007); 「『大祭司』—『収税人』—『罪の女』」 ["The High Priest," "The Tax Collector," "The Woman Who Was a Sinner" [from *Three Discourses at the Communion on Fridays*]], trans. by Masaru Otani;

— vol. 13, 『キリスト教への修練』 [*Practice in Christianity*], trans. by Tetsuyoshi Kunii and Hidetomo Yamashita; 『一つの建徳的講話』 [*An Upbuilding Discourse*], trans. by Hidetomo Yamashita;

— vol. 14, 『自省のために、現代にすすむ』 [*For Self-Examination*], trans. by Tetsuyoshi Kunii; 『汝自ら審け！』 [*Judge for Yourself*], trans. by Kinya Masugata; 『我が著作家＝活動に対する視点』 [*The Point of View for My Work as an Author*], trans. by Masaru Otani, 『我が著作家＝活動について』 [*On My Work as an Author*], trans. by Masaru Otani, 『金曜日の聖餐式における二つの談話』 [*Two Discourses at the Communion on Fridays*], trans. by Masaru Otani;

— vol. 15, 『瞬間』 [*The Moment*], trans. by Hidehiko Kondo and Testuyoshi Kondo; 『これは言われねばならない、それだからこそ今それを言うことにする』 [*This Must Be Said; So Let it Be Said*], trans. by Masaru Otani; 『官公キリスト教についてキリストの裁き給うこと』 [*What Christ Judges of Official Christianity*], trans. by Masaru Otani; 『神の不変性』 [*The Changelessness of God*], trans. by Masaru Otani.

『死にいたる病』・「現代の批判」 [*The Sickness unto Death*, "The Present Age" [from *A Literary Review*]], trans. by Keizaburo Masuda, Tokyo: Chuokoron-shinsha 2003.

『キリスト教の修練』 [*Practice in Christianity*], trans. by Yoshio Inoue, Tokyo: Shinkyo-shuppan 2004.

『あれか、これか』 [*Either/Or*], trans. by Masao Asai and Kazutomi Shiba, Tokyo: Kawadeshobo-shinsha 2005.

「ドン・ジョヴァンニ音楽的エロスについて」 ["The Immediate Erotic Stages or The Musical-Erotic" [from *Either/Or*]], trans. by Masao Asai, Tokyo: Hakusui-sha 2006.

『死に至る病』・「現代の批判」 [*The Sickness unto Death*, "The Present Age" [from *A Literary Review*]], trans. by Shinzaburo Matsunami and Munetaka Iijima, Tokyo: Hakusui-sha 2008.

「美と倫理」 ["The Esthetic Validity of Marriage" [from *Either/Or*]], trans. by Munetaka Iijima and Junko Hamada, Tokyo: Michitani 2009.

II. Secondary Literature on Kierkegaard in Japanese

阿部曜子 [Abe, Yoko], 「G. グリーンのキェルケゴール受容」 [The Reception of Kierkegaard by Graham Greene in the Case of *A Burnt-Out Case*], *Persica. Journal of the English Literary Society of Okayama*, vol. 28, 2001, pp. 57–65.

安倍能成 [Abe, Yoshishige], 「可能性に対する情熱」 [Passion for Possibility] and 「キェルケゴールの恋愛」 [Kierkegaard's Love], in his 『山中雑記』 [Notes in the Mountains], Tokyo: Iwanami-shoten 1924, pp. 256–63; pp. 264–9.

安達忠夫 [Adachi, Tadao], 「想像力について―キルケゴールおよび児童文学を中心に」 [On Imagination: In Kierkegaard and Children's Literature], 『埼玉大学紀要』 [Reports of Saitama University], vol. 21, 1985, pp. 67–88.

足立美比古 [Adachi, Yoshihiko], 「《逆説》のイロニー―キルケゴールと「音楽論」」 [Paradoxical Irony: Kierkegaard and his Ideas of Music], 『理想』 [Riso], vol. 555, 1979, pp. 62–76.

赤岩栄 [Akaiwa, Sakae], 「キエルケゴールとマルクス」 [Kierkegaard and Marx], 『学生評論』 [Students' Review], vol. 2, 1949, pp. 25–9.

秋山英夫 [Akiyama, Hideo], 『ニヒルと神―キエルケゴールとニーチェ』 [Nihil and God: Kierkegaard and Nietzsche], Tokyo: Shakaishiso-kenkyukai-shuppanbu 1951.

秋山山英 [Akiyama, Sanei], 「キエルケゴールにおける『詩人的実存』」 [The Poetic Existence in Kierkegaard], 『知と行』 [Knowledge and Action], vol. 4, 1949, pp. 33–7.

天野格之助 [Amano, Kakunosuke], 「キルケゴールにおける真理と信仰の問題」 [The Problem of Truth and Faith in Kierkegaard], 『皇学館大学紀要』[Bulletin of Kogakkan University], vol. 17, 1979, pp. 268–86.

―「『単独者』における信仰と愛―キルケゴールの婚約破棄の謎をめぐって」 [Faith and Love in "the Single Individual": About the Enigma of Kierkegaard's Breaking the Engagement], 『皇学館大学紀要』 [Bulletin of Kogakkan University], vol. 22, 1984, pp. 182–202.

天野敬太郎・万里小路通宗 [Amano, Keitaro and Michimune Madenokoji], 「日本に於けるキェルケゴール文献」 [Literature on Kierkegaard in Japan], 『関西大学学報』 [Annual Report of Kansai University], vol. 284, 1955, pp. 6–10.

雨宮久美 [Amemiya, Kumi], 「享楽か信仰か―キルケゴールの実存主義的生の諸相」 [Pleasure or Faith: Aspects of Kierkegaard's Existential Life], in 『芸術と宗教―キリスト教的視点より―』 [Art and Religion: From a Christian Perspective], ed. by Hiromichi Ishihama, Tokyo: Hokuju-shuppan 2008, pp. 43–58 (2nd ed. 2010; 3rd ed. 2012).

[Anonymous], 「キールケガールド」 [Kierkegaard], in 『近世泰西英傑伝』 第 5 巻 [The History of Great Figures of the Modern Western World], Tokyo: Dainihon-bunmei-kyokai 1911, vol. 5, pp. 84–90.

安西真 [Anzai, Makoto], 「ソークラテースをみつめるキェルケゴールとアリストパネース―キェルケゴールの『雲』評価を補足する試み」 [Kierkegaard and Aristophanes Gazing at Socrates], 『比較文化研究』 [Comparative Studies of Culture], vol. 20, 1981, pp. 73–100.

青柳進 [Aoyagi, Susumu], 「実存主義とは何か―キルケゴールからサルトルまでの系譜を追って」 [What is Existentialism? Tracing the Descent from Kierkegaard to Sartre], 『研究紀要（宇都宮短期大学）』 [Bulletin of Utsunomiya Junior College], vol. 10, 2003, pp. 23–54; republished in 『研究紀要（宇都宮短期大学）』 [Bulletin of Utsunomiya Junior College], vol. 11, 2004, pp. 31–91.

— 『現代における実存主義の意味―キルケゴールからサルトルへ』 [The Meaning of Existentialism Today: from Kierkegaard to Sartre], Tokyo: Kindaibungei-sha 2008.

荒井優 [Arai, Masaru], 「キェルケゴールにおける同時性の構造（一）」 [The Structure of "Contemporaneity" in Kierkegaard (I)], 『キェルケゴール研究』 [Kierkegaard-Studiet], no. 17, 1987, pp. 5–14.

— 「キェルケゴールにおける同時性の構造（二）」 [The Structure of "Contemporaneity" in Kierkegaard (II)], 『キェルケゴール研究』 [Kierkegaard-Studiet], no. 18, 1988, pp. 5–14.

— 「キェルケゴールにおける 2 つのキリスト教」 [Two Christianities in Kierkegaard], 『宗教研究』 [Journal of Religious Studies], vol. 65, 1991, pp. 239–67.

朝日知行 [Asahi, Tomoyuki], 「自己関係における永遠性の二義―キルケゴール『死に至る病』の考察」 [The Two Meanings of the Eternal in Self-relation], 『哲学論集』 [The Philosophical Studies], vol. 44, 1997, pp. 79–85.

浅野遼二 [Asano, Ryoji], 「キルケゴールの実存弁証法」 [Kierkegaard's Existential Dialectic], 『愛知学院大学論叢一般教育研究』 [Aichigakuin Daigaku Journal. Studies in Cultural Sciences], vol. 15, 1967, pp. 43–68.

— 「キルケゴールの不安と絶望の概念について」 [On Kierkegaard's Concepts of Anxiety and Despair], 『愛知学院大学論叢一般教育研究』 [Aichigakuin Daigaku Journal. Studies in Cultural Sciences], vol. 16, 1968, pp. 175–202.

— 「キルケゴールの『単独者』思想」 [Kierkegaard's Idea of "the Single Individual"], 『待兼山論叢』 [Machikaneyama-ronso], vol. 3, 1969, pp. 25–45.

— 「キルケゴールとニーチェの歴史哲学」 [Philosophy of History in Kierkegaard and Nietzsche], 『哲学論叢』 [Tetsugaku-ronso], vol. 4, 1979, pp. 71–92.

— 「キェルケゴールの『想起』論」 [Kierkegaard's Doctrine of Recollection], 『待兼山論叢』 [Machikaneyama-ronso], vol. 32, 1998, pp. 1–12.

麻生健 [Aso, Ken], 「キェルケゴール―<関係>としての世界」 [The World as Relation in Kierkegaard], 『帝京平成大学紀要』 [Journal of Teikyo Heisei University], vol. 15, no. 2, 2003, pp. 1–16.

大谷長博士古稀記念論集刊行会 [Association for Publishing a Memorial Volume on the Occasion of Prof. Dr. Masaru Otani's 70th Birthday] (ed.), 『キェルケゴール—デンマークの思想と言語—』 [Søren Kierkegaard: Thinking and Usage of the Language in Denmark], Osaka: Toho-shuppan 1982. (F.J. Billeskov Jansen, 「世界をめぐるキェルケゴール研究」 [Søren Kierkegaard Goes Around the World], trans. by Hikari Yabu, pp. 3–22; Jun Hashimoto, 「セーレン・キェルケゴールの遺稿文書（Papirer）について」 [An Introduction to Kierkegaard's "Papirer": Primary Sources for the Historical Understanding of Kierkegaard], pp. 23–40; Eiko Hanaoka-Kawamura, 「自由の問題」 [The Problem of Freedom], pp. 41–60; Katsumi Kitada, 「キェルケゴールにおける主体性の宗教的次元」 [The Religious Dimension of the Subjectivity in Kierkegaard], pp. 61–80; Marie Mikulová Thulstrup, 「キェルケゴールと彼の時代における東洋の神秘主義—歴史的研究—」 [Kierkegaard and the Mysticism of the Orient in his Time: A Historical Research], trans. by Kuniko Yamamoto, pp. 81–118; Kinya Masugata, 「アリストテレスとキェルケゴール—エートス（ήθος）と自己有化（Tilegnelse）」 [Aristotle and Kierkegaard—ήθος and Tilegnelse], pp. 119–54; Toshiaki Muraki, 「ホ・セ・ブラナー『騎手』—四十年代デンマーク文学—」 [On H.C. Branner: *The Rider*—the Danish Literature in the 1940s], pp. 155–172; Niels Thulstrup, 「マーク・C・テイラーのヘーゲル及びキェルケゴールとの旅を評す」 [Criticism of Mark C. Taylor's Journey with Hegel and Kierkegaard], trans. by Masaru Otani, pp. 173–212; Kazuhiko Ozaki, 「キェルケゴール著作家活動の弁証法的構造—『視点』における『弁証法的二面性』の概念の意味するもの—」 [The Dialectical Structure of Kierkegaard's Authorship], pp. 213–46; Peter Rohde, 「ポウル・メェラーとセーレン・キェルケゴール」 [Poul Møller and S. Kierkegaard], trans. by Koji Sato, pp. 247–68; Emanuel Skjoldager, 「セーレン・キェルケゴール—説教者—」 [Søren Kierkegaard the Preacher], trans. by Tetsuyoshi Kunii, pp. 269–80; Steffen Steffensen, 「三つのファウスト像」 [Three Images of Faust], trans. by Toshikazu Oya, pp. 281–94; Naomichi Takama, 「続・キェルケゴールの顔—人間知の手段としての『人相学』的な視点から」 [A Study of S. Kierkegaard's Face, Continued: From a Physiognomical Point of View], pp. 295–314; Hikari Yabu, 「ルーズヴィ・ホルベアとその喜劇」 [Ludvig Holberg and his Comedy], pp. 315–38; Hidetomo Yamashita, 「『死に至る病』の立場」 [The Standpoint of *The Sickness unto Death*], pp. 339–60; Masaru Otani, 「キェルケゴールを巡って格闘する精神達—私的回想—」 [Spirits which Fight around Kierkegaard], pp. 361–401; Kunishiro Sugawara, 「近代デンマーク語表現"den dag i dag"の起原に関する一考察」 [On the Origin of the New Danish Experssion "den dag i dag"], pp. 402–15; Hideo Mase, 「Kierkegaardという姓の発音と音声的転写」 [Pronunciation and Transliteration of the Name Kierkegaard], pp. 416–30.)

馬場智理 [Baba, Tomomichi], 「主体的行為における他者との邂逅—キェルケゴール『おそれとおののき』から」 [The Encounter with the Other in Subjective Action – Through *Fear and Trembling*], 『倫理学年報』 [Annals of Ethics], vol. 19, 2002, pp. 95–107.

——「キルケゴールにおける真理の現実性の問題」 [The Problem of the Reality of Truth in Kierkegaard], 『哲学・思想論叢』 [Miscellanea Philosophica], vol. 21, 2003, pp. 15–25.

——「キルケゴール思想における『他なるもの』への問い」 [The Question of "the Other" in Kierkegaard's Thought], 『倫理学』 [Ethics], vol. 20, 2004, pp. 121–32.

——「キルケゴールにおける懐疑の問題」 [The Problem of Doubt in Kierkegaard], 『倫理学』 [Ethics], vol. 21, 2005, pp. 35–47.

——「キルケゴール思想における他者と時間」 [The Other and Time in Kierkegaard's Thought], 『倫理学』 [Ethics], vol. 22, 2006, pp. 53–66.

——「キルケゴール思想における逆説の問題」 [The Problem of Paradox in Kierkegaard's Thought], 『倫理学』 [Ethics], vol. 23, 2007, pp. 121–34.

——「死と再生の論理—田辺哲学におけるキルケゴール思想との出会い」 [The Logic of Death and Rebirth: Encounters with Kierkegaard's Thought in Tanabe Philosophy], 『求真』 [Kyushin], vol. 15, 2008, pp. 42–56.

別所梅之助 [Bessho, Umenosuke], 「苦痛の福音—ヴィネとキェルケゴールド」 [The Gospel of Suffering: Vigny and Kierkegaard], 『聖書之研究』 [Biblical Study], vol. 125, 1910, pp. 21–31.

——「苦悩の福音」 [The Gospel of Suffering], in his 『武蔵野の一角にたちて』 [Standing on the Corner of Musashino District], Tokyo: Keiseisha-shobo 1915, pp. 435–63.

千葉泰爾 [Chiba, Taiji], 「キルケゴールにおける実存の伝達と覚醒」 [Existential Communication and Awakeing in Kierkegaard], 『東北大学教育学部研究年報』 [The Annual Reports of the Faculty of Education, Tohoku University], vol. 17, 1969, pp. 1–35.

——「キルケゴールにおける主体的実存」 [Subjective Existence in Kierkegaard], 『東北大学教育学部研究年報』 [The Annual Reports of the Faculty of Education, Tohoku University], vol. 18, 1970, pp. 1–24.

——「キルケゴールにおける実存伝達の弁証法」 [The Dialectics of Existential Communication in Kierkegaard], 『教育哲学研究』 [Studies in Philosophy of Education], vol. 22, 1970, pp. 20–36.

——「キルケゴールにおける内在と超越の弁証法」 [The Dialectics of Immanence and Transcendence in Kierkegaard], 『東北大学教育学部研究年報』 [The Annual Reports of the Faculty of Education, Tohoku University], vol. 21, 1973, pp. 37–84.

——「キルケゴールの思想の基底をめぐる諸問題」 [Problems of the Foundation of Kierkegaard's Thought], 『東北大学教育学部研究年報』 [The Annual Reports of the Faculty of Education, Tohoku University], vol. 36, 1988, pp. 1–46.

茅野蕭々 [Chino, Shosho], 「キェルケゴール」 [Kierkegaard], in 『世界文学講座第１１巻—北欧文学篇』 [Lectures on World Literature, vol. 11—Literature in Northern Europe], ed. by Yoshiaki Sato, Tokyo: Shincho-sha 1930, pp. 311–20.

——「キェルケゴールの『あれか・これか』」 [*Either/Or* by Kierkegaard], 『文藝』 [Literature], vol. 3 no. 5, 1935, pp. 85–96.

道躰滋穂子 [Dotai, Shihoko], 「キルケゴールの美的領域とパスカルの肉の秩序について」 [On the Aesthetic Field in Kierkegaard and the Discipline of the

Flesh in Pascal], 『桜美林論集』 [Journal of Social Sciences and Humanities: Obirin Ronshu], vol. 29, 2002, pp. 35–53.

江口聡 [Eguchi, Satoshi], 「沈黙のヨハンネスはなぜ眠れないのか: キェルケゴールの『恐れとおののき』における倫理的なものについて」 [Why Can't Johannes de Silentio Sleep? On the Ethical in Kierkegaard's *Fear and Trembling*], 『実践哲学研究』 [Studies of Practical Philosophy], vol. 14, 1991, pp. 1–30.

—「道徳哲学者としてのヨハネス・デ・シレンチオ—『恐れとおののき』と普遍的指令主義」 [Johannes de Silentio as a Moral Philosopher: *Fear and Trembling* and the Universal Prescriptivism], 『キェルケゴール研究』 [Kierkegaard-Studiet], no. 23, 1993, pp. 5–16.

—「『真理は主体性である』再考—キェルケゴール『後書』における逆説と倫理」 ["Truth is Subjectivity" Revisited: Ethics and Paradox in Kierkegaard's *Postscript*], 『実践哲学研究』 [Studies of Practical Philosophy], vol. 19, 1996, pp. 49–65.

—「大衆メディア批判者としてのキェルケゴール」 [Kierkegaard as a Media Critic], 『新キェルケゴール研究』 [Kierkegaard Studies], no. 1, 2001, pp. 82–101

—「キェルケゴールの『鬱』とその対策」 [Kierkegaard's "Depression" and his Philosophical Prescriptions], 『現代社会研究』 [Study of Contemporary Society], no. 15, 2012, pp. 37–54.

遠藤徹 [Endo, Toru], 「キルケゴールにおける無の問題の一考察」 [On the Problem of Nothingness in Kierkegaard], 『実存主義』 [Existentialism], vol. 49, 1969, pp. 66–78.

—「キルケゴールにおける自由の問題」 [The Problem of Freedom in Kierkegaard], 『哲学雑誌』 [The Journal of Philosophy], vol. 84, 1969, pp. 213–33.

—「キルケゴールにおける『精神』の概念」 [Kierkegaard's Concept of "Spirit"], 『山口大学文学会誌』 [Journal of the Literary Society of Yamaguchi University], vol. 22, 1971, pp. 19–33.

—「体系の可能性—キルケゴール、ニーチェを通して」 [The Possibility of System: Kierkegaard and Nietzsche], 『哲学雑誌』 [Tetsugaku-zasshi], vol. 90, 1975, pp. 80–103.

—「実践的真理の構造—キルケゴールの命題『主体性が真理である』に即して」 [Structure of the Practical Truth: On Kierkegaard's Proposition "Subjectivity is the Truth"], 『山口大学文学会誌』 [Journal of the Literary Society of Yamaguchi University], vol. 43, 1992, pp. 20–39; vol. 44, 1993, pp. 1–21.

遠藤利国 [Endo, Toshikuni], 「キェルケゴールにおけるソクラテス像の形成」 [The Formation of Kierkegaard's Image of Socrates], 『国学院雑誌』 [The Journal of Kokugakuin University], vol. 81, 1980, pp. 34–47.

榎田達美 [Enokida, Tatsumi], 「キェルケゴールにおける『主体性』概念」 [The Concept of "Subjectivity" in Kierkegaard], 『キェルケゴール研究』 [Kierkegaard-Studiet], no. 8, 1978, pp. 5–10.

—「教育者としてのキェルケゴール」 [Kierkegaard as Educator], 『キェルケゴール研究』 [Kierkegaard-Studiet], no. 9, 1978, pp. 5–14.

藤枝真 [Fujieda, Shin],「キェルケゴールの教会批判における敬虔主義の意義—シュペーナーとの比較から」[The Meaning of Pietism in Kierkegaard's Criticism of the Church: In Comparison with Spener],『哲学論集』Philosophical Studies], no. 46, 1999, pp. 81–9.

—「生成と存立—キェルケゴールの教会観の二様相」[Becoming and Existence: Two Aspects of Kierkegaard's View of the Church],『大谷大学大学院研究紀要』[Research Report in the Graduate School of Otani University], vol. 17, 2000, pp. 73–92.

—「信仰と理性—キェルケゴールにおける理性の限界と逆説への信仰」[Truth and Reason: The Limit of Reason and Faith in Paradox in Kierkegaard],『倫理学研究』[Annals of Ethical Studies], vol. 31, 2001, pp. 39–49.

—「『知られざるもの』について語ることは可能か—キェルケゴールと宗教の基礎づけ主義」[Is It Possible to Talk about "det Ubekjendte"?—Kierkegaard and Religious Foundationalism],『新キェルケゴール研究』[Kierkegaard Studies], no. 2, 2002, pp. 19–36.

藤井忠 [Fujii, Tadashi],「キェルケゴールを読みながら」[Fragmentary Thoughts on S. Kierkegaard],『横浜経営研究』[Yokohama Buisiness Review], vol. 15, 1994, pp. 170–179.

藤本浄彦 [Fujimoto, Kiyohiko],「S.キェルケゴールにおける"Begriff"の特質—IronieとAngstを契機として」[The Characteristic of "Begriff" in S. Kierkegaard],『人文学論集』[Journal of Humanistic Studies], vol. 9, 1975, pp. 1–15.

—「S.キェルケゴールにおける'Paradox'について１—特に『Philosophische Brocken <哲学的断片>』の問題として」["Paradox" in S. Kierkegaard],『仏教大学研究紀要』[Journal of Bukkyo University], vol. 62, 1978, pp. 62–78.

—「主体性と信仰をめぐる一断片—S.キェルケゴールにおける問題を契機として」[On Subjectivity and Faith],『哲学論集』[Philosophical Studies], vol. 25, 1978, pp. 19–31.

—「S.キェルケゴールにおける『erbaulich<建徳的>』ということについて—法然浄土教への関わりに立って—」[About "the Edifying" in S. Kierkegaard's Thought—in Relation to the Amida Buddhism of Honen],『キェルケゴール研究』[Kierkegaard-Studiet], no. 19, 1989, pp. 5–16.

藤本正高 [Fujimoto, Masataka],「キェルケゴールの教会批判」[Kierkegaard's Criticism of the Church],『日本聖書雑誌』[Japanese Journal for Biblical Studies], vol. 72, 1935, pp. 25–30; vol. 73, 1935, pp. 36–41; vol. 74, 1935, pp. 27–32; vol. 75, 1935, pp. 25–30; vol. 76, 1935, pp. 33–8; vol. 77, 1935, pp. 39–44; vol. 78, 1935, pp. 30–5; vol. 79, 1935, pp. 30–5.

—『キェルケゴールの教会批判』[Kierkegaard's Criticism of the Church], Matsuyama: Dohi-shoten 1937.

藤野寛 [Fujino, Hiroshi],「いかなる意味においてソクラテスをキェルケゴールはたたえるのか」[In what Sense Does Kierkegaard Praise Socrates?],『実践哲学研究』[Studies of Practical Philosophy], vol. 7, 1984, pp. 17–36.

—「ショーペンハウアーの美学とキェルケゴールの実存倫理—一つの『あれか/これか』」[The Aesthetics in Schopenhauer and the Existential Ethics in Kierkegaard],『哲学』[Philosophy], vol. 48, 1997, pp. 247–56.

—「思想の言葉　主観性／客観性をめぐる二つの思考―キルケゴール生誕二〇〇年に寄せて」 [Language of Thoughts: Two Thoughts on Subjectivity/Objectivity: In Celebration of the 200th Anniversary of Kierkegaard's Birth], 『思想』 [*Shiso*], vol. 1069, 2013, pp. 2–6.

藤尾清孝 [Fujio, Kiyotaka], 「キェルケゴールの『沈黙』について」 [On Kierkegaard's "Silence"], 『桃山学院大学キリスト教論集』 [The St. Andrew's University Journal of Christian Studies], vol. 4, 1968, pp. 1–10.

藤城優子 [Fujishiro, Yuko], 「後期西田哲学における神と人間との関係―キルケゴールの思想を手がかりにして」 [The Relationship between God and Humam Beings in Late Nishida Philosophy: Examined with Kierkegaard's Thought Used as a Clue], 『日本大学大学院総合社会情報研究科紀要』 [The Bulletin of the Graduate School of Social and Cultural Studies, Nihon University], vol. 8, 2008, pp. 197–207.

藤田健治 [Fujita, Kenji], 「キェルケゴールのヘーゲル批判」 [Kierkegaard's Criticism of Hegel], 『一橋論叢』 [The Hitotsubashi Review], vol. 30, 1953, pp. 146–68.

藤田正勝 [Fujita, Masakatsu], 「後期シェリングとキルケゴール」 [Schelling and Kierkegaard], 『キェルケゴール研究』 [Kierkegaard-Studiet], no. 24, 1994, pp. 5–14.

藤原猶華 [Fujiwara, Yuka], 「キェルケゴールにおける信仰と倫理」 [Faith and Ethics in Kierkegaard], 『倫理学年報』 [Annals of Ethics], vol. 8, 1959, pp. 89–98.

—「キルケゴールに於ける絶望の概念」 [The Concept of Despair in Kierkegaard], 『名古屋市立大学教養部紀要人文社会研究』 [Bulletin of Nagoya City University], vol. 12, 1967, pp. 1–16.

—「キルケゴールに於ける同時性について」 [On Contemporaneity in Kierkegaard], 『名古屋市立大学教養部紀要人文社会研究』 [Bulletin of Nagoya City University], vol. 13, 1968, pp. 95–106.

—「キルケゴールに於けるヘーゲル」 [Hegel in Kierkegaard], 『名古屋市立大学教養部紀要人文社会研究』 [Bulletin of Nagoya City University], vol. 14, 1970, pp. 227–45.

深井智朗 [Fukai, Tomoaki], 「Vaeren=Christen: セーレン・キェルケゴールのキリスト教理解について」 [Vaeren=Christen: On Søren Kierkegaard's Understanding of Christianity], 『聖学院大学総合研究所紀要』 [Bulletin, Seigakuin University General Research Institute], vol. 12, 1998, pp. 259–86.

福島保夫 [Fukushima, Yasuo], 「ギリシアとキェルケゴール」 [Greece and Kierkegaard], 『実存主義』 [Existentialism], vol. 49, 1969, pp. 2–12.

舟木譲 [Funaki, Jo], 「S. キェルケゴール『死に至る病』の人間理解: キェルケゴールの人間理解に関する一考察」 [An Interpretaion of Human Beings in Søren Kierkegaard's *The Sickness unto Death*], 『外国文化論集』 [Essays on Foreign Studies], vol. 2, 1999, pp. 129–46.

—「S.キェルケゴールの堕罪理解（１）: キェルケゴールの女性理解からのアプローチ」 [An Interpretation on Degeneration in Søren Kierkegaard's Thought (1)], 『言語文化論集』 [Essays on Language and Culture], vol. 1, 2000, pp. 151–62.

布施圭司 [Fuse, Keiji], 「キェルケゴールとヤスパース: 現実の意義をめぐって」 [Kierkegaard and Jaspers: On the Meaning of Reality], 『コムニカチオン』 [Communication], vol. 10, 1999, pp. 211–22.

後藤英樹 [Goto, Hideki], 「信仰の超越性と内在性—『死に至る病』を手掛かりにして—」 [Transcendence and Inwardness of Faith: Following the Path of *Sickness unto Death*], 『新キェルケゴール研究』 [Kierkegaard Studies], no. 11, 2013, pp. 16–33.

後藤平 [Goto, Taira], 「パスカルと実存主義—パスカル、ニーチェ、ケルケゴール」 [Pascal and Existentialism: Pascal, Nietzsche and Kierkegaard], 『理想』 [Riso], vol. 329, 1960.

八谷俊久 [Hachiya, Toshihisa], 「逆説から物語へ—, キェルケゴールにおけるキリスト論的思惟の変貌について」 [From Paradox to History: The Development of Christological Thought in Kierkegaard], 『新キェルケゴール研究』 [Kierkegaard Studies], no. 5, 2007, pp. 1–20.

—「生成する神—『哲学的断片』 (1844年) におけるキェルケゴールの「啓示」概念の構想」 [The Becoming God: Kierkegaard's Understanding of the Revelation in *Philosophical Fragments*], 『新キェルケゴール研究』 [Kierkegaard Studies], no. 6, 2008, pp. 1–21.

—「『まねびの類比 (Analogia Imitationis)』の提唱—キェルケゴールの『キリスト教の修練』 (1850年) におえる『神＝人』の類比 (アナロギア) 」 [Analogia Imitationis: The Possibility of the Analogy of the "God-man" in Kierkegaard's *Practice in Christianity*], 『新キェルケゴール研究』 [Kierkegaard Studies], no. 7, 2009, pp. 37–58.

—「『不安の概念』におけるキェルケゴールの『第二の倫理学』の構想—新しいキリスト教倫理学のためのプロレゴメナ (序説) 」 [Kierkegaard's Plan of "the Second Ethics" in *The Concept of Anxiety*: A Prolegomenon to New Christian Ethics], 『倫理学研究』 [Annals of Ethical Studies], vol. 39, 2009, pp. 91–101.

—「キェルケゴールにおける『真理』概念の構想—新しいキリスト教社会倫理学の基礎付けのために」 [The Concept of Truth in Kierkegaard: Prolegomena to Christian Social Ethics], 『新キェルケゴール研究』 [Kierkegaard Studies], no. 8, 2010, pp. 100–23.

—「『不安の概念』 (1844年) における『デモニスクなもの』の諸相についての社会思想史的な考察—マランツクの『不安』の分析を手掛かりにして—」 [Diagnosis of "the Demonic" in *The Concept of Anxiety*—in Regard to Malantschuk's Analysis of "Anxiety"], 『新キェルケゴール研究』 [Kierkegaard Studies], no. 9, 2011, pp. 54–71.

芳賀檀 [Haga, Mayumi], 「現代の恐怖について (1) : キェルケゴールの場合」 [On the Modern Fear: In the Case of Kierkegaard], 『人文論究』 [Humanities Review], vol. 16, 1965, pp. 11–24.

芳賀直哉 [Haga, Naoya], 「実存的真理認識の問題: キェルケゴールとティリッヒ」 [On the Problem of Existential Knowledge of Truth: Kierkegaard and Tillich], 『文化と哲学』 [Journal of Culture and Philosophy], vol. 1, 1981, pp. 49–67.

浜田恂子 [Hamada, Junko], 「キルケゴールの時間論」 [Kierkegaard's Theory of Time], 『理想』 [Riso], vol. 360, 1963, pp. 21–32.

— 「当為の根拠—キルケゴールとカント」 [The Ground of "Sollen": Kierkegaard and Kant], 『関東学院大学文学部紀要』 [Bulletin of the College of Humanities, Kanto Gakuin University], vol. 34, 1981, pp. 136–50.

— 「キルケゴールの講話にみられる倫理性と現代—『ヤコブの手紙』をめぐって」 [The Ethical Nature and Modernity Seen in Kierkegaard's Discourses], 『関東学院大学文学部紀要』 [Bulletin of the College of Humanities, Kanto Gakuin University], vol. 39, 1983, pp. 108–87.

— 「倫理的概念としての『躓き』—キルケゴール研究の一端として」 ["Offense" as an Ethical Concept], 『関東学院大学文学部紀要』 [Bulletin of the College of Humanities, Kanto Gakuin University], vol. 42, 1984, pp. 228–46.

— 『キルケゴールの倫理思想—行為の問題』 [Kierkegaard's Ethical Thinking: The Problem of Action], Tokyo: Shinchi-shobo 1986.

— 「キルケゴールの『反復』概念」 [Kierkegaard's Concept of "Repetition"], 『関東学院大学文学部紀要』 [Bulletin of the College of Humanities, Kanto Gakuin University], vol. 50, 1987, pp. 377–90.

— 「主体性の真理—キルケゴールの真理概念— 1 —」 [The Subjective Truth: Kierkegaard's Concept of Truth], 『関東学院大学文学部紀要』 [Bulletin of the College of Humanities, Kanto Gakuin University], vol. 58, 1989, pp. 326–44.

— 「ヤスパースのキルケゴール理解」 [Jaspers' Understanding of Kierkegaard], 『関東学院大学人文科学研究所報』 [Transactions of Institute of Humanities], vol. 15, 1991, pp. 138–56.

— 「発端の問い—キルケゴールの『ヨハンネス・クリマクス』断片」 [The Question of the Outset: Kierkegaard's *Johannes Climacus*], 『関東学院大学文学部紀要』 [Bulletin of the College of Humanities, Kanto Gakuin University], vol. 84, 1998, pp. 51–67.

— 『キルケゴール—主体性の真理』 [Kierkegaard: The Truth of Subjectivity], Tokyo: Sobun-sha 1999.

— 『歌舞伎随想—歌右衛門とキルケゴール』 [Essays on Kabuki: Utaemon and Kierkegaard], Tokyo: Michitani 2000.

— 「キルケゴールにおける思索と生の真理」 [The Truth of Thinking and Life in Kierkegaard], 『関東学院大学文学部紀要』 [Bulletin of the College of Humanities, Kanto Gakuin University], vol. 94, 2001, pp. 107–31.

花岡（川村）永子 [Hanaoka-Kawamura, Eiko], 「不安の問題」 [The Problem of Angst in Kierkegaard], 『宗教研究』 [Journal of Religious Studies], vol. 231, 1977, pp. 59–81.

— 「キェルケゴールにおける『単独者』の問題」 [The Problem of "the Individual" in Kierkegaard], 『キェルケゴール研究』 [Kierkegaard-Studiet], no. 7, 1977, pp. 5–10.

— 「キェルケゴールにおける愛の問題」 [The Problem of "Love" in Kierkegaard], 『キェルケゴール研究』 [Kierkegaard-Studiet], no. 8, 1978, pp. 21–30.

— 「キェルケゴールにおける実存弁証法の問題」 [The Problem of Existential Dialectic in Kierkegaard], 『宗教研究』 [Journal of Religious Studies], vol. 244, 1979, pp. 49–77.

— 「キェルケゴールにおける時と歴史の問題」 [The Problem of "Time" and "Geschichte" in Kierkegaard], 『キェルケゴール研究』 [Kierkegaard-Studiet], no. 10, 1980, pp. 29–38.

— 「キェルケゴールにおける自然の問題」 [The Problem of Nature in Kierkegaard], 『ブッディスト』 [Buddhist], vol. 11, 1982, pp. 22–9.

— 「キェルケゴールにおける実存理解の問題」 [The Problem of the Understanding of Existence in Kierkegaard], 『キェルケゴール研究』 [Kierkegaard-Studiet], no. 14, 1984, pp. 5–14.

— 「キェルケゴールにおける『時と永遠』の問題」 [The Problem of "Time and Eternity" in Kierkegaard], 『花園大学研究紀要』 [Bulletin of Hanazono University], vol. 17, 1986, pp. 25–47.

— 「日本のキリスト教とキェルケゴール」 [Christianity in Japan and Kierkegaard], 『日本の神学』 [Theological Studies in Japan], vol. 20, 1988, pp. 183–206.

— 「弁証法神学とキェルケゴール」 [Dialectical Theology and Kierkegaard], 『花園大学研究紀要』 [Bulletin of Hanazono University], vol. 20, 1989, pp. 183–206.

— 「キェルケゴールと西田哲学—死・復活による自由の問題をめぐって」 [Kierkegaard and Nishida's Philosophy: The Problem of Freedom through Death and Resurrection], 『キェルケゴール研究』 [Kierkegaard-Studiet], no. 20, 1990, pp. 19–28.

— 『キェルケゴールの研究—新しい宗教哲学的探求』 [A Study on Kierkegaard: A Pursuit of a New Philosophy], Tokyo: Kindaibungei-sha 1993.

— 「キェルケゴールにおける『自己と世界』の問題」 [The Problem of "Self and World" in Kierkegaard], 『新キェルケゴール研究』 [Kierkegaard Studies], no. 3, 2004, pp. 1–24.

— 「『己事究明』の現象学—ニヒリズムの克服の道」 [The Phenomenology of "Self-discipline": The Road to Self-overcoming of Nihilism], 『新キェルケゴール研究』 [Kierkegaard Studies], no. 8, 2010, pp. 1–23.

— 「宗教への根源的考察」 [An Original Consideration on Religion], 『新キェルケゴール研究』 [Kierkegaard Studies], no. 12, 2014, pp. 31–44.

羽入辰郎 [Hanyu, Tatsuro], 「ソクラテスはなぜ殺されたか？ —キェルケゴール『哲学的断片』を用いて」 [Why was Socrates Killed? With Reference to Kierkegaard's *Philosophical Fragments*], 『青森県立保健大学雑誌』 [Journal of Aomori University of Health and Welfare], vol. 11, 2010, pp. 21–8.

原佑 [Hara, Tasuku], 「ハイデガーとキェルケゴール」 [Heidegger and Kierkegaard], 『東京大学教養学部人文科学科紀要』 [Bulletin of University of Tokyo], vol. 57, 1974, pp. 1–16.

原田博充 [Harada, Hiromitsu], 「キェルケゴールにおける同時性の思想とその意義」 [The Concept of Contemporaneity in S. Kierkegaard and its Significance], 『大阪府立工業高等専門学校研究紀要』 [Bulletin of Osaka Prefecture University College of Technology], vol. 8, 1974, pp. 93–100.

— 「ひとり立つ人格と真の交わり—キルケゴールの『単独者』の思想を媒介として」 [The Individual Personality and True Communication], 『基督教学研究』 [Journal of Christian Studies], vol. 20, 2000 pp. 89–111.

原田信夫 [Harada, Nobuo]，「キエルケゴール Leben und Walten der Liebe に於ける愛に就いて」[Love in Kierkegaard's *Works of Love*]，『基督教研究』 [Studies in Christian Religion], vol. 13, 1936, pp. 257–66.

—「キエルケゴール Christliche Reden に現はれた辯證法について」[Dialectics in Kierkegaard's *Christian Discourses*]，『基督教研究』 [Studies in Christian Religion], vol. 14, 1936, pp. 29–35.

—「キエルケゴールの『瞬間』概念について」[The Conception of the "Moment" in Kierkegaard]，『基督教研究』 [Studies in Christian Religion], vol. 14, 1937, pp. 280–97.

—「辯證法的契機としての『躓き』の可能 —キエルケゴール研究4—」 [Kierkegaard's Conception of "Offense"]，『基督教研究』 [Studies in Christian Religion], vol. 15, 1938, pp. 289–98.

—「キエルケゴールに於けるExistierenについて」[The Conception of "Existence" in Kierkegaard]，『基督教研究』 [Studies in Christian Religion], vol. 16, 1939, pp. 253–64.

—「ケルケゴールに於けるEntweder-Oderの概念について」 [The Idea of "Either/Or" in S. Kierkegaard]，『基督教研究』 [Studies in Christian Religion], vol. 17, 1940, pp. 280–290.

—『ケルケゴールの基督教思想』 [Kierkegaard's Christian Thought], Tokyo: Shinsei-do 1937.

春名純人 [Haruna, Sumito]，「倫理と宗教—カントとキルケゴール」 [Ethics and Religion: Kant and Kierkegaard]，『関西学院大学社会学部紀要』 [Kwansei Gakuin Sociology Department Studies], vol. 15, 1967, pp. 73–83.

長谷修孝 [Hase, Nobuyuki]，「キルケゴールと懐疑」 [Kierkegaard and Skepticism]，『法政大学教養部紀要』 [Bulletin of Hosei University], vol. 96, 1996, pp. 67–85.

—「キルケゴールの様相概念について」 [On the Modal Concepts in Kierkegaard]，『法政大学教養部紀要』 [Bulletin of Hosei University], vol. 104, 1998, pp. 125–38.

長谷川宏 [Hasegawa, Hiroshi]，「単独者の内面と外界—キルケゴール『死にいたる病』」 [The Inside and Outside of the Single Individual: Kierkegaard's *The Sickness unto Death*]，『文芸』 [The Bungei Quarterly], vol. 24, 1985, pp. 136–62.

—『格闘する理性—ヘーゲル、ニーチェ、キルケゴール』 [Struggling Reason: Hegel, Nietzsche and Kierkegaard], Tokyo: Kawadeshobo-shinsha 1987 (2nd ed., Tokyo: Yosen-sha 2008).

橋本淳 [Hashimoto, Jun]，「キェルケゴールにおける苦悩について—その一・『後書』の『宗教的苦悩』—」 [On Kierkegaard's Understanding of Suffering 1— the Religious Suffering in the *Postscript*]，『キェルケゴール研究』 [Kierkegaard-Studiet], no. 1, 1964, pp. 34–42.

—「キェルケゴールによる苦悩の理解について—その二・受難のイエス像における『苦しみ』—」 [On Kierkegaard's Understanding of Suffering 2—the Sufferings of Christ]，『キェルケゴール研究』 [Kierkegaard-Studiet], vol. 2, 1965, pp. 5–15.

—「キェルケゴールによる苦悩について—その三・キリスト者と苦しみ—」 [On Kierkegaard's Understanding of Suffering 3—Christians and their

Sufferings], 『キェルケゴール研究』 [Kierkegaard-Studiet], no. 4, 1967, pp. 5–19.

——「キェルケゴールのキリスト教理解と『真理の証人』—教会闘争の一研究」 [Kierkegaard's Understanding of Christianity and "Witness to the Truth"], 『四国学院大学論集』 [Shikoku Christian College Treatises], vol. 15, 1969, pp. 23–44.

——「セーレン・キェルケゴールの葬り—H. ルンの事件をめぐって」 [The Funeral of Søren Kierkegaard], 『四国学院大学論集』 [Shikoku Christian College Treatises], vol. 21, 1971, pp. 1–20.

——「北欧におけるキェルケゴール研究の現況と問題—今後のキェルケゴール研究の方法を模索して」 [The Current Situation and Problems of Kierkegaard Studies in Northern Europe], 『四国学院大学論集』 [Shikoku Christian College Treatises], vol. 23, 1972, pp. 1–21.

——「『責めがあるのか?』—セーレン・キェルケゴールにおける『苦悩』の1章」 ["Guilty?": One Chapter of "Suffering" in Søren Kierkegaard], 『四国学院大学論集』 [Shikoku Christian College Treatises], vol. 28, 1973, pp. 69–86.

——「『真理の証人』—セーレン・キェルケゴールのキリスト教理解と教会闘争に関する一研究」 ["The Witness to the Truth": A Study on Kierkegaard's Understanding of Christianity and Church Struggle], 『四国学院大学論集』 [Shikoku Christian College Treatises], vol. 26, 1973, pp. 33–72; vol. 27, 1973, pp. 74–94.

——「日本におけるキェルケゴール研究」 [Kierkegaard Studies in Japan], 『四国学院大学論集』 [Shikoku Christian College Treatises], vol. 31, 1974, pp. 17–34.

——「晩年のセーレン・キェルケゴール—H.P. ハンセンの『スケッチ』をめぐって」 [Kierkegaard in his Late Years], 『四国学院大学論集』 [Shikoku Christian College Treatises], vol. 30, 1974, pp. 91–109.

——「キェルケゴールの建徳的著作について1」 [On Kierkegaard's Upbuilding Works, 1], 『四国学院大学論集』 [Shikoku Christian College Treatises], vol. 33, 1976, pp. 49–66.

——『キェルケゴールにおける「苦悩」の世界』 ["Suffering" in Søren Kierkegaard's Life and Authorship], Tokyo: Mirai-sha 1976.

——『逍遥する哲学者—キェルケゴール紀行』 [The Wandering Philosopher: Kierkegaard's Life and Authorship], Tokyo: Shinkyo-shuppansha 1979.

——「殉教のキリスト教—『認容』の問題をめぐって」 [Christianity as Martyrdom], 『理想』 [Riso], vol. 555, 1979, pp. 50–61.

——「キェルケゴールの著作活動と<ソクラテス的な助産術>」 [The Maieutic Method Employed in Søren Kierkegaard], 『神學研究』 [Theological Studies], vol. 27, 1979, pp. 67–85.

——「キェルケゴール『畏れとおののき』における『罪』の問題」 [On the Problem of Sin in Søren Kierkegaard's *Fear and Trembling*], 『キェルケゴール研究』 [Kierkegaard-Studiet], no. 10, 1980, pp. 5–16.

——「日本におけるキェルケゴール: (1) 吉満義彦の場合」 [Kierkegaard in Japan: (I) Prof. Yoshihiko Yoshimitsu (1904–1945). The Influence of S. Kierkegaard on his Life and Thought], 『神學研究』 [Theological Studies], vol. 29, 1981, pp. 77–98.

—「キェルケゴール『死に至る病』の研究」 [A Study of Søren Kierkegaard's *The Sickness unto Death*], 『神學研究』 [Theological Studies], vol. 34, 1986, pp. 45–63; vol. 36, 1989, pp. 55–72; vol. 37, 1990, pp. 193–210.

—『憂愁と愛』 [Melancholy and the Unhappy Love], Kyoto: Jinbun-shoin 1985.

—「日本におけるキェルケゴール—全体の展望と課題」 [Kierkegaard in Japan: Perspectives and Tasks], 『日本の神学』 [Theological Studies in Japan], vol. 27, 1988, pp. 9–24.

—「日本のキリスト教会とキェルケゴール」 [Christian Churches in Japan and Kierkegaard], 『神学研究』 [Theological Studies], special volume, 2003, pp. 85–98.

—「自然と人間—キェルケゴールにおける自然観」 [Søren Kierkegaard and his View of Nature], 『神学研究』 [Theological Studies], vol. 51, 2004, pp. 97–106.

—「若き日のセーレン・キェルケゴール—肖像画の物語」 [Søren Kierkegaard in his Youth: A Story of a Portrait], 『時計台』 [Tokeidai], vol. 83, 2013, pp. 12–16.

—「セーレン・キェルケゴール生誕200年記念日本人はキェルケゴールをどのように読んだのか ： 和辻哲郎と田辺元を中心に ：西洋精神の一つの受容」 [The 200th Anniversary of Kierkegaard's Birth: How Did the Japanese Read Kierkegaard?], 『キリスト教文化学会年報』 [Annals of the Association of Christian Culture], vol. 60, 2014, pp. 1–18.

—『セーレン・キェルケゴール　北シェランの旅』 [Søren Kierkegaard's Travel to North Zealand], Osaka: Sogen-sha 2014.

橋本鑑 [Hashimoto, Kagami], 「証人としてのスェレン＝キェルケグヌル」 [Kierkegaard as a Witness], 『復活』 [The Resurrection], vol. 1, no. 2, 1935, pp. 8–15; vol. 1, no. 3, 1935, pp. 7–15; vol. 1, no. 5, 1935, pp. 14–22.

—「スェレン＝キェルケグヌルにおける証人の意義」 [The Meaning of Witness in Kierkegaard], 『復活』 [The Resurrection], vol. 1, no. 7, 1935, pp. 7–15; vol. 1, no. 9, 1935, pp. 7–15.

服部佐和子 [Hattori, Sawako], 「個と類との間の一考察—キェルケゴール『不安の概念』を中心に」 [Consideration of the Individual and the Race: From Kierkegaard's *The Concept of Anxiety*], 『メタフュシカ』 [Metaphysica], vol. 41, 2010, pp. 49–62.

葉山万次郎 [Hayama, Manjiro], 「キールケゴールドの耶蘇教観」 [Kierkegaard's View of Christianity], 『帝國文学』 [Japanese Literature], vol. 13, no. 11, 1907, pp. 13–22.

—「キールケゴールドの人格」 [Kierkegaard's Personality], 『東亜之光』 [Light from Eastern Asia], vol. 3, no. 1, 1908, pp. 177–82.

林忠良 [Hayashi, Tadayoshi], 「キルケゴールにおける教育の問題」 [The Problem of Education in the Thought of S. Kierkegaard], 『神學研究』 [Theological Studies], vol. 20, 1972, pp. 97–134.

—「キルケゴールの教育思想」 [Kierkegaard's Educational Thought], 『キリスト教主義教育：キリスト教主義教育研究室年報』 [Journal of Christian Education], special edition, 1975, pp. 17–32.

—「キェルケゴールのヨブ論」 [Kierkegaard's Interpretation of Job], 『キェルケゴール研究』 [Kierkegaard-Studiet], no. 12, 1982, pp. 5–14.

— 「『反復』における試錬の範疇—『キルケゴールのヨブ論』補論１」
[The Category of Trial in *Repetition*], 『キリスト教学研究』 [Ronko. K.G.
Studies in Christianity], vol. 8, 1984, pp. 29–48.

— 「キルケゴールのルターへの言及—１—」 [Kierkegaard's References to
Luther (1)], 『キリスト教学研究』 [Ronko. K.G. Studies in Christianity],
vol. 11, 1990, pp. 53–98.

— 「ヨハネス・クリマクス遺稿をめぐって（一）」 [On the Nachlass "Johannes
Climacus or De omnibus dubitandum est" (1)], 『キェルケゴール研究』
[Kierkegaard-Studiet], no. 21, 1991, pp. 5–14.

— 「キルケゴールにおける死の問題—１—」 [The Problem of Death in
Kierkegaard] 『キリスト教学研究』 [Ronko. K.G. Studies in Christianity],
vol. 12, 1992, pp. 73–90.

— 「キルケゴールにおける<論理的問題>」 [The Logical Problem in
Kierkegaard], 『基督教学研究』 [Journal of Christian Studies], vol. 14, 1993,
pp. 1–38.

— 「キルケゴールのヨブ記解釈をめぐって—H.P.　ミュラーの所論にふれ
て」 [Kierkegaard's Interpretation of the Book of Job], 『キリスト教学研究』
[Ronko. K.G. Studies in Christianity], vol. 15, 1995, pp. 104–32.

— 「キルケゴールにおける"Confinium"の問題」 [The Problem of "Confinium"
in Kierkegaard], 『基督教学研究』 [Journal of Christian Studies], vol. 23,
2003, pp. 1–24.

— 「著作『反復』の成立—キルケゴールの<反復>の思想序説」 [The Forma-
tion of *Repetition*], 『基督教学研究』 [Journal of Christian Studies], vol. 27,
2007, pp. 21–53.

東専一郎 [Higashi, Senichiro], 「キェルケゴールに於ける信仰と倫理」
[Faith and Ethics in Kierkegaard], 『哲学研究』 [The Journal of Philosophical
Studies], vol. 36, 1953, pp. 488–518.

— 「宗教的死と宗教的時間—ハイデッガー・キェルケゴール・道元」
[Religious Death and Time: Heidegger, Kierkegaard and Dogen], 『理想』
[Riso], vol. 443, 1970, pp. 17–28 (part 1); 『関西大学哲学』 [Kansai University
Philosophy], vol. 2, 1971, pp. 48–68 (part 2).

— 「西田哲学とキェルケゴール—『行為的直観』の問題をめぐって—」
[The Philosophy of Nishida and Kierkegaard—on the Problem of "Active Intuition"],
『キェルケゴール研究』 [Kierkegaard-Studiet], no. 10, 1980, pp. 17–28.

平林孝裕 [Hirabayashi, Takahiro], 「ヘーゲルの『美学講義』とキルケゴール:
『あれかこれか』における「悲劇論」を中心として」 [Hegel's *Lectures
on Aesthetics* and Kierkegaard], 『哲学・思想論叢』 [Miscellanea Philosoph-
ica], vol. 6, 1988, pp. 101–12.

— 「キルケゴールのトレンデレンブルクに対する関係: ヘーゲル哲学批判
の視座から」 [Kierkegaard's Relations to Trendelenburg], 『哲学・思想論叢』
[Miscellanea Philosophica], vol. 9, 1991, pp. 41–53.

— 「キルケゴールにおける反復の問題」 [The Problem of Repetition in
Kierkegaard], 『宗教研究』 [Journal of Religious Studies], vol. 68, 1994,
pp. 285–308.

——「信仰と倫理: キェルケゴール『おそれとおののき』再読」 [Faith and Ethics: Kierkegaard's *Fear and Trembling* Reread], 『神學研究』 [Theological Studies], vol. 46, 1999, pp. 23–43.

——「セーレン・キェルケゴールの新版全集（刊行著作部門）の特徴とその意義: 『不安の概念』からの実例を通じて照明した」 [On the Characters and Significance of the New Textual-Critical Edition of Søren Kierkegaard Writings (Published Works), with some Examples from *The Concept of Anxiety*], 『神學研究』 [Theological Studies], vol. 47, 2000, pp. 83–105.

——「S. キェルケゴールの心理学的方法—心理学的実験をめぐって」 [The Psychological Method of S. Kierkegaard – About his Psychological Experiment], 『神学研究』 [Theological Studies], vol. 50, 2003, pp. 105–17.

——「セーレン・キェルケゴールにおける≪心理学的実験≫の構成とその方法論的意義」 [The Structure of Søren Kierkegaard's "Psychological Experiment" and its Methodological Meanings], 『神学研究』 [Theological Studies], vol. 51, 2004, pp. 107–15.

——「セーレン・キルケゴールにおける≪心理学≫の問題—一つの歴史的研究」 [The Problem of "Psychology" in Søren Kierkegaard: A Historical Study], 『理想』 [Riso], vol. 676, 2006, pp. 37–56.

——「セーレン・キルケゴールとデンマーク中世」 [On Søren Kierkegaard's View of the Middle Ages in Denmark], 『神学研究』 [Theological Studies], vol. 55, 2008, pp. 49–62.

平松義郎 [Hiramatsu, Yoshiro], 「現代を救ふもの—キエルケゴール復興—」 [Saving the Present Age], 龍南 [Ryunan], vol. 254, 1944, pp. 10–20.

弘瀬潔 [Hirose, Kiyoshi], 『キェルケゴールの実存哲学』 [Kierkegaard's Existential Philosophy], Tokyo: Heibon-sha 1949.

——「『デモーニッシュなるもの』について」 [On "the Demonic"], 『理想』 [Riso], vol. 269, 1955.

久野晋良 [Hisano, Shinryo], 「S. キルケゴール『死にいたる病』における精神の問題」 [On the Problem of Spirit in Kierkegaard's *The Sickness unto Death*], 『大阪経大論集』 [Journal of Osaka University of Economics], vol. 172, 1986, pp. 347–66.

北条照由 [Hojo, Teruyoshi], 「キルケゴールにおける『悟性』と『絶対的逆説』について」 ["Understanding" and "Absolute Paradox" in Kierkegaard], 『白山哲学』 [Hakusan-tetsugaku], vol. 13, 1979, pp. 125–38.

本多謙三 [Honda, Kenzo], 「審美的と実存的」 [The Aesthetical and the Existential], 『一橋文芸』 [Ikkio bungei], vol. 1, 1933, pp. 120–91.

本田誠也 [Honda, Masaya], 「他者への言葉—キェルケゴールの言語思想」 [Words for Others: Kierkegaard's Thoughts on Language], 『倫理学研究』 [Annals of Ethical Studies], vol. 30, 2000, pp. 45–56.

——「信仰における隣人の他性—レヴィナスによるキェルケゴールの宗教性批判に応えて」 [The Otherness of the Neighbor in Kierkegaardian Faith: Response to Levinas' Criticism of Kierkegaard's Religiousness], 『新キェルケゴール研究』 [Kierkegaard Studies], no. 2, 2002, pp. 37–58.

— 「時間性の獲得—キェルケゴールの信仰におけるエロスとアガペーの関係」 [Agape and Eros in Kierkegaard's Faith], 『新キェルケゴール研究』 [Kierkegaard Studies], no. 3, 2004, pp. 82–101.

堀剛 [Hori, Tsuyoshi], 「ヴィトゲンシュタインとキェルケゴールにおける神及び伝達の理解の類似性」 [The Resemblance of the Understandings of God and Communication between Wittgenstein and Kierkegaard], 『四国学院大学論集』 [Shikoku Christian College Treatises], vol. 92, 1996, pp. 1–24.

堀岡弥寿子 [Horioka, Yasuko], 「キェルケゴールの思想における主体性」 [Subjectivity in the Thought of Søren Kierkegaard], 『キェルケゴール研究』 [Kierkegaard-Studiet], vol. 2, 1965, pp. 16–24.

細羽嘉子 [Hosoba, Yoshiko], 「キェルケゴールにみる反省の二重性」 [Duplicity of Reflection in Kierkegaard], 『哲学』 [Philosophy], no. 52, 2000, pp. 51–60.

— 「キェルケゴールの女優論—『危機』についての考察」 [Kierkegaard's Argument about Actresses: Through *The Crisis and a Crisis in the Life of an Actress*], 『哲学』 [Philosophy], vol. 55, 2003, pp. 57–68.

— 「和辻哲郎のキェルケゴール理解—1910年代の和辻の著作をてがかりに」 [Watsuji Tetsuro and Kierkegaard], 『新キェルケゴール研究』 [Kierkegaard Studies], no. 3, 2004, pp. 159–75.

細谷昌志 [Hosoya, Masashi], 「キェルケゴールにおける『直接性』の問題とカントの『物自体』—キェルケゴールの存在論への試み—」 [The Problem of "the Immediacy" in Kierkegaard and Kant's "Ding an sich": An Essay on Kierkegaard's Ontology], 『キェルケゴール研究』 [Kierkegaard-Studiet], no. 8, 1978, pp. 11–20.

— 「『逆対応』の論理と『逆超越』—キェルケゴールの『死にいたる病』をめぐって」 ["Inverse Transcendence" and the Logic of "Inverse Correspondence": In the Light of Kierkegaard's *The Sickness unto Death*], 『親鸞教学』 [The Otani Journal of Shin Buddhism], vol. 94, 2009, pp. 60–78.

市沢正則 [Ichizawa, Masanori], 「キェルケゴールにおける殉教の意義」 [The Meaning of Martyrdom in Kierkegaard], 『清泉女学院短期大学研究紀要』 [Bulletin of Seisenjogakuin Junior College], vol. 20, 2001, pp. 49–69.

— 「絶対服従による至福への道—キェルケゴール的思考」 [A Way to Supreme Bliss through the Absolute Obedience: Kierkegaard's Way of Thinking], 『清泉女学院短期大学研究紀要』 [Bulletin of Seisenjogakuin Junior College], vol. 21, 2002, pp. 1–27.

飯島宗享 [Iijima, Munetaka], 「キェルケゴール『死に至る病』」 [Kierkegaard's *The Sickness unto Death*], 『基督教文化』 [Christian Culture], vol. 40, 1949, pp. 29–37.

— 「キェルケゴールに於けるロマンティシズムの問題」 [The Problem of Romanticism in Kierkegaard], 『理想』 [Riso], vol. 198, 1949, pp. 66–75.

— 「キェルケゴールにおけるキリスト教と教会について」 [Christianity and Church in Kierkegaard], 『理想』 [Riso], vol. 269, 1955.

— 「キェルケゴールの保守性 1」 [Kierkegaard's Conservatism (1)], 『東洋大学紀要文学部篇』 [Bulletin of Toyo University], vol. 15, 1961.

— 『キェルケゴール』 [Kierkegaard], Tokyo: Heibon-sha 1976 (*Series of the World's Thinkers*, vol. 15) (2nd ed., Tokyo: Michitani 2012).

池島重信 [Ikejima, Shigenobu], 「キェルケゴールの人間学」 [Kierkegaard's Anthropology], 『浪漫古典』 [Roman Classics], vol. 7, 1934, pp. 83–9.

—「キェルケゴールと今日の文学の問題」 [Kierkegaard and the Problem of the Literature Today], 『文藝』 [Literature], vol. 2, no. 12, 1934, pp. 135–9.

—「ニイチェとキェルケゴール」 [Nietzsche and Kierkegaard], 『理想』 [Riso], vol. 62, 1935, pp. 88–100.

今井尚生 [Imai, Naoki], 「キルケゴールの処方箋―可能性の不安に対峙する思索の試み」 [Kierkegaard's Prescription: An Attempt to Face the Anxiety of Possibility], 『同志社大学ヒューマン・セキュリティ研究センター年報』 [Annual Report : Doshisha Research Center for Human Security], vol. 3, 2006, pp. 35–50.

稲葉稔 [Inaba, Minoru], 「キエルケゴール『不安の概念』の『序論』について」 [On "the Preface" of *The Concept of Anxiety*], 『大阪工業大学紀要人文社会篇』 [Memoirs of the Osaka Institute of Technology. Series B, Liberal Arts], vol. 13, 1969, pp. 23–46.

稲村秀一 [Inamura, Shuichi], 「キルケゴールの人間学」 [Kierkegaard's Anthropology], 『岡山大学文学部紀要』 [Journal of the Faculty of Letters, Okayama University], vol. 6, 1985, pp. 37–55; vol. 7, 1986, pp. 17–33; vol. 11, 1989, pp. 27–46; vol. 12, 1989, pp. 17–35; vol. 14, 1990, pp. 29–42; vol. 16, 1991, pp. 11–36; vol. 17, 1992, pp. 43–62; vol. 18, 1992, pp. 25–37; vol. 22, 1994, pp. 1–20; vol. 23, 1995, pp. 1–17; vol. 24, 1995, pp. 1–18; vol. 25, 1996, pp. 1–17; vol. 26, 1996, pp. 1–22; vol. 27, 1997, pp. 1–13.

—「キルケゴールにおける宗教的実存の二形態」 [Two Forms of Religious Existence in Kierkegaard], 『岡山大学文学部紀要』 [Journal of the Faculty of Letters, Okayama University], vol. 33, 2000, pp. 1–15; vol. 34, 2000, pp. 19–34.

稲山聖修 [Inayama, Kiyonobu], 「拡大し続ける単独者の交わり: 『不安の概念』におけるキルケゴールの罪理解の一考察」 [Expanding Communion of the Single Individual: A Study on Kierkegaard's Thoughts on Sin in *The Concept of Anxiety*], 『基督教研究』 [Studies in the Christian Religion], vol. 57, 1995, pp. 56–83.

石居正己 [Ishii, Masami], 「ルターとキェルケゴール」 [Luther and Kierkegaard], 『テオロギア・ディアコニア』 [Teologia Diakonia], vol. 26, 1992, pp. 1–23.

石井誠士 [Ishii, Seishi], 「宗教的死と愛―キェルケゴールを通して」 [Religious Death and Love], 『哲学研究』 [The Journal of Philosophical Studies], vol. 45, 1972, pp. 53–84; vol. 45, 1973, pp. 35–61; vol. 45, 1974, pp. 33–59.

石津照璽 [Ishizu, Teruji], 「ヘーゲルとキェルケゴールの対比」 [Hegel and Kierkegaard in Comparison], 『理想』 [Riso], vol. 20, 1930, pp. 101–9.

—「宗教的実存の実存的課題―キェルケゴール諸著作の位置と意義」 [The Existential Tasks of the Religious Existence], 『哲学研究』 [The Journal of Philosophical Studies], vol. 33, 1950, pp. 1–24; vol. 34, 1950, pp. 1–30.

—「憂鬱の哲学―キェルケゴールにおける現代的意義」 [The Philosophy of Melancholy], 『改造』 [Kaizo], vol. 31, 1950, pp. 50–7.

—「北欧のキルケゴール研究その他」 [Kierkegaard Studies in North Europe], 『理想』 [Riso], vol. 269, 1955.

— 「キェルケゴール思想の基盤」 [The Foundation of Kierkegaard's Thought], 『文化』 [Culture], vol. 19, 1955.

— 「キェルケゴールに於ける『宗教的著者』と伝達の問題」 [The Problems of "the Religious Author" and Communication in Kierkegaard], 『宗教研究』 [Journal of Religious Studies], vol. 148, 1957.

— 「宗教の根拠に関する研究—キュルケゴールとハイデッガーの所論の吟味に沿って」 [A Study on the Ground of Religion: Kierkegaard and Heidegger], 『東北大学文学部研究年報』 [The Annual Reports of the Faculty of Arts and Letters, Tohoku University], vol. 8, 1958.

— 「天理図書館蔵キェルケゴール全著作の初版本」 [The First Edition of Kierkegaard's Works in Tenri University Library], 『ビブリア天理図書館報』 [Bulletin of Tenri Central Library], vol. 23, 1962; vol. 24, 1963.

— 『キェルケゴール研究』 [A Study of Kierkegaard], Tokyo: Sobun-sha 1974.

— 『宗教的人間』 [A Religious Person], Tokyo: Sobun-sha 1980 (Studies of the Philosophy of Religion, vol. 5).

伊藤源一郎 [Ito, Genichiro], 「キェルケゴールのソクラテス的なるものにおける実存哲学概念」 [The Concept of Existential Philosophy in the Socratic according to Kierkegaard], 『哲学論集』 [Philosophical Studies], vol. 2, 1935, pp. 138–82.

— 「単独者と我と汝—ブーバーのキェルケゴール論について—」 [The Single Individual and I and Thou: On Buber's Understanding of Kierkegaard], 『キェルケゴール研究』 [Kierkegaard-Studiet], no. 1, 1964, pp. 43–56.

伊藤潔志 [Ito, Kiyoshi], 「キェルケゴールにおける『単独者』の自由」 [Freedom of "the Single Individual" in Kierkegaard], 『教育思想』 [The Journal of Educational Theories], vol. 26, 1999, pp. 15–24.

— 「自己生成へと導く教育方法としての間接伝達（１）キェルケゴールにおける『実存の三段階』説の構造」 [Indirect Communication as an Educational Means to Lead People to Self-becoming], 『教育思想』 [The Journal of Educational Theories], vol. 27, 2000, pp. 63–76.

— 「キェルケゴールにおける義務と良心—カントとの比較を手がかりとして」 [Duty and Conscience in Kierkegaard – Compared with Kant], 『教育思想』 [The Journal of Educational Theories], vol. 28, 2001, pp. 17–30.

— 「キェルケゴールにおける教育関係の原理と構造」 [The Principle and Structure of the Educational Relationship in Kierkegaard], 『東北大学大学院教育学研究科研究年報』 [Annals of the Graduate School of Pedagogy], vol. 50, 2002, pp. 15–30.

— 「キェルケゴールにおける絶望の教育学的考察」 [Pedagogical Study of Despair in the Thought of S. Kierkegaard], 『新キェルケゴール研究』 [Kierkegaard Studies], no. 3, 2004, pp. 142–58.

— 「キェルケゴールにおけるユーモアの教育学的考察」 [Pedagogical Study of Humor in the Thought of S. Kierkegaard], 『理想』 [Riso], vol. 676, 2006, pp. 57–66.

— 「キェルケゴールにおける自然の教育学的考察」 [Pedagogical Study of Nature in the Thought of S. Kierkegaard], 『新キェルケゴール研究』 [Kierkegaard Studies], no. 5, 2007, pp. 21–39.

—「キルケゴールにおけるフモール概念の成立—キルケゴールの中のハーマン」 [Formation of the Concept of "Humor" in Kierkegaard: Hamann in Kierkegaard], 『教育思想』 [The Journal of Educational Theories], vol. 35, 2008, pp. 39–50.

—「キルケゴールにおけるイロニーの教育学的考察」 [Pedagogical Study of Irony in the Thought of S. Kierkegaard], 『山陽学園短期大学紀要』 [Bulletin of Sanyogakuen-College], vol. 40, 2009, pp. 17–32.

—「キルケゴールにおける人間存在と教育」 [Human Being and Education in the Thought of Kierkegaard], 『山陽学園短期大学紀要』 [Bulletin of Sanyogakuen-College], vol. 42, 2011, pp. 17–28.

—「キルケゴールにおける実存伝達の教育」 [Education as Existential Communication in the Thought of S. Kierkegaard], 『山陽学園短期大学紀要』 [Bulletin of Sanyogakuen-College], no. 43, 2012, pp. 8–15.

—「キェルケゴールにおける歴史の教育学的考察」 [Pedagogical Study of History in the Thought of S. Kierkegaard], 『新キェルケゴール研究』 [Kierkegaard Studies], no. 11, 2013, pp. 1–15.

伊藤幸子 [Ito, Sachiko], 「瞬間と同時性（２）—キルケゴールの瞬間」 [The Moment and Contemporaneity (2): The Moment in Kierkegaard], 『一般教育総合センター紀要』 [Kitasato Journal of Liberal Arts and Sciences], no. 2, 1997, pp. 161–75.

伊藤之雄 [Ito, Yukio], 「キルケゴールと聖書—現代神学との関連で」 [Kierkegaard and the Bible], 『実存主義』 [Existentialism], vol. 49, 1969, pp. 13–22.

—「詩と弁証法: キルケゴールの『美』の概念をめぐって」 [Poetry and Dialectics: The Role of the Beautiful in the Faith of Kierkegaard], 『論集』 [Ronshu], vol. 9, 1970, pp. 2–15.

—「キルケゴールの信仰: 試論」 [The Faith of Kierkegaard], 『研究紀要』 [The Studies], vol. 12, 1973, pp. 3–10.

—「ヘーゲル宗教哲学の問題点: ヘーゲルからキルケゴールへ」 [Problems of Hegelian Philosophy of Religion], 『研究紀要』 [The Studies], vol. 15, 1976, pp. 3–13.

—「キルケゴールの信仰: その罪概念をめぐって」 [The Faith of Kierkegaard: His Conception of Sin], 『研究紀要』 [The Studies], vol. 16, 1977, pp. 3–9.

岩佐満雄 [Iwasa, Mitsuo], 「キェルケゴールの『畏れとおののき』におけるディレンマの問題」 [On the Problem of Dilemma in Kierkegaard's *Fear and Trembling*], 『公民論集』 [Komin Ronshu], vol. 6, 1998, pp. 33–55.

岩田靖夫 [Iwata, Yasuo], 『神なき時代の神—キルケゴールとレヴィナス』 [God in an Age Devoid of God: Kierkegaard and Levinas], Tokyo: Iwanami-shoten 2001.

泉治典 [Izumi, Harunori], 「中世における条然性の概念とキルケゴール」 [The Concept of Contingency in the Middle Ages and Kierkegaard], 『実存主義』 [Existentialisim], vol. 49, 1969, pp. 23–31.

神保全孝 [Jinbo, Zenko], 「キルケゴールにおける自条—可能的考察１—」 [The Concept of Freedom in Kierkegaard], 『芦屋大学論叢』 [Ashiyadaigaku-ronso], vol. 8, 1981, pp. 85–130.

— 「S・キェルケゴールに於ける自由: 其の可能的考察（其の二）」 [The Concept of Freedom in the Case of the Father-Son Relation of Kierkegaard], 『姫路獨協大学一般教育部紀要』 [Bulletin, College of Liberal Arts, Himeji Dokkyo University], vol. 1, 1990, pp. 37–46.

甲斐友朗 [Kai, Tomoaki], 「キェルケゴールにおける自由の問題」 [On the Problem of Freedom in Kierkegaard], 『同志社哲学年報』 [Societas Philosophiae Doshisha], vol. 32, 2009, pp. 35–41.

— 「キェルケゴールにおけるキリストの倣いと隣人愛の関係」 [The Relationship between the Imitation of Christ and Neighbor-Love in Kierkegaard], 『新キェルケゴール研究』 [Kierkegaard Studies], no. 9, 2011, pp. 20–40.

掛川典子 [Kakegawa, Noriko], 「近代家族と女性像、その女性史的考察に向けて: （1）キェルケゴールの結婚観」 [Women's Image and the Modern Family: From the Perspective of Women's History: (1) Kierkegaard's View of Marriage], 『昭和女子大学女性文化研究所紀要』 [Bulletin of the Institute of Women's Culture, Showa Women's University], vol. 8, 1991, pp. 17–31.

鎌数学 [Kamakazu, Manabu], 「キェルケゴールと親鸞」 [Kierkegaard and Shinran], 『キェルケゴール研究』 [Kierkegaard-Studiet], no. 21, 1991, pp. 15–24.

上村和宏 [Kamimura, Kazuhiro], 「キェルケゴールにおける倫理と逆説」 [Kierkegaard's Ethics and Paradox], 『哲学倫理学研究』 [Studies on Philosophy and Ethics], vol. 5, 2001, pp. 21–37.

金子淳人 [Kaneko, Atsuhito], 「キェルケゴールとレヴィナス―,他者論としての実存思想」 [Kierkegaard and Levinas: The Existential Thought as the Theory of the Other], 『哲学世界』 [World of Philosophy], vol. 26, 2003, pp. 21–38.

金子筑水 [Kaneko, Chikusui], 「キヤーケゴールドの人生観」 [Kierkegaard's View of Life], 『早稲田文学』 [Waseda Literature], vol. 3, no. 9, 1906, pp. 113–49.

金子武蔵 [Kaneko, Takezo], 「ケルケゴールと現代思想」 [Kierkegaard and Modern Thought], 『心』 [Kokoro], vol. 9, 1956.

— 『キェルケゴールからサルトルへ―実存思想の歩み』 [From Kierkegaard to Sartre: The Development of Existential Thought], Tokyo: Shimizu-kobundo 1967.

金子琢磨 [Kaneko, Takuma], 「キルケゴールとカフカ―婚約をめぐって―」 [Kierkegaard and Kafka on Engagement], 『思想と文化』 [Thoughts and Culture], 1986, pp. 371–83.

柏原 啓一 [Kashiwabara, Keiichi], 「キルケゴールとシェリング―可能性から現実性への移行の問題」 [Kierkegaard and Schelling: The Problem of the Transition from Possibility to Reality], 『理想』 [Riso], vol. 360, 1963, pp. 11–20.

— 「キルケゴールに於ける可能性の問題―ハイデガーを手掛りにして」 [The Problem of Possibility in Kierkegaard: From the Viewpoint of Heidegger], 『哲学雑誌』 [The Journal of Philosophy], vol. 81, 1966, pp. 178–97.

— 「キルケゴールにおける絶望の意味」 [The Meaning of Despair in Kierkegaard], 『理想』 [Riso], vol. 411, 1967, pp. 16–24.

— 「キルケゴール『死にいたる病』」 [Kierkegaard's *The Sickness unto Death*], 『理想』 [Riso], vol. 422, 1968, pp. 38–46.

——「デカルトの懐疑とキルケゴールの懐疑」 [The Skepticism in Descartes and Kierkegaard], 『実存主義』 [Existentialism], vol. 49, 1969, pp. 40–8.

——「歴史の終わりと始まり—キルケゴールの歴史哲学と、それにもとづくささやかなレーヴィット批判」 [The End and the Beginning of History: Kierkegaard's Philosophy of History and Some Criticism of Löwith], 『理想』 [Riso], vol. 491, 1974, pp. 22–37.

——「ハイデガーの<転回>について—キルケゴールを顧慮しつつ」 [On the "Evolution" in Heidegger: With Respect to Kierkegaard], 『思索』 [Meditations], vol. 13, 1980, pp. 1–20.

加藤典子 [Kato, Noriko], 「現象学的子供論とキルケゴールにおける子供像」 [Phenomenological Theory about Children and Images of Children in the Works of Kierkegaard], 『昭和女子大学女性文化研究所紀要』 [Bulletin of the Institute of Women's Culture, Showa Women's University], vol. 4, 1989, pp. 44–54.

加藤隆生 [Kato, Takao], 「キェルケゴールに於ける『瞬間と愛』」 ["The Moment and Love" in Kierkegaard], 『大谷学報』 [The Journal of Buddhist Studies and Humanities], vol. 44, 1964.

——「フィヒテの『絶対我に於ける自覚』とキルケゴールの『絶対他者に於ける自覚』」 [Fichte and Kierkegaard on Awakening], 『同朋学報』 [The Journal of Buddhism and Cultural Science], vol. 13, 1966, pp. 24–48.

——「実存論的な歴史概念について—ハイデッガー、キェルケゴール」 [On the Existential Concept of History: Heidegger and Kierkegaard], 『同朋大学論叢』 [The Journal of Buddhism and Cultural Science], vol. 31, 1974, pp. 113–31.

——「人間と言葉—キェルケゴール・ハイデッガーを中心として」 [Human Beings and Language: From Kierkegaard and Heidegger], 『同朋大学論叢』 [The Journal of Buddhism and Cultural Science], vol. 36, 1977, pp. 33–57.

——「師と弟子—キェルケゴールに於ける想起と反復」 [Recollection and Repetition in Kierkegaard], 『同朋大学論叢』 [The Journal of Buddhism and Cultural Science], vols. 44–5, 1981, pp. 579–600.

可藤豊文 [Kato, Toyofumi], 「キルケゴール晩年の思想」 [Kierkegaard's Thought in his Late Years], 『研究紀要』 [Kenkyu-kiyo], vol. 18, 1980, pp. 154–67.

——「キルケゴール: Det guddommelige Claudatur」 [Kierkegaard: Det guddommelige Claudatur], 『研究紀要』 [Kenky-kiyo], vol. 22, 1984, pp. 27–41.

加藤保義 [Kato, Yasuyoshi], 「キルケゴールにおける信仰の問題」 [The Problem of Faith in Kierkegaard], 『関西学院哲学研究年報』 [Yearbook of Philosophical Studies], vol. 9, 1968, pp. 67–103.

川戸好武 [Kawado, Yoshitake], 「人間的実存の綜合性格—キルケゴール・ハイデッガー・フィヒテにおける」 [The Synthetic Character of Human Existence: Kierkegaard, Heidegger and Fichte], 『キリスト教学』 [Christian Studies], vol. 22, 1980, pp. 69–93.

河合孝昭 [Kawai, Takaaki], 「キルケゴールにおけるアイロニーとユーモアの概念—『実存領域の境界』の本質をめぐって」 [The Concepts of Irony and Humor in Kierkegaard],『哲学世界』 [Philosophical World], vol. 20, 1997, pp. 63–76.

川井義男 [Kawai, Yoshio],「マックス・フリッシュへのキェルケゴールの影響」 [The Influence of Max Frisch on Kierkegaard],『キェルケゴール研究』 [Kierkegaard-Studiet], no. 15, 1985, pp. 5–16.

—「キェルケゴールとカフカ」 [Kierkegaard and Kafka],『キェルケゴール研究』 [Kierkegaard-Studiet], no. 16, 1986, pp. 5–18.

—「キェルケゴールと『ファウスト博士』」 [Kierkegaard and *Doctor Faust*],『キェルケゴール研究』 [Kierkegaard-Studiet], no. 19, 1989, pp. 17–26.

—「キェルケゴールとH. ブロッホ『夢遊の人々』」 [Kierkegaard and H. Broch's *The Sleepwalkers*],『キェルケゴール研究』 [Kierkegaard-Studiet], no. 20, 1990, pp. 5–18.

—「キェルケゴールとドイツ語圏文学」 [Kierkegaard and the German Language Literature],『新キェルケゴール研究』 [Kierkegaard Studies], no. 1, 2001, pp. 23–45.

河上正秀 [Kawakami, Shoshu],「キルケゴールにおける実存と時間」 [Existence and Time in Kierkegaard],『倫理學年報』 [Annals of Ethics], vol. 21, 1972, pp. 83–96.

—「『沈黙』と『言語』―キルケゴールにおいて」 ["Silence" and "Language" in Kierkegaard],『哲学』 [The Philosophy], vol. 23, 1973, pp. 97–110.

—「仮名と著作―沈黙の語り出すもの」 [Pseudonymity and Works],『理想』 [Riso], vol. 555, 1980, pp. 143–52.

—「ドイツ今世紀初頭におけるキルケゴール思想の影響・受容の局面」 [The Influence and Reception of Kierkegaard's Thought in Germany in the Early Part of this Century],『実践女子大学文学部紀要』 [The Faculty of Letters in Jissen Women's College Annual Reports of Studies], vol. 27, 1985, pp. 155–74 (part 1);『哲学・思想論集』 [Studies in Philosophy and Thoughts], vol. 15, 1990, pp. 137–53 (part 2); vol. 16, 1991, pp. 31–51 (part 3);『倫理学』 [Ethics], vol. 10, 1992, pp. 1–14 (part 4);『哲学・思想論集』 [Studies in Philosophy and Thoughts], vol. 18, 1993, pp. 1–18 (part 5); vol. 19, 1993, pp. 1–18 (part 6).

—『ドイツにおけるキルケゴール思想の受容―20 世紀初頭の批判哲学と実存哲学』 [Kierkegaard's Reception in Germany: The Critical Philosophy and Existential Philosophy at the Beginning of the Twentieth Century], Tokyo: Sobun-sha 1999.

—「ウィトゲンシュタインのキルケゴールへのまなざし：『倫理的なもの』をめぐって」 [Wittgenstein's View of Kierkegaard: On "the Ethical"],『哲学・思想論叢』 [Miscellanea Philosophica], vol. 17, 1999, pp. 71–82.

—「キルケゴールと倫理: 戦後日本の受容史断面」 [Kierkegaard and Ethics: A Phase of the History of Reception in Postwar Japan],『哲学・思想論集』 [Studies in Philosophy and Thoughts], vol. 26, 2000, pp. 1–15.

—「実存から他者へ―レヴィナス、デリダのキルケゴール読解」 [From Existence to the Other: Kierkegaard Read by Levinas and Derrida],『哲学「思想論集』 [Studies in Philosophy and Thoughts], vol. 21, 2001, pp. 1–17.

—「非同一の主体性—実存思想以後のキルケゴール読解」 [Unidentical Subjectivity: Reading of Kierkegaard after Existentialism], 『理想』 [Riso], vol. 676, 2006, pp. 2–12.

河上徹太郎 [Kawakami, Tetsutaro], 『ドン＝ジョヴァンニ—キルケゴールのモツアルト論』 [Don Giovanni: Kierkegaard's Discussions about Mozart], Tokyo: Hosokawa-shoten 1951.

川村三千雄 [Kawamura, Michio], 「實存の倫理: キルケゴールを中心として」 [The Ethics of Existence: From the Perspective of Kierkegaard], 『經濟再建の諸問題』 [Problems of Economics], vol. 1, 1948, pp. 105–36.

川中子義勝 [Kawanago, Yoshikatsu], 「ハーマンとキルケゴール・序説」 [Hamann and Kierkegaard], 『外国語科研究紀要』 [The Proceedings of the Department of Foreign Languages and Literatures, College of General Education, University of Tokyo], vol. 39, 1991, pp.161–89.

河中正彦 [Kawanaka, Masahiko], 「キルケゴールとカフカ 1 —カフカのキルケゴール受容—」 [Kierkegaard and Kafka 1: Kafka's Reception of Kierkegaard], 『山口大学教養部紀要人文科学篇』 [Journal of the Faculty of Liberal Arts, Yamaguchi University. Humanities and Social Sciences], vol. 16, pp. 165–79.

木田元 [Kida, Gen], 「シェリングとキルケゴール」 [Schelling and Kierkegaard], 『大航海』 [Voyages into Thought, Literature and History], vol. 14, 1997, pp. 170–9.

木瀬康太 [Kinose, Kota], 「三土興三の『酔歌』—大正期におけるキルケゴール受容の一例」 [Kozo Mitsuchi's *Song of a Drunken Man*: An Example of Kierkegaard Reception in the Taisho Era], 『比較文学・文化論集』 [Proceedings of Comparative Literature & Culture], vol. 26, 2009, pp. 45–58.

—「和辻哲郎の『個人主義』論—キルケゴール受容を手がかりとして」 [Tetsuro Watsuji's Criticism of Individualism: Examining his Reception of Kierkegaard], 『超域文化科学紀要』 [Interdisciplinary Cultural Studies], vol. 18, 2013, pp. 173–89.

— 「戦時下日本におけるキルケゴール受容—クリスチャンの知識人の活動を中心に」 [The Reception of Kierkegaard in Wartime Japan], 『比較文学・文化論集』 [Proceedings of Comparative Literature & Culture], vol. 29, 2013, pp. 29–36.

北田勝巳 [Kitada, Katsumi], 「単独者の弁証法的構造」 [The Dialectical Structure of the Single Individual], 『人文論究』 [The Journal of the Literary Association of Kwansei Gakuin University], vol. 8, 1957, pp. 108–28.

—「若きキルケゴールにおける宗教的実存の成立」 [The Formation of Religious Existence in Young Kierkegaard], 『人文論究』 [The Journal of the Literary Association of Kwansei Gakuin University], vol. 13, 1962, pp. 57–9.

—「キルケゴールにおける主体性と逆説」 [Subjectivity and Paradox in Kierkegaard], 『関西学院哲学研究年報』 [Yearbook of Philosophical Studies], vol. 3, 1963.

—「キルケゴールにおける『第二の直接性』について」 ["Second Immediacy" in Kierkegaard], 『キェルケゴール研究』 [Kierkegaard-Studiet], vol. 2, 1965, pp. 25–30.

—「キルケゴールにおける信仰と理性―キリスト教弁証論の試み」 [Faith and Reason in Kierkegaard], 『関西学院哲学研究年報』 [Yearbook of Philosophical Studies], vol. 6, 1966, pp. 36–43.

—「キェルケゴールにおけるキリスト教の弁証」 [The Christian Apologetics in the Works of Kierkegaard], 『キェルケゴール研究』 [Kierkegaard-Studiet], no. 5, 1968, pp. 5–18.

—「キェルケゴールにおける実存的懐疑の成立」 [The Formation of Existential Doubt in Kierkegaard], 『キェルケゴール研究』 [Kierkegaard-Studiet], no. 8, 1978, pp. 31–40.

—「キルケゴールの遺稿『ヨハンネス・クリマクス』について」 [On Kierke-gaard's Nachlass "Johannes Climacus"], 『大阪電気通信大学研究論集人文・社会科学篇』 [Reports of the College of Ōsaka, Electro-Communications, Social Sciences and Humanities], vol. 17, 1981, pp. 145–50.

—「キェルケゴールにおける自己の根本構造」 [The Basic Structure of the Self in Kierkegaard], 『キェルケゴール研究』 [Kierkegaard-Studiet], no. 14, 1984, pp. 15–26.

—「キェルケゴールにおける『教化的講話』の一考察」 [On "Upbuilding Discourses" in Kierkegaard], 『大阪電気通信大学研究論集人文・社会科学篇』 [Reports of the College of Ōsaka Electro-Communication. Social Science and Humanity], vol. 25, 1990, pp. 1–6.

—「和辻哲郎における『ゼエレン・キェルケゴール』解釈」 [An Interpretation of *Søren Kierkegaad* by Tetsuro Watsuji], 『大阪電気通信大学研究論集人文・社会科学篇』 [Reports of the College of Ōsaka Electro-Communication. Social Science and Humanity], vol. 27, 1992, pp. 1–8; vol. 28, 1993, pp. 1–6.

—「キェルケゴールにおける間接的伝達の問題」 [The Problem of Indirect Communication in S. Kierkegaard], 『大阪電気通信大学研究論集人文・社会科学篇』 [Reports of the College of Ōsaka Electro-Communication. Social Science and Humanity], vol. 31, 1996, pp. 1–10.

喜田川信 [Kitagawa, Shin], 「キェルケゴールにおける倫理的なもの―逆説と実存―」 ["The Ethical" in the Thought of Søren Kierkegaard: Paradox and Existence], 『キェルケゴール研究』 [Kierkegaard-Studiet], no. 3, 1966, pp. 5–12.

—『キェルケゴールと現代の神学』 [Kierkegaard and Modern Theology], Tokyo: Shinkyo-shuppansha 1971.

—「キェルケゴールの現代的意義」 [Kierkegaard's Significance for Today], 『キェルケゴール研究』 [Kierkegaard-Studiet], no. 25, 1995, pp. 21–4.

北野裕通 [Kitano, Hiroyuki], 「キェルケゴールの魔論―『魔』＝『間』の思想から見られた―」 [An Interpretation of Kierkegaard's Demonology], 『キェルケゴール研究』 [Kierkegaard-Studiet], no. 11, 1981, pp. 5–14.

—「大西祝とヘフディングの『キェルケゴール』」 [Hajime Ohnishi and Harald Høffding's *Kierkegaard*], 『キェルケゴール研究』 [Kierkegaard-Studiet], no. 17, 1987, pp. 15–28.

鬼頭英一 [Kito, Eiichi], 「キェルケゴールとハイデッガー」 [Kierkegaard and Heidegger], in his 『ハイデッガーの存在学』 [Heidegger's Ontology], Tokyo: Toyo-shuppan 1935, pp. 183–189.

—「キエルケゴールに於ける『ヘーゲル』」 [Hegel in Kierkegaard], 『理想』 [Riso], vol. 198, 1949, pp. 36–45.

黄綿昶行 [Kiwata, Choko], 「キルケゴールの思想における『匿名』の表現形式と発表形式」 [Pseudonymity in Kierkegaard's Thought], 『哲学会誌』 [Bulletin of Philosophy], vol. 8, 1972, pp. 8–16.

小林謙一 [Kobayashi, Kenichi], 「日記に見るキルケゴールのキリスト教理解: 『本来のキルケゴール』の問題に寄せて」 [Kierkegaard's Understanding of Christianity in his Journals: On the Problem of "the True Kierkegaard"], 『横浜国立大学人文紀要第一類,哲学・社会科学』 [The Journal of Yokohama National University], vol. 20, 1974, pp. 1–20.

—「キルケゴールにおける愛の問題: 『愛のわざ』を中心として」 [The Problem of Love in Kierkegaard: From *Works of Love*], 『桐朋学園大学研究紀要』 [Toho Gakuen School of Music Faculty Bulletin], vol. 1, 1975, pp. 41–64.

小林修 [Kobayashi, Osamu], 「キルケゴールに於ける『イロニー克服』の問題について」 [On the Conquest of Irony by Kierkegaard], 『一橋論叢』 [The Hitotsubashi Review], vol. 60, 1968, pp. 215–25.

小林茂 [Kobayashi, Shigeru], 「キルケゴールにおける歴史理解」 [Kierkegaard's Understanding of History], 『白山哲学』 [Bulletin of Toyo University], vol. 4, 1966, pp. 20–37.

—「キルケゴールの宗教・歴史哲学—その歴史的背景の一考察」 [Kierkegaard's Philosophy of Religion and History], 『経済論集』 [Journal of Economics], vol. 8, 1967, pp. 81–96.

—「弁証法的思考の方法とその前提—キルケゴールの場合」 [The Method and Presupposition of the Dialectical Thought in Kierkegaard], 『理想』 [Riso], vol. 419, 1968, pp. 75–85.

—「キルケゴールの実存弁証法」 [Kierkegaard's Existential Dialectics], 『大東文化大学紀要教養編』 [Daito Bunka University General Course Bulletin], vol. 1, 1968, pp. 57–67.

—「キルケゴールのキリスト教界批判」 [Kierkegaard's Criticism of Christendom], 『大東文化大学紀要教養編』 [Daito Bunka University General Course Bulletin], vol. 2, 1969, pp. 93–109.

—「キルケゴールにおける逆説と信仰の問題」 [The Problem of Paradox and Faith in Kierkegaard], 『大東文化大学紀要教養編』 [Daito Bunka University General Course Bulletin], vol. 3, 1970, pp. 131–41.

児島洋 [Kojima, Hiroshi], 「単独者と社会を結ぶもの—ブーバーのキルケゴール批判」 [The Connection between the Single Individual and Society: Buber's Criticism of Kierkegaard], 『理想』 [Riso], vol. 338, 1961, pp. 57–66.

近藤重明 [Kondo, Shigeaki], 「逆説と超越—キルケゴールとヤスパース」 [Paradox and Transcendence: Jaspers and Kierkegaard], 『哲学論叢』 [The Philosophical Miscellany], vol. 24, 1967, pp. 155–65.

小坂国継 [Kosaka, Kunitsugu], 「逆対応とパラドックス: 西田幾多郎とキルケゴールにおける信仰の論理」 [Gyakutaio (Inverse Polarity) and Paradox: Logic of Faith in K. Nishida and S. Kierkegaard], 『比較思想研究』 [Studies in Comparative Philosophy], vol. 19, 1992, pp. 39–48.

高坂正顕 [Kosaka, Masaaki], 「キェルケゴールと道化芝居—『反復』の一考察」 [Kierkegaard and a Farce: On *Repetition*], 『芸文』 [Geibun], vol. 1, 1948, pp. 94–104.

— 『キェルケゴールからサルトルへ—実存哲学研究』 [From Kierkegaard to Sartre: A Study of Existential Philosophy], Tokyo: Kobun-do 1949.

上妻精 [Kozuma, Tadashi], 「キルケゴール文献」 [Kierkegaard Literature], 『実存主義』 [Existentialism], vol. 26, 1962, pp. 123–33.

— 「キルケゴール文献目録」 [List of Kierkegaard Literature], 『理想』 [Riso], vol. 555, 1979, pp. 97–141.

— 「ヘーゲルから見たキルケゴール—キルケゴールのヘーゲル批判をめ ぐって」 [Kierkegaard Viewed by Hegel], 『理想』 [Riso], vol. 555, 1979, pp. 153–68.

工藤綏夫 [Kudo, Yasuo], 「キルケゴールに於ける自己生成の倫理について」 [On the Ethics of Self-becoming in Kierkegaard], 『秋田大学学芸学部研究紀要 人文科学・社会科学・教育科学』 [Bulletin of Akita University], vol. 6, 1956.

— 『キェルケゴール—人と思想』 [Kierkegaard: His Life and Thought], Tokyo: Shimizu-shoin 1966.

工藤宜延 [Kudo, Yoshinobu], 「キェルケゴールにおける内在から超越への 弁証法—その一—」, [Kierkegaard's Dialectics from the Immanence to the Transcendence], 『キェルケゴール研究』 [Kierkegaard-Studiet], no. 10, 1980, pp. 39–48.

— 「キェルケゴールの人間観の一側面」 [An Aspect of Kierkegaard's Understanding of Human Beings], 『キェルケゴール研究』 [Kierkegaard-Studiet], no. 14, 1984, pp. 27–36.

熊野義孝 [Kumano, Yoshitaka], 「キェルケゴールの人と思想」 [Kierkegaard's Personality and Thought], 『経済往来』 [The Economy Today], vol. 10, no. 5, 1935, pp. 166–75; republished in his 『現代の神学』 [Modern Theology], Tokyo: Shinsei-do 1936, pp. 209–28.

— 「キエルケゴールとバルト—神学的弁正法について」 [Kierkegaard and Barth: On Theological Dialectics], 『理想』 [Riso], vol. 198, 1949, pp. 13–23.

国井哲義 [Kunii, Tetsuyoshi], 「キェルケゴールにおける弁証法の意味」 [The Meaning of the Dialectics in Kierkegaard], 『キェルケゴール研究』 [Kierkegaard-Studiet], no. 7, 1977, pp. 11–14.

— 「キェルケゴールのヘーゲル批判とその思想的立場について」 [Kierkegaard's Criticism of Hegel and his Standpoint], 『キェルケゴール研 究』 [Kierkegaard-Studiet], no. 10, 1980, pp. 49–56.

— 「キェルケゴールの思想の社会的、政治的側面」 [The Social and Political Aspects of Kierkegaard's Thought], 『大阪工業大学紀要人文社会篇』 [Memoirs of the Osaka Institute of Technology. Series B, Liberal Arts], vol. 33, 1989, pp. 131–50.

— 「キェルケゴールにおける実存人間観」 [A Study of the Human Being from Kierkegaard's Existential Viewpoint], 『キェルケゴール研究』 [Kierkegaard-Studiet], no. 11, 1981, pp. 15–24.

— 「キェルケゴールとマルクス」 [Kierkegaard and Marx], 『大阪工業大学 紀要人文社会篇』 [Memoirs of the Osaka Institute of Technology. Series B, Liberal Arts], vol. 37, 1992, pp. 49–68.

—「キェルケゴールの教会攻撃」 [Kierkegaard's Attack upon the Christian Church], 『キェルケゴール研究』 [Kierkegaard-Studiet], no. 25, 1995, pp. 25–38.

—「キェルケゴールにおける瞬間の概念」 [The Concept of Instant in Kierkegaard], 『金蘭短期大学研究誌』 [The Review of Kinran Junior College], no. 28, 1997, pp. 1–26.

—「キェルケゴールとレギーネ」 [Kierkegaard and Regine], 『金蘭短期大学研究誌』 [The Review of Kinran Junior College], no. 29, 1998, pp. 1–12.

—「キェルケゴールにおける『間接伝達』」 ["Indirect Communication" in Kierkegaard], 『金蘭短期大学研究誌』 [The Review of Kinran Junior College], no. 31, 2000, pp. 1–12.

—「レギーネと間接伝達」 [Regine and Indirect Communication], 『新キェルケゴール研究』 [Kierkegaard Studies], no. 2, 2002, pp. 1–18.

—『苦悩と愛—キェルケゴール論』 [Suffering and Love: Treatise on Kierkegaard], Fukuoka: Sogen-sha 2002.

—「キェルケゴールの段階理論」 [The Theory of Stages in Kierkegaard], 『金蘭短期大学研究誌』 [The Review of Kinran Junior College], vol. 33, 2002, pp. 1–13; vol. 34, 2003, pp. 1–14.

国谷純一郎 [Kuniya, Junichiro], 「誘惑者—キェルケゴールに於ける美的実存」 [The Seducer: Aesthetic Existence in Kierekgaard], 『初雁』 [Hatsukari], vol. 19, 1949, pp. 4–6.

久野昭 [Kuno, Akira], 「キェルケゴールと『自己』の問題」 [A Wild Goose and Tame Geese: Kierkegaard and the Problem of "the Self"], 『キェルケゴール研究』 [Kierkegaard-Studiet], no. 7, 1977, pp. 15–20.

倉内利美 [Kurauchi, Rimi], 「S. キルケゴールにおける知の評価」 [Evaluation of Knowledge in S. Kierkegaard], 『比較思想の途』 [Ways of Comparative Thought], vol. 4, 1985, pp. 91–2.

—「S. キルケゴールにおける生成の概念—『哲学的断片』『間奏曲』の章に関する一考察」 [The Concept of Becoming in S. Kierkegaard], 『宗教研究』 [Journal of Religious Studies], vol. 58, 1985, pp. 261–86.

紅松保雄 [Kurematsu, Yasuo], 「キェルケゴールの審美的著作について」 [On Kierkegaard's Aesthetic Works], 『研究』 [Studies], vol. 6, 1955, pp. 96–116.

—「キェルケゴールのドン・ジュアン像」 [Kierkegaard's Idea of Don Juan], 『研究』 [Studies], vol. 15, 1957, pp. 24–43.

—「キェルケゴールの審美的著作とレギーネ・オルセン体験」 [Kierkegaard's Aesthetic Works and his Experience with Regine Olsen], 『近代』 [Kindai], vol. 40, 1967, pp. 31–49; vol. 41, 1967, pp. 21–34; vol. 42, 1968, pp. 19–42.

桑原浄信 [Kuwabara, Joshin], 「キルケゴールに於ける苦悩について」 [On Suffering in Kierkegaard], 『真宗研究会紀要』 [Bulletin of Shinshu-Kenkyukai], vol. 35, 2003, pp. 69–84.

—「キルケゴールにおける実存の三段階」 [Three Existential Stages in Kierkegaard], 『真宗研究会紀要』 [Bulletin of Shinshu-Kenkyukai], vol. 36, 2004, pp. 58–74.

桑田秀延 [Kuwata, Hidenobu], 「キェルケゴールの弁証法神学」 [Kierkegaard's Dialectical Theology], 『理想』 [Riso], vol. 62, 1935, pp. 2–21.

久山康 [Kuyama, Yasushi],「キェルケゴールとドストエフスキイ」[Kierkegaard and Dostoevsky],『関西学院哲学研究年報』[Yearbook of Philosophical Studies], vol. 2, 1961.

万里小路通宗 [Madenokoji, Michimune],「日本におけるキェルケゴール文献」[Kierkegaard Literature in Japan],『キェルケゴール研究』[Kierkegaard-Studiet], no. 1, 1964, pp. 139–49.

—「日本におけるキェルケゴール文献」[Kierkegaard Literature in Japan, Parts 1–2],『キェルケゴール研究』[Kierkegaard-Studiet], no. 7, 1977, pp. 72–7; no. 8, 1978, pp. 95–103.

牧野仁 [Makino, Jin],「親鸞とキェルケゴールの宗教的実存」[Religious Existence in Shinran and Kierkegaard],『龍谷大学大学院文学研究科紀要』[Ryukoku University the Bulletin of the Graduate School of Letters], vol. 22, 2000, pp. 100–3.

丸山良治 [Maruyama, Ryoji],「キルケゴールの実存の思考」[Kierkegaard's Existential Thought],『天理大学学報』[Bulletin of Tenri University], vol. 15, 1963.

桝田啓三郎 [Masuda, Keizaburo],「キェルケゴールの根本思想」[Kierkegaard's Fundamental Thought],『理想』[Riso], vol. 62, 1935, pp. 74–87.

—「キェルケゴールの日記から」[From Kierkegaard's Journals],『高原』[Kogen], vol. 9, 1949, pp. 127–36; vol. 10, 1949, pp. 64–70.

—「キェルケゴール文献解説—研究者への手びきとして」[Introduction to the Literature on Kierkegaard],『理想』[Riso], vol. 198, 1949, pp. 86–104.

—「単独者と超人—キェルケゴールとニーチェ」[The Single Individual and Superman: Kierkegaard and Nietzsche],『理想』[Riso], vol. 24. 1950, pp. 64–75.

—「文献—著作・文献目録・略年譜・解説」[Kierkegaard Literature, Secondary Literature, his Chronological Record and Commentary],『理想』[Riso], vol. 269, 1955, pp. 104–58.

—「恋と罪」[Love and Sin],『文庫』[Bunko], vol. 55, 1956.

—「キルケゴールにおける『大地震』の休験について—キルケゴール研究の覚え書」[On Kierkegaard's "Great Earthquake"],『人文学報』[The Journal of Social Sciences and Humanity], vol. 27, 1962.

—「キルケゴール研究の意義と方法—ひとつの弁明」[The Meaning and Method of Kierkegaard Studies],『哲学誌』[Historia Philosophiae], vol. 7, 1965.

桝形公也 [Masugata, Kinya],「懐疑—絶望—真摯—キェルケゴール青年期における問い—」[Doubt—Despair—Earnestness—Kierkegaard's Question in his Youth],『キェルケゴール研究』[Kierkegaard-Studiet], no. 8, 1978, pp. 41–50.

—「キェルケゴールにおける可能性の概念について」[Kierkegaard's Concept of Possibility],『キェルケゴール研究』[Kierkegaard-Studiet], no. 9, 1978, pp. 15–24.

—「キェルケゴールの言語理解—キェルケゴール青年期における問い（二）—」[Kierkegaard's Understanding of Language: Some Notes on Kierkegaard's Questions in his Youth (2)], 『キェルケゴール研究』 [Kierkegaard-Studiet], no. 11, 1981, pp. 25–34.

—「言葉と倫理: キェルケゴールの言語観を手がかりにして」 [Language and Ethics: Kierkegaard's View of Language as a Clue], 『実践哲学研究』 [Studies on Practical Philosophy], vols. 3–4, 1981, pp. 13–42.

—「キェルケゴール—善と救い—」 [Kierkegaard: The Good and Salvation], in 『善の本質と諸相』 [The Nature and the Varieties of the Good], ed. by Shozo Fukatani and Shunsuke Terasaki, Kyoto: Showado 1983, pp. 195–212.

—「実存主義1—キェルケゴール、ヤスパース」 [Existentialism I: Kierke-gaard and Jaspers] in 『西洋倫理思想の形成2』 [The Formation of the Western Ethical Thinking, II], ed. by Seiki Oguma, Hidekazu Kawshima and Shozo Fukatani, Kyoto: Koyo Shobo 1986, pp. 21–40.

—「愛について—キェルケゴールの『愛の業』に即して」 [On Love: Kierkeg-aard's *Works of Love*], in 『変革期の思索』 [Thought in the Age of Reforma-tion], ed. by Tsutomu Kubota, Kyoto: Minerva-shobo 1989, pp. 160–77.

—「日本におけるキェルケゴール受容史」 [The History of the Reception of Kierkegaard in Japan], 『大阪教育大学紀要I人文科学』 [Memoirs of Osaka Kyoiku University I, Humanities], vol. 38, 1989, pp. 49–66.

—「明治時代とキェルケゴール—キェルケゴール受容史」 [The History of Kierkegaard's Reception: The Meiji Era and Kierkegaard], 『キェルケゴール 研究』 [Kierkegaard-Studiet], no. 20, 1990, pp. 29–40; no. 22, 1992, pp. 5–12.

—「キェルケゴール—仮名の謎」 [The Riddle of Kierkegaard's Pseudonyms], in 『哲学のエポック』 [The Epoch of Philosophy], ed. by Koichi Tsujiura, Kyoto: Minerva- shobo 1991, pp. 233–43.

—「実存」 [Existence], in 『現代哲学を学ぶ人のために』 [An Aid for the Study of Contemporary Philosophy], ed. by Takashi Maruyama, Kyoto: Sekaishisosha, 1992, pp. 4–17.

—「キェルケゴールのStemning（気分・情調）の概念について」 [The Concept of "Stemning" in Kierkegaard], in 『現代医療の光と影』 [Light and Shadow of Medical Services], ed. by Tomio Ota, Kyoto: Koyo Shobo 1996, pp. 171–86.

—「ディレンマの意味論—キェルケゴールの『畏れとおののき』をめぐって」 [Semantics of Dilemma: On Kierkegaard's *Fear and Trembling*], 『人間存在 論』 [Menschenontologie of Kyoto University], vol. 3, 1997, pp. 583–93.

—「キェルケゴールにおける『誘惑』概念の役割」 [The Possibility of Interpretation of Kierkegaard's Text as Seduction], 『比較思想研究』 [Studies in Comparative Philosophy], vol. 25, 1998, pp. 76–7.

—「キェルケゴールにおける『誘惑』としてのテキスト」 [Texts as "Seduc-tion" in Kierkegaard], 『倫理学研究』 [Annals of Ethical Studies], vol. 30, 2000, pp. 1–8.

—「キェルケゴールの魅力—日本語によるキェルケゴール研究—」 [Attractiveness of Kierkegaard: Kierkegaard Studies in Japanese], 『新キェル ケゴール研究』 [Kierkegaard Studies], no. 12, 2014, pp. 1–13.

松田明 [Matsuda, Akira], 「モーツァルトとキルケゴール—歌劇<ドン・ジ ョヴァンニ>をめぐる考察」 [Mozart and Kierkegaard: A Consideration on

Don Giovanni], 『芸術』 [Journal of Osaka University of Arts], vol. 22, 1999, pp. 200–12.

松田幸子 [Matsuda, Sachiko], 「キェルケゴールの『倫理的生き方』について」 [On Kierkegaard's "Ethical Way of Life"], 『紀要』 [Bulletin of Ueda Junior College], no. 20, 1997, pp. 1–7.

松木真一 [Matsuki, Shinichi] (ed.), 『キェルケゴールとキリスト教神学の展望』 [New Perspective of Studies on Kierkegaard and the Scope of Contemporary Christian Theology], Hyogo: Kwansei Gakuin University Press 2006. (Finn H. Mortensen, 「キェルケゴールと現代」 [Søren Kierkegaard and "the Modern"], trans. by Tadayoshi Hayashi, pp. 1–44; Niels Jørgen Cappelørn, 「セーレン・キェルケゴールの新版原典全集の刊行」 [Søren Kierkegaard's Writings in the New Edition], trans. by Jun Hashimoto, pp. 45–76; Jae-Myeong Pyo, 「韓国におけるゼーレン・キェルケゴール」 [Kierkegaard in Korea], pp. 77–112; Shoshu Kawakami, 「キルケゴール『現代の批判』とわれわれの『現代』」 [S. Kierkegaard's *The Present Age* vs. the Present Age of our Own], pp. 113–26; Jo Funaki, 「キェルケゴールにおける教会批判の射程」 [A Study of Søren Kierkegaard's Attack upon "Christendom"], pp. 127–44; Takahiro Hirabayashi, 「セーレン・キェルケゴールにおける≪不死性≫論争と実存的真理の地平—ひとはいかに≪私≫になるのか?」 [Søren Kierkegaard on the Immortality of the Soul: About the Horizon of his Subjective Thought], pp. 145–66; Mitsuko Inoue, 「デンマークの武装中立と国際商業」 ["Armed Neutrality" in the Perspective of Danish Commercial History], pp. 167–81; Wataru Mizugaki, 「キリスト教思想の構造のモデルとしての≪中心と円≫—ルター『ガラテヤ書講義』の一テクストについての覚え書」 ["Center and Circle" as a Model of the Structure of Christian Thought: An Interpretation of a Text in Luther's Lecture on the Galatians (1531)], pp. 181–94; Hitoshi Ishihara, 「モルトマン初期三部作に見る三位一体論の形成」 [Trinitarianism in an Early Triology of Moltman], pp. 195–212; Go Kondo, 「神の国と涅槃—ティリッヒと久松真一の対話」 [Kingdom of God and Nirvana: a Dialogue between Paul Tillich and Hisamatsu Shin'ichi], pp. 213–34; Shinichi Matsuki, 「パウロの『唯一の神』理解—第一コリント八・四ー六の釈義的解釈学的考察」 [Monotheism in Paul: Interpretation of I Corinthians 8: 4–6], pp. 235–54; Keisuke Masuda, 「父の思い出—桝田啓三郎とキェルケゴール」 [My Father Keizaburo Masuda: His Life as a Scholar and Translator of Søren Kierkegaard], pp. 255–70; Jun Hashimoto, 「キェルケゴール協会(大阪)の草創期」 [Memory of Prof. Masaru Otani, his Foundation of Kierkegaard Society in Japan (Osaka) and its Earlier Years], pp. 271–78; Tadayoshi Hayashi, 「武藤一雄のキェルケゴール論」 [The Late Prof. Kazuo Muto: His Contribution to Søren Kierkegaard Studies], pp. 279–92; Jun Hashimoto, 「遥かなデンマーク—キェルケゴールの国」 [My Studies on Søren Kierkegaard in Denmark as a Fairy Tale: Reminiscences of Late Prof. N.H. Søe, Prof. N. Thulstrup, Dr. G. Malantschuk and Others], pp. 293–321.)

松本良彦 [Matsumoto, Yoshihiko], 「ケルケゴールの不安論—特に神経症的な不安の論について」 [Kierkegaard's Concept of Anxiety], 『岡山大学法文学部学術紀要』 [Bulletin of Okayama University], vol. 16, 1964, pp. 32–46.

—「ケルケゴールにおける『悪魔的なるもの』について」 ["The Demonic" in Kierkegaard], 『岡山大学法文学部学術紀要』 [Bulletin of Okayama University], vol. 20, 1964.

松山康国 [Matsuyama, Yasukuni], 「キェルケゴールのソクラテス解釈とドイツ・ロマン主義理解」 [Kierkegaard's Interpretation of Socrates and German Romanticism], 『商学論究』 [Journal of Business Administration of Kwansei Gakuin University], vol. 12, 1965.

松塚豊茂 [Matsuzuka, Toyoshige], 「絶望の論理: キルケゴール『死に至る病』の研究」 [The Logic of Despair: A Study of *The Sickness unto Death*], 『島根大学法文学部紀要文学科編』 [Memoirs of the Faculty of Law and Literature], vol. 11, 1978, pp. 233–55; vol. 14, 1990, pp.1–42; vol. 16, 1991, pp.1–29; vol. 19, 1992, pp.1–34; vol. 20, 1993, pp.1–24.

—『絶望の論理—キルケゴール『死にいたる病』の研究』 [The Logic of Despair: A Study of *The Sickness unto Death*], Tokyo: Kindaibungei-sha 1995.

松井吉康 [Matsui, Yoshiyasu], 「エックハルトとキェルケゴール—『内面性』を手がかりとして」 [Eckhart und Kierkegaard], 『キェルケゴール研究』 [Kierkegaard-Studiet], no. 23, 1993, pp. 17–26.

三村徹也 [Mimura, Tetsuya], 「キェルケゴールにおける信仰のパラドクス—『おそれとおののき』研究」 [The Paradox of Faith in Kierkegaard], 『哲学論集』 [Philosophical Studies], vol. 41, 1994, pp. 56–62.

南コニー [Minami, Connie], 「サルトルとキェルケゴールに於けるモラルの相関性について」 [Correspondence of the Moral in Kierkegaard and Sartre], 『関西フランス語フランス文学』 [Kansai Studies of French Language and Literature], vol. 12, 2006. pp. 58–69.

—「サルトルのキェルケゴール論—『単独的普遍』の解釈をめぐって」 [Sartre's Understanding of Kierkegaard: On the Interpretation of the Concept "Singular Universal"], *Études de langue et littérature françaises*, no. 103, 2013, pp. 185–99.

源宣子 [Minamoto, Nobuko], 「キェルケゴールの『不安』の構造について」 [The Structure of Kierkegaard's "Anxiety"], 『人間文化研究年報』 [Bulletin of the Graduate School of Humanities and Sciences], vol. 18, 1994, pp. 104–10.

—「キェルケゴールとソクラテス—特にイロニーの問題について」 [Kierkegaard and Socrates on Irony], 『目白学園女子短期大学研究紀要』 [Memoirs of the Mejiro Gakuen Women's Junior College], vol. 32, 1995, pp. 175–86.

—「キェルケゴールにおける『単独者』と他者の問題について」 ["The Single Individual and Others" in the Philosophy of Kierkegaard], 『宗教研究』 [Journal of Religious Studies], vol. 313, 1997, pp. 21–41.

—「キェルケゴールの『不安の概念』における『罪』と『自由』について」 [On "Sin" and "Freedom" in Kierkegaard's *The Concept of Anxiey*], 『人間文化論叢』 [Journal of the Graduate School of Humanities and Sciences], vol. 1, 1998, pp. 15–22.

源哲麿 [Minamoto, Tetsumaro], 「キェルケゴールの"Dichter"批判とその視点—ロマンテーク批判をめぐって」 [Kierkegaard's Criticism of "Dichter" and his Viewpoint], 『専修大学論集』 [Senshu University Review], vol. 34, 1964.

— 「キルケゴールの結婚観—特にその 『レギーネ体験』との関聯について」 [Kierkegaard's View on Marriage], 『専修大学論集』 [Senshu University Review], vol. 4, 1967, pp. 35–64.

蓑輪秀邦 [Minowa, Shuho], 『キェルケゴールと親鸞—宗教的真理の伝達者たち』 [Kierkegaard and Shinran: Communicators of the Religious Truth], Kyoto: Minerva-shobo 2000.

— 「宗教的世界における師と弟子の関係について—キルケゴールと親鸞の場合」 [A Study of the Teacher-Pupil Relationship in the Religious World: From the Viewpoints of Kierkegaard and Shinran], 『仁愛大学研究紀要』 [Research Journal of Jin-Ai University], vol. 4, 2005, pp. 1–14.

三土興三 [Mitsuchi, Kozo], 「酔歌」 [Song of a Drunken Man], 『講座』 [Lectures], vol. 11, 1923, pp. 143–74 (part 1); vol. 11, 1924, pp. 162–92 (part 2) (2nd ed. Tokyo: Koubun-do 1948 (part 2)).

見附陽介 [Mitsuke, Yosuke], 「M.M. バフチンとS. キルケゴール—対話と実存について」 [M.M. Bakhtin and S. Kierkegaard: On Dialogue and Existence], 『ロシア語ロシア文学研究』 [Bulletin of the Japanese Association of Russian Scholars], vol. 42, 2010, pp. 41–8.

三浦永光 [Miura, Nagamitsu], 「キルケゴールのイロニー理解」 [Kierkegaard's Understanding of Irony], 『哲学誌』 [Historia Philosophiae], vol. 8, 1966, pp. 55–74.

— 「実存と普遍の問題—キルケゴールの例外者論」 [The Problem of Existence and Universality], 『哲学誌』 [Historia Philosophiae], vol. 11, 1968, pp. 89–109.

— 「実存と歴史—キルケゴールに即して」 [Existence and History], 『理想』 [Riso], vol. 431, 1969, pp. 35–43.

— 「F. シュレーゲルとキルケゴール—『ルチンデ』をめぐって」 [F. Schlegel and Kierkegaard: On "Lucinde"], 『理想』 [Riso], vol. 448, 1970, pp. 75–87.

— 「客体世界の喪失—キルケゴールの『インサイレントなもの』をめぐって」 [Losing Objective World], 『高崎経済大学論集』 [Journal of Takasaki City University of Economics], vol. 17, 1975, pp. 195–228.

宮地たか [Miyachi, Taka], 『倫理と宗教の間—カントとキルケゴールに関連して』 [Between Ethics and Religion – In Relation to Kant and Kierkegaard], Hiroshima: Keisui-sha 2002.

宮原晃一郎 [Miyahara, Koichiro], 「キェルケゴール」 [Kierkegaard], in 『大思想エンサイクロペデア2 —文芸思想2』 [Encyclopedia, Part 2—Literary Thoughts, Part 2], ed. by Toyoho Kanda, Tokyo: Shunju-sha 1929, pp. 325–6.

— 「憂愁孤独の思想家キェルケゴール」 [Kierkegaard as a Melancholic and Solitary Thinker], 『思想春秋』 [Philosophy Today], vol. 34, 1934, pp. 9–10.

— 「キェルケゴールの芸術観」 [Kierkegaard's View of Art], 『浪漫古典』 [Roman Classics], vol. 7, 1934, pp. 71–82.

宮坂いち子 [Miyasaka, Ichiko], 「キルケゴールの倫理的実存」 [The Ethical Existence in Kierkegaard], 『倫理學年報』 [Annals of Ethics], vol. 20, 1971, pp. 133–45.

— 「キルケゴールの死と永遠性」 [Kierkegaard on Death and Eternity], 『研究紀要』 [Bulletin of Seitoku University], vol. 6, 1995, pp. 9–15.

宮田玲 [Miyata, Akira]，「創世記２２章の旧約解釈と『おそれとおののき』」 [Exegesis on Genesis 22:1–19 and *Fear and Trembling*]，『新キェルケゴール 研究』 [Kierkegaard Studies], no. 3, 2004, pp. 124–41.

宮澤幸恵 [Miyazawa, Yukie]，「キェルケゴール『あれか、これか』における 『美的なもの』と『倫理的なもの』の関係」 [The Relationship between "the Aesthetic" and "the Ethical" in Kierkegaard's *Either/Or*]，『創価大学大学院紀要』 [The Bulletin of the Graduate School, Soka University], vol. 33, 2011, pp, 211–33.

溝井高志 [Mizoi, Takashi]，「ゼーレン・キェルケゴールにおける精神の概念 と絶望の諸相」 [The Concept of Spirit and Aspects of Despair in Kierkegaard]，『阪南論集』 [The Hannan-ronshu], vol. 13, 1978, pp. 59–87.

— 「ゼーレン・キェルケゴールにおける愛の概念」 [The Concept of Love in Kierkegaard]，『阪南論集』 [The Hannan-ronshu], vol. 14, 1979, pp. 129–63.

— 「キェルケゴールの視点から見たゲーテのメフィスト観」 [Goethe's Mephistopheles from Kierkegaard's Point of View]，『同志社哲学年報』 [Societas Philosophiae Doshisha], vol. 24, 2001, pp. 1–22.

水垣渉 [Mizugaki, Wataru]，「パウロにおける≪私≫とキェルケゴールにおけ る≪自己≫—キリスト教的人間理解の基礎—」 ["I" in Paul and the "Self" in Kierkegaard: The Basis of the Christian Understanding of Human Being]，『キェルケゴール研究』 [Kierkegaard-Studiet], no. 23, 1993, pp. 17–26.

水田信 [Mizuta, Makoto]，「キェルケゴールにおける『神・人』の逆説につ いて」 [On the Paradox of "God-Man" in Kierkegaard]，『東海大学紀要文 学部』 [The Bulletin of the Faculty of Literature of Tokai University], vol. 13, 1969, pp. 59–68.

— 「キェルケゴールの『自己』についての一考察」 [A Study of "the Self" in Kierkegaard]，『東海大学紀要文学部』 [The Bulletin of the Faculty of Literature of Tokai University], vol. 15, 1971, pp. 94–108.

— 「キェルケゴールとブーバー—『単独者』の概念を中心に—」 [Kierkegaard and Buber: On the Concept of "the Single Individual"]，『キェル ケゴール研究』 [Kierkegaard-Studiet], no. 18, 1988, pp. 15–26.

— 「森有正とキェルケゴール—１つの比較論的試み」 [Arimasa Mori and Kierkegaard]，『哲学論文集』 [Tetsugaku-ronbunshu], vol. 26, 1990, pp. 1–20.

— 「滝沢克己とキェルケゴール：『宗教性』の問題を中心に」 [Katsumi Takizawa and Kierkegaard: Concerning "Religiousness"]，『比較思想研究』 [Studies in Comparative Philosophy], vol. 19, 1992, pp. 58–64.

— 『キェルケゴールと現代の実存—比較思想と対話の精神』 [Kierkegaard and Existence in Modern Times: The Comparative Thoughts and Dialogue], Fukuoka: Soubun-sha 1998.

— 「夏目漱石とセーレン・キェルケゴール：『自己』への問いと発見」 [Soseki Natsume and Søren Kierkegaard: Their Quest for "Self"]，『比較思想研究』 [Studies in Comparative Philosophy], vol. 27, 2000, pp. 90–6.

— 「近代的個人主義の超克—漱石とキェルケゴールに学ぶ」 [Overcoming Modern Individualism – Through Souseki and Kierkegaard]，『自然と文化』 [Nature and Culture], vol. 28, 2001, pp. 19–28.

— 「キェルケゴールに学ぶ—キェルケゴールと今日の我々」 [Meaning of a Study under/with Kierkegaard: Kierkegaard and Us in Present-day]，『新キェ ルケゴール研究』 [Kierkegaard Studies], no. 3, 2004, pp. 25–36.

森岡治夫 [Morioka, Haruo], 「十九世紀デンマーク文学とキェルケゴール」 [Nineteenth-Century Danish Literature and Kierkegaard], 『キェルケゴール研究』 [Kierkegaard-Studiet], no. 3, 1966, pp. 13–23.

森田美芽 [Morita, Mime], 「キェルケゴールの『宗教性』について」 [On Kierkegaard's Religiousness], 『待兼山論叢』 [Machikaneyama-ronso], vol. 19, 1985, pp. 29–44.

— 「キェルケゴールにおける愛の倫理」 [The Ethics of Love in Kierkegaard], 『キェルケゴール研究』 [Kierkegaard-Studiet], no. 17, 1987, pp. 29–38.

— 「キェルケゴールの女性論（1）：『ある女優の生涯における危機とある危機』に見る女性的なもの」 [Kierkegaard on Womanhood: Femininity in *The Crisis and a Crisis in the Life of an Actress*], 『神学と人文』 [Theology and Humanity], vol. 35, 1995, pp. 129–38.

— 「キェルケゴールの女性論（2）：キェルケゴールの宗教性と女性」 [A Feminist Interpretation of Kierkegaard (2): the Womanhood and the Religious in Kierkegaard's Religious Writings], 『神学と人文』 [Theology and Humanity], vol. 39, 1999, pp. 133–44.

— 「キェルケゴールにおける女性と女性論の問題」 [Analyzing Feminist Interpretations of Kierkegaard], 『新キェルケゴール研究』 [Kierkegaard Studies], no. 1, 2001, pp. 46–65.

— 「キェルケゴールの女性論（3）—レギーネとキェルケゴール」 [A Feminist Interpretation of Kierkegaard (3): Regine and Kierkegaard], 『神学と人文』 [Theology and Humanity], vol. 43, 2003, pp. 53–60; vol. 44, 2004, pp. 75–89.

— 「レギーネとキェルケゴール—その関係の再考察」 [Regine and Kierkegaard: Rethinking their Relationship], 『新キェルケゴール研究』 [Kierkegaard Studies], no. 4, 2005, pp. 23–41.

— 「キェルケゴールにおけるキリスト教と女性」 [The Relationship between Christianity and Woman in Kierkegaard], 『日本の神学』 [Theological Studies in Japan], vol. 44, 2005, pp. 41–62.

— 「森有正とキェルケゴール—主体性と他者性についての一つの試み」 [Arimasa Mori and Kierkegaard], 『同志社大学ヒューマン・セキュリティ研究センター年報』 [Annual Report: Doshisha Research Center for Human Security], vol. 3, 2006, pp. 51–70.

— 「キェルケゴールの女性論（4）美的実存における女性像とその意味（上）」 [A Feminist Interpretation of Kierkegaard (4): Images and Meanings of Woman in the Aesthetic Existence (part 1)], 『神学と人文』 [Theology and Humanity], vol. 46, 2006, pp. 79–87.

— 「キェルケゴールの女性論（5）文学批評『二つの時代』における女性の問題」 [A Feminist Interpretation of Kierkegaard (5): The Problems of Woman in *A Literary Review of Two Ages*], 『神学と人文』 [Theology and Humanity], vol. 47, 2007, pp. 155–68.

— 「キェルケゴール『不安』と『絶望』における女性性の問題—身体、心、性」 [The Problem of Femininity in Kierkegaard's "Anxiety" and "Despair"], 『研究論集』 [Kenkyu-ronshu], vol. 4, 2007, pp. 225–41.

— 「キェルケゴールの女性論—実存、他者、宗教性」 [Feminist Interpretation of Kierkegaard's Thought and Life: Existence, Others, Religiosity], 『新キェルケゴール研究』 [Kierkegaard Studies], no. 8, 2010, pp. 24–47.

— 『キェルケゴールの女性論』 [Feminist Interpretation of Kierkegaard], Fukuoka: Sogen-sha 2010.

— 「不安と絶望—キェルケゴールの人間論」 [Anxiety and Despair: Humanity in Kierkegaard's Thought], 『改革派神学』 [Reformed Churches], vol. 38, 2011, pp. 4–31.

— 「キェルケゴールのソクラテス論—レオ・シュトラウスとのかかわりを求めて—」 [Kierkegaard's Image of Socrates—in Comparison with Leo Strauss], 』新キェルケゴール研究』 [Kierkegaard Studies], no. 10, 2012, pp. 1–15.

— 「生誕200周年記念シンポジウム『キェルケゴールの魅力』：『キェルケゴールの魅力—いま私たちはキェルケゴールをどう読むか—』の意義」 [Kierkegaard Bicentennial Symposium "How Do We Read Kierkegaard?"], 『新キェルケゴール研究』 [Kierkegaard Studies], no. 12, 2014, pp. 45–53.

諸富祥彦 [Morotomi, Yoshihiko], 「人格形成における『絶望』の深化の意義—S.キルケゴールの『死に至る病』の検討を中心に」 [The Meaning of Deepening Despair in Forming Personality], 『関東教育学会紀要』 [Pedagogica Centrajapona: Annual Report of the Kanto Educational Research Society], vol. 16, 1989, pp. 23–30.

— 「『実存的自己生成への導き入れ』の方法: S. キルケゴールの所論の検討を中心に」 [A Method of "Introducing the Other into the Process of Self-Becoming": An Examination of S. Kierkegaard's Theory of Existential Communication], 『教育方法学研究』 [Research Journal of Educational Methods], vol. 15, 1990, pp. 19–27.

— 「キルケゴールの『倫理的伝達』による実存の覚醒: 『ソクラテス的産婆術』の受容と批判的展開」 [The Awakening to Existence through Kierkegaard's "Ethical Transmission": Reception and Critical Development of Socrates' "Maieutic Method"], 『教育哲学研究』 [Studies in the Philosophy of Education], vol. 66, 1992, pp. 43–58.

村上暁子 [Murakami, Akiko], 「レヴィナスにおけるキルケゴール読解を通じた主体性概念の改鋳について—講演『神人？』における特異な受肉理解をめぐって」 [The Idea of Subjectivity in Levinas Built through his Reading of Kierkegaard], 『哲学』 [Philosophy], vol. 131, 2013, pp. 153–80.

村上恭一 [Murakami, Kyoichi], 「キルケゴールにおける個の論理—ヘーゲル哲学との対決において」 [The Logic of Individuality in Kierkegaard: In Contrast to Hegelian Philosophy], 『理想』 [Riso], vol. 398, 1966, pp. 78–87.

— 「キルケゴールのヘーゲル批判」 [Kierkegaard's Critique of Hegel], 『法政大学教養部紀要』 [Bulletin of Hosei University], vol. 66, 1988, pp. 89–106.

— 「キルケゴールの時間論—とくに『不安の概念』における『瞬間』概念についての若干の注釈から」 [Kierkegaard's Theory about Time], 『フィロソフィア』 [Philosophia], vol. 76, 1988, pp. 69–84.

— 「キルケゴールの『パン屑』讃歌」 "Kierkegaard's Praise of a Breadcrumb],『図書』 [Books], vol. 661, 2004, pp. 15–19.

村岡晋一 [Muraoka, Shinichi], 「キルケゴールの時間論」 [Kierkegaard's Argument about Time], 『中央大学文学部紀要』 [Bulletin of Faculty of Humanities, Chuo University], vol. 192, 2002, pp. 27–50.

村瀬学 [Murase, Manabu], 『新しいキルケゴール』 [The New Understanding of Kierkegaard: An Essay on the Concept of the Theory of Plural Selves], Tokyo: Daiwa-shobo 1986.

村瀬良子 [Murase, Yoshiko], 「キルケゴールにおける批判的主体の形成:『現代の批判』の教育論的意義」 [Formation of Critical Subjectivity in S.A. Kierkegaard: The Pedagogical Significance of *The Present Age*], 『国際基督教大学学報I-A教育研究』 [International Christian University Publications. I-A, Educational Studies], vol. 23, 1980, pp. 57–87.

村田俊郎 [Murata, Toshiro], 「苦悩する実存—パスカルとキルケゴール」 [The Suffering Existence: Pascal and Kierkegaard], 『世紀』 [The Century], no. 391, 1982, pp. 63–72.

室伏高信 [Murobuse, Koshin], 「あれか・これか」 [Either/Or], in his 『青年の書』 [Books for Youth], Tokyo: Seinen-shobo 1936, pp. 1–9.

室井光広 [Muroi, Mitsuhiro], 『キルケゴールとアンデルセン』 [Kierkegaard and Andersen], Tokyo: Kodan-sha 2000.

務台理作 [Mutai, Risaku], 「キルケゴールの現代的意義」 [The Meaning of Kierkegaard for Today], 『理想』 [Riso], vol. 269, 1955.

— (ed.), 『セーレン＝キルケゴール—その人と思想』 [Søren Kierkegaard: His Life and Thoughts], Tokyo: Riso-sha 1956.

武藤一雄 [Muto, Kazuo], 「キルケゴールに於ける時間性の問題」 [The Problem of Time in Kierkegaard], 『基督教文化』 [Christian Culture], vol. 33, 1949, pp. 40–3.

— 「宗教的実存と現代的課題—キエルケゴールに就いての一考察」 [The Religious Existence and its Task for Today], 『理想』 [Riso], vol. 198, 1949, pp. 24–35.

— 『信仰と倫理—キエルケゴールの問題』 [Faith and Ethics: Problems of Kierkegaard], Kyoto: Hozo-kan 1950.

— 「キルケゴールの現代的意義」 [The Meaning of Kierkegaard for Today], 『福音と世界』 [Gospel and World], vol. 10, 1955.

— 「キルケゴールの宗教哲学」 [Kierkegaard's Philosophy of Religion], 『理想』 [Riso], vol. 269, 1955.

— 『キエルケゴール—その思想と信仰』 [Kierkegaard: His Thought and Faith], Tokyo: Sobun-sha 1967.

— 「キルケゴールへの問い」 [Questions to Kierkegaard], 『理想』 [Riso], vol. 555, 1979, pp. 37–49.

武藤光朗 [Muto, Mitsuro], 「キエルケゴールとマルクス」 [Kierkegaard and Marx], 『理想』 [Riso], vol. 198, 1949, pp. 56–65.

長江弘晃 [Nagae, Hiroaki], 「青年ヘーゲルとキルケゴール—『対立』、『生』、そして『イエス・キリスト』をめぐって」 [Young Hegel and Kierkegaard], 『精神科学』 [Science of Mind], vol. 12, 1973, pp. 96–104.

長島要一 [Nagashima, Yoichi],「『作家』キルケゴールの虚と実―婚約者レ ギーネの日記から」[Falsehood and Truth in Kierkegaard as an Author: From Fiancée Regine's Diaries],『図書』[Tosho], no. 776, 2013, pp. 22–8; no. 777, 2013, pp. 30–6.

中村憲司 [Nakamura, Kenji],「キルケゴールにおける<自己>と<躓き>につい て」[On "the Self" and "Offense" in Kierkegaard],『西日本工業大学紀要人 文社会科学編』[Memoirs of Nishinippon Institute of Technology. Humanities and Social Sciences], vol. 3, 1987, pp. 1–7.

中村幸平 [Nakamura, Kohei],「キルケゴールにおける主体性」 [Kierkegaard's Subjectivity],『大阪女子学園短期大学紀要』[Bulletin of Osaka Joshigakuen Junior College], vol. 2, 1958, pp. 49–58; vol. 3, 1959, pp. 1–13.

―「キルケゴールに於ける大衆と単独者の二重性」[The Duplicity of the Mass and the Single Individual in Kierkegaard],『大阪女子学園短期大学紀 要』[Bulletin of Osaka Joshigakuen Junior College], vol. 4, 1960, pp. 1–17.

―「キルケゴールの人間の概念」[Kierkegaard's Concept of the Human],『 大阪女子学園短期大学紀要』[Bulletin of Osaka Joshigakuen Junior College], vol. 5, 1961, pp. 85–96; vol. 6, 1962, pp. 62–77; vol. 7, 1963, pp. 139–67.

―「キルケゴールの人間と科学の関係についての一考察」[On the Rela- tionship of Human Being and Science in Kierkegaard],『キルケゴール研究』 [Kierkegaard-Studiet], no. 1, 1964, pp. 66–77.

―「キルケゴールにおける人間の概念：自己否定について」[On Kierke- gaard's Concept of the Human],『大阪女子学園短期大学紀要』[Bulletin of Osaka Joshigakuen Junior College], vol. 9, 1965, pp. 147–67.

―「キルケゴールの自己の概念」[The Concept of the Self in Kierkegaard], 『キルケゴール研究』[Kierkegaard-Studiet], vol. 2, 1965, pp. 31–40.

―「キルケゴールの自己と現存在」[The Self in Kierkegaard and Heidegger's Dasein],『キルケゴール研究』[Kierkegaard-Studiet], no. 6, 1969, pp. 5–21.

―「キルケゴールの宗教的実存と宗教美術への一考察」 [An Essay on Kierkegaard's Religious Existence and Religious Art],『キルケゴール研 究』[Kierkegaard-Studiet], no. 7, 1977, pp. 21–7.

中尾隆司 [Nakao, Takashi],「ヘーゲルとキエルケゴール」[Hegel and Kierkegaard],『神戸山手女子短期大学紀要』[Kobe Yamate Women's Junior College Annual Report], vol. 2, 1957, pp. 31–8.

中山剛史 [Nakayama, Takeshi],「西田幾多郎とキルケゴール：自己の根底にお ける<絶対のパラドックス>をめぐって」[Kitaro Nishida and Kierkegaard: On the Absolute Paradox in the Ground of the Self],『比較思想』[Studies in Comparative Philosophy], vol. 9, 1996, pp. 21–33.

中里巧 [Nakazato, Satoshi],「キルケゴール―末期医療と土着的自然観の 再生」[Kierkegaard: Terminal Care and Restoration of Indigenous View of Nature],『理想』[Riso], vol. 650, 1992, pp. 29–40.

―『キルケゴールとその思想風土―北欧のロマンティークと敬虔主義』 [Kierkegaard and the Climate of Traditional Thought: Romanticism and Pietism in Northern Europe], Tokyo: Sobun-sha 1994.

—「キルケゴール思想における『実存』概念解釈について—『実存』概念の研究方法をめぐる試論」 [An Interpretation of the Concept "Existence" in Kierkegaard's Thought: An Essay on the Methodology of the Study of "Existence"], 『白山哲学』 [Bulletin of Toyo University], vol. 30, 1996, pp. 41–61.

—「悪魔的絶望と覚醒」 [Demonic Despair and Awakening], 『理想』 [Riso], no. 676, 2006, pp. 13–23.

—「キェルケゴール思想研究にともなうアポリアについて—実存的思索とキリスト教の問題性」 [Aporia in Kierkegaard's Thoughts: The Problems of the Existential Thinking and the Christian Faith], 『新キェルケゴール研究』 [Kierkegaard Studies], no. 7, 2009, pp. 78–97.

—「マザー＝テレサとキェルケゴール—神の不在とイエスの遍在—」 [Mother Teresa and S. Kierkegaard: God's Absence and Omnipotence of Jesus], 『新キェルケゴール研究』 [Kierkegaard Studies], no. 9, 2011, pp. 1–19.

—「呪詛と自己犠牲—キェルケゴール思想における祈りの本質—」 [The Curse and the Self-sacrifice: The Essence of Prayer in S. Kierkegaard's Thoughts], 『新キェルケゴール研究』 [Kierkegaard Studies], no. 11, 2013, pp. 34–47.

中澤英雄 [Nakazawa, Hideo], 『カフカとキルケゴール』 [Kafka and Kierkegaard], Tokyo: Onbook 2006.

中沢洽樹 [Nakazawa, Koki], 「若きキエルケゴールに於ける宗教的実存の問題—レギーネ事件を中心として」 [The Problem of Religious Existence in the Young Kierkegaard], 『理想』 [Riso], vol. 198, 1949, pp. 76–85.

—「キェルケゴールの基督教」 [Kierkegaard's Christianity], 『独立』 [Dokuritsu], vol. 18, 1950, pp. 23–33.

中澤臨川・生田長江 [Nakazawa, Rinsen and Choko Ikuta], 「キアルケガールドとイプセン」 [Kierkegaard and Ibsen], in their (eds.) 『近代思想16講』 [Sixteen Lectures on Modern Ideas], Tokyo: Shincho-sha 1915, pp. 265–9.

成川武夫 [Narukawa, Takeo], 「美的実存—キルケゴールとベッカーとの対比において」 [The Aesthetic Existence: Comparing Kierkegaard with Becker], 『東京芸術大学美術学部紀要』 [Bulletin of the Faculty of Fine Arts, Tokyo University of Arts], vol. 9, 1973, pp. 1–32.

新畑耕作 [Niihata, Kosaku], 「キェルケゴールの『善に対する不安』という概念」 [Kierkegaard's Concept of "Anxiety for the Good"], 『倫理學年報』 [Annals of Ethics], vol. 22, 1973, pp. 125–36.

—「キェルケゴールの時間論」 [Kierkegaard's Concept of Time], 『実存主義』 [Existentialism], vol. 66, 1973, pp. 54–63.

—「後期シェリングとキェルケゴール」 [Schelling in the Late Period and Kierkegaard], 『理想』 [Riso], vol. 510, 1975, pp. 25–30.

二条秀政 [Nijo, Hidemasa], 「親鸞における『単独者』の問題—キェルケゴールとの類比的考察」 [The Problem of "the Single Individual" in Shinran: Comparative Study with Kierkegaard], 『眞宗研究』 [Journal of Shinshu-studies], vol. 4, 1959.

—「キエルケゴールの『倫理的なるもの』」 ["The Ethical" in Kierkegaard], 『哲学論集』 [The Philosophical Studies], vol. 9, 1963.

—「主体的真理、実存における自由—キェルケゴール的『自己理解』」[Subjective Truth and Freedom in Existence], 『哲学論集』[Philosophical Studies], vol. 12, 1966, pp. 59–88.

—「実存哲学における基本概念としての個体と人類—キェルケゴールの思想を中心として」[The Individuality and Mankind as Basic Concepts of Existential Philosophy], 『大谷学報』[The Journal of Buddhist Studies and Humanities], vol. 48, 1969, pp. 50–64.

西川武夫 [Nishikawa, Takeo], 「キェルケゴールにおける超越と逆説—その現代倫理学に与える示唆」[Transcendence and Paradox in Kierkegaard], 『立命館文學』[Ritsumeikan Literature], vol. 285, 1969, pp. 1–14.

西倉直樹 [Nishikura, Naoki], 「キェルケゴールにおける殉教者の理念」[The Idea of a Martyr in Kierkegaard], 『キェルケゴール研究』[Kierkegaard-Studiet], no. 19, 1989, pp. 27–40.

西村恵信 [Nishimura, Eshin], 「キェルケゴールにおける歴史の問題」[The Problem of History in Kierkegaard], 『禪學研究』[Zen Studies], vol. 56, 1968, pp. 35–66.

—「禅とキェルケゴールの通路」[Zen and Kierkegaard—Issue of the Self-pursuit], 『キェルケゴール研究』[Kierkegaard-Studiet], no. 24, 1994, pp. 15–26; republished in 『駒沢大学禅研究所年報』[Annual Report of the Zen Institute, Komazawa University], vol. 13, 2002, pp. 1–10 and 『京都哲学撰書』[Kyoto Philosophy Collections], ed. by Shizuteru Ueda, Kyoto: Toei-sha 2006, pp. 362–83.

西崎等恵 [Nishizaki, Toe], 「親鸞とキェルケゴール」[Shinran and Kierkegaard], 『龍谷大学大学院紀要文学研究科』[The Bulletin of the Graduate School of Ryukoku University], vol. 6, 1985, pp. 139–42.

丹羽治男 [Niwa, Haruo], 「トオマス・マンの聖書ロマンにおけるアブラハムとヨゼフ: ゼーレン・キルケゴールとトオマス・マン」[Abraham and Joseph in the Biblical Novel of Thomas Mann: Kierkegaard and Thomas Mann], 『大阪経大論集』[Journal of Osaka University of Economics], vol. 79, 1971, pp. 66–93.

信岡茂浩 [Nobuoka, Shigehiro], 「キェルケゴール『死に至る病』の『キリスト教的理解』」[Kierkegaard's Christian Understanding in *The Sickness unto Death*], 『基督教学研究』[Journal of Christian Studies], vol. 10, 1988, pp. 144–54.

野口芳雄 [Noguchi, Yoshio], 「ケルケゴールに於ける絶望と実存」[Despair and Existence in Kierkegaard], 『三重大学学芸学部教育研究所研究紀要』[Bulletin of the Faculty of Education, Mie University], vol. 13, 1955, pp. 15–22.

—「キェルケゴールにおける実存と倫理」[Existence and Ethics in Kierkegaard], 『三重大学学芸学部教育研究所研究紀要』[Bulletin of the Faculty of Education, Mie University], vol. 26, 1962.

—「キェルケゴールにおける時代と実存」[The Ages and Existence in Kierkegaard Studies], 『三重大学学芸学部教育研究所研究紀要』[Bulletin of the Faculty of Education, Mie University], vol. 31, 1964.

—「キェルケゴールにおける愛の構造」[The Structure of Love in Kierkegaard], 『哲学』[Philosophy], vol. 17, 1965.

— 「キェルケゴールの倫理的実存とその限界」 [Kierkegaard's Ethical Existence and its Limit], 『三重大学教育学部教育研究所研究紀要』 [Bulletin of the Faculty of Education, Mie University], vol. 37, 1967, pp. 21–32.

野村知佐子 [Nomura, Chisako], 「バタイユとキルケゴールにおける罪の概念」 [The Concept of Sin in Bataille and Kierkegaard], *Stella: Etudes de langue et litterature francaises*, vol. 22, 2003, pp. 115–29.

落合健一 [Ochiai, Kenichi], 「単独者」 [The Single Individual], 『ふじ』 [Fuji], vol. 5, 1956.

小川圭治 [Ogawa, Keiji], 「実存の三段階と倫理の問題」 [Three Existential Stages and the Problem of Ethics], 『理想』 [Riso], vol. 269, 1955.

— 「愛の無常と永遠—キルケゴール『愛のわざ』について」 [Uncertainty and Eternity of Love], 『福音と世界』 [Gospel and World], vol. 13, 1958.

— 「近代主義の成立とその問題点: キルケゴール研究への序章」 [The Making of Modern Spirit and its Problem: An Introduction to the Study on S.A. Kierkegaard], 『東京女子大學論集』 [Science Reports of Tokyo Woman's Christian College], vol. 11, 1960, pp. 1–26.

— 「キルケゴール解釈の問題」 [The Problem of the Interpretation of Kierkegaard], 『東京女子大學論集』 [Science Reports of Tokyo Woman's Christian College], vol. 14, 1964, pp. 41–63.

— 「三木清とセーレン・キルケゴール: 実存主義の受容をめぐって」 [Kiyoshi Miki and Søren Kierkegaard : On the Acceptance of Existentialism in Japan], 『東京女子大學附屬比較文化研究所紀要』 [Annals of the Institute for Comparative Studies of Culture, Tokyo Woman's Christian University], vol. 22, 1966, pp. 1–43.

— 「西田幾多郎のキルケゴール理解」 [Kitaro Nishida's Understanding of Kierkegaard], 比較文化 [Comparative Studies of Culture], vol. 15, 1969, pp. 59–89.

— 「西田幾多郎とS・キルケゴール」 [Kitaro Nishida and S. Kierkegaard], 『東京女子大學論集』 [Science Reports of Tokyo Woman's Christian College], vol. 19, 1969, pp. 77–82.

— 「キルケゴールと現代思想」 [Kierkegaard and Modern Thought], 『実存主義』 [Existentialism], vol. 49, 1969, pp. 79–97.

— 「S. キルケゴール『哲学的断片へのあとがき』の構成と成立について」 [On the Structure and Formation of Kierkegaard's *Postscript*], 『宗教研究』 [The Journal of Religious Studies], vol. 47, 1974, pp. 23–52.

— 『主体と超越—キルケゴールからバルトへ』 [The Subject and Transcendence: From Kierkegaard to Barth], Tokyo: Sobun-sha 1975.

— 『キルケゴール』 [Kierkegaard], Tokyo: Kodan-sha 1979 (*Series of the Intellectual Heritage of Mankind*).

— 「キルケゴール研究の方法について」 [On the Methods of Studying Kierkegaard], 『基督教学研究』 [Journal of Christian Studies], vol. 3, 1980, pp.1–33.

— 「日本におけるキルケゴール—西田幾多郎・田辺元の場合」 [Kierkegaard in Japan: in Kitaro Nishida and Hajime Tanabe], 『日本の神学』 [Theological Studies in Japan], vol. 27, 1988, pp. 25–48.

荻原樂 [Ogiwara, Madoka]，「続・信仰のパラドックス―キルケゴールに
  したがって」[The Paradox of Faith (2): Following Kierkegaard]，『東京国
  際大学論叢商学部編』[The Journal of Tokyo International University. The
  Department of Commerce]，vol. 37, 1988, pp. 47–62.

小原信 [Ohara, Shin]，「キルケゴールにおける倫理と言語」[Ethics and
  Language in Kierkegaard]，『日本の神学』[Theological Studies in Japan]，
  vol. 6, 1967, pp. 185–92.

――「キルケゴールにおける言語と伝達の問題 ―近似と間接的伝達をめぐっ
  て」[Language and Communication in the Thought of Kierkegaard]，『倫理學
  年報』[Annals of Ethics]，vol. 18, 1969, pp. 79–88.

――「キルケゴールにおける言語と宗教」[Language and Religion in Kierke-
  gaard]，『科学哲学』[Philosophy of Science]，vol. 2, 1969, pp. 91–7.

――「科学と宗教―キルケゴールの学問論」[Kierkegaard on Science and
  Religion]，『倫理學年報』[Annals of Ethics]，vol. 19, 1970, pp. 69–80.

――「わが国における最近のキルケゴール研究」[Recent Kierkegaard Studies
  in Japan]，『実存主義』[Existentialism]，vol. 53, 1970, pp. 88–92.

――「キルケゴールと内村鑑三」[Kierkegaard and Kanzo Uchimura]，『日本の
  神学』[Theological Studies in Japan]，vol. 27, 1988, pp. 180–92.

岡林洋 [Okabayashi, Hiroshi]，「沈黙のパラドックス―ロマン的イロニー批
  判以後のキェルケゴールと芸術概念」[The Paradox of Silence]，『文化
  学年報』[Annual Report of Cultural Studies – Doshisha University]，vol. 39,
  1990, pp. 216–35.

岡林克己 [Okabayashi, Katsumi]，「キルケゴールの『無限断念』に就い
  て―現代倫理の動向と目的論的中断の意義」[On Kierkegaard's "Infinite
  Renunciation"]，『島根大学論集人文科学』[Bulletin of Shimane University]，
  vol. 11, 1962, pp. 38–52.

沖野政弘 [Okino, Masahiro]，「キルケゴールの実存弁証法―主体性と逆説
  との弁証法的関係」[Kierkegaard's Existential Dialectics]，『大阪電気通信
  大学研究論集人文・社会科学編』[Reports of Osaka Electro-Communication
  University. Social Science and Humanity]，vol. 2, 1966, pp. 1–25.

――「キルケゴールにおける教義学と弁証法」[Dogmatics and Dialectics in
  Kierkegaard]，『関西学院哲学研究年報』[Yearbook of Philosophical Studies]，
  vol. 6, 1966, pp. 80–97.

大小島真二 [Okojima, Shinji]，『キルケゴールの実存哲学』[Kierkegaard's
  Existential Philosophy]，Osaka: Kahori-shobo 1947.

奥山裕介 [Okuyama, Yusuke]，「境界人の詩学としての『あれか=これか』―
  セーアン・キェルケゴールのユラン旅行と１８４０年代コペンハーゲン
  における遊歩者像の形成」[*Either/Or* as Poetics of a Boundary Man]，
  『独文学報』[Studia Germanica Osacensia]，no. 29, 2013, pp. 27–54.

大峯顕 [Omine, Akira]，「実存弁証法と有限性の形而上学―キルケゴール対
  フィヒテのための序章―」[The Existential Dialectic and the Metaphysics of the
  Finite]，『キェルケゴール研究』[Kierkegaard-Studiet]，no. 3, 1966, pp. 24–31.

――「近代的自己意識の問題としてのキェルケゴールとフィヒテ」
  [Kierkegaard and Fichte on the Problem of Reflection]，『キェルケゴール研
  究』[Kierkegaard-Studiet]，no. 4, 1967, pp. 20–8.

—「キェルケゴールとヘーゲルの絶対的認識」 [Kierkegaard and Hegel's Absolute Cognition], 『キェルケゴール研究』 [Kierkegaard-Studiet], no. 6, 1969, pp. 22–31.

大西優香 [Onishi, Yuka], 「キェルケゴールにおける真摯の意味—『不安の概念』の読解を中心に」 [The Meaning of the Concept "Earnestness" in Kierkegaard], 『新キェルケゴール研究』 [Kierkegaard Studies], no. 8, 2010, pp. 48–65.

小野蓮明 [Ono, Renmyo], 「瞬間と反復—キェルケゴールに就ての一考察」 [The Moment and Repetition], 『哲学論集』 [The Philosophical Studies], vol. 8, 1962.

—「キェルケゴールにおける『主体性』の問題」 [The Problem of "Subjectivity" in Kierkegaard], 『金沢経済大学論集』 [Journal of Kanazawa College of Economics], vol. 1, 1967, pp. 99–128.

小野雄介 [Ono, Yusuke], 「キルケゴール『反復』の成立と構成について—仮名の問題を手がかりに」 [On the Composition and Construction of Kierkegaard's *Repetition:* The Problem of his Use of Pseudonyms], 『茨城大学人文科学研究』 [Ibaraki Studies in Humanities], vol. 3, 2011, pp. 1–11.

大野木哲 [Onogi, Satoshi], 「キルケゴールにおける『反復』の概念」 [The Concept of Repetition in Kierkegaard], 『鳥取大学教育学部研究報告人文社会科学』 [The Journal of the Faculty of Education. Cultural Science], vol. 22, 1971, pp. 53–61.

小野島康雄 [Onojima, Yasuo], 「キルケゴール『反復』について」 [On Kierkegaard Repetition], 『白山哲学』 [Bulletin of Toyo University], vol. 10, 1976, pp. 111–34.

—「キルケゴール『後書』におけるフモールについて」 [On Humor in Kierkegaard's *Postscript*], 『白山哲学』 [Bulletin of Toyo University], vol. 18, 1984, pp. 147–63.

—「キルケゴールにおける主体性の問題—原罪と信仰をめぐって」 [The Problem of Subjectivity in Kierkegaard], 『白山哲学』 [Bulletin of Toyo University], vol. 23, 1989, pp. 126–48.

—「キルケゴールと懐疑」 [Kierkegaard and Skepticism], 『白山哲学』 [Bulletin of Toyo University], vol. 24, 1990, pp. 39–62.

大貫敦子 [Onuki, Atsuko], 「自己犠牲の弁証法—アドルノのキルケゴール論をめぐって」 [Dialectics of Self-sacrifice: On Adorno's Interpretation of Kierkegaard], 『現代思想』 [Gendai-shiso], vol. 16, 1989, pp. 102–15.

大類雅敏 [Ori, Masatoshi], 『内村鑑三とキェルケゴール』 [Kanzo Uchimura and Kierkegaard], Tokyo: Eiko-shuppansha 1997.

太田裕信 [Ota, Hironobu], 「西田幾多郎の『場所の論理』と罪悪の問題—キェルケゴールとの関わりにおいて」 ["The Logic of Locus" and the Concept of Sin in Nishida Kitaro: In Relation to Kierkegaard], 『宗教研究』 [Journal of Religious Studies], vol. 86–1, 2012, pp. 53–78.

大田孝太郎 [Ota, Kotaro], 「キルケゴールのソクラテス像—『イロニーの概念』をめぐって」 [Kierkegaard's Image of Socrates: On *The Concept of Irony*], 『待兼山論叢』 [Machikaneyama-ronso], vol. 14, 1980, pp. 1–17.

—「キルケゴールにおける『否定的なもの』の意義」 [The Meaning of "the Negative" in Kierkegaard], 『哲学論叢』 [Journal of Philosophy], vol. 9, 1981, pp. 43–65.

太田早苗 [Ota, Sanae], 「回想と耳の思想家—キェルケゴールのレギーネ宛の手紙から」 [A Thinker of Recollection and Ear: Kierkegaard's Letters to Regine], 『明星大学研究紀要人文学部』 [Research Bulletin of Meisei University. Humanities and Social Sciences], vol. 8, 1972, pp. 13–20.

—「『これか—あれか』の娘、レギーネ・オルセン」 [The Girl of *Either/Or*: Regine Olsen], 『キェルケゴール研究』 [Kierkegaard-Studiet], no. 22, 1992, pp. 45–52.

大谷愛人 [Otani, Hidehito], 「キェルケゴールの思惟方法: 主体性及びイロニーの概念の哲学方法論的意味」 [Thought-Method of S. Kierkegaard: Methodological Sense of Conceptions of "Subjectivity" and "Irony"], 『哲學』 [Philosophy], vol. 29, 1953, pp. 67–98.

—「キルケゴールにおける逆説の概念」 [The Concept of Paradox in Kierkegaard], 『理想』 [Riso], vol. 269, 1955.

—「キルケゴールによるアンデルセン批評の歴史的背景: 処女出版『いまなお生ける者の手記より』について」 [The Historical Background of Kierkegaard's Criticism of Andersen], 『哲學』 [Philosophy], vol. 40, 1961, pp. 69–112.

—「デンマーク的ユーモアとキルケゴール」 [Danish Humor and Kierkegaard], 『理想』 [Riso], vol. 351, 1962.

—「キルケゴール文献目録」 [List of Kierkegaard Literature], 『理想』 [Riso], vol. 360, 1963, pp. 80–94.

—「19世紀前半におけるデンマーク教会史素描—キルケゴール登場のデンマーク教会史的背景」 [A Brief Sketch on the History of Danish Church in the Early 19th Century], 『理想』 [Riso], vol. 360, 1963.

—『キルケゴール青年時代の研究』正・続 [A Study of Kierkegaard in his Youth], vols. 1–2, Tokyo: Keiso-shobo 1966–1968.

—「19世紀前半世紀デンマークにおける反ヘーゲル主義思想の系譜: キルケゴール理解のための一つの前提」 [Genealogy of Anti-Hegelians in Denmark in the Mid-Nineteenth Century: One Premise for Understanding the Thought of S. Kierkegaard], 『哲學』 [Philosophy], vol. 50, 1967, pp. 23–46.

—「S・キルケゴールのアイロニー理解:その序論的考察のためのノートとして」 [S. Kierkegaard's Understanding of Irony], 『哲學』 [Philosophy], vol. 56, 1970, pp. 21–58.

—「キルケゴール実存の段階説の起源」 [The Origin of Kierkegaard's Theory of the Existential Stages], 『理想』 [Riso], vol. 481, 1973, pp. 71–90.

—「『時と永遠』という問題—キルケゴールを介して」 [The Problem of "Time and Eternity": From Kierkegaard's Viewpoint], 『理想』 [Riso], vol. 489, 1974, pp. 61–73.

—『キルケゴール著作活動の研究 前篇—青年時代を中心に行われた文学研究の実態』 [A Study on Kierkegaard's Authorship, Part 1: The Realities of the Young Kierkegaard's Studies of Literature], Tokyo: Keiso-shobo 1989.

—『キルケゴール著作活動の研究 後編—全著作構造の解明』 [A Study on Kierkegaard's Authorship, Part 2: Investigation in the Structure of the Entirety of his Works], Tokyo: Keiso-shobo 1991.

—『キルケゴール教会闘争の研究』 [A Study on Kierkegaard's Attack on Christendom], Tokyo: Keiso-shobo 2007.

大谷愛人・泉治典 [Otani, Hidehito and Harunori Izumi], 『キルケゴール—死にいたる病』 [Kierkegaard: The Sickness unto Death], Tokyo: Yuikaku 1980.

大谷愛人・柏原啓一 [Otani, Hidehito and Keiichi Kashiwabara], 「キルケゴールと現代—日本のキルケゴール研究を回顧しつつ」 [Kierkegaard and Modernity], 『理想』 [Riso], vol. 555, 1979, pp. 2–36.

大谷長 [Otani, Masaru], 「キエルケゴール『単独者』概念成立史の一考察」 [On the Formation of Kierkegaard's Concept of "the Single Individuality"], 『哲学雑誌』 [Journal of Philosophy], vol. 66, 1951, pp. 51–78.

— 『キエルケゴールにおける授受の弁証法』 [The Dialectic of Indirect Communication in Kierkegaard], Tokyo: Kobun-do 1952; republished as vol. 1 of 大谷長著作集 [Masaru Otani's Selected Works], vols. 1–3, Fukuoka: Sogen-sha 2001–2003.

— 「キルケゴールの『受取り直し』」 ["Repetition" in Kierkegaard], 『哲学研究』 [The Journal of Philosophical Studies], vol. 35, 1952, pp. 608–26.

— 「キヤケゴーアとドン・キホーテ」 [Kierkegaard and Don Quixote], 『大阪外国語大学学報』 [Journal of Osaka University of Foreign Studies], vol. 6, 1958.

— 「キヤケゴーアに於ける『大地震』の今一つの説明—カール・サガウ『責めありや—責めなきや』に関連して」 [Another Explanation of Kierkegaard's "Great Earthquake"], 『大阪外国語大学学報』 [Journal of Osaka University of Foreign Studies], vol. 7, 1959.

— 「デンマーク・ソェーヤン・キヤケゴーア協会の現況」 [The Current Situation of the Kierkegaard Society in Denmark], 『哲学研究』 [The Journal of Philosophical Studies], vol. 40, 1959.

— 「キヤケゴーアに於ける著作活動の宗教的発展」 [The Religious Development of Kierkegaard's Authorship], 『宗教研究』 [Journal of Religious Studies], vol. 160, 1959.

— 「キヤケゴーアの爪の痕—モゥエンス・ボウルセン『キヤケゴーア的運命の人々』に関連して」 [Kierkegaard's Scratch], 『大阪外国語大学学報』 [Journal of Osaka University of Foreign Studies], vol. 10, 1961.

— 「矛盾原理論争—キヤケゴーア理解のための寄与」 [Dispute over the Principle of Contradiction: for Understanding Kierkegaard], 『大阪外国語大学学報』 [Journal of Osaka University of Foreign Studies], vol. 11, 1962.

— 『キエルケゴールにおける真理と現実性』 [Truth and Reality in Kierkegaard], Tokyo: Sobun-sha 1963; republished as vol. 2 of 大谷長著作集 [Masaru Otani's Selected Works], vols. 1–3, Fukuoka: Sogen-sha 2001–2003.

— 「現実性の逆説性—シュレーヤーのキエルケゴール研究に関連する単純な心理学的考察—」 [The Paradox in the Reality: A Simple Psychological Consideration of Henning Schröer's Study on Kierkegaard], 『キエルケゴール研究』 [Kierkegaard-Studiet], no. 1, 1964, pp. 78–88.

— 「キエルケゴールの『後書』における『滑稽なもの』について」 [On "the Comical" in Kierkegaard's *Postscript*], 『キエルケゴール研究』 [Kierkegaard-Studiet], vol. 2, 1965, pp. 41–8.

— 「人間破滅性の凝視—キエルケゴールに関連する複視的序説—」 [Staring at the Human Loss: A Diploic Introduction to Kierkegaard's Thought], 『キエルケゴール研究』 [Kierkegaard-Studiet], no. 3, 1966, pp. 32–9.

—「キェルケゴールの『不安』における自由の自己顕示について」 [Self-Manifestation of Freedom in "Anxiety" in Kierkegaard], 『キェルケゴール研究』 [Kierkegaard-Studiet], no. 4, 1967, pp. 29–37.

—『キェルケゴールにおける自由と非自由』 [Freedom and Non-Freedom in Kierkegaard], Tokyo: Sobun-sha 1977; republished as vol. 3 of 大谷長著作集 [Masaru Otani's Selected Works], vols. 1–3, Fukuoka: Sogen-sha 2001–2003.

—「キェルケゴールにおける『絶望』概念の二つの顔」 [Janus-Faces of the Concept of "the Despair" in Kierkegaard], 『キェルケゴール研究』 [Kierke-gaard-Studiet], no. 7, 1977, pp. 28–37

—「キェルケゴールの神概念との浄土真宗の理念的な可能的接触について」 [On the Possibility of Ideal Contact between the Japanese Shin-Buddhism of Pure Land and the Concept of God by Kierkegaard], 『キェルケゴール研究』 [Kierkegaard-Studiet], no. 9, 1978, pp. 25–42.

—「キェルケゴールを巡って格闘する精神達（その二）—私的回想—」 [Spirits which Fight around Kierkegaard (2)], 『キェルケゴール研究』 [Kierkegaard-Studiet], no. 12, 1982, pp. 15–26.

—「キェルケゴールにおける倫理的なものと『単独者』の殉教」 [The Ethi-cal and the Martyrdom of the Single Individual in Kierkegaard], 『キェルケゴール研究』 [Kierkegaard-Studiet], no. 14, 1984, pp. 37–50.

—「キェルケゴールの著作表題の持つ問題性（I）—『哲学的断片』の表題における諸問題を中心として—」 [On the Problematic Points in the Titles of Kierkegaard's Works (I)], 『キェルケゴール研究』 [Kierkegaard-Studiet], no. 15, 1985, pp. 17–28.

—「キェルケゴールの著作表題の持つ問題性（II）—『視点』、『我が著作家＝活動について』の表題解釈—」 [On the Problematic Points in the Titles of Kierkegaard's Works (II)], 『キェルケゴール研究』 [Kierkegaard-Studiet], no. 16, 1986, pp. 19–30.

—「キェルケゴールの著作表題の持つ問題性（III）—『汝自ら審け！』、『建徳的談話』、『人生行路の諸段階』—」 [On the Problematic Points in the Titles of Kierkegaard's Works (III)], 『キェルケゴール研究』 [Kierkegaard-Studiet], no. 17, 1987, pp. 39–48.

—「『最も不幸な者』（『これか—，あれか』の中の一編）をどう読むか」 [Reading "The Unhappiest One" (in *Either/Or*)], 『キェルケゴール研究』 [Kierkegaard-Studiet], no. 18, 1988, pp. 15–26.

—「キェルケゴールの著作表題の持つ問題性（IV）—『これか—あれか』の二重性とその表し方—」 [On the Problematic Points in the Titles of Kierkegaard's Works (IV)], 『キェルケゴール研究』 [Kierkegaard-Studiet], no. 19, 1989, pp. 41–52.

—「キェルケゴール『文学批評』の救済的意義」 [Relief Character of Kierkeg-aard's *A Literary Review*], 『キェルケゴール研究』 [Kierkegaard-Studiet], no. 20, 1990, pp. 41–8.

—「キェルケゴール『或る女優の危機』における『変貌』の弁証法—著作家活動の宗教的貫徹性への示顕—」 [Dialectics of "Metamorphosis" in Kierkegaard's *The Crisis of an Actress*: Manifestation of the Religious Consistency of his Work as an Author], 『キェルケゴール研究』 [Kierkegaard-Studiet], no. 21, 1991, pp. 25–36.

—「理念と行為の衝突—『諸段階』の『挿入編』への註解—」 [The Colli-
sion between Idea and Acts: An Interpretation of "Insertions" in *Stages*], 『キェ
ルケゴール研究』 [Kierkegaard-Studiet], no. 25, 1995, pp. 7–20.

大谷長・大屋憲一 [Otani, Masaru and Kenichi Oya] (eds.) 『キェルケゴールと
日本の仏教・哲学』 [Kierkegaard and Japanese Buddhism and Philosophy],
Osaka: Toho-shuppan 1992. (Kiyohiko Fujimoto, 「キェルケゴールと法
然—宗教的人間観の形成—」 [Kierkegaard and Honen: The Formation of
the Religious View on Human Beings], pp. 3–22; Masaru Otani, 「キェル
ケゴールと親鸞における絶対他者啓示信仰の普遍性」 [Universality of
Faith in the Revelation of the Absolute Other by Kierkegaard and Shinran],
pp. 23–44; Toshikazu Oya, 「『同時性』と『自然』—キェルケゴールと
親鸞—」 ["Contemporaneity" and "Nature": Kierkegaard and Shinran], pp. 45–68;
Hidetomo Yamashita, 「自己生成の論理—親鸞とキェルケゴール—」 [The
Logic of Self-becoming: Shinran and Kierkegaard], pp. 69–86; Eiko Hanaoka-
Kawamura, 「キェルケゴールと禅の教え—宗教の新しい可能性を求め
て—」 [Kierkegaard and the Teaching of Zen: Seeking for the New Possibilities
of Religion], pp. 87–110; Koji Sato, 「キェルケゴールと鈴木禅学—二つ
の『非』—」 [Kierkegaard and Zen Buddhism of Suzuki: Two Negations],
pp. 111–36; Akira Omine, 「西田幾多郎の著作に現れたキェルケゴール」
[Kierkegaard in the Works of Kitaro Nishida], pp. 137–46; Senichiro Higashi,
「西田哲学とキェルケゴール—『行為的直観』の問題をめぐって—」
[The Philosophy of Nishida and Kierkegaard: On the Problem of "Active
Intuition"], pp. 147–66; Shudo Tsukiyama, 「田辺元の『懺悔道としての
哲学』とキェルケゴールの実存思想」 [Hajime Tanabe's *Philosophy as
Metanoia* and Kierkegaard's Existential Thought], pp. 167–90; Hiroyuki Kitano,
「三木清とキェルケゴール」 [Kiyoshi Miki and Kierkegaard], pp. 191–214;
Yoshio Kawai, 「キェルケゴールと三土興三—和辻哲郎とのかかわりを
基軸に—」 [Kierkegaard and Kozo Mitsuchi: From the Perspective of their
Relations to Tetsuro Watsuji], pp. 215–40; Makoto Mizuta, 「キェルケゴー
ルと滝沢克己」 [Kierkegaard and Katsumi Takizawa], pp. 241–64; Kinya
Masugata, 「日本に於けるキェルケゴール受容史」 [The History of the
Reception of Kierkegaard in Japan], pp. 265–85; Arild Christensen, 「キェ
ルケゴールは仏教と対比し得るか」 [Can Kierkegaard be Compared with
Buddhism?], trans. by Takayuki Okubo, pp. 289–98; George Pattison, 「永遠
の孤独—キェルケゴールと禅における芸術と宗教」 [The Eternal Solitude:
Kierkegaard and Art and Religion in Zen Buddhisim], trans. by Kinya Masugata,
pp. 299–324; Walter Lowrie, 「マハヤナ・クリスチアニティ」 [Mahayana-
Christianity], trans. by Masaru Otani, pp. 325–34.)

大利裕子 [Otoshi, Hiroko], 「キェルケゴールのキリスト像—その著作活動
を規定するものとしての—」 [Kierkegaard's Image of Christ: The Principle
which Informed his Writing Activity], 『キェルケゴール研究』 [Kierkegaard-
Studiet], no. 24, 1994, pp. 27–34.

—「キェルケゴール仮名著作の語り」 [Narrative in Kierkegaard's Pseudonymous
Works], 『宗教研究』 [Journal of Religious Studies], vol. 68, 1994, pp. 47–66.

——「キェルケゴールの倫理理解」 [Kierkegaard's Understanding of Ethics], 『倫理学研究』 [Ethical Studies], vol. 27, 1997, pp. 74–83.

——「キェルケゴールにおける他者の問題」 [The Problem of Others in Kierkegaard], 『比較思想研究』 [Studies in Comparative Philosophy], vol. 23, 1997, pp. 45–7.

——「キェルケゴールにおける主体性と逆説:『後書』における弁証論」 [Kierkegaard on Subjectivity and Paradox: Apologetic Arguments in Postscript], 『外国文化論集』 [Essays on Foreign Studies], vol. 2, 1999, pp. 111–28.

——「キェルケゴールにおける『苦しみ』の概念」 [Kierkegaard on the Concept of Suffering], 『新キェルケゴール研究』 [Kierkegaard Studies], no. 1, 2001, pp. 66–81.

大内惇 [Ouchi, Atsushi], 「S.キルケゴールの真理論」 [S. Kierkegaard's Theory of Truth], 『清和女子短期大学紀要』 [The Bulletin of Seiwa Women's Junior College], vol. 10, 1981, pp. 65–76; vol. 11, 1982, pp. 63–8; vol. 13, 1984, pp. 1–11; vol. 16, 1987, pp. 55–62; vol. 25, 1996, pp. 31–40.

大屋憲一 [Oya, Toshikazu], 「キルケゴールに於ける『綜合』の批判」 [The Criticism of "Synthesis" in Kierkegaard], 『大谷大学研究年報』 [The Annual Report of Researches of Otani University], vol. 20, 1967, pp. 255–303.

——「キルケゴールに於ける『現実性』の意味あるもの」 ["Reality" in Kierkegaard], 『哲学論集』 [Philosophical Studies], vol. 15, 1968, pp. 1–14.

——「キルケゴールにおける『隠れ』の意味するもの」 [What it Means to "Hide" in Kierkegaard], 『大谷学報』 [The Journal of Buddhist Studies and Humanities], vol. 50, 1970, pp. 19–31.

——「キルケゴールにおける『実存』の特質」 [Characteristics of "Existence" in Kierkegaard], 『哲学論集』 [Philosophical Studies], vol. 20, 1974, pp. 47–62.

——「キルケゴールとニーチェ—その『生成』の問題」 [Kierkegaard and Nietzsche on "Becoming"], 『大谷大学研究年報』 [The Annual Report of Researches of Otani University], vol. 33, 1980, pp. 61–98.

——「キェルケゴールにおける『普遍』と『個』」 ["The Universal" and "the Individual" in Kierkegaard], 『キェルケゴール研究』 [Kierkegaard-Studiet], no. 12, 1982, pp. 27–36.

——「キェルケゴールにおける『魔的なもの』について」 [On "the Demonic" in Kierkegaard], 『大谷学報』 [The Journal of Buddhist Studies and Humanities], vol. 62, 1982, pp. 1–13.

——「キェルケゴールの思索の歩み」 [The Development of Kierkegaard's Thought], 『哲学論集』 [Philosophical Studies], vol. 30, 1983, pp. 62–77.

——「『単独者』について—M. ブーバーとS. キェルケゴール」 [On "the Single Individual": M. Buber and S. Kierkegaard], 『大谷学報』 [The Journal of Buddhist Studies and Humanities], vol. 66, 1986, pp. 1–12.

——「キェルケゴールにおける不安とその超克」 [Anxiety and the Overcoming of it in Kierkegaard], 『キェルケゴール研究』 [Kierkegaard-Studiet], no. 22, 1992, pp. 33–44

大屋憲一・細谷昌志 [Oya, Toshikazu and Masashi Hosoya] (eds.), 『キェル
ケゴールを学ぶ人のために』 [For Those Who Study Kierkegaard], Kyoto:
Sekaishiso-sha 1996. (Hidetomo Yamashita, 「キェルケゴールの生涯と思
想」 [The Life and Thought of Kierkegaard], pp. 4–35; Hiroshi Fujino, 「逆
説弁証法」 [The Paradoxical Dialectics], pp. 36–54; Nobuko Minamoto,
「イロニーとフモール」 [Irony and Humor], pp. 55–73; Katsumi Kitada,
「間接的伝達」 [Indirect Communication], pp. 74–91; Hiroko Otoshi, 「実存」
[Existence], pp. 92–107; Tatsumi Enokida, 「単独者」 [The Single Individual],
pp. 108–23; Masashi Hosoya, 「憂愁・不安・絶望」 [Melancholy, Anxiety
and Despair], pp. 124–39; Yoshio Kawai, 「美的・倫理的・宗教的段階」
[The Aesthetic, Ethical, and Religious Stages], pp. 140–57; Shudo Tsukiyama,
「瞬間」 [The Moment], pp. 158–75; Toshikazu Oya, 「反復」 [Repetition],
pp. 176–90; Koji Sato, 「同時性」 [Contemporaneity], pp. 191–206; Masashi
Hosoya, 「神」 [God], pp. 207–21; Kuniko Yamamoto, 「躓き」 [Offense],
pp. 222–36; Eiko Hanaoka-Kawamura, 「宗教性B」 [Religiousness B], pp. 237–53;
Kinya Masugata, 「愛」 [Love], pp. 254–70; Tetsuyoshi Kunii, 「キェルケゴ
ールと社会」 [Kierkegaard and Society], pp. 271–86; Mime Morita, 「キェル
ケゴールと女性論」 [Kierkegaard and Femininity], pp. 287–304.)

尾崎和彦 [Ozaki, Kazuhiko], 「キェルケゴールにおける時間と永遠―時間性
の問題をめぐって―」 [Time and Eternity in Kierkegaard: On the Problem
of Temporality], 『キェルケゴール研究』 [Kierkegaard-Studiet], no. 4, 1967,
pp. 38–56.

—「キェルケゴールにおける恩寵の問題―キリスト模倣の思想との関連に
おいて」 [The Problem of Grace in Kierkegaard], 『岡山商大論叢』 [Journal
of Okayama Shoka University], vol. 3, 1967, pp. 35–61.

—「模範と和解者としてのキリスト―キェルケゴールのキリスト論の一
断面―」 [Christ as a Model and Reconciler: A Phase of Søren Kierkegaard's
Christology], 『キェルケゴール研究』 [Kierkegaard-Studiet], no. 6, 1969,
pp. 32–9.

—「キェルケゴールにおける自由と思寵―同時性の場面をめぐって」
[Freedom and Grace in Kierkegaard], 『明治大学教養論集』 [The Bulletin of
Arts and Sciences, Meiji University], vol. 105, 1976, pp. 46–65.

—「キェルケゴールの結婚観―エロティークとキリスト教の相剋」
[Kierkegaard's View on Marriage], 『明治大学人文科学研究所紀要』
[Memoirs of the Institute of Cultural Sciences, Meiji University], vol. 16, 1977,
pp. 1–31.

—「実存弁証法的自由の心理構造―キェルケゴール『不安の概念』に
おける」 [Psychological Structure in Freedom of Existential Dialectic in
Kierkegaard's *The Concept of Anxiety*], 『明治大学人文科学研究所紀要』
[Memoirs of the Institute of Cultural Sciences, Meiji University], vol. 15, 1977,
pp. 1–28; vol. 19, 1980, pp. 1–36.

—「キェルケゴールと政治・社会問題」 [Kierkegaard and Political-Social
Problems], 『キェルケゴール研究』 [Kierkegaard-Studiet], no. 8, 1978,
pp. 51–60; no. 10, 1980, pp. 57–64.

—「キェルケゴールの個人主義解釈の視点―研究史を通しての一つの方法
論的反省」 [Viewpoint for the Interpretation of Kierkegaard's Individualism],

『明治大学教養論集』 [The Bulletin of Arts and Sciences, Meiji University], vol. 112, 1978, pp. 121–202.

—「キェルケゴールの『Corrective』の範疇の解釈について—キェルケゴール研究史を通して」 [On the Interpretation of Kierkegaard's Category of "Corrective"], 『明治大学教養論集』 [The Bulletin of Arts and Sciences, Meiji University], vol. 154, 1982, pp. 1–30.

—「実存弁証法的自由の心理構造—キェルケゴール『不安の概念』における」 [The Psychological Structure of Existential Dialectic in Kierkegaard's *The Concept of Anxiety*], 『明治大学人文科学研究所紀要』 [Memoirs of the Institute of Cultural Sciences, Meiji University], vol. 23, 1984, pp. 33–75.

—「キェルケゴール原罪論における『歴史的関係』の意義」 [The Meaning of "Historical Relationship" in Kierkegaard's Theory of Original Sin], 『明治大学教養論集』 [The Bulletin of Arts and Sciences, Meiji University], vol. 178, 1985, pp. 125–62.

—「キェルケゴールとブレクナーの『将来の哲学』の理念（上）—十九世紀デンマークにおける「信仰—知」論争の行方—」 [Kierkegaard and the Idea of "the Future Philosophy" in Hans Brøchner], 『キェルケゴール研究』 [Kierkegaard-Studiet], no. 16, 1986, pp. 31–42.

—「キェルケゴールとウプサラ学派の価値ニヒリスム」 [Kierkegaard and Value Nihilism of Uppsala Schools], 『明治大学教養論集』 [The Bulletin of Arts and Sciences, Meiji University], vol. 194, 1986, pp. 63–89.

—「キェルケゴールとブレクナーの『将来の哲学』の理念（続き）—十九世紀デンマークにおける「信仰—知」論争の行方—」 [Kierkegaard and the Idea of "the Future Philosophy" in Hans Brøchner (II)], 『キェルケゴール研究』 [Kierkegaard-Studiet], no. 17, 1987, pp. 49–60.

—「１９世紀デンマークにおける第１期『信仰—知』論争—R. ニエルセンとP.M. スティリングのキェルケゴール的立場からのマーテンセン『キリスト教教義学』批判」 [The First Stage of "Faith-Knowledge" Dispute in Denmark in the 19th Century: Kierkegaardian Criticism of Martensen's *Christian Dogmatics*], 『明治人学教養論集』 [The Bulletin of Arts and Sciences, Meiji University], vol. 221, 1989, pp. 57–136.

—「信仰と知—１９世紀デンマークにおけるポスト・キェルケゴールの問題」 [Knowledge and Faith: The Problem of Post-Kierkegaard in Denmark in the 19th Century], 『明治大学教養論集』 [The Bulletin of Arts and Sciences, Meiji University], vol. 228, 1990, pp. 1–164.

—「キェルケゴールの神話論」 [Kierkegaard's Understanding of Mythology], 『キェルケゴール研究』 [Kierkegaard-Studiet], no. 22, 1992, pp. 13–32.

—「１９世紀デンマークにおける『信仰一知』論争—ポスト・キェルケゴールの問題」 [Dispute over "Faith-Knowledge" in Denmark in the 19th Century], 『明治大学人文科学研究所紀要』 [Memoirs of the Institute of Cultural Sciences, Meiji University], vol. 35, 1994, pp. 227–37.

—「ブレクナーとキェルケゴール、ニールセン」 [Brøchner, Kierkegaard and Nielsen], 『明治大学人文科学研究所紀要』 [Memoirs of the Institute of Cultural Sciences, Meiji University], vol. 53, 2003, pp. 1–27.

—「H. ブレクナーのキェルケゴール理解—１９世紀デンマークにおける『信—知論争』考察の方法論を求めて」 [H. Brøchner's Interpretation of

Kierkegaard], 『明治大学教養論集』 [The Bulletin of Arts and Sciences, Meiji University], vol. 427, 2008, pp. 1–56.

三枝博音 [Saekusa, Hiroo], 「キェルケゴールの弁証法」 [Kierkegaard's Dialectic], in his 『弁証法談叢』 [Arguments about Dialectics], Tokyo: Chuokoron-sha 1935, pp. 199–242.

斎藤信治 [Saito, Shinji], 「キエルケゴールに於けるイロニーの概念」 [The Concept of Irony in Kierkegaard], 『理想』 [Riso], vol. 198, 1949, pp. 46–55.

—「キェルケゴールのソクラテス解釈」 [Kierkegaard's Interpretation of Socrates], 『理想』 [Riso], vol. 239, 1953, pp. 78–92; vol. 240, 1953, pp. 66–80.

—『ソクラテスとキェルケゴール—イロニーの概念』 [Socrates and Kierkegaard: The Concept of Irony], Tokyo: Gakugei-shobo 1955.

—「『死に至る病』に至る迄」 [Unto *The Sickness unto Death*], 『文庫』 [Bunko], vol. 62, 1956.

斎藤末弘 [Saito, Suehiro], 「キェルケゴールと椎名麟三」 [Kierkegaard and Rinzo Shiina], 『日本の神学』 [Theological Studies in Japan], vol. 27, 1988, pp. 193–200.

崎川修[Sakikawa, Osamu], 「沈黙と信仰—キルケゴールとウィトゲンシュタインをめぐる3章」 [Silence and Faith: Philosophy of Religion in Kierkegaard and Wittgenstein], 『上智哲学誌』 [Sophia Philosophica], vol. 12, 1999, pp. 49–62.

阪口尚弘 [Sakaguchi, Naohiro], 「S・キェルケゴール邦語文献目録」 [List of Literature in Japanese on S. Kierkegaard], 『桃山学院大学キリスト教論集』 [The St. Andrew's University Journal of Christian Studies], vol. 3, 1967, pp. 110–47.

酒井一郎 [Sakai, Ichiro], 「おしゃべりのメディオロジーへ—キェルケゴールの『現代の批判』を視座において」 [On the Way to Mediology of Talking], 『人間学紀要』 [Studies in Philosophical Anthropology], vol. 38, 2008, pp. 55–85.

讃岐和家 [Sanuki, Kazuie], 「キェルケゴールにおける倫理性の問題」 [Ethical Ideas of Kierkegaard], 『倫理學年報』 [Annals of Ethics], vol. 2, 1953, pp. 12–23.

早乙女禮子 [Saotome, Reiko], 「ルターとキェルケゴール」 [Kierkegaard und Luther], 『キェルケゴール研究』 [Kierkegaard-Studiet], no. 18, 1988, pp. 37–46; no. 19, 1989, pp. 53–60.

—「キェルケゴールにおけるルター批判—信仰とわざ」 [Kierkegaard's Criticism of Luther], 『大阪体育大学紀要』 [Bulletin of Osaka College of Physical Education], vol. 22, 1991, pp. 169–79.

—「キェルケゴールと新渡戸稲造」 [S.A. Kierkegaard and Nitobe Inazo], 『新キェルケゴール研究』 [Kierkegaard Studies], no. 6, 2008, pp. 41–62.

笹田恭史 [Sasada, Takafumi], 「キルケゴール美学的=感性的段階における『直接的なもの』」 ["The Immediate" in Kierkegaard's Aesthetic Stage], 『立命館言語文化研究』 [Ritsumeikan Studies in Language and Culture], vol. 6, 1994, pp. 215–25.

佐々木一義 [Sasaki, Kazuyoshi], 「キェルケゴールの実存哲学に於ける自己の問題」 [The Problem of the Self in Kierkegaard's Existential Philosophy], 『哲学年報』 [Annual of Philosophy], vol. 10, 1950, pp. 107–35.

— 「キェルケゴールにおける実存生成の論理」 [The Logic of the Existential Becoming in Kierkegaard], 『キェルケゴール研究』 [Kierkegaard-Studiet], no. 1, 1964, pp. 98–121.

— 「ヘルマン・ディームのキェルケゴール論における実存弁証法理解」 [Hermann Diem's Understanding of Kierkegaard's Existential Dialectic], 『キェルケゴール研究』 [Kierkegaard-Studiet], no. 5, 1968, pp. 19–33.

— 「キェルケゴールにおける実存の存在論的基本構造」 [The Ontological Basic Structure of Existence in Kierkegaard], 『哲学論文集』 [Journal of Philosophy], vol. 5, 1969, pp. 87–96.

— 「キェルケゴールにおける自己存在の実存論的構造分析」 [Existential Analysis of Self-Being in S. Kierkegaard], 『キェルケゴール研究』 [Kierkegaard-Studiet], no. 7, 1977, pp. 38–43.

佐々木徹 [Sasaki, Toru], 「キェルケゴールにおける詩と沈黙」 [Poetry and Silence in Kierkegaard], 『キェルケゴール研究』 [Kierkegaard-Studiet], no. 4, 1967, pp. 57–66.

— 「キェルケゴールに関する一断想」 [A Fragmentary Thought on Kierkegaard], 『関西学院哲学研究年報』 [Yearbook of Philosophical Studies], vol. 8, 1967, pp. 130–8.

— 「キェルケゴールにおける愛と死」 [Love and Death in Kierkegaard], 『キェルケゴール研究』 [Kierkegaard-Studiet], no. 5, 1968, pp. 34–45.

— 「キェルケゴールにおける美的実存」 [The Aesthetic Existence in Kierkegaard], 『追手門学院大学文学部紀要』 [Literary Department Review, Otemon Gakuin University], vol. 7, 1973, pp. 11–18.

佐々木行宏 [Sasaki, Yukihiro], 『キルケゴールの『イロニー論』について』 [On Kierkegaard's Concept of Irony], Tokyo: Maruzen 2010.

佐藤啓介 [Sato, Keisuke], 「死の後をめぐる幸福な記憶と忘却—キェルケゴールとホワイトヘッドを読むリクールの思索を手がかりに」 [Being Remembered by Forgetting about Death during Life: Ricoeurian Thought via Kierkegaard and Whitehead], 『死生学年報』 [Annual of the Institute of Thanatology], 2013, pp. 131–48.

佐藤潔人 [Sato, Kiyoto], 「原体験と思想形成について—キェルケゴールとカフカの場合」 [The Original Experience and Formation of Thought], 『学苑』 [Gakuen], vol. 360, 1969, pp. 12–19; vol. 374, 1971, pp. 48–58.

佐藤幸治 [Sato, Koji], 「生成の課題—キェルケゴールの『瞬間』論」 [The Problem of the Coming into Existence: The Thesis of "the Moment" by Kierkegaard], 『キェルケゴール研究』 [Kierkegaard-Studiet], no. 11, 1981, pp. 35–44.

— 「認容と殉教—キェルケゴールの宗教哲学・試論—」 [Admission and Martyrdom: An Essay on Kierkegaard's Religious Philosophy], 『キェルケゴール研究』 [Kierkegaard-Studiet], no. 15, 1985, pp. 29–40.

— 「キェルケゴールの自由論—『不安の概念』の一考察」 [Kierkegaard's Theory of Freedom], 『宗教研究』 [Journal of Religious Studies], vol. 60, 1986, pp. 213–35.

佐藤平 [Sato, Taira], 「キェルケゴールはどこにいる—思想を実存と思惟の連関として理解する視点からの仮名の問題の一考察」 [Where is Kierkegaard?],

『大谷女子大学紀要』 [Bulletin of Otani Women's College], vol. 6, 1972, pp. 38–51; vol. 7, 1973, pp. 47–64; vol. 8, 1974, pp. 66–80.

— 「キェルケゴールにおける自己の概念の研究」 [A Study on Kierkegaard's Concept of Self], 『大谷女子大学紀要』 [Bulletin of Otani Women's College], vol. 24, 1989, pp. 109–40.

佐藤卓司 [Sato, Takuji], 「アルベール・カミユの不条理とキルケゴール」 [Absurdity in A. Camus and Kierkegaard], 『学園論集』 [The Gakuen Review], vol. 31, 1977, pp. 61–86.

薩川秀樹 [Satsukawa, Hideki], 「罪意識と恩寵体験: もう一つのキルケゴール像」 [Consciousness of Sins and Experience of Grace: Another Image of Kierkegaard], 『東北哲学会年報』 [Bulletin of Tohoku Philosophical Association], vol. 8, 1992, pp. 1–14.

清徳光文 [Seitoku, Mitsubumi], 「キルケゴールにおける実存の三段階」 [Three Existential Stages of Kierkegaard], 哲学論集 [Journal of Philosophy], vol. 4, 1958, pp. 80–97.

世良寿男 [Sera, Toshio], 「キェルケゴールに於ける絶対的逆説」 [The Absolute Paradox in Kierkegaard], 『大谷学報』 [The Journal of Buddhist Studies and Humanities], vol. 34, 1955.

釋徹宗 [Shaku, Tesshu], 「日本浄土教思想とキルケゴール」 [Japanese Pure Land Buddhism and Kierkegaard], 『比較思想研究』 [Studies in Comparative Philosophy], vol. 26, 1999, pp. 52–9.

信太正三 [Shida, Shozo], 「水平化問題の一系譜—ヤスパースとキルケゴール」 [On the Problem of Horizontalization: Jaspers and Kierkegaard], 『実存』 [Existence], vol. 4, 1953, pp. 36–45.

清水徹 [Shimizu, Toru], 「キルケゴールについての誤解—特にパラドックスについて—」 [Misunderstandings about Kierkegaard: Especially on the Paradox], 『熊本工業大学研究報告』 [Bulletin of the Kumamoto Institute of Technology], vol. 14, 1989, pp. 1–10; vol. 15, 1990, pp. 1–5.

— 「世界史的段階について—キルケゴールの思想における」 [On the Stage of the World History in Kierkegaard], 『熊本工業大学研究報告』 [Bulletin of the Kumamoto Institute of Technology], vol. 18, 1993, pp. 1–9.

宍戸好子 [Shishido, Yoshiko], 「キールケゴールにおけるVorbildとしてのキリスト」 [Christ as "Vorbild" in Kierkegaard], 『神学』 [Journal of Theology], vol. 26, 1964.

相馬御風 [Soma, Gyofu], 「キャールケガァルドとイプセン」 [Kierkegaard and Ibsen], in his 『個人主義思想』 [The Thought of Individualism], Tokyo: Tenkodo-shobo 1915, pp. 99–118.

スザ・ドミンゴス [Sousa, Domingos], 「親鸞とキルケゴール」 [Shinran and Kierkegaard], 『大谷大学大学院研究紀要』 [Research Report in the Graduate School of Otani University], vol. 19, 2002, pp. 1–29.

— 「罪と悪の問題—キュルケゴールと親鸞の比較考察」 [The Problem of Sin and Evil: Comparative Study of Kierkegaard and Shinran], 『南山神学』 [Nanzan Journal of Theological Studies], vol. 26, 2003, pp. 33–56.

— 「信仰と歴史の問題—キェルケゴールの立場」 [Faith and History: Kierkegaard's Perspective], 『宗教研究』 [Journal of Religious Studies], vol. 79, 2005, pp. 1–24.

—「信仰行為における神の恩恵と人間の決断」 [Grace and Freedom in the Act of Faith: A Study in Kierkegaard's Thought], 『新キェルケゴール研究』 [Kierkegaard Studies], no. 6, 2008, pp. 22–40.

—「愛は義務になり得るのか—キェルケゴールのキリスト教倫理」 [Can Love Be Commanded? Kierkegaard's Christian Ethics], 『宗教研究』 [Journal of Religious Studies], vol. 83, 2009, pp. 765–87.

—「キェルケゴールの自己論—非社会的個人主義であるのか—」 [Kierkegaard's Conception of the Self: Proponent of Asocial Individualism?], 『新キェルケゴール研究』 [Kierkegaard Studies], no. 10, 2012, pp. 16–30.

須藤茂明 [Sudo, Shigeaki], 「内在的真理の伝達をめぐっての『教える者』と『学ぶ者』との関係: S・キルケゴールの理論を手がかりとして」 [Relation between the Teacher and Learner in Conveying Immanent Truth: A Study Based on the Theory of Søren Kierkegaard], 『筑波社会科研究』 [Tsukuba Annals for the Education of Social Studies], vol. 3, 1984, pp. 20–7.

杉本吉雄 [Sugimoto, Yoshio], 「知識のアポリアを巡って キルケゴールとプロチノス」 [Kierkegaard and Plotinos, the "Aporia" Concerning the Acquisition of Knowledge], 『紀要』 [Yamawaki Studies of Arts and Science], vol. 34, 1996, pp. 1–24.

杉山好 [Sugiyama, Yoshimu], 「キルケゴールのキリスト像」 [Kierkegaard's Image of Christ], 『理想』 [Riso], vol. 360, 1963.

皇紀夫 [Sumeragi, Norio], 「キエルケゴールにおける実存の内的構造」 [The Internal Structure of Existence in Kierkegaard], 『京都大学教育学部紀要』 [Bulletin of Kyoto University], vol. 15, 1969, pp. 33–41.

—「キルケゴールにおける『自己』の実存的生成について」 [On the Existential Becoming of Self in Kierkegaard], 『理想』 [Riso], vol. 487, 1973, pp. 88–100; vol. 497, 1974, pp. 152–64.

須藤孝也 [Suto, Takaya], 「キルケゴールによる『超越的人間学』の発見: 『内在か超越か』という解釈枠組みからのキルケゴールの解放」 [The Discovery of "Transcendent Anthropology" by Kierkegaard: Liberating Kierkegaard from the Interpretative Frame, "Either Immanence or Transcendence"], 『一橋論叢』 [The Hitotsubashi Review], vol. 124–2, 2000, pp. 327–42.

—「キルケゴールにおける『自己愛（Selvkjerlighed）』に関して」 [On the "Self-love" in Kierkegaard], 『新キェルケゴール研究』 [Kierkegaard Studies], no. 2, 2002, pp. 77–93.

—「キェルケゴールとヨーロッパ—キリスト教の受容と改編」 [Kierkegaard and Europe: The Reception of and Change in Christianity], 『理想』 [Riso], vol. 670, 2003, pp. 24–33.

—「キェルケゴール思想における倫理とキリスト教の相補性について」 [On the Complementarity of Ethics and Christianity in Kierkegaard's Thought], 『新キェルケゴール研究』 [Kierkegaard Studies], no. 3, 2004, pp. 102–23.

—「歴史における実践—キルケゴールとフーコーの捩れた関係」 [Practice in History: Twisted Relationship between Kierkegaard and Foucault], 『理想』 [Riso], vol. 676, 2006, pp. 67–76.

—「キルケゴールと『規範』」 [Kierkegaard and "the Norm"], 『宗教と倫理』 [Religion and Ethics], vol. 6, 2006, pp. 3–16.

——「遜りとポレミックの弁証法—ハーマンからキルケゴールへ」 [The Dialectic of Humility and Polemics: From Hamann to Kierkegaard], 『宗教研究』 [Journal of Religious Studies], vol. 83, 2009, pp. 1–23.

——「霊性の思想家としてのキルケゴール：　フーコーの霊性理解に照らして」 [Kierkegaard as a Spiritual Thinker: Compared with Foucault's Understanding of Spirituality], in 『宗教史学論叢１５：　スピリチュアリティの宗教史』 [A Collection of Studies of Religious History, 15], ed. by Hidetaka Fukasawa et al., Tokyo: Riton-sha 2010, pp. 349–72.

——「卑賤の実存　—キルケゴールとキュニコス主義—」 [The Humble Existence: Kierkegaard and Cynicism], 『一橋社会科学』 [Hitotsubashi Bulletin of Social Sciences], no. 5, 2013, pp. 1–13.

——『キルケゴールと「キリスト教界」』 [Kierkegaard and "Christendom"], Tokyo: Sobun-sha 2014.

陶山務 [Suyama, Tsutomu], 『キェルケゴールの思想と生涯』 [Kierkegaard's Thought and Life], Tokyo: Soubun-sha 1948.

——「キェルケゴールの恋愛と性格」 [Kierkegaard's Love and Character], 『知と行』 [Knowledge and Action], vol. 5, 1950, pp. 44–50.

鈴木三郎 [Suzuki, Saburo], 「キルケゴールとヤスパース」 [Kierkegaard and Jaspers], 『理想』 [Riso], vol. 269, 1955.

鈴木俊吉 [Suzuki, Shunkichi], 「ヘフディング『パスカルとキルケゴール』」 [*Pascal and Kierkegaard* by H. Høffding], 『倫理研究』 [Ethical Studies], vol. 21, 1933, pp. 2–9.

鈴木祐丞 [Suzuki, Yusuke], 「キェルケゴールの１８４８年の信仰的突破について」 [On Kierkegaard's Religious Breakthrough in 1848], 『新キェルケゴール研究』 [Kierkegaard Studies], no. 5, 2007, pp. 40–52.

——「キェルケゴールの信仰観についての一考察—『反省のあとの直接性』とは何か」 [On Kierkegaard's View of Faith: What Is "Immediacy after Reflection"?], 『新キェルケゴール研究』 [Kierkegaard Studies], no. 7, 2009, pp. 20–36.

——「『死に至る病』における『絶望の弁証法』についての考察」 [On "the Dialectic of Despair" in *The Sickness unto Death*], 『新キェルケゴール研究』 [Kierkegaard Studies], no. 8, 2010, pp. 66–82.

——「『死に至る病』における信仰の定義についての考察」 [On the Definition of Faith in *The Sickness unto Death*], 『哲学・思想論叢』 [Miscellanea Philosophica], no. 28, 2010, pp. 69–79.

——「キェルケゴールの新版原典全集 (*SKS*) の特徴と意義について」 [The Distinction and Importance of *Søren Kierkegaards Skrifter* (*SKS*)], 『名古屋商科大学論集』 [NUCB Journal of Economics and Information Science], vol. 58, 2014, pp. 167–74.

——「生に対する真剣さ—キェルケゴールの魅力—」 [Being Serious about Life: My Attraction to Kierkegaard], 『新キェルケゴール研究』 [Kierkegaard Studies], no. 12, 2014, pp. 54–62.

——『キェルケゴールの信仰と哲学　生と思想の全体像を問う』 [Kierkegaard's Philosophy and Faith: Examining the Whole Picture of his Life and Thought], Kyoto: Minerva-shobo 2014.

— 「ウィトゲンシュタインのキェルケゴール体験—『キリスト教の修練』の宗教哲学を生きること—」 [Wittgenstein's Encounters with Kierkegaard: Kierkegaard's Philosophy of Religion in *Practice in Christianity*], 『宗教研究』 [Journal of Religious Studies], vol. 88, no. 3, 2014, pp. 647–71.

平良信勝 [Taira, Shinsho], 「キェルケゴールにおける主体的真理について—実存の生成に即して—」 [On "Subjectivity is Truth" in Kierkegaard: Concerning the Becoming of Existence], 『キェルケゴール研究』 [Kierkegaard-Studiet], no. 5, 1968, pp. 46–52.

— 「西田哲学における『逆対応』とキェルケゴール哲学における『逆説』」 ["Inverse Polarity" in Nishida's Philosophy and "Paradox" in Kierkegaard's Philosophy], 『琉球大学教育学部紀要』 [Bulletin of the Division of Education, the University of the Ryukyus], vol. 15, 1972, pp. 17–25.

高藤直樹 [Takafuji, Naoki], 『キェルケゴール思想へのいざない—エロス・理性・聖性の音楽家としての』 [Invitation to Kierkegaard's Thought: A Musician of Eros, Reason and Holiness], Tokyo: Binebaru-shuppan 1996.

高橋文雄 [Takahashi, Fumio], 「人と神—キェルケゴールの絶望論『死に至る病』の思索を辿って、キリスト者の『人と神』の関係を究明する」 [Human Being and God], 『法学紀要』 [Hogaku-kiyo], vol. 10, 1968, pp. 289–344.

高橋亘 [Takahashi, Wataru], 『絶対と深淵—ヘーゲルとキェルケゴール—』 [The Absolute and the Abyss: Hegel and Kierkegaard], Tokyo: Ikuei-shoin 1942.

— 『キェルケゴール』 [Kierkegaard], Tokyo: Shinkyo-shuppansha 1950.

高間直道 [Takama, Naomichi], 「キェルケゴールの顔—人相学的な視点から—」 [A Study of S. Kierkegaard's Face—From a Physiognomical Point of View], 『キェルケゴール研究』 [Kierkegaard-Studiet], no. 3, 1966, pp. 40–71.

高本茂 [Takamoto, Shigeru], 『松下昇とキェルケゴール』 [Noboru Matsushita and Kierkegaard], Tokyo: Yudachi-sha 2010.

武林泰男 [Takemura, Yasuo], 「カントとキルケゴール」 [Kant and Kierkegaard], 『実存主義』 [Existentialism], vol. 49, 1969, pp. 49–56.

— 「キェルケゴール・デ・シレンチオ」 [Kierkegaard de silentio], 『キェルケゴール研究』 [Kierkegaard-Studiet], no. 9, 1978, pp. 43–50.

— 「意味連関の構造—キルケゴールに即して」 [The Structure of the Connection of Meanings], 『三重大学教育学部研究紀要』 [Bulletin of Mie University], vol. 30, 1979, pp. 67–76.

竹之内裕文 [Takenouchi, Hirobumi], 「ハイデガーとキルケゴール—実存的カテゴリーの問題をめぐって」 [Heidegger and Kierkegaard: The Problem of the Existential Categories], 『思索』 [Shisaku], vol. 35, 2002, pp. 61–80.

— 「『瞬間』（Augenblick）と『突如』（exaiphnes）—ハイデガーのキルケゴール批判をめぐって」 ["The Moment" and "the Sudden": Heidegger's Criticism of Kierkegaard], 『東北大学哲学会年報』 [Annual Reports of Tohoku Philosophical Association], vol. 19, 2003, pp. 29–45.

竹下直之 [Takeshita, Naoyuki], 「キェルケゴールの実存弁証法」 [Kierkegaard's Existential Dialectics], 『理想』 [Riso], vol. 62, 1935.

竹内寛 [Takeuchi, Hiroshi], 「大地震」 [The Great Earthquake], 『立教大学神学年報』 [The Annual Report of Theology], vol. 2, 1954, pp. 183–9.

—「不安・絶望・罪」 [Anxiety, Despair and Sin],『立教大学神学年報』 [The Annual Report of Theology], vol. 6, 1959, pp. 97–110.

田窪一郎 [Takubo, Ichiro], 「形成の原理とキェルケゴールの生成について」 [On the Principle of Formation and the Becoming in Kierkegaard],『キェルケゴール研究』 [Kierkegaard-Studiet], vol. 2, 1965, pp. 49–54.

玉井治 [Tamai, Osamu], 「キェルケゴールの『言葉』」 [Kierkegaard's "Words"],『東海大学短期大学部紀要一般研究』 [Bulletin of Tokai University], vol. 2, 1967, pp. 37–43.

—「キェルケゴールの『哲学以前』」 ["Before Philosophy" in Kierkegaard],『哲学論叢』 [The Philosophical Miscellany], vol. 24, 1967, pp. 265–74.

—「『段階』について: キェルケゴール研究」 [Kierkegaard's Concept of "Stage"],『東海大学紀要文学部』 [Proceedings of the Faculty of Letters of Tokai University], vol. 15, 1971, pp. 1–13.

—「反復の概念の成立: キェルケゴール研究」 [The Origin of Kierkegaard's Concept "Repetition"],『東海大学紀要文学部』 [Proceedings of the Faculty of Letters of Tokai University], vol. 18, 1972, pp. 9–16.

玉井茂 [Tamai, Shigeru], 「キェルケゴールの美的実存」 [The Aesthetic Existence of Kierkegaard],『紀要』 [Bulletin], vol. 2, 1956, pp. 1–7.

玉置保巳 [Tamaki, Yasumi], 「人間性の限界に就いて―キェルケゴールとレッシング」 [On the Limit of Humanity: Kierkegaard and Lessing],『愛知大学文学論叢』 [Bulletin of Aichi University], vols. 22–3, 1962; vol. 25, 1963.

田村恭一 [Tamura, Kyoichi], 「キェルケゴールにおけるイデア的なものの主体化をめぐって」 [On Subjectification of the Ideal in Kierkegaard],『思索』 [Shisaku], vol. 14, 1981, pp. 61–81.

田辺元 [Tanabe, Hajime], 『実存と愛と実践』 [Existence, Love and Praxis], Tokyo: Chikuma-shobo 1948; republished as vol. 9 in 田辺元全集第9巻 [Hajime Tanabe's Complete Works], Tokyo: Chikuma-shobo 1963.

田辺保 [Tanabe, Tamotsu], 「キェルケゴールとパスカル」 [Kierkegaard and Pascal],『キェルケゴール研究』 [Kierkegaard-Studiet], vol. 2, 1965, pp. 55–65.

—「キェルケゴールとシモーヌ・ヴェイユ」 [Kierkegaard and Simone Weil],『キェルケゴール研究』 [Kierkegaard-Studiet], no. 6, 1969, pp. 40–8.

田中一馬 [Tanaka, Kazuma], 「『倫理的―宗教的』とは如何なる意味か」 [On the Meaning of "Ethical-Religious" in the *Postscript*],『キェルケゴール研究』 [Kierkegaard-Studiet], no. 24, 1994, pp. 35–44.

—「『判定基準』から何が導き出されるのか? ―キェルケゴール『アズラーについての書』をめぐって」 [What is Concluded from the "Criteria"? Concerning Kierkegaard's *The Book on Adler*],『新キェルケゴール研究』 [Kierkegaard Studies], no. 3, 2004, pp. 56–81.

谷口竜男 [Taniguchi, Tatsuo], 「実存の展開について―キェルケゴールの倫理的実存を中心として」 [On the Development of Existence (1)],『フィロソフィア』 [Philosophia], vol. 43, 1962.

—「キェルケゴールに於ける個と普遍―倫理の問題を中心にして」 [The Individuality and Universality in Kierkegaard],『理想』 [Riso], vol. 360, 1963.

——「実存の展開について—キルケゴールの宗教的実存を中心にして」 [On the Development of Existence (2)], 『フィロソフィア』 [Philosophia], vol. 51, 1967, pp. 23–43.

——「キルケゴールの『単独者』の概念」 [Kierkegaard's Concept of "the Single Individual"], 『早稲田大学大学院文学研究科紀要』 [Bulletin of the Graduate Division of Literature of Waseda University], vol. 27, 1981, pp. 1–16.

——「実存と他者—キルケゴールの実存の倫理を中心として」 [Existence and Others], 『フィロソフィア』 [Philosophia], vol. 72, 1984, pp. 1–23.

——『キルケゴール研究』 [A Study of Kierkegaard], Tokyo: Hokuju-shuppan 1988.

谷口郁夫 [Tanikuchi, Ikuo], 「キルケゴールの原罪論: 人間の根源的状態の理解として」 [The Doctrine of the Original Sin in Kierkegaard], 『哲学・思想論叢』 [Miscellanea Philosophica], vol. 4, 1986, pp. 59–70.

——「レッシングとキルケゴール: 飛躍概念を巡って」 [Lessing and Kierkegaard on the Concept of "Leap"], 『哲学・思想論叢』 [Miscellanea Philosophica], vol. 5, 1987, pp. 29–40.

——「レッシングとキルケゴール: 歴史的なものに対する関係を巡って」 [Lessing and Kierkegaard on the Historical], 『哲学・思想論叢』 [Miscellanea Philosophica], vol. 6, 1988, pp. 19–30.

立川健二 [Tatsukawa, Kenji], 「キルケゴール、ブレンダル、イェルムスレウ<デンマーク構造主義>にかんする覚え書」 [Kierkegaard, Brøndal and Hjelmslev: On Danish Structuralism], 『現代思想』 [Gendai-shiso], vol. 16, 1988, pp. 151–81.

手川誠士郎 [Tegawa, Seishiro], 「明治期におけるキルケゴールとニーチェの思想」 [The Thought of Kierkegaard and Nietzsche in the Meiji Era] 『立正大学人文科学研究所年報』 [Annual Bulletin of the Institute of Humanistic Sciences, Rissho University], vol. 17, 1980, pp. 54–63.

——「永遠と時の間で: S. キルケゴールと M. ウナムーノにおける人間について」 [Between an Eternity and a Moment: On Human Beings according to S. Kierkegaard and M. Unamuno], 『立正大学文学部論叢』 [The Journal of the Department of Literature, Rissho University], vol. 98, 1993, pp. 99–114.

戸田伊助 [Toda, Isuke], 「ルターとキエルケゴール」 [Luther and Kierkegaard], 『基督教文化』 [Christian Culture], vol. 57, 1951, pp. 31–44.

東城国裕 [Tojo, Kunihiro], 「キルケゴールvs. ヘーゲル—アブラハムを巡って」 [Kierkegaard against Hegel: About Abraham], 『日本の科学者』 [Journal of Japanese Scientists], vol. 399, 2001, pp. 181–5.

鳥居正夫 [Torii, Masao],「実存哲学研究—キエルケゴールからハイデッガーへ」 [A Study on Existential Philosophy: From Kierkegaard to Heidegger], 『午前』 [Gozen], vol. 3, no. 8, 1948, pp. 2–13; vol. 3, no. 9, 1948, pp. 41–62; vol. 4, no. 2, 1949, pp. 19–28.

豊福淳一 [Toyofuku, Junichi], 「キルケゴールとヘーゲル—旧約のアブラハムをめぐって」 [Kierkegaard and Hegel on Abraham], 『理想』 [Riso], vol. 360, 1963.

— 「キルケゴールの『想定された機会における三つの講話』について」 [On Kierkegaard's *Three Discourses on Imagined Occasions*], 『哲学誌』 [Historia Philosophiae], vol. 7, 1965.

— 「キルケゴールにおけるソクラテスのイロニー解釈—ヘーゲルとの対比において」 [Kierkegaard's Understanding of Socrates' Interpretation of Irony – In Comparison to Hegel], 『倫理學年報』 [Annals of Ethics], vol. 18, 1969, pp. 69–78.

— 「キルケゴールの『不安』の概念について—ヘーゲルとの対立をめぐって」 [On Kierkegaard's Concept of "Anxiety": In Contrast to Hegel], 『釧路論集』 [Reports of Hokkaido University of Education (Kushiro)], vol. 1, 1970, pp. 1–20.

— 「キルケゴールにおける絶望の弁証法」 [The Dialectic of Despair in Kierkegaard], 『倫理學年報』 [Annals of Ethics], vol. 20, 1971, pp. 119–32.

— 「キルケゴールにおける二重の反省と倫理的真理」 [The Duplicate Reflection and Ethical Truth in Kierkegaard], 『釧路論集』 [Reports of Hokkaido University of Education (Kushiro)], vol. 3, 1972, pp. 1–18.

— 「キルケゴール初期講集話の研究」 [On Kierkegaard's Early Discourses], 『北海道教育大学紀要第一部A人文科学編』 [Journal of Hokkaido University of Education. Section 1. A, Humanities], vol. 24, 1973, pp. 1–14.

— 「ヘーゲルとキルケゴールの悲劇観」 [Hegel's and Kierkegaard's Views on Tragedy], 『北海道教育大学紀要第一部A人文科学編』 [Journal of Hokkaido University of Education. Section 1. A, Humanities], vol. 24, 1974, pp. 57–70.

— 「キルケゴールにおける宗教的実存の課題—内在と超越」 [The Task in the Religious Existence in Kierkegaard], 『防衛大学校紀要人文科学分冊』 [Studies in Humanities and Social Sciences. Humanities Series], vol. 30, 1975, pp. 225–51.

— 「キルケゴールの反復をめぐって」 [On Kierkegaard's Repetition], 『防衛大学校紀要人文科学分冊』 [Studies in Humanities and Social Sciences. Humanities Series], vol. 32, 1976, pp. 1–30.

— 「キルケゴールの１８４３年の『三つの講話』」 [Kierkegaard's "Three Discourses" in 1843], 『防衛大学校紀要人文科学分冊』 [Studies in Humanities and Social Sciences. Humanities Series], vol. 33, 1976, pp. 1–28.

— 「キルケゴールと肉中の刺」 [Kierkegaard and Thorn in the Flesh], 『防衛大学校紀要人文科学分冊』 [Studies in Humanities and Social Sciences. Humanities Series], vol. 35, 1978, pp. 1–44.

— 『ヘーゲルとキルケゴール』 [Hegel and Kierkegaard], Tokyo: Kobun-do 1979.

— 「キルケゴールとロマン的イロニー」 [Kierkegaard and the Romantic Irony], 『防衛大学校紀要人文科学分冊』 [Studies in Humanities and Social Sciences. Humanities Series], vol. 40, 1980, pp. 1–34.

— 「キルケゴールにおける宗教的愛の闘争性」 [The Struggling Nature of the Religious Love in Kierkegaard], 『防衛大学校紀要人文科学分冊』 [Studies in Humanities and Social Sciences. Humanities Series], vol. 46, 1983, pp. 1–37.

— 「キルケゴールにおける人間と神の相剋」 [Conflict between God and Human in Kierkegaard], 『防衛大学校紀要人文科学分冊』 [Studies in Humanities and Social Sciences. Humanities Series], vol. 50, 1985, pp. 1–39; vol. 51, 1985, pp. 67–114.

— 「ヘーゲルとキルケゴールのアンティゴネ解釈」 [The Interpretations of Antigone by Hegel and Kierkegaard], 『防衛大学校紀要人文科学分冊』 [Studies in Humanities and Social Sciences. Humanities Series], vol. 59, 1989, pp. 1–40.

— 「キルケゴールの倫理的愛」 [Kierkegaard's Ethical Love], 『防衛大学校紀要人文科学分冊』 [Studies in Humanities and Social Sciences. Humanities Series], vol. 62, 1991, pp. 1–22.

— 「キルケゴールにおける倫理的自己の自律性」 [Autonomy of Ethical Self in Kierkegaard], 『防衛大学校紀要人文科学分冊』 [Studies in Humanities and Social Sciences. Humanities Series], vol. 64, 1992, pp. 51–75.

— 『キルケゴールの実存思想—ヘーゲルと対比しつつ』 [Kierkegaard's Existential Thought – Compared with Hegel], Tokyo: Kobundo-shuppansha 1994.

— 「デンマークの教会とキルケゴール」 [Danish Church and Kierkegaard], 『防衛大学校紀要人文科学分冊』 [Studies in Humanities and Social Sciences. Humanities Series], vol. 68, 1995, pp. 1–49.

— 「G.マランツクによるキルケゴールの『肉中の刺』解釈」 [G. Malantschuk's Interpretation of Kierkegaard's "Thorn in the Flesh"], 『防衛大学校紀要人文科学分冊』 [Studies in Humanities and Social Sciences. Humanities Series], vol. 71, 1995, pp. 1–17.

— 「キルケゴールの講話『苦難の福音』の意義」 [The Meaning of Kierkegaard's Discourse "The Gospel of Suffering"], 『防衛大学校紀要人文科学分冊』 [Studies in Humanities and Social Sciences. Humanities Series], vol. 73, 1996, pp. 1–31.

— 「キルケゴールの『キリスト教講話』における厳しいものの意義」 [The Meaning of Strictness in Kierkegaard's *Christian Discourses*], 『防衛大学校紀要人文科学分冊』 [Studies in Humanities and Social Sciences. Humanities Series], vol. 74, 1997, pp. 55–89.

土村啓介 [Tsuchimura, Keisuke], 「キェルケゴールにおける神話と意識の問題」 [Relation between Myth and Consciousness in Kierkegaard], 『新キェルケゴール研究』 [Kierkegaard Studies], no. 8, 2010, pp. 83–99.

— 「『イロニーの概念』における全体的真理の地平」 [The Level of Comprehensive Truth in *The Concept of Irony*], 『新キェルケゴール研究』 [Kierkegaard Studies], no. 9, 2011, pp. 41–53.

— 「『イロニーの概念』のプラトン理解からみた意識の現実性」 [The Reality of Consciousness in Kierkegaard: "The Concept of Irony" from Platonic Perspective], 『新キェルケゴール研究』 [Kierkegaard Studies], no. 10, 2012, pp. 31–42.

— 「『イロニーの概念』に見られるギリシア哲学史」 [The History of Greek Philosophy Found in *The Concept of Irony*], 『新キェルケゴール研究』 [Kierkegaard Studies], no. 12, 2014, pp. 1–13.

辻厚治 [Tsuji, Koji], 「キェルケゴール『死に至る病』を読み解く」 [Reading Kierkegaard's *The Sickness unto Death*], 『臨床心理学』 [Clinical Psychology], vol. 1, 2004, pp. 75–89; vol. 2, 2005, pp. 1–14; vol. 3, 2006, pp. 1–8.

築山修道 [Tsukiyama, Shudo], 「キェルケゴールにおける『瞬間』の構造と宗教的意味」 [The Structure and Meaning of "the Moment" in Kierkegaard], 『大谷学報』 [The Journal of Buddhist Studies and Humanities], vol. 64, 1984, pp. 45–59.

—「キェルケゴールにおける人間実存と不安」 [Human Existence and Anxiety in Kierkegaard], 『キェルケゴール研究』 [Kierkegaard-Studiet], no. 15, 1985, pp. 41–52.

—「宗教と実存 1 —キェルケゴールにおける実存の根本形式とその宗教性」 [Religion and Existence (1)], 『哲学論集』 [Philosophical Studies], vol. 32, 1985, pp. 62–77.

—「『自己』究明をめぐる東西の宗教思想：　西田幾多郎とキェルケゴール（一）」 [On Self-Understandings of Kitaro Nishida and Søren Kierkegaard], 『比較思想研究』 [Studies in Comparative Philosophy], vol. 13, 1986, pp. 107–13.

—「キェルケゴールの実存思想に対する西田哲学と田辺哲学」 [The Philosophical Relations of Nishida and Tanabe to Kierkegaard], 『キェルケゴール研究』 [Kierkegaard-Studiet], no. 21, 1991, pp. 37–50.

鶴真一 [Tsuru, Shinichi], 「他者へのかかわりとしての言語—キェルケゴールとレヴィナス」 [The Language as a Relation to Others—Kierkegaard and Levinas], 『新キェルケゴール研究』 [Kierkegaard Studies], no. 2, 2002, pp. 59–76.

鶴田英也 [Tsuruta, Hidenari], 「キルケゴールの反復と固有名」 [Repetition and Proper Nouns in Kierkegaard], 『日本病跡学雑誌』 [Japanese Bulletin of Pathography], vol. 63, 2002, pp. 64–73.

内田克孝 [Uchida, Katsutaka], 「キェルケゴールにおける宗教的恍惚体験との関連における憂愁と絶望」 [Thorn in the Flesh and Religious Experience: S. Kierkegaard's Case, Dialectically Understood], 『キェルケゴール研究』 [Kierkegaard-Studiet], no. 5, 1968, pp. 53–63.

—「キェルケゴール　ウィトゲンシュタインと私」 [Kierkegaard and Wittgenstein], 『キェルケゴール研究』 [Kierkegaard-Studiet], no. 23, 1993, pp. 39–48.

内村鑑三 [Uchimura, Kanzo], 「大野心」 [The Great Ambition], 『聖書之研究』 [Biblical Study], vol. 9, no. 7, 1906, pp. 3–4.

上田敏 [Ueda, Bin], 「イブセン」 [Ibsen], 『早稲田文学』 [Waseda Literature], vol. 3, no. 7, 1906, pp. 83–94.

魚木忠一 [Uoki, Tadakazu], 「ヘーゲルの辨證法に對するキェルケゴール並にバルトの修正」 [Hegel's Dialectic as Corrected by Kierkegaard and Karl Barth], 『基督教研究』 [Studies in Christian Religion, Doshisha University], vol. 9, no. 2, 1931, pp. 184–98.

若松謙 [Wakamatsu, Ken], 「キルケゴールにおける美的実存」 [The Aesthetic Existence in Kierkegaard], 『奈良教育大学紀要人文・社会科学』 [Bulletin of Nara University of Education. Cultural and Social Science], vol. 34, 1985, pp. 87–106.

— 「キルケゴールにおける倫理的実存」 [The Ethical Existence in Kierke-gaard], 『奈良教育大学紀要人文・社会科学』 [Bulletin of Nara University of Education. Cultural and Social Science], vol. 35, 1986, pp. 101–21; vol. 36, 1987, pp. 23–43.

— 「キルケゴールにおける宗教的実存」 [The Religious Existence in Kierke-gaard], 『奈良教育大学紀要人文・社会科学』 [Bulletin of Nara University of Education. Cultural and Social Science], vol. 37, 1988, pp. 15–35.

— 『若松謙思想論集—カント・ロック・キェルケゴール』 [Ken Wakamatsu's Collection of Philosophical Treatises: Kant, Locke and Kierkegaard], Osaka: Sogen-sha 1990.

若山玄芳 [Wakayama, Genpo], 「キルケゴールの倫理観」 [Kierkegaard's View on Ethics], 『哲学誌』 [Historia Philosophiae], vol. 7, 1965; vol. 8, 1966, pp. 13–31.

渡部光男 [Watabe, Mitsuo], 「キルケゴールに於けるキリスト教理解の諸傾向」 [Some Tendencies in Kierkegaard's Understanding of Christianity], 『宗教研究』 [Journal of Religious Studies], vol. 38, 1965.

— 「キルケゴールとヘーゲル左派」 [S. Kierkegaard and Left Hegelians], 『酪農学園大学紀要』 [Journal of the College of Dairying], vol. 2, 1965, pp. 181–199; republished in 『キェルケゴール研究』 [Kierkegaard-Studiet], no. 3, 1966, pp. 72–87.

— 「キルケゴールの『教会闘争』の一側面」 [An Aspect of Kierkegaard's "Church Struggle"], 『哲学』 [Annals of the Philosophical Society of Hokkaido University], vol. 3, 1967, pp. 125–52.

— 「キェルケゴールの思想的背景としてのフランツ・フォン・バーダー」 [Franz von Baader as a Background of Søren Kierkegaard], 『キェルケゴール研究』 [Kierkegaard-Studiet], no. 4, 1967, pp. 67–81.

— 「キェルケゴールの『後書』第一部研究」 [A Study of Kierkegaard's *Postscript, Part I*], 『基督教学』 [Christian Studies], vol. 3, 1968, pp. 50–4.

— 『キェルケゴールの研究』 [A Study of Kierkegaard], Tokyo: Hosaka-shuppann 1969.

— 「１９世紀思想とキルケゴール」 [The Thinking of the 19th Century and Kierkegaard], 『実存主義』 [Existentialism], vol. 49, 1969, pp. 57–65.

— 「キェルケゴールの『後書』第一部の聖書観」 [Kierkegaard's View of the Bible in the First Part of the *Postscript*], 『キェルケゴール研究』 [Kierke-gaard-Studiet], no. 6, 1969, pp. 49–66.

— 「キェルケゴールの実存関係の弁証法」 [S. Kierkegaard's Dialectic of "Existents-Forhold"], 『酪農学園大学紀要』 [Journal of the College of Dairy-ing], 1971, vol. 4, pp. 61–74.

— 「キェルケゴールに於ける『建揚』の概念の発展」 [Kierkegaard's Con-cept of "Upbuilding"], 『基督教学』 [The Christian Studies], vol. 13, 1978, pp. 125–35.

— 「キェルケゴールにおける『希望』概念」 [Kierkegaard's Concept of "Hope"], 『キェルケゴール研究』 [Kierkegaard-Studiet], no. 12, 1982, pp. 37–46.

— 『初期ヘーゲル・キェルケゴール・ティリッヒ』 [Kierkegaard's and Tillich's Relations to the Young Hegel], Tokyo: Sugiyama-shoten 1984.

— 「キェルケゴールにおける悔恨の概念」 [Kierkegaard's Concept of Repentance], 『酪農学園大学紀要人文・社会科学編』 [Journal of the College of Dairying. Cultural and Social Science], vol. 10, 1984, pp. 557–75.

— 「キェルケゴール『後書』までの『悔い』の概念の展開」 [The Development of the Concept of "Anger" in Kierkegaard's Authorship until the *Postscript*], 『キェルケゴール研究』 [Kierkegaard-Studiet], no. 16, 1986, pp. 43–56.

— 「キェルケゴールにおける懐疑の問題」 [Analysis of Kierkegaard's Concept of Doubt], 『キェルケゴール研究』 [Kierkegaard-Studiet], no. 18, 1988, pp. 47–58.

渡辺明照 [Watanabe, Akiteru], 「キルケゴールの絶望をめぐって」 [On Kierkegaard's Concept of Despair], 『哲学年誌』 [Annual of Philosophy], no. 8, 2002, pp. 88–102.

渡辺護 [Watanabe, Mamoru], 「キェルケゴールの音楽美学」 [Kierkegaard's Aesthetics of Music], 『美学』 [Aesthetics], vol. 8, 1957, pp. 21–9.

— 「キェルケゴールのドン・ジョヴァンニ論」 [Kierkegaard's Concept of Don Juan], 『フィルハーモニー』 [Philharmony], vol. 29, 1957.

和辻哲郎 [Watsuji, Tetsuro], 『ゼエレン＝キェルゴオル』 [Søren Kierkegaard], Tokyo: Uchidarokakuho 1915 (2nd ed., Tokyo: Chikuma-shobo 1947); republished as vol. 1 in 和辻哲郎全集第1巻 [Tetsuro Watsuji's Complete Works], Tokyo: Iwanami-shoten 1961.

八木武三郎 [Yagi, Busaburo], 「『実存に於ける真理の根源』—ハイデッガーとキルケゴール」 [The Root of the Truth in Existence: Heidegger and Kierkegaard], 『福島大学学芸学部論集』 [Bulletin of Fukushima University], vol. 1, 1950, pp. 41–56.

山田衛 [Yamada, Mamoru], 「単独者の信仰—キェルケゴールにおける実存の一側面」 [Faith of the Single Individual], 『哲学論集』 [Philosophical Studies], vol. 26, 1979, pp. 75–9.

— 「石津照璽のキェルケゴール論（上）」 [Kierkegaard-Theory of Ishizu Teruji, I], 『新キェルケゴール研究』 [Kierkegaard Studies], no. 3, 2004, pp. 37–55.

山松勇太 [Yamamatsu, Yuta], 「『ドゥーヴの動と不動』におけるヘーゲルとキルケゴールの思想」 [Thoughts of Hegel and Kierkegaard in *Du Mouvement Et De L'Immobilite De Douve*], 『仏語仏文学研究』 [Revue de langue et littérature françaises], no. 46, 2013, pp. 71–95.

山本邦子 [Yamamoto, Kuniko], 「キェルケゴールにおける『躓きの可能性』の積極性」 [On the Positivity of "the Possibility of Offense" in Kierkegaard], 『キェルケゴール研究』 [Kierkegaard-Studiet], no. 9, 1978, pp. 51–60.

— 「キェルケゴールによる我々の時代への示唆」 [What is Suggested by Kierkegaard to our Times], 『キェルケゴール研究』 [Kierkegaard-Studiet], no. 11, 1981, pp. 45–52.

— 「キェルケゴールと生老病死の問題」 [Kierkegaard and "Shō-rō-byō-shi"], 『キェルケゴール研究』 [Kierkegaard-Studiet], no. 20, 1990, pp. 49–60.

— 「キェルケゴールにおける『現代』にまつわる一考察—ヘッカー、ゾフィーとともに」 [On "Modernity" in Kierkegaard with Th. Haecker and S. Scholl], 『新キェルケゴール研究』 [Kierkegaard Studies], no. 7, 2009, pp. 59–76.

山本忠義 [Yamamoto, Tadayoshi],「キェルケゴールの『自己の定義』について」 [On Kierkegaard's Definition of the Self],『基督教学研究』 [Journal of Christian Studies], vol. 9, 1986, pp. 131–44.

—「キェルケゴールの『罪』理解—『死に至る病』を手掛かりに」 [Kierkegaard's Understanding of "Sin": From *The Sickness unto Death*],『基督教学研究』 [Journal of Christian Studies], vol. 18, 1998, pp. 175–93.

—「キェルケゴールの『自由の可能性』—『永遠的なもの』を目指して」 ["Possibility of Freedom" in Kierkegaard],『基督教学研究』 [Journal of Christian Studies], vol. 25, 2005, pp. 171–90.

山本泰生 [Yamamoto, Yasuo],「渦動と水平線—キルケゴールとアドルノ」 [Vortex and Horizon: Kierkegaard and Adorno],『理想』 [Riso], vol. 676, 2006, pp. 24–36.

山中博心 [Yamanaka, Hiroshi],「マックス・フリッシュとキルケゴール—『シュテイラー』に見る『私』からの遁走」 [Max Frisch and Kierkegaard],『福岡大学人文論叢』 [Fukuoka University Review of Literature & Humanities], vol. 22, 1990, pp. 155–85.

山下秀智 [Yamashita, Hidetomo],「親鸞とキェルケゴール」 [Shinran and Kierkegaard],『理想』 [Riso], vol. 485, 1973, pp. 100–11.

—「実存の深み—キェルケゴールの根本思想—」 [On the Depth of Existence: Kierkegaard's Basic Ideas],『キェルケゴール研究』 [Kierkegaard-Studiet], no. 7, 1977, pp. 44–8.

—『絶対否定と絶対肯定—キェルケゴールと親鸞の問題』 [The Absolute Negation and Affirmation: A Problem of Kierkegaard and Shinran], Tokyo: Hokuju-shuppan 1978.

—「キェルケゴールにおける反省の概念」 [The Concept of Reflection in Kierkegaard],『キェルケゴール研究』 [Kierkegaard-Studiet], no. 9, 1978, pp. 61–70.

—「根底の自覚—キェルケゴールと唯識思想—」 [Realization of the Ground of Life: Kierkegaard and the Thought of Yogācāra School in Buddhism],『キェルケゴール研究』 [Kierkegaard-Studiet], no. 25, 1995, pp. 39–50.

—『宗教的実存の展開—キェルケゴールと親鸞』 [The Development of the Religious Existence: Kierkegaard and Shinran], Fukuoka: Sogen-sha 2000.

—「無常性の克服—『神の不変性』を読む」 [The Concept of Impermanence],『新キェルケゴール研究』 [Kierkegaard Studies], no. 1, 2001, pp. 1–22.

—『キェルケゴール『死に至る病』』 [Kierkegaard's *The Sickness unto Death*], Kyoto: Koyo-shobo 2011.

—「キェルケゴールの魅力—信仰を支える逆説弁証法—」 [Charm of the Paradoxical Dialectic in Kierkegaard],『新キェルケゴール研究』 [Kierkegaard Studies], no. 12, 2014, pp. 82–9.

山下太郎 [Yamashita, Taro],「キェルケゴールの実存弁証法における若干の問題—ヘーゲルとキェルケゴール」 [A Few Problems in Kierkegaard's Existential Dialectics: Hegel and Kierkegaard],『精神科学』 [Science of Mind], vol. 24, 1985, pp. 81–98.

山内清郎 [Yamauchi, Seiro],「キェルケゴール『イロニーの概念』におけるソクラテス像: 教師としてのイロニカー、イロニカーとしての教師」

[Kierkegaard's Image of Socrates in *The Concept of Irony*], 『京都大学大学院教育学研究科紀要』 [Kyoto University Research Studies in Education], vol. 46, 2000, pp. 274–86.

—「覚醒的な教師としてのキルケゴール—著作活動を通しての伝達、フモリストがひらくトポス」 [Kierkegaard as the Awakening Teacher: A Communication through Authorship and the Topos which the Humorist Unfolds], 『臨床教育人間学:年報』 [Clinical Pedagogy and Anthropology: Annual Report], vol. 4, 2002, pp. 53–70.

—「キルケゴールの、死んでも癒されぬ病である『絶望』とは」 [What is the Incurable Disease, which Kierkegaard Calls "Despair"?], 『哲学論集』 [Philosophical Studies], vol. 50, 2003, pp. 55–72.

—「笑うキルケゴールのニヒリズム—コーヒーと散歩と実存とわたし」 [The Nihilism of the Smiling Kierkegaard], 『教育哲学研究』 [Studies in the Philosophy of Education], vol. 94, 2006, pp. 91–7.

—「キルケゴールの語りのスタイルの根本衝動—『文体の根本衝動』『物語の真実性』の観点から」 [Fundamental Impulse of Kierkegaard's Style of Speech], 『大谷学報』 [The Journal of Buddhist Studies and Humanities], vol. 87, 2008, pp. 24–40.

柳堀素雅子 [Yanagibori, Sugako], 「キルケゴールにおける『他者』の問題」 [S. Kierkegaard's "the Other"], 『大正大学大学院研究論集』 [Journal of the Graduate School, Taisho University], vol. 15, 1991, pp. 107–17.

—「キルケゴールの教会批判」 [Kierkegaard's Criticism of the Church], 『大正大学大学院研究論集』 [Journal of the Graduate School, Taisho University], vol. 17, 1993, pp. 141–50.

—「キェルケゴール解釈における仏教とキリスト教」 [Buddhism and Christianity in Kierkegaard's Interpretation], 『大正大学総合仏教研究所年報』 [Annual of the Institute for Comprehensive Studies of Buddhism, Taisho University], vol. 23, 2001, pp. 112–17.

—「日本人とキルケゴール」 [The Japanese and Kierkegaard], 『大正大学総合仏教研究所年報』 [Annual of the Institute for Comprehensive Studies of Buddhism, Taisho University], vol. 25, 2003, pp. 110–19.

栁沢貴司 [Yanagisawa, Takashi], 「キェルケゴールにおける絶望の弁証法」 [The Dialectic of Despair in Kierkegaard], 『倫理学研究』 [Ethical Studies], vol. 26, 1996, pp. 48–57.

—「キェルケゴールにおける倫理的段階と宗教性A」 [The Ethical Stage and Religiousness A in Kierkegaard], 『京都大学総合人間学部紀要』 [The Integrated Human Studies], vol. 5, 1998, pp. 99–110.

—「キェルケゴールにおける『逆説』と『悟性』」 ["Paradox" and "Understanding" in Kierkegaard], 『哲學』 [The Philosophy], vol. 49, 1998, pp. 239–48.

—「信仰の矛盾—キェルケゴールのキリスト教信仰論」 [The Contradiction of Faith: Kierkegaard's Theory of Christian Faith], 『総合人間科学』 [Toua Journal of Human Science], vol. 4, 2004, pp. 43–52.

—「キェルケゴールのアンチ哲学」 [Kierkegaard's Antiphilosophy], 『新キェルケゴール研究』 [Kierkegaard Studies], no. 12, 2014, pp. 63–72.

安本行雄 [Yasumoto, Yukio], 「キェルケゴールにおける宗教的実存」 [The Religious Existence in Kierkegaard], 『哲学研究』 [The Journal of Philosophical Studies], vol. 39, 1956.

——「キルケゴールにおけるパトス的内面性の論理—実存弁証法」 [The Logic of Pathetic Interiority in Kierkegaard], 『理想』 [Riso], vol. 442, pp. 54–63.

横山喜之 [Yokoyama, Yoshiyuki], 「キルケゴールと内村鑑三」 [Kierkegaard and Kanzo Uchimura], 『理想』 [Riso], vol. 269, 1955.

米沢一孝 [Yonezawa, Kazutaka], 「キェルケゴールにおける歌劇受容について」 [On the Problem of Opera in Kierkegaard's Thought], 『新キェルケゴール研究』 [Kierkegaard Studies], no. 4, 2005, pp. 42–59.

——「実存の領域論は『実存』と矛盾するのか?—アドルノによるキルケゴール批判の検討」 [Is the Theory of Existential Stages Contradictory to "Existence"?], 『東北哲学会年報』 [Annual of the Philosophical Society of Tohoku], vol. 21, 2005, pp. 1–13.

——「キルケゴールにおける美的媒体論について」 [On Kierkegaard's Theory of Aesthetic Media], 『日本リズム協会年報』 [Annual of the Japan Institute of Rhythm], vol. 12, 2008, pp. 50–63.

米沢紀 [Yonezawa, Toshi], 「キィルケゴールに於ける罪の問題」 [The Problem of Sin in Kierkegaard], 『宗教研究』 [Journal of Religious Studies], vol. 133, 1952, pp. 330–2.

——「キェルケゴールの『説教集』について」 [On Kierkegaard's Discourses], 『弘前学院大学・弘前学院短期大学紀要』 [The Bulletin of Hirosaki Gakuin College], vol. 13, 1977, pp. 42–50; vol. 15, 1979, pp. 39–45; vol. 16, 1980, pp. 165–74.

——「S. キェルケゴールの『キリスト教講話』について」 [On S. Kierkegaard's *Christian Discourses*], 『宗教研究』 [Journal of Religious Studies], vol. 54, 1980, pp. 79–98.

——「S. キルケゴールの『不安の概念』における罪観」 [Kierkegaard's View of Sin in *The Concept of Anxiety*], 『弘前学院大学・弘前学院短期大学紀要』 [The Bulletin of Hirosaki Gakuin College], vol. 17, 1981, pp. 131–48.

——「S. キルケゴールの『死に至る病』、『哲学的断片』、『哲学的断片への結びとしての非学問的あとがき』における罪観」 [Kierkegaard's View of Sin in *The Sickness unto Death, Philosophical Fragments* and the *Postscript*], 『弘前学院大学・弘前学院短期大学紀要』 [The Bulletin of Hirosaki Gakuin College], vol. 18, 1982, pp. 71–8.

——「セーレン・キェルケゴールの生涯と思想」 [The Life and Thought of Søren Kierkegaard], 『弘前学院大学・弘前学院短期大学紀要』 [The Bulletin of Hirosaki Gakuin College], vol. 19, 1983, pp. 13–18; vol. 20, 1984, pp. 45–8; vol. 22, 1986, pp. 1–6; vol. 24, 1988, pp. 9–14; vol. 26, 1990, pp. 1–6.

吉田敬介 [Yoshida, Keisuke], 「キルケゴール・ルネッサンスの影—両大戦間期ドイツにおける決断主義的・非合理主義的解釈に関する受容史研究」 [The Shadow of the Kierkegaard Renaissance], 『学習院大学人文科学論集』 [Studies in Humanities], no. 22, 2013, pp. 1–27.

——「『かけら』としての哲学—キェルケゴールにおける非学問的な学問としての哲学」 [The Philosophy as "Fragment"], 『学習院大学人文科学論集』 [Studies in Humanities], vol. 18, 2009, pp. 1–30.

— 「キェルケゴールにおける『実存』への問い直し」 [Renewed Question of "Existence" in Kierkegaard], 『哲学会誌』 [Journal of Philosophy], no. 34, 2010, pp. 21–39.

— 「キェルケゴールが追い求めた真理とは」 [What is the Truth that Kierkegaard Sought?], 『哲学会誌』 [Journal of Philosophy], no. 35, 2011, pp. 25–48.

— 「ヨハンネス・クリマクスの『一断片の哲学』における断絶の弁証法」 [The Dialectic of the Break in "Fragmental Philosophy" by Johannes Climacus], 『新キェルケゴール研究』 [Journal of Philosophy], no. 9, 2011, pp. 72–89.

— 「キルケゴールは観念論者か—アドルノのキルケゴール論をめぐって—」 [Is Kierkegaard an Idealist? With Reference to Adorno's Theory of Kierkegaard], 『新キェルケゴール研究』 [Journal of Philosophy], no. 12, 2014, pp. 14–30.

吉満義彦 [Yoshimitsu, Yoshihiko], 「キェルケゴール的思惟について」 [On Kierkegaard's Way of Thinking], in his 『文化倫理の根本問題』 [The Fundamental Problems of Culture and Ethics], Tokyo: Shinsei-shobo 1936, pp. 83–7.

吉村博次 [Yoshimura, Hiroji], 『キェルケゴール絶望の概念—「死にいたる病」とその周辺』 [The Concept of Despair in Kierkegaard: Concerning *The Sickness unto Death*], Tokyo: Natsume-shoten 1947.

吉野要 [Yoshino, Kaname], 「『エロス』の謎—キェルケゴールのエロス論—」 [Mystery of Eros: Eros in Kierkegaard], 『公民論集』 [Komin-ronshu], vol. 4, 1996, pp. 19–37.

吉沢慶一 [Yoshizawa, Keiichi], 「倫理的実存と宗教的実存—キルケゴールとドフトエフスキイの実存的思想をめぐって」 [The Ethical and Religious Existence: On the Existential Thoughts of Kierkegaard and Dostoevsky], 『明治学院大学キリスト教研究所紀要』 [The Bulletin of Christian Research Institute, Meiji Gakuin University], vol. 9, 1976, pp. 49–72.

湯浅南海男 [Yuasa, Namio], 「キェルケゴールの作品における論理性についての私見」 [On the Logicality of Kierkegaard's Works], 『キェルケゴール研究』 [Kierkegaard-Studiet], no. 1, 1964, pp. 143–52.

結城敏也 [Yuki, Toshiya], 「『キェルケゴール』の視差」 [The Parallax of "Kierkegaard"], 『国際基督教大学学報I-A教育研究』 [International Christian University Publications. I-A, Educational Studies], vol. 28, 1986, pp. 49–66.

行武宏明 [Yukutake, Hiroaki], 「キェルケゴール思想における実存概念—1841-1841–1842年におけるキルケゴールのシェリング哲学受容」 [The Concept of Existence in Kierkegaard's Thought: His Reception of Schelling's Philosophy in 1841–1842], 『東洋大学大学院紀要』 [Bulletin of the Graduate School, Toyo University], vol. 44, 2007, pp. 43–65.

— 「アンチ＝クリマクスによる絶望の治療について」 [On Curing Despair by Anti-Climacus], 『新キェルケゴール研究』 [Kierkegaard Studies], no. 7, 2009, pp. 1–19.

由良哲次 [Yura, Tetsuji], 「キェルケゴールの人及びその思想」 [Kierkegaard's Life and Thought], in his 『人生観の問題』 [The Problems of the View of Life], Tokyo: Meguro-shoten 1935, pp. 190–205.

— 「キェルケゴールの人生観」 [Kierkegaard's View of Life], 『教育学術雑誌』 [Journal of Educational Review], vol. 9, 1935, pp. 7–22; vol. 10, 1935, pp. 49–67; vol. 11, 1935, pp. 2–21; vol. 12, 1935, pp. 12–30.

是影生 [Ze, Eisei], 「キィルケゴオルドの戀日記」 [Kierkegaard's Diary of Love], 『層雲』 [A Stratus Cloud], vol. 1, no. 2, 1911, pp. 1–17.

III. Translated Secondary Literature on Kierkegaard in Japanese

Adorno, Theodor W., 『キルケゴール—美的なものの構成』 [Kierkegaard: Konstruktion des Ästhetischen], trans. by Nagamitsu Miura and Yukio Ito, Saitama: Izara-shobo 1974; trans. by Yasuo Yamamoto, Tokyo: Misuzu-shobo 1974.

Arbaugh, George E., 「キルケゴールとフォイエルバッハ」 [Kierkegaard and Feuerbach], trans. by Katsumi Kitada, 『キルケゴール研究』 [Kierkegaard-Studiet], no. 13, 1983, pp. 5–8.

Brandt, Frithiof, 『七つのキルケゴール研究』 [Seven Kierkegaard Studies], trans. by Masaru Otani, Tokyo: Tokai University Press 1981.

— 『キルケゴールの生涯と作品』 [Søren Kierkegaard (1813–1855): His Life, his Works], trans. by Katsumi Kitada and Tami Kitada, Kyoto: Horitsubunka-sha 1991.

Bukdahl, Jørgen K., 「『心の通暁者』キルケゴール—両義性に対するキェルケゴールの両義的関係について—」 ["Connoisseur of the Heart": Kierkegaard], trans. by Shozo Fujiki, 『キェルケゴール研究』 [Kierkegaard-Studiet], no. 5, 1968, pp. 64–79.

— 「セーレン・キェルケゴールとハイネ」 [Søren Kierkegaard and Heine], trans. by Masaru Otani, 『キェルケゴール研究』 [Kierkegaard-Studiet], no. 13, 1983, pp. 9–12.

Burgess, Andrew J., 「情念と信仰に関するスピノザとキルケゴール」 [Spinoza and Kierkegaard on Passion and Faith], trans. by Masashi Hosoya, 『キルケゴール研究』 [Kierkegaard-Studiet], no. 9, 1978, pp. 71–6.

Cauly, Olivier, 『キルケゴール』 [Kierkegaard], trans. by Kyoichi Murakami and Masami Kobayashi, Tokyo: Hakusui-sha 1995.

Christensen, Arild, 「キルケゴールは仏教と対比し得るか」 [Can Kierkegaard be Compared with Buddhism?], trans. by Takayuki Okubo, 『キルケゴール研究』 [Kierkegaard-Studiet], no. 1, 1964, pp. 8–12.

Christensen, Villads, 「キルケゴールはどんな外見をしていたか」 [How did Kierkegaard Look?], trans. by Haruo Morioka, 『キルケゴール研究』 [Kierkegaard-Studiet], no. 3, 1966, pp. 94–8.

Deyton, C. Edward, 『愛について—キルケゴールの場合』 [Speaking of Love: Kierkegaard's Plan for Faith], trans. by Katsumi Kitada and Tami Kitada, Kyoto: Horitsubunka-sha 1997.

Diem, Hermann, 「キルケゴールと後世」 [Kierkegaard und die Nachwelt], trans. by Kohei Nakamura and Masaru Otani, 『キルケゴール研究』 [Kierkegaard-Studiet], no. 1, 1964, pp. 13–27.

— 『キルケゴールの実存弁証法』 [Die Existenzdialektik von Sören Kierkegaard], trans. by Kazuyoshi Sasaki and Masaru Otani, Fukuoka: Sogen-sha 1969.

Dietz, Walter, R., 「新たな国際的研究の光を浴びるキルケゴール」 [Kierkegaard im Licht der neuren internationalen Forschung], trans. by Shin Fujieda, 『新キルケゴール研究』 [Kierkegaard Studies], no. 1, 2001, pp. 122–41.

Fabro, Cornelio, 「『真理の主体性』とキルケゴールの解釈」 [The "Subjectivity of Truth" and the Interpretation of Kierkegaard], trans. by Sanae Fukuyama, 『キルケゴール研究』 [Kierkegaard-Studiet], no. 1, 1964, pp. 28–33.

Fenger, Henning, 「キェルケゴールの水曜日の交信—キェルケゴールのレギー
　　ネ・オルセン宛の手紙の日附に関する試論—」 [Kierkegaard's Correspond-
　　ence on Wednesdays], trans. by Kazuhiko Ozaki and Masaru Otani, 『キェルケゴ
　　ール研究』 [Kierkegaard-Studiet], no. 6, 1969, pp. 67–91.

Gardiner, Patrick L., 『キェルケゴール』 [Kierkegaard], trans. by Jun Hashimoto
　　and Takahiro Hirabayashi, Tokyo: Kyobunkwan 1996.

Geismar, Eduard O., 『キェルケゴールの宗教思想』 [Lectures on the Religious
　　Thought of Søren Kierkegaard], trans. by Kazuhiko Ozaki et al., Tokyo: Tokai
　　University Press 1978.

Gerdes, Hayo, 『キルケゴール—その生涯と著作』 [Sören Kierkegaard: Leben
　　und Werk], trans. by Yasuo Takemura, Tokyo: Bokutaku-sha 1976.

Giles, James, 「内面性から空性へ—キェルケゴールとヨーガチャーラ仏教」
　　[From Inwardness to Emptiness: Kierkegaard and Yogācāra Buddhism], trans.
　　by Akira Miyata, 『新キェルケゴール研究』 [Kierkegaard Studies], no. 2,
　　2002, pp. 94–144.

Grimsley, Ronald, 「キェルケゴールとモンテーニュ」 [Kierkegaard and
　　Montaigne], trans. by Hiroyuki Kitano, 『キェルケゴール研究』 [Kierkegaard-
　　Studiet], no. 13, 1983, pp. 13–22.

Hessel, R.A. Egon, 「キェルケゴールとカフカ」 [Kierkegaard und Kafka],
　　trans. by Jun Hashimoto, 『キェルケゴール研究』 [Kierkegaard-Studiet],
　　no. 3, 1966, pp. 88–93.

Hirsch, Emanuel, 「ゼーレン・キェルケゴールによる伝承的摂理信仰の改革」
　　[Die Umbildung des überlieferten Vorsehungsglaubens durch Sören Kierkegaard],
　　trans. by Mime Morita, 『キェルケゴール研究』 [Kierkegaard-Studiet],
　　no. 24, 1994, pp. 45–54; no. 25, 1995, pp. 51–60.

Hohlenberg, Johannes, 『セーレン・キェルケゴール伝』 [Søren Kierkegaard],
　　trans. by Masaru Otani et al., Kyoto: Minerva-shobo 1967.

Holm, Søren, 「キェルケゴールと『ギリシャ性』」 [Søren Kierkegaard and "the
　　Greeks"], trans. by Jun Hashimoto, 『キェルケゴール研究』 [Kierkegaard-
　　Studiet], vol. 2, 1965, pp. 79–88.

Høffding, Harald, 『哲學者としてのキェルケゴール』 [Søren Kierkegaard as a
　　Philosopher], trans. by Hiroo Torii, Tokyo: Daiichi-shobo 1935.

Hultberg, Helge, 「セーレン・キェルケゴールにおけるフモール」 [Humor in
　　Kierkegaard], trans. by Toshikazu Oya, 『キェルケゴール研究』 [Kierkegaard-
　　Studiet], no. 17, 1987, pp. 61–77; no. 18, 1988, pp. 59–68; no. 19, 1989,
　　pp. 61–74; no. 20, 1990, pp. 61–72.

Hügli, Anton, 「キェルケゴールの概念性がドイツ哲学に与えた影響」 [Der
　　Einfluss von Kierkegaards Begrifflichkeit auf die deutsche Philosophie], trans.
　　by Kinya Masugata, 『キェルケゴール研究』 [Kierkegaard-Studiet], no. 10,
　　1980, pp. 65–80.

Jansen, F.J. Billeskov, 「北欧諸国におけるキェルケゴールの遺産」 [L'Héritage
　　de Kierkegaard dans les Pays Nordiques], trans. by Hirokazu Nakahori and Tamotsu
　　Tanabe, 『キェルケゴール研究』 [Kierkegaard-Studiet], no. 1, 1964, pp. 57–65.

—「単独者への訴え—セーレン・キェルケゴール・生死の道案内—」 [The
　　Appeal to the Single Individual], trans. by Toshiaki Muraki, 『キェルケゴール
　　研究』 [Kierkegaard-Studiet], no. 11, 1981, pp. 77–91.

— 『キェルケゴール—セーレン・キェルケゴールの生涯と思想への手引き』 [Kierkegaard: Introduction to the Life and Thought of Søren Kierkegaard], trans. by Masaru Otani, Fukuoka: Sogen-sha 1997.

Kim, Madeleine, 『単独者と普遍—キェルケゴールにおける人間の自己実現への道』 [Der Einzelne und das Allgemeine], trans. by Ichiro Sakai, Tokyo: University of Tokyo Press 1988.

Kiær, Uffe, 「ただの詩人—セーレン・キェルケゴールと芸術について—」 [Only a Poet: Søren Kierkegaard and Art], trans. by Masaru Otani, 『キェルケゴール研究』 [Kierkegaard-Studiet], no. 21, 1991, pp. 51–8.

Kloeden, Wolfdietrich v., 「時間—永遠問題に対してS・キェルケゴールによって新たに展開された諸相—神学的人間学への寄与—」 [Neu entwickelte Aspekte zum Zeit-Ewigkeits-Problem bei S. Kierkegaard: Ein Beitrag zur theologischen Anthropologie], trans. by Reiko Saotome, 『キェルケゴール研究』 [Kierkegaard-Studiet], no. 15, 1985, pp. 53–64.

Lowrie, Walter, 『キェルケゴール小傳』 [A Short Life of Kierkegaard], trans. by Masaru Otani, Tokyo: Sobun-sha 1958.

Löwith, Karl, 『キェルケゴールとニーチェ』 [Kierkegaard und Nietzsche oder theologische und philosophische Überwindung des Nihilismus: Zur Problematik der Humanität in der Philosophie nach Hegel], trans. by Hideyasu Nakagawa, Tokyo: Kobundo-shobo 1943 (2nd ed., Tokyo: Mirai-sha 1967; 3rd ed., Tokyo: Mirai-sha 2002).

— 『ヘーゲル・マルクス・キェルケゴール』 [L'achèvement de la philosophie classique par Hegel et sa dissolution chez Marx et Kierkegaard], trans. by Jisaburo Shibata, Tokyo: Kaname-shobo 1951 (2nd ed., Tokyo: Mirai-sha 1967).

— 『ヘーゲルからニーチェへ』 [Von Hegel zu Nietzsche], trans. by Jisaburo Shibata, Tokyo: Iwanami-shoten 1952.

Malantschuk, Gregor, 「想起の概念とセーレン・キェルケゴールの著作におけるその諸相」 [The Concept of Recollection and its Aspects in Kierkegaard's Authorship], trans. by Masaru Otani, 『キェルケゴール研究』 [Kierkegaard-Studiet], no. 3, 1966, pp. 99–110.

— 『キェルケゴール—その著作の構造』 [Introduction to Søren Kierkegaard's Authorship], trans. by Shozo Fujiki, Tokyo: Yorudan-sha 1976.

— 「セーレン・キェルケゴールにおける倣いの思想の帰結」 [Consequences of Kierkegaard's Thought of Imitation], trans.by Masaru Otani, 『キェルケゴール研究』 [Kierkegaard-Studiet], no. 7, 1977, pp. 49–57.

— 「キェルケゴールとニーチェ」 [Kierkegaard and Nietzsche], trans. by Tetsuyoshi Kunii, 『キェルケゴール研究』 [Kierkegaard-Studiet], no. 13, 1983, pp. 23–36.

— 『キェルケゴールの弁証法と実存』 [Dialectic and Existence in Kierkegaard], trans. by Masaru Otani, Osaka: Toho-shuppan 1984.

— 「セーレン・キェルケゴールにおける相対的自由と絶対的自由をめぐる諸問題（遺稿）」 [Problems of Relative Freedom and Absolute Freedom in Kierkegaard (Posthumous Manuscript)], trans. by Kinya Masugata, 『キェルケゴール研究』 [Kierkegaard-Studiet], no. 14, 1984, pp. 51–64.

— 「セーレン・キルケゴールにおける内在と超越の概念」 [The Concepts of Immanence and Transcendence in Søren Kierkegaard], trans. by Tadayoshi

Hayashi, 『関西学院大学キリスト教学研究』 [Kwansei Gakuin University Journal of Christian Studies], vol. 1, 1998, pp. 79–120.

— 「セーレン・キェルケゴールにおける肉の内なる刺」 ["Thorn in the Flesh" in Søren Kierkegaard], trans. by Tomoaki Kai, 『哲学論究』 [Philosophical Research], vol. 24, 2010, pp. 1–14.

桝形公也 [Masugata, Kinya] (ed.), 『キェルケゴール―新しい解釈の試み―』 [Kierkegaard: New Interpretations], Kyoto: Showado 1993. (George Pattison, 「美学と『美学的なるもの』」 [Aesthetics and "the Aesthetic"], trans. by Satoshi Eguchi, pp. 3–24; Sylvia I. Walsh, 「絶望の『女性的』ならびに『男性的』形態について」 [On "Feminine" and "Masculine" Forms of Despair], trans. by Hiroko Otoshi, pp. 25–44; Robert L. Perkins, 「思慮分別（Klogskab）―美徳から悪徳へ」 [Prudence, From Virtue to Vice], trans. by Katsuaki Tanaka, pp. 45–67; Poul Lübcke, 「キェルケゴールを道徳哲学者として分析的に解釈すること」 [An Analytical Interpretation of Kierkegaard as Moral Philosopher], trans. by Ken Takahashi, pp. 68–91; Edward Harris, 「キェルケゴールの『倫理的断片』に見られる道徳的行為主体」 [The Reality of the Act of Choice in Kierkegaard's Forms Despair], trans. by Masahiro Ito, pp. 92–108; Edward F. Mooney, 「アブラハムとディレンマ―キェルケゴールの目的論的停止再考―」 [Abraham and Dilemma; the Teleological Suspension Revisited], trans. by Wataru Wada, pp. 109–34; Julia Watkin, 「倫理的＝宗教的行為の基準―キェルケゴールとアドルフ・アズラー―」 [The Criteria of Authentic Ethical-Religious Authority: Kierkegaard and Adolf Adler], trans. by Kazuma Tanaka, pp. 135–60; Steven M. Emmanuel, 「キェルケゴールの教義論―一つのポスト・モダン解釈―」 [Kierkegaard on Doctrine: A Post-Modern Interpretation], trans. by Satoshi Nakazato, pp. 161–89; Alastair Hannay, 「自己の道徳心理学をめぐってキェルケゴールがはたした貢献の再評価」 [Kierkegaard's Contribution to an Understanding of Selfhood], trans. by Kazuma Tanaka, pp. 190–219; Daphne Hampson 「キェルケゴールの自己論」 [Kierkegaard on the Self], trans. by Akihisa Matsushima, pp. 220–44; Alastair McKinnon, 「キェルケゴールによる善の提示」 [Kierkegaard's Presentation of the Good], trans. by Kinya Masugata, pp. 245–77; Abrahim H. Khan, 「キェルケゴールとパトス―『後書』における一概念の研究」 [Kierkegaard and Pathos], trans. by Hiroko Otoshi, pp. 278–308.)

— 『宗教と倫理―キェルケゴールにおける実存の言語性―』 [Religion and Ethics: Language of Existence in Kierkegaard], Kyoto: Nakanishiya-shuppan 1998. (Steven Shakespeare, 「キェルケゴール―異言で語る―」 [Kierkegaard: Speaking in Tongues], trans. by Tadayoshi Hayashi, pp. 4–24; C. Stephen Evans, 「宗教的言語の誤用―キェルケゴールと『神の受肉の神話』について―」 [Mis-Using Religious Language: Something about Kierkegaard and "The Myth of God Incarnate"], trans. by Mime Morita, pp. 25–41; Peter Kemp, 「倫理と言語―レヴィナスからキェルケゴールへ」 [Ethics and Language: from Levinas to Kierkegaard], trans. by Akihisa Matsushima, pp. 42–72; Andrew J. Burgess, 「レトリックと喜劇的なもの―キェルケゴールとケネス・バーク」 [Kierkegaard and Kenneth Burke on the Rhetoric of the Comic], trans. by Yoshinobu Kudo, pp. 73–83; Joakim Garff, 「『わが親愛なる読者よ』―好意的な気持ちを抑えながら読んだキェルケゴール―」 ["My Dear Reader!"

Kierkegaard Read with Restrained Affection], trans. by Takahiro Hirabayashi, pp. 86–107; Helmuth Vetter, 「魔力（デモニー）と啓示—キェルケゴールにおける『言葉と救済』」 [Demonic and Revelation: On "Language and Redemption" in Kierkegaard], trans. by Kazumichi Yamashita, pp. 108–25; George Pattison, 「『建徳的談話』における言語とコミュニケーション」 [The Theory and Practice of Language and Communication in Kierkegaard's Upbuilding Discourses], trans. by Shudo Tsukiyama, pp. 126–45; Julia Watkin, 「キェルケゴールの著作活動における『透明性』概念」 [The Concept of "Gennemsigtighed" in Kierkegaard's Authorship], trans. by Satoshi Nakazato, pp. 146–58; Alastair McKinnon, 「キェルケゴールの言語論」 [Kierkegaard on Language], trans. by Nobuyuki Hase, pp. 159–77; Haim Gordon, 「『畏れとおののき』に対するブーバー的批判—リーダーシップおよび悪との闘いへの関わりにおいて—」 [Implication for Leadership and Fighting Evil: A Buberian Critique of *Fear and Trembling*], trans. by Hiroko Otoshi, pp. 180–95; Edward F. Mooney, 「カントはアブラハムを認めるべきか？」 [Should Kant Approve of Abraham?], trans. by Kazuma Tanaka, pp. 196–208; John Donnelly 「『畏れとおののき』における『信仰を保つこと』」 [Keeping Faith in Kierkegaard's *Fear and Trembling*], trans. by Satoshi Eguchi, pp. 209–26; Wilfried Greve, 「『死に至る病』における倫理的なものの欠落」 [Where does the Ethical Remain in Kierkegaard's *The Sickness unto Death*?], trans. by Takashi Yanagisawa, pp. 227–43.)

McDonald, William, 「個人から組織へ、そしてまた個人へ」 [From the Individual to the Institution to the Individual: A Tribute to Julia Watkin's Contribution to Kierkegaard's Philosophical Reception in Australia], trans. by Takaya Suto, 『新キェルケゴール研究』 [Kierkegaard Studies], no. 5, 2007, pp. 53–70.

McKinnon, Alastair, 「キェルケゴールの作品における＜汝＞—＜ひと＞の対極性」 [The Du-man Polarity in Kierkegaard's Works], trans. by Hiroyuki Kitano, 『キェルケゴール研究』 [Kierkegaard-Studiet], no. 12, 1982, pp. 47–60.

Meerpohl, Bernhard, 『絶望の形而上学—キェルケゴール『死に至る病』の問題』 [Die Verzweifelung als metaphysisches Phänomen in der Philosophie Sören Kierkegaards], trans. by Kazuhiko Ozaki, et al., Tokyo: Tokai University Press 1980.

Mikulová Thulstrup, Marie, 「セーレン・キェルケゴールの殉教者概念」 [Søren Kierkegaard's Concept of Martyr], trans. by Sanae Fukuyama, 『キェルケゴール研究』 [Kierkegaard-Studiet], vol. 2, 1965, pp. 66–78.

— 「キェルケゴールと教父たち」 [Kierkegaard and the Church Fathers], trans. by Kuniko Yamamoto, 『キェルケゴール研究』 [Kierkegaard-Studiet], no. 13, 1983, pp. 65–74.

Mortensen, Finn H., 「アンデルセンとキェルケゴール: 世界文学における二巨匠」 [Andersen and Kierkegaard: An Introduction to Two Masters of the World], trans. by Ken Takahashi, 『姫路獨協大学一般教育部紀要』 [Bulletin, College of Liberal Arts, Himeji Dokkyo University], vol. 3, 1992, pp. 75–89.

— 「キェルケゴールのデンマーク語テキストの問題とその再構成について: 批評的新版の刊行を求めて」 [A Critical Edition of Søren Kierkegaard's Texts in Database and in Book Form], trans. by Jun Hashimoto, 『神學研究』 [Theological Studies], vol. 40, 1993, pp. 103–41.

—「デンマーク文学とキリスト教—キェルケゴールとアンデルセンを中心に」 [Danish Literature and Christianity: Around Kierkegaard and Andersen], trans. by Takahiro Hirabayashi 『神學研究』 [Theological Studies], special volume, 2003, pp. 99–109.

Müller, Paul, 「キェルケゴールにおける『建徳的なもの』という概念」 [The Concept of "the Upbuilding" in Kierkegaard], trans. by Kinya Masugata, 『キェルケゴール研究』 [Kierkegaard-Studiet], no. 16, 1986, pp. 57–74.

—「キェルケゴールの思想における伝達の倫理」 [The Ethics of Communication in Kierkegaard's Thought], trans. by Kazuma Tanaka, 『キェルケゴール研究』 [Kierkegaard-Studiet], no. 23, 1993, pp. 49–58.

Nielsen, S. Aage, 「キェルケゴールの著作活動についての陪審判事ヴィルヘルムの見解—倫理的段階が最高のものである—」 [Judge William's View on Kierkegaard's Authorship], trans. by Masashi Hosoya, 『キェルケゴール研究』 [Kierkegaard-Studiet], no. 6, 1969, pp. 92–105.

大谷長 [Otani, Masaru] (ed.), 『キェルケゴールと悪』 [Kierkegaard and the Evil], Osaka: Toho-shuppan 1982. (Karl Jaspers, 「キェルケゴール」 [Kierkegaard], trans. by Hiroyuki Kitano, pp. 3–19; Emil Brunner, 「カントとキェルケゴールにおける哲学の根本問題」 [The Basic Problem of Philosophy in Kant and Kierkegaard], trans. by Kuniko Yamamoto, pp. 20–51; Alfred Baeumler, 「ヘーゲルとキェルケゴール」 [Hegel and Kierkegaard], trans. by Tetsuyoshi Kunii, pp. 52–76; Richard Kroner, 「キェルケゴールのヘーゲル理解」 [Kierkegaard's Understanding of Hegel], trans. by Tetsuyoshi Kunii, pp. 77–97; Jean Wahl, 「ヤスパース、キェルケゴール、そして実存」 [Notes on Some Relations of Jaspers to Kierkegaard and Heidegger], trans. by Hiroyuki Kitano, pp. 98–130; Paul Ricoeur, 「キェルケゴールと悪」 [Kierkegaard and Evil], trans. by Akihisa Matsushima, pp. 131–55; Liselotte Richter, 「キェルケゴールを哲学することはいかにして可能であるか」 [Philosophy after Kierkegaard], trans. by Akihisa Matsushima, pp. 156–86; Helmut Fahrenbach, 「キェルケゴールの倫理的実存分析」 [Kierkegaard's Analysis of Ethical Existence], trans. by Kinya Masugata, pp. 187–232.)

Pedersen, Olaf, 「ガブリエル・マルセルとキェルケゴール」 [Gabriel Marcel], trans. by Koji Sato, 『キェルケゴール研究』 [Kierkegaard-Studiet], no. 13, 1983, pp. 37–40.

Pelikan, Jaroslav J., 『ルターからキェルケゴールまで』 [From Luther to Kierkegaard], trans. by Toshikazu Takao, Tokyo: Seibun-sha 1967.

Perkins, Robert L., 「十九世紀における二つのソクラテス解釈—ヘーゲルとキェルケゴール」 [Two Nineteenth Century Interpretations of Socrates: Hegel and Kierkegaard], trans. by Kazuhiko Ozaki, 『キェルケゴール研究』 [Kierkegaard-Studiet], no. 4, 1967, pp. 82–7.

Perrot, Maryvonne, 「ユーモアから信仰へ—『セーレン・キェルケゴール例外者』最終章—」 [De l'humour à la foi ('Sören Kierkegaard, l'exception')], trans. by Akihisa Matsushima, 『キェルケゴール研究』 [Kierkegaard-Studiet], no. 21, 1991, pp. 59–66.

Plekon, Michael, 「キェルケゴールと近代解釈」 [Kierkegaard and the Interpretation of Modernity], trans. by Masashi Hosoya, 『キェルケゴール研究』 [Kierkegaard-Studiet], no. 11, 1981, pp. 53–64.

Richter, Liselotte, 「キェルケゴールと量的時代」 [Kierkegaard und das Quantitative Zeitalter], trans. by Masaru Otani, 『キェルケゴール研究』 [Kierkegaard-Studiet], no. 1, 1964, pp. 89–97.

Rohde, H. Peter, 「キェルケゴールの一引用の解明―彼の蔵書の競売記録を手引きとして―」 [Elucidating a Citation by Kierkegaard], trans. by Masaru Otani, 『キェルケゴール研究』 [Kierkegaard-Studiet], no. 5, 1968, pp. 64–9.

―『キェルケゴールの行路における謎の諸段階』 [Mysterious Stages on Kierkegaard's Way], trans. by Masaru Otani, Tokyo: Tokai University Press 1977.

―「一片の詩香」 [A Scent of Poetry], trans. by Masaru Otani, 『キェルケゴール研究』 [Kierkegaard-Studiet], no. 8, 1978, pp. 61–8.

Roos, Heinrich, 『キルケゴールとカトリシズム』 [Kierkegaard and Catholicism], trans. by Taira Goto and Minoru Mita, Tokyo: Sozo-sha 1972.

Sartre, Jean-Paul et al., 『生けるキェルケゴール』 [Kierkegaard Vivant] trans. by Shinzaburo Matsunami et al., Kyoto: Jinbun-shoin 1967.

Shakespeare, Steven, 「キリスト教の修練―躓きの諸範疇」 [Kierkegaard im Licht der neueren internationalen Forschung], trans. by Akira Miyata, 『新キェルケゴール研究』 [Kierkegaard Studies], no. 1, 2001, pp. 102–21.

Skjoldager, Emanuel, 「『自分自身を選ぶこと』についてのセーレン・キェルケゴールの見解」 [Søren Kierkegaard on "Choosing Oneself"], trans. by Kazuhiko Ozaki, 『キェルケゴール研究』 [Kierkegaard-Studiet], no. 5, 1968, pp. 80–4.

Sløk, Johannes, 「ハイデッガー、サルトル、キェルケゴールにおける実存の概念」 [The Concept of Existence in Heidegger, Sartre and Kierkegaard], trans. by Kazuhiko Ozaki, 『キェルケゴール研究』 [Kierkegaard-Studiet], no. 13, 1983, pp. 41–50.

―「キェルケゴールの人間論」 [Die Anthropologie Kierkegaards], trans. by Kazuhiko Ozaki, 『明治大学教養論集』 [The Bulletin of Arts and Sciences, Meiji University], no. 447, 2009, pp. 1–35; no. 448, 2009, pp. 29–134; no. 453, 2010, pp. 1–48; no. 456, 2010, pp. 25–72.

Søe, Niels H., 「生存における意義は何かという問いに対するキェルケゴールの答え」 [Søren Kierkegaard's Answer to the Question of the Meaning in Existence], trans. by Masaru Otani, 『キェルケゴール研究』 [Kierkegaard-Studiet], no. 1, 1964, pp. 122–32.

Stack, George J., 『キェルケゴールの実存倫理学』 [Kierkegaard's Existential Ethics], trans. by Mitsuo Watanabe, Tokyo: Sugiyama-shoten 1985.

Steffensen, Steffen, 「キェルケゴールとハマン」 [Kierkegaard und Hamann], trans. by Masaru Otani, 『キェルケゴール研究』 [Kierkegaard-Studiet], no. 4, 1967, pp. 88–106.

―「カスナーとキェルケゴール―一つの講演―」 [Kassner und Kierkegaard: Ein Vortrag], trans. by Masaru Otani, 『キェルケゴール研究』 [Kierkegaard-Studiet], no. 10, 1980, pp. 81–90.

―"キェルケゴール、ニーチェとニヒリズム" [Kierkegaard, Nietzsche and Nihilism], trans. by Masaru Otani, 『キェルケゴール研究』 [Kierkegaard-Studiet], no. 12, 1982, pp. 61–6.

―「二十世紀ドイツ語圏文学へのキェルケゴールの影響」 [Die Einwirkung Kierkegaards auf die deutschsprachige Literatur des 20. Jahrhunderts], trans. by Toshikazu Oya, 『キェルケゴール研究』 [Kierkegaard-Studiet], no. 14, 1984, pp. 65–72.

Stengren, George, L., 「トマス・アクィナスにおける一致体験による知識とキェルケゴールの主体性」 [Connatural Knowledge in Aquinas and Kierkegaardian Subjectivity], trans. by Katsutaka Uchida, 『キェルケゴール研究』 [Kierkegaard-Studiet], no. 13, 1983, pp. 51–6.

Strathern, Paul, 『９０分でわかるキルケゴール』 [Kierkegaard in 90 Minutes], trans. by Shogo Asami, Tokyo: Aoyama-shuppansha 1998.

Struve, Wolfgang, 「キェルケゴールとシェリング」 [Kierkegaard und Schelling], trans. by Eiko Kawamura, 『キェルケゴール研究』 [Kierkegaard-Studiet], no. 13, 1983, pp. 57–64.

Thomte, Reidar, 『キェルケゴールの宗教哲学』 [Kierkegaard's Philosophy of Religion], trans. by Katsumi Kitada and Tami Kitada, Kyoto: Horitsubunka-sha 1987.

Thielst, Peter, 「セーレンとレギーネ—キェルケゴールの婚約史梗概」 [Søren and Regine], trans. by Masaru Otani, 『キェルケゴール研究』 [Kierkegaard-Studiet], no. 9, 1978, pp. 77–98.

Thulstrup, Niels, 「キェルケゴールとヘーゲルの間の不一致」 [Le Désaccord entre Kierkegaard et Hegel], trans. by Tamotsu Tanabe, 『キェルケゴール研究』 [Kierkegaard-Studiet], no. 1, 1964, pp. 133–42.

— 「劇作家としての学生セーレン・キェルケゴール」 [Student Søren Kierkegaard in the Role as a Dramatist], trans. by Haruo Morioka and Masaru Otani, 『キェルケゴール研究』 [Kierkegaard-Studiet], vol. 2, 1965, pp. 89–105.

— 「哲学的並びに神学的伝統についてのキェルケゴールの知識—或は、至難な企て事をするセーレン・キェルケゴール」 [Kierkegaard's Knowledge of the Philosophical and Theological Tradition], trans. by Masaru Otani, 『キェルケゴール研究』 [Kierkegaard-Studiet], no. 7, 1977, pp. 58–71.

— 『キェルケゴールのヘーゲルへの関係』 [Kierkegaard's Relation to Hegel], trans. by Masaru Otani, Osaka: Toho-shuppan 1980.

— 「キェルケゴールによるピエール・ベールの使い方」 [Kierkegaard's Use of Bayle], trans. by Koji Sato, 『キェルケゴール研究』 [Kierkegaard-Studiet], no. 13, 1983, pp. 75–8.

Vetlesen, Alf, 「セーレン・キェルケゴールとゲオルグ・クリストフ・リヒテンベルグ」 [Søren Kierkegaard and Georg Christoph Lichtenberg], trans. by Hikaru Yabu, 『キェルケゴール研究』 [Kierkegaard-Studiet], no. 13, 1983, pp. 79–84.

Vries, Hent de, 『暴力と証し: キルケゴール的省察』 [Religion and Violence], trans. by Takaaki Kawai, Tokyo: Getsuyo-sha 2009.

— 「キェルケゴールとロマン主義」 [Kierkegaard et le Romantisme], trans. by Akihisa Matsushima, 『キェルケゴール研究』 [Kierkegaard-Studiet], no. 24, 1994, pp. 55–60.

Korean

Jae-myeong Pyo and Min-Ho Lee

I. Korean Translations of Kierkegaard's Works

『죽음에 이르는 병』 [*The Sickness unto Death*], trans. by Hyung-suk Kim, Seoul: Gyeongjisa 1956.

『죽음에 이르는 병』 [*The Sickness unto Death*], trans. by Chun-gap Rim, Seoul: Changrimsa 1957.

『유혹자의 일기』 ["The Seducer's Diary" [from *Either/Or*]], trans. by Chun-gap Rim, Seoul: Changrimsa 1960.

「세리」 ["The Tax Collector" [from *Three Discourses at the Communion on Fridays*]], trans. by Jae-myeong Pyo, 『기독교사상』 [Christian Thought], vol. 4, no. 8, 1960, pp. 54–7.

『인생행로의 제 단계』 [*Stages on Life's Way*], trans. by Eun-yeong Lee, Seoul: Cheongsan Munhwasa 1962.

『이것이냐 저것이냐』 (抄譯) [*Either/Or* [selections]], trans. by Yeong-cheol Kim, Seoul: Hwimun Chulpansa 1962.

「주께서 잡히시던 밤에」 ["I Corinthians 11:23" [from *Christian Discourses*]], trans. by Jae-myeong Pyo, 『기독교사상』 [Christian Thought], vol. 6, no. 5, 1962, pp. 62–7.

『사랑이 남긴 이야기』 [*Fear and Trembling*], trans. by Hak-cheol Kang, Seoul: Hwimun Chulpansa 1966.

『이 아름다운 고독』 [*Repetition*], trans. by Yeong-taek Song, Seoul: Sinjo Munhwasa 1966.

『불안의 개념』 [*The Concept of Anxiety*], trans. by Jae-eon Shim, Seoul: Cheongsan Munhwasa 1968.

『사랑의 철학』 (抄譯) [*Works of Love* [selections]], trans. by Jae-eon Shim, Seoul: Cheongsan Munhwasa 1968.

『불안의 개념, 죽음에 이르는 병』 [*The Concept of Anxiety* and *The Sickness unto Death*], trans. by Byeong-ok Kim, Seoul: Daeyang Seojeok 1970 (세계사상대전집 [*Great Thoughts of the World*], vol. 9).

『불안의 개념』 [*The Concept of Anxiety*], trans. by Chun-gap Rim, Seoul: Pyeonghwa Chulpansa 1972.

『철학적 단편, 공포와 전율, 현대의 비판 [제3부 抄譯], 죽음에 이르는 병』 [*Philosophical Fragments, Fear and Trembling, A Literary Review* [selections from Part Three] and *The Sickness unto Death*], trans. by Jae-myeong Pyo, Bok-rok Gwak, Du-shik Kang and Hwan-deok Park, Seoul: Hwimun Chulpansa 1972 (세계의 대사상 [*Great Books of the World*], vol. 9).

『죽음에 이르는 병, 이것이냐 저것이냐 [抄譯], 불안의 개념』 [*The Sickness unto Death, Either/Or* [selections] and *The Concept of Anxiety*], trans. by Yoon-Sup Kim, Seoul: Cheongsan Munhwasa 1973 (세계대사상전집 [*Great Thoughts of the World*], vol. 1).

『공포와 전율, 반복』 [*Fear and Trembling* and *Repetition*], trans. by Chun-gap Rim, Seoul: Pyeonghwa Chulpansa 1973.

『철학적 단편』 [*Philosophical Fragments*], trans. by Jae-myeong Pyo, Seoul: Pyeonghwa Chulpansa 1973.

『유혹자의 일기, 불안의 개념, 죽음에 이르는 병』 ["The Seducer's Diary" [from *Either/Or*], *The Concept of Anxiety* and *The Sickness unto Death*], trans. by Seong-wi Kang, Seoul: Dongseo Munhwasa 1975 (세계문학사상전집 [*World's Great Books*], vol. 24).

「철학적 단편」 [*Philosophical Fragments*], trans. by Seong-beom Yun, in 『세계기독교사상전집』 [Christian Thoughts in the World], ed. by Sintaeyangsa, Seoul: Sintaeyangsa 1975, vol. 2, pp. 7–138.

『철학적 단편 또는 한 조각의 철학』 [*Philosophical Fragments*], trans. by Jae-myeong Pyo, Seoul: Jongno Seojeok 1975.

「단독자—나의 저작활동에 대한 두 개의 각서」 ["'The Single Individual.' Two 'Notes' Concerning My Work as an Author" [from *The Point of View for My Work as an Author*]], trans. by Jae-myeong Pyo, in 『세계사상대전집』 [Great Thoughts of the World], ed. by Daeyang Seojeok, Seoul: Daeyang Seojeok 1975, vol. 48, pp. 61–86.

『두려움과 떨림』 [*Fear and Trembling*], trans. by Hak-cheol Kang, Seoul: Joyang Munhwasa 1976.

『공포와 전율, 철학적 단편, 죽음에 이르는 병, 반복』 [*Fear and Trembling, Philosophical Fragments, The Sickness unto Death* and *Repetition*], trans. by Jae-jun Sohn, Seoul: Samseong Chulpansa 1976 (세계사상전집 [*Great Books of the World*], vol. 15).

『그리스도교의 훈련』 [*Practice in Christianity*], trans. by Chun-gap Rim, Seoul: Pyeonghwa Chulpansa 1978.

『유혹자의 일기』 ["The Seducer's Diary" [from *Either/Or*]], trans. by Chun-gap Rim, Seoul: Jongno Seojeok 1979.

『공포와 전율, 반복』 [*Fear and Trembling* and *Repetition*], trans. by Chun-gap Rim, Seoul: Jongno Seojeok 1979 (2nd ed., Seoul: Dasan Geulbang 2007; 3rd ed., Seoul: Chiu 2011).

『불안의 개념』 [*The Concept of Anxiety*], trans. by Chun-gap Rim, Seoul: Jongno Seojeok 1979 (2nd ed., Seoul: Dasan Geulbang 2007; 3rd ed., Seoul: Chiu 2011).

『사랑의 역사』 [*Works of Love*], trans. by Chun-gap Rim, vols. 1–2, Seoul: Jongno Seojeok 1979 (2nd ed., Seoul: Dasan Geulbang 2007; 3rd ed., Seoul: Chiu 2011).

『관점, 현대의 비판 [제3부 抄譯]』 [*The Point of View for My Work as an Author* and *A Literary Review* [selections from Part Three]], trans. by Chun-gap Rim, Seoul: Jongno Seojeok 1980 (2nd ed., Seoul: Dasan Geulbang 2007; 3rd ed., Seoul: Chiu 2011).

『죽음에 이르는 병』 [*The Sickness unto Death*], trans. by Chun-gap Rim, Seoul: Jongno Seojeok 1979 (2nd ed., Seoul: Dasan Geulbang 2007; 3rd ed., Seoul: Chiu 2011).

『순간』 [*The Moment*], trans. by Chun-gap Rim, Seoul: Jongno Seojeok 1979 (2nd ed., Seoul: Dasan Geulbang 2007; 3rd ed., Seoul: Chiu 2011).

『들의 백합 공중의 새』 [*The Lily in the Field and the Bird of the Air* and *Three Discourses at the Communion on Fridays*], trans. by Jae-myeong Pyo, Seoul: Jongno Seojeok 1980.

「인간은 진리를 위하여 피살될 권리가 있는가」 ["Does a Human Being Have the Right to Let Himself Be Put to Death for the Truth?" [from *Two Ethical-Religious Essays*]], trans. by Chun-gap Rim, 『기독교사상』 [Christian Thought], vol. 25, no. 4, 1981, pp. 79–108.

『이것이냐 저것이냐』 [*Either/Or*], trans. by Chun-gap Rim, vols. 1–4, Seoul: Jongno Seojeok 1982 (2nd ed., Seoul: Dasan Geulbang 2008; 3rd ed., Seoul: Chiu 2012).

『그리스도교의 훈련』 [*Practice in Christianity*], trans. by Chun-gap Rim, Seoul: Jongno Seojeok 1983 (2nd ed., Seoul: Dasan Geulbang 2007; 3rd ed., Seoul: Chiu 2011).

『불안의 개념』 [*The Concept of Anxiety*], trans. by Seok-cheon Choi, Seoul: Sangseogak 1984.

『사랑과 영혼의 기로에서』 [*A Kierkegaard Anthology*], trans. and ed. by Hyeok-sun Choi, Seoul: Eulji Chulpansa 1988.

『키에르케고르 선집』 [*A Kierkegaard Anthology*], trans. and ed. by Hyeok-sun Choi, Seoul: Jipmundang 1989.

『코끝의 땀방울을 바라보는 즐거움: 이것이냐 저것이냐—키에르케고르의 철학 우화』 [*Parables of Kierkegaard* (ed. by Thomas C. Oden, Princeton: Princeton University Press 1978)], trans. by Heon-sik Hwang, Seoul: Saramgwa Saram 1993.

『철학적 조각들 혹은 한 조각의 철학』 [*Philosophical Fragments*], trans. by Pil-ho Hwang, Seoul: Jipmundang 1998.

『불안의 개념』 [*The Concept of Anxiety*], trans. by Gyu-jeong Im, Seoul: Hangilsa 1999.

『유혹자의 일기』 ["The Seducer's Diary" [from *Either/Or*]], trans. by Gyu-jeong Im and Hee-weon Yeon, Seoul: Hangilsa 2001.

『키에르케고르의 기도』 [*The Prayers of Kierkegaard* (ed. by Perry D. Lefevre, Chicago: University of Chicago Press 1963)], trans. by Chang-seung Lee, Seoul: The United Christian Newspaper 2004.

『들의 백합화 공중의 새』 [*The Lily in the Field and the Bird of the Air*], trans. by Jae-myeong Pyo, Seoul: Preaching Academy, 2005.

『예수께서 잡히시던 밤에—금요일 성찬식 때에 할 강화』 [*Christian Discourses*, Part Four], trans. by Jae-myeong Pyo, Seoul: Preaching Academy 2005.

『이방인의 염려』 [*Christian Discourses*, Part One], trans. by Jae-myeong Pyo, Seoul: Preaching Academy 2005.

『적게 사함을 받은 사람은 적게 사랑한다』 [*Three Discourses at the Communion on Fridays, An Upbuilding Discourse* and *Two Discourses at the Communion on Fridays*], trans. by Jae-myeong Pyo, Seoul: Preaching Academy 2005.

『죽음에 이르는 병』 [*The Sickness unto Death*], trans. by Yong-il Kim, Daegu: Keimyung University Press 2006.

『키에르케고어와 함께 하는 52주 묵상여행』 [*A Kierkegaard Anthology*], trans. and ed. by Hong-deok Choi, Seoul: Pastor's House 2006.

『죽음에 이르는 병』 [*The Sickness unto Death*], trans. by Gyu-jeong Im, Paju: Hangilsa 2007.

『철학의 부스러기 또는 부스러기의 철학』 [*Philosophical Fragments*], trans. by Jae-myeong Pyo, Seoul: Preaching Academy 2007.

『결혼에 관한 약간의 성찰』 (抄譯) ["Some Reflections on Marriage in Answer to Objections by a Married Man" [from *Stages on Life's Way*]], trans. by Gyu-jeong Im, Seoul: ZMANZ 2008.

『신앙의 기대』 [*Two Upbuilding Discourses* (1843) and *Three Upbuilding Discourses* (1843)], trans. by Jae-myeong Pyo, Seoul: Preaching Academy 2008.

『공포와 전율: 변증법적 서정시』 (抄譯) [*Fear and Trembling* [selections]], trans. by Gyu-jeong Im, Seoul: ZMANZ 2009.

『직접적이며 에로틱한 관계들 또는 음악적이고 에로틱한 것』 (抄譯) ["The Immediate Erotic Stages or The Music-Erotic" [from *Either/Or*]], trans. by Gyu-jeong Im, Seoul: ZMANZ 2009.

『주신이도 여호와시오 거두신 이도 여호와시오니』 [*Four Upbuilding Discourses* (1843) and "'The Single Individual.' Two 'Notes' Concerning My Work as an Author" [from *The Point of View for My Work as an Author*]], trans. by Jae-myeong Pyo, Yongin: Preaching Academy 2010.

『주체적으로 되는 것』 ["Becoming Subjective" [from *Concluding Unscientific Postscript*]], trans. by Gyu-jeong Im and Eun-jae Song, Seoul: ZMANZ 2012.

II. Secondary Literature on Kierkegaard in Korean

안병욱 [Ahn, Byeong-uk], 「실존주의의 계보」 [The Genealogy of Existentialism], 『사상계』 [Sasanggye], vol. 3, no. 4, 1955, pp. 77–100.

— 『키엘케골』 [Kierkegaard], Seoul: Sasanggyesa 1959; republished as 『키에르케고르』 [Kierkegaard], Seoul: Jimungak 1966. (Review: 최동희 [Choi, Dong-hee], review in 『사상계』 [Sasanggye], vol. 8, no. 12, 1960, pp. 426–7.)

— 『키에르케고르 사상』 [Kierkegaard's Thought], Seoul: Samyuk Chulpansa 1973.

안병무 [Ahn, Byung-Mu], 「불안과 신앙: 킬게고오르를 중심해서 (1)」 [Anxiety and Faith: with Special Reference to Kierkegaard (1)], 『현존』 [Presence], vol. 7, 1970, pp. 23–30.

변주환 [Byun, Joo Hwan], 「자기관계와 자기됨—키에르케고어의 『죽음에 이르는 병』을 중심으로」 [Self-Relation and "Becoming Oneself": With Special Reference to *The Sickness unto Death* of Kierkegaard], 『해석학연구』 [Hermeneutic Studies], vol. 21, 2008, pp. 241–66.

장인식 [Chang, Einsik], 「나다니엘 호손의 시와 단상(斷想)에 나타난 실존주의적 경향」 [The Existential Tendency in Nathaniel Hawthorne's Poems and Fragmentary Thoughts], 『신영어영문학』 [New Studies of English Language and Literature], vol. 33, 2006, pp. 107–28.

장문정 [Chang, Moon Jeong], 「예술, 아이러니한 슬픔과 웃음의 문턱— 예술의 구원 가능성에 대한 키에르케고어적 이해」 [Art, the Threshold of Ironical Sadness and Laughter: A Kierkegaardian Apprehension of the Possibility of Salvation through Art], 『대동철학』 [Journal of the Daedong Philosophical Association], vol. 30, 2005, pp. 179–204.

——「어떻게 진리가 가능한가—라깡과 키에르케고어의 '말할 수 없는 것'의 말하기」 [How to Reach the Truth: Saying "What Cannot Be Said" in Lacan and Kierkegaard], 『대동철학』 [Journal of the Daedong Philosophical Association], vol. 46, 2009, pp. 113–37.

——「왜 페미니스트가 신을 말하는가? 페미니스트들의 키에르케고어되기와 키에르케고어의 여성되기」 [Why Do Feminists Speak of God? Feminists' "Becoming Kierkegaard" and Kierkegaard's "Becoming Feminine"], 『대동철학』 [Journal of the Daedong Philosophical Association], vol. 59, 2012, pp. 245–66.

장성식 [Chang, Sung-Shik], 「찰스 하지(Charles Hodge)의 하나님의 섭리로 본 데리다의 '코라'(khora)와 키에르케고어의 '믿음의 역설'(Paradox of Faith)」 [Derrida's "Khora" and Kierkegaard's "Paradox of Faith," Viewed through Charles Hodge's "Providence of God"], 『교회와 문화』 [The Church and Culture], vol. 24, 2010, pp. 153–84.

조가경 [Cho, Kah Kyung], 「키엘케고올의 역설적 실존」 [Kierkegaard's "Paradoxical Existence"], in his 『실존철학』 [Philosophy of Existence], Seoul: Pakyoungsa 1961, pp. 57–63.

최종호 [Choi, Jongho], 「키에르케고르의 인간이해에 대한 교육학적 성찰」 [An Educational Reflection on Kierkegaard's View of the Human Being], 『기독교교육정보』 [Christian Education and Information Technology], vol. 35, 2012, pp. 361–84.

최상욱 [Choi, Sang-Wook], 「헤겔과 키에르케고르에 있어 신앙의 본질」 [The Essence of Faith According to Hegel and Kierkegaard], 『인문과학논집』 [Journal of Humanities (Kangnam University)], vol. 3, 1997, pp. 49–78.

최승일 [Choi, Seung-il], 「키에르케고어의 죄성에 대한 고찰」 [Considerations on Kierkegaard's "Original Sin"], 『철학연구』 (대한철학회) [Journal of the Korean Philosophical Society], vol. 85, 2003, pp. 317–37.

정대현 [Chung, Daihyun], 「슬픔: 또 하나의 실존 범주」 [Sorrow as an Existential Category], 『철학』 [Cheolhak], vol. 100, 2009, pp. 47–73.

도양술 [Do, Yang-sul], 「키엘케골의 역설신학」 [Kierkegaard's Theology of Paradox], 『신학지남』 [Presbyterian Theological Quarterly], vol. 25, no. 1, 1958, pp. 119–25.

엄태동 [Eom, Tae Dong], 「키에르케고르 간접전달과 교육적 인식론」 [Kierkegaard's Indirect Communication and Educational Epistemology], 『교육원리연구』 [Journal of Educational Principles], vol. 1, no. 1, 1996, pp. 85–126.

——「키에르케고르의 間接傳達과 遠隔敎育의 原理」 [Kierkegaard's Indirect Communication and Principles of Distance Education], 『방송통신교육논총』

[Korea National Open University Journal of Education], vol. 10, 1997, pp. 183–206.

——「키에르케고르(S. Kierkegaard) 간접전달의 인식론적 의의: 인식론의 딜레마와 교육적 해결」 [The Epistemological Significance of Kierkegaard's Indirect Communication: Dilemmas in Epistemology and Educative Solutions], 『교육철학연구』 [The Korean Journal of Philosophy of Education], vol. 19, 1998, pp. 117–43.

——「키에르케고르 가명저작의 방편성」 [Kierkegaard's Pseudonymous Works as Educational Means] 『교육학연구』 (한국교육학회) [Korean Journal of Educational Research], vol. 36, no. 4, 1998, pp. 71–95.

——「'비언어적 체험의 언어적 전달'이라는 역설로서의 교육: 장자와 키에르케고르를 중심으로」 [Education as Verbal Communication of the Non-Verbal Experience: With Special Reference to Chuang Tzu and Kierkegaard], 『초등교육연구』 [The Journal of Elementary Education], vol. 20, no. 2, 2007, pp. 27–52.

하일선 [Ha, Ilseon], 「현대사회에서 교육자의 자기이해: 소크라테스의 아이러니 논쟁을 중심으로」 [The Educator's Self-Understanding in Contemporary Society: With Special Reference to the Controversy about Socrates' Irony], 『교육철학연구』 [The Korean Journal of Philosophy of Education], vol. 47, 2010, pp. 203–23.

하선규 [Ha, Sun Kyu], 「예술과 문화—칸트, Fr. 슐레겔, 키에르케고어, 니체를 돌이켜보며」 [Art and Culture: With Special Reference to Kant, F. Schlegel, Kierkegaard and Nietzsche], 『인문학연구』 (조선대학교 인문학연구원) [Humanities Research (Chosun University)], vol. 39, 2010, pp. 7–54.

——「랩 음악에 대한 매체미학적 고찰: 키에르케고어, 크라카우어, 벤야민으로부터」 [Considerations on Rap Music from the Perspective of Media Aesthetics: With Special Reference to Kierkegaard, Kracauer and W. Benjamin], 『미학예술학연구』 [The Journal of Aesthetics and Science of Art], vol. 31, 2010, pp. 139–84.

——「키에르케고어 철학에 있어 심미적 실존과 예술의 의미에 관한 연구—『이것이냐/저것이냐』, 『불안의 개념』, 『반복』, 『철학적 조각들』을 중심으로」 [The Meanings of Aesthetic Existence and Art in Kierkegaard: Focusing on *Either/Or, The Concept of Anxiety, Repetition* and *Philosophical Fragments*], 『미학』 [The Korean Journal of Aesthetics], vol. 76, 2013, pp. 219–68.

허양수 [Heo, Yang-su], 「키엘케골에 있어서의 실존이해, 절망, 역설을 중심으로」 [Kierkegaard's Conception of Existence: A Study Focusing on Despair and Paradox], 『논문집』 (기전여자전문대학교) [Journal of Kijeon Women's Junior College], vol. 2, 1981, pp. 127–37.

홍준기 [Hong, Joon-Kee], 「불안과 그 대상에 관한 연구: 프로이트ㅁ라캉 정신분석학과 키에르케고르를 중심으로」 [Anxiety and Its Object: A Comparative Study of Freudo-Lacanian Psychoanalysis and Kierkegaard], 『철학과 현상학 연구』 [Research in Philosophy and Phenomenology], vol. 17, 2001, pp. 234–67.

홍경실 [Hong, Kyoung-sil], 「키에르케고어와 레비나스의 주체성 비교: 우리 시대의 새로운 인간 이해를 위하여」 [A Comparison of Kierkegaard and Levinas on Subjectivity: Looking for a New Understanding of the Human Being for Our Time], 『철학연구』 (고려대학교) [Philosophical Studies], vol. 27, 2004, pp. 143–72.
—「키에르케고어와 베르그송의 사랑에 대한 이해 비교」 [A Comparison of Kierkegaard and Bergson on Love], 『인문과학』 (성균관대학교) [Journal of the Humanities (Sungkyunkwan University)], vol. 44, 2009, pp. 71–89.
—「키에르케고어와 수운의 인간 이해 비교—동학과 서학의 만남」 [A Comparison of Kierkegaard's and Su-un's Views of the Human Being], 『동학학보』 [The Korea Journal of Donghak Studies], vol. 19, 2010, pp. 113–41.
—「시간에 대한 이해를 중심으로 한 키에르케고어의 실존의 삼 단계설」 [Kierkegaard's Theory of Three Stages of Existence: Focusing on Time], 『인문학연구』 (경희대학교) [The Journal of Humanities (Kyunghee University)], vol. 20, 2011, pp. 179–205.
홍문표 [Hong, Mun-pyo], 『신학적 구원과 시적 구원—기독교적 구원의 두 양상 연구: 키에르케고르와 김현승의 고독에서 구원까지』 [Theological Salvation and Poetic Salvation. A Study of Two Aspects of Christian Salvation: From Solitude to Salvation in Kierkegaard and Kim Hyeon-seung], Seoul: Changjo Munhaksa 2005.
홍순명 [Hong, Sun-myeong], 「키엘케골의 교회공격」 [Kierkegaard's Attack on the Church], 『성서연구』 [Bible Studies], vol. 106, 1963, pp. 5–13.
—「키엘케골의 『그리스도교의 훈련』 (1)」 [Kierkegaard's *Practice in Christianity* (1)], 『성서연구』 [Bible Studies], vol. 113, 1963, pp. 10–14.
—「키엘케골의 『그리스도교의 훈련』 (2)」 [Kierkegaard's *Practice in Christianity* (2)], 『성서연구』 [Bible Studies], vol. 114, 1963, pp. 9–12.
—「키엘케골의 생애와 역사적 의미 (1)」 [The Life and Historical Significance of Kierkegaard (1)], 『성서연구』 [Bible Studies], vol. 136, 1965, pp. 11–13.
—「키엘케골의 생애와 역사적 의미 (2)」 [The Life and Historical Significance of Kierkegaard (2)], 『성서연구』 [Bible Studies], vol. 137, 1965, pp. 9–12.
—「키엘케골의 생애와 역사적 의미 (3)」 [The Life and Historical Significance of Kierkegaard (3)], 『성서연구』 [Bible Studies], vol. 138, 1966, pp. 8–10.
—「키엘케골의 생애와 역사적 의미 (4)」 [The Life and Historical Significance of Kierkegaard (4)], 『성서연구』 [Bible Studies], vol. 139, 1966, pp. 14–15.
—「무엇이 정상인가—키엘케골의 『너 스스로를 심판하라』」 [What is Normal? Kierkegaard's *Judge for Yourself!*], 『성서연구』 [Bible Studies], vol. 151, 1967, pp. 9–15.
—「키엘케골의 『사랑의 행위』」 [Kierkegaard's *Works of Love*], 『성서연구』 [Bible Studies], vol. 154, 1967, pp. 6–12.
—「키엘케골의 강화, 『들의 나리 하늘의 새』」 [Kierkegaard's Discourses, *The Lily in the Field and the Bird of the Air*], 『성서연구』 [Bible Studies], vol. 162, 1968, pp. 2–8.
—「「사랑은 많은 죄를 덮는다」: 키엘케골의 강화」 [Kierkegaard's Discourse: "Love Will Hide a Multitude of Sins"], 『성서연구』 [Bible Studies], vol. 173, 1969, pp. 6–10.

— 「키엘케골의 강화 「세리」: 누가복음 18장 9–14절」 [Kierkegaard's Discourse: "The Tax Collector"— Luke 18:9–14], 『성서연구』 [Bible Studies], vol. 180, 1969, pp. 8–13.

황종환 [Hwang, Jong-Hwan], 「키르케고아와 카시러의 종교성 비교연구」 [A Comparative Study of Kierkegaard and Cassirer on Religiosity], 『철학논총』 (새한철학회) [Journal of the New Korean Philosophical Association], vol. 51, 2008, pp. 351–69.

— 「'윤리적인 것의 목적론적 정지'의 도덕교육적 함의: 환경의식을 중심으로」 [Implications of the "Teleological Suspension of the Ethical" to Moral Education: Focusing on Environmental Consciousness], 『도덕윤리과교육연구』 [Journal of the Korean Society for the Study of Moral and Ethics Education], vol. 26, 2008, pp. 125–44.

— 「키르케고아에서 불안의 의미—도덕교육과 관련하여」 [The Meaning of Anxiety in Kierkegaard: In Connection with Moral Education], 『윤리연구』 [Journal of Ethics], vol. 71, 2008, pp. 255–75.

— 「키르케고아의 실존에서 본 미래윤리 의식(意識)」 [Future Ethics and Kierkegaard's "Existence"], 『도덕윤리과교육연구』 [Journal of the Korean Society for the Study of Moral and Ethics Education], vol. 29, 2009, pp. 107–26.

— 「키르케고아에서 도덕 환경적 요소로서 노래 부르기」 [The Moral and Environmental Meanings of Singing in Kierkegaard], 『윤리교육연구』 [Journal of Ethics Education Studies], vol. 23, 2010, pp. 133–50.

— 「키르케고아에서 실존적 변형(metamorphosis)으로서 용서(容恕)의 간접전달」 [Indirect Communication of Forgiveness as an Existential Metamorphosis in Kierkegaard], 『철학논총』 [Journal of the New Korean Philosophical Association], vol. 63, 2011, pp. 451–71.

— 「키에르케고어에서 환경윤리의 근거화로서 인간본성」 [Human Nature as the Foundation of Environmental Ethics in Kierkegaard], 『철학논총』 [Journal of the New Korean Philosophical Association], vol. 69, 2012, pp. 363–82.

— 「키에르케고어의 『사랑의 역사』의 종교 윤리적 함의」 [Implications of Kierkegaard's *Works of Love* to Religious Ethics], 『철학연구』 (고려대학교) [Philosophical Studies], vol. 47, 2013, pp. 131–57.

— 「키에르케고어에서 불안과 도덕적 행위」 [Anxiety and Moral Acts in Kierkegaard], 『철학논총』 [Journal of the New Korean Philosophical Association], vol. 75, 2014, pp. 313–33.

— 「키르케고아에서 '영원한 행복'의 도덕교육적 이해」 [Understanding Kierkegaard's "Eternal Happiness" in Connection with Moral Education], 『도덕윤리과교육』 [Journal of Moral and Ethics Education], vol. 42, 2014, pp. 69–92.

황필호 [Hwang, Pil-ho], 「키에르케고르의 작품세계」 [Kierkegaard's Œuvre], 『종교연구』 (한국종교학회) [The Journal of the Korean Association for the History of Religions], vol. 4, 1988, pp. 99–112.

— 「키에르케고르의 삶과 사상의 관계」 [The Relation of Kierkegaard's Life to His Thought], 『종교연구』 [The Journal of the Korean Association for the History of Religions], vol. 5, 1989, pp. 43–59.

— 「키에르케고르의 문학철학」 [Kierkegaard's Philosophy of Literature], in his 『문학철학 산책: 플라톤, 아리스토파네스, 파스칼, 키에르케고르』 [Promenades in Philosophy of Literature: Plato, Aristophanes, Pascal and Kierkegaard], Seoul: Jipmundang 1996, pp. 253–308.

황순환 [Hwang, Sun-hwan], 「키에르케고어의 인간실존에 관한 고찰」 [Considerations on Kierkegaard's View of Human Existence], 『신학과 문화』 (장로회대전신학교) [Theology and Culture (Daejeon Theological University)], vol. 4, 1995, pp. 255–92.

임규정 [Im, Gyu-jeong], 「키에르케고르의 변증법과 그리이스 사상」 [Kierkegaard's Dialectic and Greek Thought], 『철학연구』 (고려대학교) [Philosophical Studies], vol. 13, 1988, pp. 341–59.

— 「키에르케고르의 정열의 개념에 관하여」 [On Kierkegaard's Concept of Passion], 『철학연구』 (고려대학교) [Philosophical Studies], vol. 14, 1989, pp. 71–83.

— 「『철학적 단편』에서 분석되고 있는 가능성과 필연성에 대한 논리적 고찰: 생성(Werden)에 관하여」 [Logical Considerations on Possibility and Necessity in *Philosophical Fragments*: On "Becoming" (*Werden*)], 『철학연구』 (고려대학교) [Philosophical Studies], vol. 17, 1993, pp. 123–45.

— 「키에르케고어를 어떻게 읽을 것인가: 1843년의 『두 편의 건덕적 강화』를 중심으로」 [How to Read Kierkegaard: Considerations Focusing on *Two Upbuilding Discourses* of 1843], 『논문집』 (군산대학교) [Journal of Kunsan National University], vol. 21, 1994, pp. 113–30.

— 「키에르케고어의 『불안의 개념』에 대한 일 고찰」 [A Study of *The Concept of Anxiety* of Kierkegaard], 『논문집』 (군산대학교) [Journal of Kunsan National University], vol. 24, 1997, pp. 51–72.

— 「'실존 단계'에 대한 일 고찰: 홀머의 키에르케고어 해석을 중심으로」 [A Study of Kierkegaard's "Stages of Existence": With Special Reference to Holmer's Interpretation of Kierkegaard], 『철학논총』 (새한철학회) [Journal of the New Korean Philosophical Association], vol. 15, 1998, pp. 203–29.

— 「'거룩한 기만': 익명성의 문제에 관하여」 [The "Holy Deception": On the Problem of Pseudonymity], 『철학연구』 (대한철학회) [Journal of the Korean Philosophical Society], vol. 69, 1999, pp. 321–39.

— 「플라톤의 변증법과 키에르케고어의 실존 철학에 관한 일 고찰」 [Plato's Dialectic and Kierkegaard's Philosophy of Existence], 『범한철학』 [Pan-Korean Philosophy], vol. 19, 1999, pp. 177–96.

— 「키에르케고르의 '주체성의 지양'과 '죄책감'에 대한 고찰」 [The "Sublation" of Subjectivity and the Consciousness of Guilt in Kierkegaard], 『철학연구』 (대한철학회) [Journal of the Korean Philosophical Society], vol. 76, 2000, pp. 255–74.

— 「키에르케고르의 사랑의 개념에 관한 일 고찰」 [A Study of Kierkegaard's Concept of Love], 『범한철학』 [Pan-Korean Philosophy], vol. 31, 2003, pp. 261–88.

— 「키에르케고르 읽기의 문제—펭거의 키에르케고르 해석을 중심으로」 [The Problem of Reading Kierkegaard: A Critical Examination of Fenger's Interpretation of Kierkegaard], 『철학연구』 (대한철학회) [Journal of the Korean Philosophical Society], vol. 87, 2003, pp. 369–86.

— 「키에르케고르: 해체인가 아닌가? 텍스트 이론과 간접전달」 [Kierkegaard: Deconstruction or Not? Text Theory and Indirect Communication], 『철학연구』 (대한철학회) [Journal of the Korean Philosophical Society], vol. 89, 2004, pp. 341–64.

— 「키에르케고르의 '말할 수 있음 또는 없음'에 관한 고찰」 ["To Be Able to Speak or Not to Be Able to Speak," According to Kierkegaard], 『철학연구』 (대한철학회) [Journal of the Korean Philosophical Society], vol. 96, 2005, pp. 391–417.

— 「키에르케고르의 절망의 형태와 삶의 단계의 상응에 관한 연구」 [The Correspondence of the Types of Despair with the Stages of Life in Kierkegaard], 『철학연구』 (대한철학회) [Journal of the Korean Philosophical Society], vol. 105, 2008, pp. 351–72.

— 「가능성의 현상학—키르케고르의 실존의 삼 단계에 관한 소고」 [The Phenomenology of Possibility: An Essay on Kierkegaard's "Three Stages of Existence"], 『범한철학』 [Pan-Korean Philosophy], vol. 55, 2009, pp. 281–325.

— 「시인의 실존: 키르케고르의 시인과 시의 개념에 관한 연구 1」 [A Poet's Existence: A Study of Kierkegaard's Concepts of Poet and Poetry (1)], 『철학, 사상, 문화』 [Philosophy, Thought, Culture], vol. 14, 2012, pp. 185–213.

임규정 [Im, Gyu-jeong], 최춘영 [Choi, Chun-yeong], 「정치와 종교의 관계에 관한 철학적 고찰: 키에르케고어에 대한 올바른 이해를 위한 하나의 시도」 [Philosophical Considerations on the Relationship between Politics and Religion: An Attempt at a Correct Understanding of Kierkegaard], 『군산수산전문대학 연구보고』 [Journal of Kunsan Fisheries College], vol. 28, no. 1, 1993, pp. 175–89.

정항균 [Jeong, Hang-Kyun], 「종교적 예외의 반복에서 미학적 창조의 반복으로: 키르케고르와 니체의 반복 개념 연구」 [From the Religious Exception's Repetition to the Aesthetic Creation's: A Study of the Concept of Repetition in Kierkegaard and Nietzsche], 『카프카연구』 [Franz Kafka], vol. 19, 2008, pp. 233–63.

정재걸 [Jeong, Jae-geol], 「키에르케고르의 主觀的 知識과 教育」 [Kierkegaard's "Subjective Knowledge" and Education], 『도덕교육연구』 [The Journal of Moral Education], vol. 2, no. 1, 1984, pp. 53–70.

정재현 [Jeong, Jae-Hyeon], 「참됨과 나: 키에르케고르의 주체적 진리관의 탈근대적 함의」 [Being Truthful and the *I*: Post-Modern Implications of Kierkegaard's View of Subjective Truth], 『신학사상』 (한국신학연구소) [The Theological Thought (Korea Theological Study Institute)], vol. 89, 1995, pp. 153–80.

정정숙 [Jeong, Jeong-suk], 「실존주의 철학의 인간관과 교육이론」 [The Existentialist View of the Human Being and Theory of Education], 『교육연구』 (이화여자대학교) [Educational Studies (Ewha Women's University)], vol. 37, 1971, pp. 140–53.

강학철 [Kang, Hak-cheol], 「지식의 반어」 [The Irony of Knowledge], 『기독교사상』 [Christian Thought], vol. 12, no. 6, 1968, pp. 118–26.

—「키아케고오아의 파토스론」 [Kierkegaard on Pathos], in Søren Kierkegaard, 『두려움과 떨림』 [*Fear and Trembling*], trans. by Hak-cheol Kang, Seoul: Joyang Munhwasa 1976, pp. 243–59.

—『도상의 실존: 키아케고오아 논구』 [Existence on the Road: Kierkegaard Research], Seoul: The Christian Literature Society of Korea 1977. (Review: 조요한 [Zoh, Johann], review in 『기독교사상』 [Christian Thought], vol. 21, no. 8, 1977, pp. 164–5.)

—「쇠얀 키아케고어의 실존적 인간학」 [Søren Kierkegaard's Existential Anthropology], 『논문집』 (대한신학교) [Journal of Daehan Theological Seminary], vol. 2, 1982, pp. 1–38.

—「S. 키아케고어의 실존적 시간론」 [S. Kierkegaard's Existential Conception of Time], 『논문집』 (대한신학교) [Journal of Daehan Theological Seminary], vol. 3, 1983, pp. 505–37.

—「S. 키아케고어에 있어서의 허무주의의 문제」 [The Problem of Nihilism in S. Kierkegaard], 『논문집』 (서울여자대학교) [Journal of Seoul Women's University], vol. 14, 1985, pp. 325–40.

—「S. 키아케고어의 '악마적인 것'의 개념」 [S. Kierkegaard's Concept of the Demonic], 『논문집』 (서울여자대학교) [Journal of Seoul Women's University], vol. 16, 1987, pp. 87–103.

—「S. 키아케고어의 실족의 개념」 [S. Kierkegaard's Concept of Offense], 『인문사회과학논총』 (서울여자대학교) [Journal of Humanities and Social Sciences (Seoul Women's University)], vol. 3, 1988, pp. 51–69.

—「S. 키아케고어의 사회적 실존」 [S. Kierkegaard's Social Existence], 『인문사회과학논총』 (서울여자대학교) [Journal of Humanities and Social Sciences (Seoul Women's University)], vol. 4, 1989, pp. 5–28.

—「S. 키아케고어의 단독자의 변증법」 [S. Kierkegaard's Dialectic of the Single Individual], 『인문사회과학논총』 (서울여자대학교) [Journal of Humanities and Social Sciences (Seoul Women's University)], vol. 6, 1991, pp. 15–34.

—「S. 키아케고어의 정치적 실존」 [S. Kierkegaard's Political Existence], 『인문사회과학논총』 (서울여자대학교) [Journal of Humanities and Social Sciences (Seoul Women's University)], vol. 9, 1994, pp. 201–21.

—「S. 키아케고어의 정치적 자유의 개념」 [S. Kierkegaard's Concept of Political Freedom], 『인문논총』 (서울여자대학교) [The Journal of the Institute of Humanities (Seoul Women's University)], vol. 3, 1996, pp. 269–302.

—「S. 키아케고어의 권위의 개념」 [S. Kierkegaard's Concept of Authority], 『인문논총』 (서울여자대학교) [The Journal of the Institute of Humanities (Seoul Women's University)], vol. 4, 1997, pp. 349–75.

—『무의미로부터의 자유』 [Freedom from Meaninglessness], Seoul: Dong-myeongsa 1999. (Review: 김경서 [Kim, Gyeong-seo], review in 『서울여자대학보』 [Seoul Women's University Biweekly], June 7, 1999, p. 3.)

강희천 [Kang, Hee Chun], 「불안 경험과 기독교 교육」 [The Experience of Anxiety and Christian Education], 『현대와 신학』 (연세대학교) [Theology and Modern Times], vol. 25, 2000, pp. 137–71.

강일구 [Kang, Il-gu], 「키엘케골이 제시한 '삶과 잠재능력(潛在能力)'에 대한 小考」 [An Essay on Life and Potentiality According to Kierkegaard], 『인문논총』 (호서대학교) [Journal of the Humanities (Hoseo University)], vol. 16, 1997, pp. 37–58.

강성일 [Kang, Seong-il], 「키에르케골 사상의 주체적 진리」 [The Subjective Truth in Kierkegaard's Thought], 『기독교사상』 [Christian Thought], vol. 15, no. 4, 1971, pp. 118–25.

강영안 [Kang, Young Ahn], 「키에르케고어에서 주체와 개인의 문제」 [The Subject and the Individual in Kierkegaard], in his 『주체는 죽었는가: 현대 철학의 포스트 모던 경향』 [Is the Subject Dead? The Post-Modern Tendency of Contemporary Philosophy], Seoul: Moonye Publishing Co. 1996, pp. 132–53.

강윤희 [Kang, Yun-hee], 「고르넬리오 파브로(Cornelio Fabro)의 키에르케고르의 단독자(單獨者) 이해」 [Cornelio Fabro's Understanding of Kierkegaard's "Single Individual"], 『누리와 말씀』 [World and Word], vol. 22, 2007, pp. 149–77.

김철손 [Kim, Cheol-son], 「키엘케골의 생애와 사상」 [Kierkegaard's Life and Thought], 『사상계』 [Sasanggye], vol. 6, no. 4, 1958, pp. 192–202.

김기석 [Kim, Gi-seok], 「칸트와 켈케고르: 신앙사에서 본 그들의 지위 (1)」 [Kant and Kierkegaard: Their Statuses in the History of Christianity (1)], 『기독교사상』 [Christian Thought], vol. 1, no. 3, 1957, pp. 58–63.

—「칸트와 켈케고르: 신앙사에서 본 그들의 지위 (2)」 [Kant and Kierkegaard: Their Statuses in the History of Christianity (2)], 『기독교사상』 [Christian Thought], vol. 1, no. 5, 1957, pp. 35–9.

김균진 [Kim, Gyun-jin], 「헤겔과 키에르케고르」 [Hegel and Kierkegaard], in his 『헤겔과 바르트』 [Hegel and Barth], Seoul: Daehan Christian Press 1983, pp. 143–66.

—「헤겔의 체계에 대한 마르크스와 키에르케골의 비판」 [Marx's and Kierkegaard's Critiques of Hegel's System], 『철학연구』 (철학연구회) [Journal of the Society of Philosophical Studies], vol. 18, 1983, pp. 45–61.

김하자 [Kim, Ha-ja], 「Søren Kierkegaard의 주체적 진리와 실존적 교육」 [The "Subjective Truth" of Søren Kierkegaard and Existential Education], 『연구논문집』 (성신여자대학교) [Sungshin Journal], vol. 22, 1985, pp. 265–90.

—「킬케골의 실존 윤리와 교육」 [The Existential Ethics of Kierkegaard and Education], 『연구논문집』 (성신여자대학교) [Sungshin Journal], vol. 28, 1989, pp. 109–65.

—『키에르케고어와 교육』 [Kierkegaard and Education], Seoul: Sungshin Women's University Press 2004.

김형석 [Kim, Hyung-suk], 「켈케고르와 죽음에 이르는 병」 [Kierkegaard and the Sickness unto Death], 『기독교사상』 [Christian Thought], vol. 2, no. 1, 1958, pp. 58–63.

—「절망의 변증법: 변증법의 실천적 성격 (Kierkegaard에 있어서의 일례)」 [Despair's Dialectic: the Dialectic's Practical Character (an Example in Kierkegaard)], 『인문과학』 (연세대학교) [Journal of the Humanities (Yonsei University)], vol. 4, 1959, pp. 31–52.

— 「키엘케고올의 생애와 사상」 [Kierkegaard's Life and Thought], in his 『현대인을 위한 세계관』 [A World-View for the Present Age], Seoul: Dongbangsa 1963, pp. 280–303.

— 「현대 철학의 발생과 주체성의 문제—S. Kierkegaard의 경우」 [The Genesis of Modern Philosophy and the Problem of Subjectivity: The Case of Kierkegaard], in 『연세대학교 80주년 기념 논문집: 인문과학편』 [Yonsei University the 80th Anniversary Thesis Collection: Liberal Arts], ed. by the Committee for the Publication of Papers in Celebration of the 80th Anniversary of Yonsei University, Seoul: Yonsei University 1965, pp. 101–19.

— 「시간의 종말론적 성격과 그 구조」 [The Eschatological Nature of Time and Its Structure], 『인문과학』 (연세대학교) [Journal of the Humanities (Yonsei University)], vols. 14–15, 1966, pp. 301–21.

김종두 [Kim, Jong-Doo], 「S. Kierkegaard의 실존개념 (1)」 [Kierkegaard's Concept of Existence (1)], 『신학지남』 [Presbyterian Theological Quarterly], vol. 54, no. 1, 1987, pp. 158–91.

— 「S. Kierkegaard의 실존개념 (2)」 [Kierkegaard's Concept of Existence (2)], 『신학지남』 [Presbyterian Theological Quarterly], vol. 54, no. 2, 1987, pp. 134–70.

— 「S. Kierkegaard의 실존개념 (3)」 [Kierkegaard's Concept of Existence (3)], 『신학지남』 [Presbyterian Theological Quarterly], vol. 54, no. 3, 1987, pp. 186–200.

— 「키르케고르에 있어서 지성과 신앙 (1)」 [Reason and Faith in Kierkegaard (1)], 『교수논총』 (한세대학교) [Journal of Hansei University], vol. 10, 1997, pp. 235–55.

— 「키르케고르에 있어서 지성과 신앙 (2)」 [Reason and Faith in Kierkegaard (2)], 『교수논총』 (한세대학교) [Journal of Hansei University], vol. 11, 1997, pp. 188–208.

— 「키르케고르에 있어서 지성과 신앙 (3)」 [Reason and Faith in Kierkegaard (3)], 『교수논총』 (한세대학교) [Journal of Hansei University], vol. 12, 1998, pp. 215–42.

— 『키에르케고르의 실존사상과 현대인의 자아 이해』 [Kierkegaard's Existential Thought and Modern Man's Self-Understanding], Seoul: M-Ad 2002.

김광민 [Kim, Kwang-Min], 「교과교육과 간접전달」 [Subject Matter Education and Indirect Communication], 『도덕교육연구』 [The Journal of Moral Education], vol. 22, no. 2, 2011, pp. 193–215.

김이섭 [Kim, Lee-Seob], 「뵐과 키에르케고르의 동질성에 관한 연구」 [A Study of the Homogeneity between Böll and Kierkegaard], 『독일어문학』 [Deutsche Sprach- und Literaturwissenschaft], vol. 23, 2003, pp. 91–112.

김선희 [Kim, Sun-Hye], 「앎에 이르는 길로서 산파법, 변증법—소크라테스, 낭만주의, 헤겔, 키에르케고어를 중심으로」 [Maieutic and Dialectic as Ways to Knowledge: With Special Reference to Socrates, Romanticism, Hegel and Kierkegaard], 『동서철학연구』 [Studies in Philosophy East-West], vol. 47, 2008, pp. 235–56.

— 「실존의 고통과 실존 치료—키에르케고어를 중심으로」 [The Suffering of Existence and Existential Therapy: With Special Reference to Kierkegaard],

『동서철학연구』 [Studies in Philosophy East-West], vol. 49, 2008, pp. 347–66.

김성곤 [Kim, Sung-Kon], 「키에르케고어의 미적 실존과 돈 후안」 [Kierkegaard's "Aesthetic Existence" and Don Juan], 『뷔히너와 현대문학』 [Büchner und Moderne Literatur], vol. 41, 2013, pp. 95–117.

김영한 [Kim, Yeong-han], 「칼 바르트의 『로마서』에 있어서의 키에르케고르의 변증법의 영향, 개혁주의적 이해와 비판」 [The Kierkegaardian Dialectic's Influence on *The Epistle to the Romans* of Karl Barth: A Reformed Theological Understanding and Critique], 『현대사조』 [Hyundai Sajo], no. 6, 1978, pp. 74–82.

김영만 [Kim, Yeong-man], 「Kierkegaard의 不安에 관한 硏究」 [A Study of Kierkegaard's "Anxiety"], 『철학사상』 (동국대학교) [Philosophical Thought (Dongguk University)], vols. 10–11, 1989, pp. 105–34.

김용환 [Kim, Yong-hwan], 「스피노자와 키에르케고르의 자기실현에 관한 비교연구」 [A Comparative Study of Spinoza and Kierkegaard on Self-Realization], 『윤리교육연구』 [Journal of Ethics Education Studies], vol. 6, 2004, pp. 203–25.

— 「키에르케고르의 실존과정 연구」 [A Study of the Process of Existence According to S. Kierkegaard], 『윤리연구』 [Journal of Ethics], vol. 72, 2009, pp. 225–45.

김용일 [Kim, Yong-il], 「자기 상실과 자기됨의 이중적 규정성으로서의 절망에 대하여: Kierkegaard의 『죽음에 이르는 병』을 중심으로」 [Despair in Its Double Meaning of "Losing Oneself" and "Becoming Oneself": With Special Reference to *The Sickness unto Death* of Kierkegaard], 『현대와 종교』 (현대종교문화연구소) [The Contemporary and Religion], vol. 17, 1994, pp. 217–35.

— 「키아케고어의 자아관: 키아케고어의 인간이해」 [Kierkegaard's View of the Self: Kierkegaard's Understanding of the Human Being], 『국제학논총』 (계명대학교 국제학연구소) [Journal of International Studies (Keimyung University)], vol. 1, 1996, pp. 277–93.

— 「키아케고어의 실존해석학」 [Kierkegaard's Existential Hermeneutics], 『철학연구』 (대한철학회) [Journal of the Korean Philosophical Society], vol. 68, 1998, pp. 63–84.

— 「키아케고어의 인간 존재론: 기술시대를 주도할 하나의 인간상 모색」 [Kierkegaard on the Human Being: Looking for a View of the Human Being for the Age of Technology], 『철학연구』 (대한철학회) [Journal of the Korean Philosophical Society], vol. 70, 1999, pp. 135–56.

— 「주체성은 진리인가? 키아케고어의 진리관」 [Is Subjectivity Truth? Kierkegaard's View of Truth], 『철학연구』 (대한철학회) [Journal of the Korean Philosophical Society], vol. 82, 2002, pp. 49–72.

— 「키아케고어와 니체」 [Kierkegaard and Nietzsche], 『철학연구』 (대한철학회) [Journal of the Korean Philosophical Society], vol. 86, 2003, pp. 23–45.

— 「실존철학에 나타난 기독교의 인간 이해—키아케고어를 통한 기독교적 인간 이해」 [The Christian View of the Human Being in Philosophy of Existence: A Christian Understanding of the Human Being through Kierkegaard],

『철학논총』 [Journal of the New Korean Philosophical Association], vol. 64, 2011, pp. 129–49.

김윤섭 [Kim, Yoon-Sup], 「F. Kafka 의 작품에 나타난 S. Kierkegaard 의 실존적 이념: 『Das Urteil』 에 투영된 『Furcht und Zittern』 의 문학성」 [S. Kierkegaard's Existential Idea in F. Kafka: the Literary Characteristics of *Fear and Trembling* Reflected in *Das Urteil*], 『독일문학』 [Dokil Munhak], vol. 35, 1985, pp. 71–99.

한국키에르케고어학회 편 [Korean Kierkegaard Academy] (ed.), 『다시 읽는 키에르케고어』 [Re-reading Kierkegaard], Seoul: Cheolhakgwa Hyeonsilsa 2003. (Mi-ja Sa, 「프로이트와 키에르케고어의 인간관 비교」 [A Comparison between Freud's and Kierkegaard's Views of the Human Being], pp. 9–43; Ha-ja Kim, 「키에르케고어의 생의 세 단계와 비연속성의 교육」 [Kierkegaard's "Stages of Life" and Education of Discontinuity], pp. 44–77; Min-Ho Lee, 「『아이러니의 개념)에 나타난 소크라테스」 [Socrates in *The Concept of Irony*], pp. 78–99; Seung Goo Lee, 「키에르케고어의 '종교성A'와 슐라이어마허의 종교) [Kierkegaard's "Religiousness A" and Schleiermacher's Religion], pp. 100–44; Sang Hoon Lee, 「키에르케고어로 읽는 종교다원주의) [Kierkegaard and Religious Pluralism], pp. 145–75; Seung-il Choi, 「하버마스와 키에르케고어에 있어서의 주체성 비교) [Subjectivity in Habermas and Kierkegaard: A Comparative Study], pp. 176–95; Yong-il Kim, 「키에르케고어의 실존철학과 한국 교회) [Kierkegaard's Philosophy of Existence and the Korean Church], pp. 196–223; Hak-cheol Kang, 「키에르케고어와 포스트모던 의식) [Kierkegaard and Post-Modern Consciousness], pp. 224–36; Abraham Kwang Koh, 「주체적 사상가와 자아 논리」 [The Subjective Thinker and the Logic of the Self], pp. 237–57; Pil-ho Hwang, 「키에르케고어와 동양 사상」 [Kierkegaard and Eastern Thoughts], pp. 258–89; Shoshu Kawakami, 「일본에서의 키에르케고어 수용사」 [The History of Japanese Reception of Kierkegaard], pp. 290–310; Jae-myeong Pyo, 「한국에서의 키에르케고어 수용사」 [The History of Korean Reception of Kierkegaard], pp. 311–49.)

— (ed.), 『키에르케고어에게 배운다』 [Learning from Kierkegaard], Seoul: Cheolhakgwa Hyeonsilsa 2005. (Pil-ho Hwang, 「언어와 침묵—『들의 백합, 공중의 새』 를 중심으로」 [Language and Silence: With Special Reference to *The Lily in the Field and the Bird of the Air*], pp. 9–31; Makoto Mizuta, 「종교와 언어—커뮤니케이션의 문제」 [Religion and Language: The Problem of Communication], pp. 32–44; Hea Jung Lee, 「사이버 공간과 간접 전달— 키에르케고어적 관점에서 본 인터넷의 간접 전달」 [Cyberspace and Indirect Communication: Indirect Communication on the Internet Viewed from the Kierkegaardian Standpoint], pp. 45–71; Satoshi Nakazato, 「키에르케고어와 생명윤리—종교와 윤리의 관점에서」 [Kierkegaard and Bioethics: From the Religious and Ethical Perspectives], pp. 72–80; Abraham Kwang Koh, 「키에르케고어와 자아의 문법」 [Kierkegaard and the Grammar of the Self], pp. 81–105; Min-Ho Lee, 「종교적 실존과 지성」 [Religious Existence and Understanding], pp. 106–25; Seung Goo Lee, 「합리주의적 윤리와 신앙의 윤리의 관계—『두려움과 떨림』 에 나타난 아브라함의 시련을 중심으로」 [The Relation between Rationalistic Ethics and Ethics of Faith: With Special Reference to Abraham's Trial in *Fear and Trembling*], pp. 126–88; Jae-myeong

Pyo, 「한국어 키에르케고어 문헌 목록」 [Kierkegaard Bibliography in Korean], pp. 189–209.)

곽은혜 [Kwag, Eun-Hye], 「키에르케고르의 주관적 지식과 도덕교육」 [Kierkegaard's "Subjective Knowledge" and Its Implication to Moral Education], 『도덕교육연구』 [The Journal of Moral Education], vol. 23, no. 1, 2011, pp. 153–82.

권기철 편 [Kwon, Gi-cheol] (ed.), 『키에르케고오르: 생애와 사상』 [Kierkegaard: Life and Thought], Seoul: Yupung Chulpansa 1979.

권교화 [Kwon, Gyo Hwa], 「키르케고르의 간접적 의사소통에 근거한 기독교교육 교수법에 관한 일 연구」 [A Study of the Teaching Method Based on Kierkegaard's Indirect Communication in Christian Education], 『교육교회』 (장로회신학대학교) [Education Church], vol. 195, 1992, pp. 75–107.

이강빈 [Lee, Gang-bin], 「키에르케고어의 '단독자'에서 나타나는 시민성 연구」 ["The Single Individual" of Kierkegaard and Citizenship], 『인문사회과학연구』 (부경대학교) [Journal of Humanities and Social Sciences (Pukyong National University)], vol. 13, no. 2, 2012, pp. 21–44.

이교상 [Lee, Gyo-sang], 「현대 철학과 문학의 일 단면: 배덕과 신앙」 [A Facet of Contemporary Philosophy and Literature: The Absurd and Faith], 『사상계』 [Sasanggye], vol. 2, no. 6, 1954, pp. 166–74.

이규민 [Lee, Gyu-min], 「구원과 기독교 교육: 제사장 모델 VS. 산파 모델—키엘케골적 접근」 [Salvation and Christian Education: The Priest Model *versus* the Midwife Model – a Kierkegaardian Approach], 『복음과 교육』 (영남신학대학교) [The Gospel and Education (Youngnam Theological University and Seminary)], vol. 25, 1996, pp. 10–21.

이혜정 [Lee, Hea Jung], 「키에르케고어에 관한 일반적 고찰」 [Some General Considerations on Kierkegaard], 『기독교철학연구』 [Journal of Christian Philosophy], vol. 1, 2004, pp. 191–219.

이일수 [Lee, Il-su], 임규정 [Im, Gyu-jeong], 「키에르케고르의 실존철학 서설」 [An Introduction to Kierkegaard's Philosophy of Existence], 『현대이념연구』 (군산대학교) [Studies of Contemporary Ideas (Kunsan National University)], vol. 5, 1990, pp. 65–88.

이인건 [Lee, In-geon], 「Kierkegaard에 있어서 生成의 문제에 관한 고찰」 [On the Problem of "Becoming" in S. Kierkegaard], 『논문집』 (부산외국어대학교) [Theses Collection (Busan College of Foreign Studies)], vol. 2, 1984, pp. 117–31.

이인옥 [Lee, In-ok], 「Kierkegaard에 있어서의 '不安'과 '瞬間'」 ["Anxiety" and "the Moment" in Kierkegaard], 『코기토』 (부산대학교) [Cogito (Pusan National University)], vol. 14, 1975, pp. 339–57.

이재만 [Lee, Jae-man], 「現代精神狀況과 키엘케콜의 思想」 [The Spiritual Situation of Our Time and Kierkegaard's Thought], 『명대논문집』 [Journal of Myongji University], vol. 9, 1976, pp. 151–76.

이종성 [Lee, Jong-Seong], 「키에르케고르의 실존주의」 [Kierkegaard's Existentialism], in his 『신학적 인간학』 [Theological Anthropology], Seoul: Daehan Christian Press 1979, pp. 81–5.

이정배 [Lee, Jung-Bae], 「한국교회를 향한 돌의 소리들: 고독하라, 저항하라 그리고 상상하라—키에르케고어, 본회퍼, 李信의 苦言」 [Voices of Stones for the Korean Church: Love Solitude, Resist and Imagine – Kierkegaard, Bonhoeffer and Lee Shinn], 『신학사상』 [Theological Thought], vol. 156, 2012, pp. 45–84.

이기상 [Lee, Ki-Sang], 「키에르케고르의 실존적 결단 『이것이냐 저것이냐』」 [Kierkegaard's "Existential Decision": *Either/Or*], 『철학윤리교육연구』 [Studies of Philosophical and Ethical Education], vol. 10, no. 21, 1994, pp. 95–104.

이규호 [Lee, Kyu-ho], 「키에르케골의 실존의 변증법」 [Kierkegaard's Dialectic of Existence], and 「키에르케골의 실존」 [Kierkegaard's "Existence"]," in his 『현대철학의 이해』 [Understanding Contemporary Philosophy], Seoul: Sung-uisa 1964, pp. 46–9, pp. 157–65.

이경옥 [Lee, Kyung Ook], 「키에르케고르의 불안의 개념과 실존의 3단계의 관점에서 『리어왕』 읽기」 [A Reading of *King Lear* from the Perspective of Kierkegaard's Concept of Anxiety and "Three Stages of Existence"], 『셰익스피어 비평』 [Shakespeare Review], vol. 49, no. 3, 2013, pp. 425–50.

이민호 [Lee, Min-Ho], 「실존과 진리—키에르케고어의 『철학적 단편 후서』를 중심으로」 [Existence and Truth: With Special Reference to Kierkegaard's *Concluding Unscientific Postscript*], 『철학연구』 (고려대학교) [Philosophical Studies], vol. 25, 2002, pp. 65–83.

— 「키에르케고어의 시대 진단」 [Kierkegaard's Diagnosis of His Age], 『철학연구』 (고려대학교) [Philosophical Studies], vol. 27, 2004, pp. 173–201.

이명곤 [Lee, Myung-gon], 「키르케고르의 '실존적 권태'와 '심미적 실존'의 의의」 [The Significance of Kierkegaard's "Existential Boredom" and "Aesthetic Existence"], 『철학연구』 (대한철학회) [Journal of the Korean Philosophical Society], vol. 127, 2013, pp. 135–68.

— 「키르케고르: 윤리적 실존의 양상과 사랑의 윤리학」 [Kierkegaard: Ethical Existence and Ethics of Love], 『철학연구』 (대한철학회) [Journal of the Korean Philosophical Society], vol. 129, 2014, pp. 167–91.

이상철 [Lee, Sang-cheol], 「Kierkegaard에 있어서의 순간과 반복」 ["The Moment" and "Repetition" in Kierkegaard], 『사대논총』 (서울대학교) [Journal of the College of Education (Seoul National University)], vol. 14, 1976, pp. 17–27.

이선숙 [Lee, Seon-suk], 「Kierkegaard, Nietzsche, Jaspers, Heidegger: 實存 哲學의 倫理」 [Ethics in Philosophy of Existence: Kierkegaard, Nietzsche, Jaspers and Heidegger], 『철학사상』 (동국대학교) [Philosophical Thought (Dongguk University)], vol. 5, 1983, pp. 129–43.

이승구 [Lee, Seung Goo], 「키에르케고르에의 개혁 신학적 한 접근」 [A Reformed Theological Approach to Kierkegaard], in his 『개혁 신학 탐구』 [Studies in Reformed Theology], Seoul: Hana 1999, pp. 247–382.

— 「그리스도와 제자도에 대한 키에르케고르의 이해」 [Kierkegaard on Christ and Christian Discipleship], 『국제신학』 (국제신학원대학교) [International Theological Journal], vol. 1, 1999, pp. 222–62.

— 「키에르케고르의 기독교적 진리 이해와 그 자신의 실존적 고백」 [Kierkegaard's Christian Understanding of Truth and His Own Existential Confession], 『한국개혁신학회 논문집』 [Korea Reformed Theology], vol. 9, 2001, pp. 286–318.

— 「『철학적 단편』에 대한 신학적 읽기의 한 시도」 [A Theological Reading of Kierkegaard's *Philosophical Fragments*], 『백석저널』 [Baekseok Christian Journal], vol. 3, 2003, pp. 135–68.

— 「키에르케고어의 『사랑의 역사』에 나타난 '사랑의 윤리'」 [Ethics of Love in Kierkegaard's *Works of Love*], 『신앙과 학문』 [Faith and Scholarship], vol. 11, no. 1, 2006, pp. 103–45.

이우찬 [Lee, Woo-chan], 「키에르케고르의 『죽음에 이르는 병』에 대한 고찰」 [Considerations on *The Sickness unto Death* of Kierkegaard], 『논문집』 (경남전문대학교) [Journal of Kyungnam Junior College], vol. 25, 1997, pp. 535–41.

이양호 [Lee, Yang Ho], 「키에르케고르의 종교적 실존주의」 [Kierkegaard's Religious Existentialism], 『현대와 종교』 [The Contemporary and Religion], vol. 20, 1997, pp. 269–307.

— 「키에르케고르: 종교적 실존의 길」 [Kierkegaard: The Way to Religious Existence], in his 『초월의 행보: 칸트ㅁ키에르케고르ㅁ셸러의 길』 [Steps of Transcendence: Kant, Kierkegaard and Scheler], Seoul: Damronsa 1998, pp. 157–224.

이영문 [Lee, Young-Mun], 「키에르케고르의 자아발달론과 도덕교육」 [Kierkegaard's Theory of the Development of the Self and Moral Education], 『교육연구』 (춘천교육대학교) [Journal of Education Research (Chuncheon National University of Education)], vol. 14, 1996, pp. 99–115.

— 「키에르케고르의 도덕교육론」 [Kierkegaard on Moral Education], 『인문사회교육연구』 (춘천교육대학교) [Journal of Humanities and Social Science Education (Chuncheon National University of Education)], vol. 2, 1998, pp. 311–31.

임병덕 [Lim, Byung-Duk], 「키에르케고르의 상심의 개념: 교육적 전달에 주는 시사」 [Kierkegaard's Concept of Offense and Its Implication to Educative Communication], 『교육이론』 (서울대학교) [Educational Theories (Seoul National University)], vol. 5, no. 1, 1990, pp. 65–85.

— 「키에르케고르의 실존의 개념: 도덕교육에 주는 시사」 [Kierkegaard's Concept of Existence and Its Implication to Moral Education], 『도덕교육연구』 [The Journal of Moral Education], vol. 9, no. 1, 1997, pp. 127–48.

— 『키에르케고르의 간접전달』 [Kierkegaard's Indirect Communication], Seoul: Kyoyook Book 1998 (2nd ed., Seoul: Seonggyeongjae 2003).

— 「키에르케고르와 왕양명: 교육원리로서의 주관성」 [Kierkegaard and Wang Yangming: Subjectivity as a Principle of Education], 『도덕교육연구』 [The Journal of Moral Education], vol. 13, no. 1, 2001, pp. 27–50.

— 「칸트와 키에르케고르: 언어의 한계와 가능성」 [Kant and Kierkegaard: The Limits and Possibility of Language], 『도덕교육연구』 [The Journal of Moral Education], vol. 16, no. 1, 2004, pp. 29–49.

— 「교육목적으로서의 자기지식」 [Self-Knowledge as an Aim of Education], 『도덕교육연구』 [The Journal of Moral Education], vol. 18, no. 2, 2007, pp. 143–69.

——「키에르케고르와 비트겐슈타인: 심성함양의 방법적 원리」 [Kierkegaard and Wittgenstein: Methodological Principles for Self-Cultivation], 『도덕교육연구』 [The Journal of Moral Education], vol. 20, no. 2, 2009, pp. 27–48.

——「소크라테스와 키에르케고르: 교육원리로서의 아이로니」 [Socrates and Kierkegaard: Irony as an Educational Principle], 『도덕교육연구』 [The Journal of Moral Education], vol. 22, no. 2, 2011, pp. 217–38.

——「키에르케고르의 자아이론: 자아실현의 계기로서의 절망」 [Kierkegaard's Theory of the Self: Despair as a Moment of Self-Realization], 『도덕교육연구』 [The Journal of Moral Education], vol. 23, no. 2, 2011, pp. 69–92.

——「키에르케고르의 실존윤리학: 도덕교육의 이론으로서의 윤리학」 [Kierkegaard's Existential Ethics: Ethics as a Theory of Moral Education], 『도덕교육연구』 [The Journal of Moral Education], vol. 24, no. 3, 2012, pp. 45–66.

——「교육의 목적으로서의 인내: 키에르케고르의 관점」 [Patience as an Aim of Education: A Kierkegaardian Perspective], 『도덕교육연구』 [The Journal of Moral Education], vol. 25, no. 3, 2013, pp. 1–17.

마스가타 킨야 (桝形公也) [Masugata, Kinya], 「'유혹' 개념으로 읽는 키에르케고어의 저작」 [Reading Kierkegaard's Works through the Concept of Seduction], 『철학연구』 (고려대학교) [Philosophical Studies], vol. 28, 2004, pp. 45–53.

노희직 [Noh, Heejik], 「키에르케고르에 있어서 아이러니 개념」 [The Concept of Irony in Kierkegaard], 『독일문학』 [Dokil Munhak], vol. 88, 2003, pp. 201–18.

오신택 [Oh, Sin-taek], 「롤로 메이의 실존주의 심리치료의 철학적 기초— 키에르케고어의 불안개념과 연관하여」 [A Philosophical Foundation of Rollo May's Existential Psychotherapy: In Connection with Kierkegaard's Concept of Anxiety], 『철학연구』 (대한철학회) [Journal of the Korean Philosophical Society], vol. 130, 2014, pp. 135–59.

백도근 [Paeg, Do-Geon], 「키에르케고르의 변명」 [Kierkegaard's Apology], 『신앙과 지성』 (한국신학원) [Intelligence and Beyond], vol. 16, 1999, pp. 98–116.

박병준 [Park, Byoung-Jun], 「자유의 인간학적 의미」 [The Anthropological Meaning of Freedom], in 『현대 사회와 자유』 [Contemporary Society and Freedom], ed. by the Christian Philosophy Institute, Seoul: Cheolhakgwa Hyeonsilsa 2001, pp. 60–84.

——「사랑에 대한 철학적 성찰」 [A Philosophical Reflection on Love], 『해석학연구』 [Hermeneutic Studies], vol. 14, 2004, pp. 307–34.

——「키르케고르의 '죄(성)'의 개념에 대한 인간학적 해석」 [An Anthropological Approach to Kierkegaard's Concept of Original Sin], 『철학』 [Cheolhak], vol. 93, 2007, pp. 159–84.

박찬국 [Park, Chan-Kook], 「키에르케고르와 하이데거의 불안 개념에 대한 비교 연구」 [A Comparative Study of Kierkegaard's and Heidegger's Concepts of Anxiety], 『시대와 철학』 [Epoch and Philosophy], vol. 10, no. 1, 1999, pp. 188–219.

——「키에르케고르—실존의 도약」 [Kierkegaard: The Leap of Existence], in his 『현대철학의 거장들』 [Masters in Contemporary Philosophy], Seoul: Cheolhakgwa Hyeonsilsa 2005, pp. 50–80.

박창균 [Park, Chang Kyun], 「튜링과 키에르케고어: 수학적 모델을 통한
    이해」 [Understanding Turing and Kierkegaard through a Mathematical Model],
    『한국수학사학회지』 [Journal for History of Mathematics], vol. 27, no. 2,
    2014, pp. 139–52.
박환덕 [Park, Hwan-deok], 「키에르케고르와 『죽음에 이르는 병』」
    [Kierkegaard and *The Sickness unto Death*], in his 『문학과 소외』 [Literature
    and Alienation], Seoul: Bumwoosa 1981, pp. 211–40.
박인성 [Park, In-Sung], 「Hegel에서 Kierkegaard에로」 [From Hegel to Kierkegaard],
    『범한철학』 [Pan-Korean Philosophy], vol. 12, 1996, pp. 319–39.
박인철 [Park, In Cheol], 「후설과 키에르케고르: 차이의 극복을 중심으로」
    [Husserl and Kierkegaard: Focusing on Their Internal Connection],
    『철학연구』 (철학연구회) [Journal of the Society of Philosophical Studies],
    vol. 89, 2010, pp. 5–35.
박종홍 [Park, Jong-hong], 「키에르케고어의 고독한 실존」 [Kierkegaard's
    Solitary Existence], in his 『철학개설』 [Introduction to Philosophy], Seoul:
    Baekyeongsa 1954, pp. 156–62.
박종서 [Park, Jong Seu], 「영화 「봄, 여름, 가을, 겨울 그리고 봄」에 관하여—
    키에르케고어의 사상을 중심으로」 [On the Film "Spring, Summer, Autumn,
    Winter and Spring": With Special Reference to Kierkegaard], 『기독교철학』
    [Journal of Christian Philosophers in Korea], vol. 8, 2009, pp. 143–69.
박상현 [Park, Sang-hyeon], 「키에르케골의 실존적 사유」 [Kierkegaard's
    Existential Thought], in his 『인간과 실존』 [The Human Being and Existence],
    Seoul: Changsin Munhwasa 1963, pp. 155–66.
박성은 [Park, Sung Eun], 「중년여성의 실존의미 상실로부터 본래적 자아로의
    회귀—키에르케고어의 실존개념을 중심으로」 [The Middle-Aged Woman's
    Return from the Loss of Meaning of Life to the Authentic Self: With Special
    Reference to Kierkegaard's Concept of Existence], 『기독교철학연구』
    [Journal of Christian Philosophy], vol. 4, 2005, pp. 73–105.
박원빈 [Park, Won Bin], 「쇠렌 키에르케고르와 에마뉘엘 레비나스의 윤리적
    주체성에 대한 연구」 [A Study of Søren Kierkegaard and Emmanuel Levinas
    on Ethical Subjectivity], 『한국기독교신학논총』 [Korean Journal of
    Christian Studies], vol. 62, 2009, pp. 227–48.
—「초월을 향한 끊임없는 도전: 철학적 에로스와 신앙—소크라테스와
    키르케고르를 중심으로」 [The Constant Attempts to Transcend: The
    Philosophical "Eros" and Faith – with Special Reference to Socrates and
    Kierkegaard], 『미학예술학연구』 [The Journal of Aesthetics and Science of
    Art], vol. 35, 2012, pp. 83–113.
—「윤리를 넘어 신앙으로—키에르케고르의 『두려움과 떨림』에 대한
    신학적 해제」 [Beyond the Ethical: A Theological Interpretation of Kierkegaard's
    Concept of Faith in *Fear and Trembling*], 『한국기독교신학논총』 [Korean
    Journal of Christian Studies], vol. 90, 2013, pp. 169–95.
박이문 [Park, Ynhui], 「키에르케고르와 실존」 [Kierkegaard and Existence],
    『세계의 문학』 [World Literature], vol. 16, 1980, pp. 66–80.
표재명 [Pyo, Jae-myeong], 「키에르케고르의 역설의 개념」 [Kierkegaard's
    Concept of Paradox], 『철학연구』 (철학연구회) [Journal of the Society of
    Philosophical Studies], vol. 10, 1975, pp. 153–65.

—「고난의 철학: 키에르케고오르의 주체사상」 [Philosophy of Suffering: Kierkegaard's Thought of Subjectivity], 『문학사상』 [Munhak Sasang], vol. 31, 1975, pp. 426–40.

—「키에르케고르의 그리스도상」 [Kierkegaard on Christ], 『현존』 [Presence], vol. 83, 1977, pp. 22–30.

—「키에르케고르의 실존의 3단계설—시간적 계기로 본」 [Kierkegaard's Theory of Three Stages of Existence: A Study Focusing on the Problem of Time], 『사색』 (숭실대학교) [Pensée (Soongsil University)], vol. 5, 1977, pp. 93–126.

—「키에르케고르의 주체성-진리 사상」 [Kierkegaard's Idea of Subjectivity-Truth], 『철학연구』 (고려대학교) [Philosophical Studies], vol. 5, 1978, pp. 193–207.

—「키에르케고어와 정치 사회 문제」 [Kierkegaard and Social-Political Problems], 『철학연구』 (고려대학교) [Philosophical Studies], vol. 7, no. 1, 1982, pp. 151–78.

—「루카치의 키에르케고어 비판」 [Lukács' Critique of Kierkegaard], 『철학연구』 (고려대학교) [Philosophical Studies], vol. 13, 1988, pp. 221–30.

—「키에르케고어의 단독자에 대한 부버의 비판」 [Buber's Critique of Kierkegaard's "Single Individual"], in 『현대 사회와 윤리』 [Contemporary Society and Ethics], ed. by Yeong-cheol Kim et al., Seoul: Seokwangsa 1989, pp. 153–66.

—『키에르케고어의 단독자 개념』 [Kierkegaard's Concept of the Single Individual], Seoul: Seokwangsa 1992. (Review: 신옥희 [Shin, Ock-Hee], review in 『출판저널』 (한국출판금고) [The Korean Publishing Journal], no. 112, 1992, p. 8.)

—「키에르케고어의 큰 지진의 체험」 [Kierkegaard's Experience of the "Great Earthquake"], 『철학연구』 (고려대학교) [Philosophical Studies], vol. 17, 1993, pp. 7–25.

—『키에르케고어 연구』 [Kierkegaard Studies], Seoul: Jiseong-ui Saem 1995 (2nd revised and enlarged ed., 『키에르케고어를 만나다』 [Encounter with Kierkegaard], Seoul: Chiu 2012). (Reviews: 강학철 [Kang, Hak-cheol], review in 『출판저널』 (한국출판금고) [The Korean Publishing Journal], no. 175, 1995, p. 27; 박범수 [Park, Bum-Soo], review in 『철학연구』 (철학연구회) [Journal of the Society of Philosophical Studies], vol. 37, 1995, pp. 287–94.)

—「키에르케고어」 [Kierkegaard], in 『위대한 교육사상가들』 [Great Thinkers on Education], ed. by Philosophy of Education Study Group at Yonsei University, vol. 4, Seoul: Kyoyook Book 2000, pp. 1–50.

—「키에르케고어 연구를 통해 본 열암 선생」 [Yeol-Am Seen through His Kierkegaardian Studies], in 『박종홍 철학의 재조명』 [Park Jong-hong's Philosophy Revisited], ed. by Yeol-Am Memorial Association, Seoul: Cheonji 2003, pp. 333–50.

변선환 [Pyun, Sun-hwan], 「단독자와 대중적 인간」 [The Single Individual and the Mass Man], 『북악』 (국민대학교) [Buk-Ak (Kookmin University)], vol. 36, 1984, pp. 91–100.

나동광 [Ra, Dong-Kwang], 「S.A. Kierkegaard의 실존적 자기 이해와 상담」 [S.A. Kierkegaard's Existential Self-Understanding and Psychological

Counseling], 『한국기독교상담학회지』 [Korean Journal of Christian Counseling], vol. 6, 2003, pp. 39–65.

임춘갑 [Rim, Chun-gap], 「키르케고르의 죄관」 [Kierkegaard's View of Sin], 『기독교사상』 [Christian Thought], vol. 2, no. 10, 1958, pp. 16–23.

— 「Søren Kierkegaard의 「현대의 비판」 소고」 [An Essay on the Third Part of Søren Kierkegaard's *A Literary Review*], 『논문집』 (강남사회복지학교) [Journal of Kangnam Social Welfare School], vol. 10, 1982, pp. 7–22.

— 「Johannes Climacus와 Anti-Climacus」 [Johannes Climacus and Anti-Climacus], 『논문집』 (강남사회복지학교) [Journal of Kangnam Social Welfare School], vol. 11, 1983, pp. 45–60.

— 「Kierkegaard 研究 1: Michael Kierkegaard와 Søren Kierkegaard」 [Kierkegaard Studies 1: Michael Kierkegaard and Søren Kierkegaard], 『논문집』 (강남사회복지학교) [Journal of Kangnam Social Welfare School], vol. 12, 1983, pp. 53–71.

— 「Kierkegaard 研究 2: S. Kierkegaard와 Regine Olsen」 [Kierkegaard Studies 2: S. Kierkegaard and Regine Olsen], 『논문집』 (강남사회복지학교) [Journal of Kangnam Social Welfare School], vol. 13, 1984, pp. 51–66.

— 「Soren Kierkegaard 연구 3: Kierkegaard와 Corsair」 [Kierkegaard Studies 3: Kierkegaard and *The Corsair*], 『논문집』 (강남사회복지학교) [Journal of Kangnam Social Welfare School], vol. 15, 1985, pp. 72–86.

— 「S. Kierkegaard 연구 4: 그리스도교계에 대한 공격」 [Kierkegaard Studies 4: Attack upon Christendom], 『논문집』 (강남사회복지학교) [Journal of Kangnam Social Welfare School], vol. 16, 1986, pp. 45–64.

— 「S. Kierkegaard 연구 5: 그의 교계 공격과 죽음」 [Kierkegaard Studies 5: His Attack upon Christendom and Death], 『논문집』 (강남사회복지학교) [Journal of Kangnam Social Welfare School], vol. 17, 1987, pp. 9–27.

— 「키르케고르 연구: 키르케고르와 그의 시대」 [Kierkegaard Studies: Kierkegaard and His Times], 『논문집』 (강남사회복지학교) [Journal of Kangnam Social Welfare School], vol. 19, 1989, pp. 389–408.

유양선 [Ryu, Yang-seon], 「尹東柱의 詩에 나타난 宗敎的 實存: 「돌아와 보는 밤」 分析」 [Religious Existence in Yoon Dong-ju's Poems: An Analysis of "The Night I Returned"], 『어문연구』 (한국어문교육연구회) [Language Literary Research], vol. 35, no. 2, 2007, pp. 195–219.

사미자 [Sa, Mi-ja], 「키에르케고어의 관점에서 본 인간 발달 과정에 관한 한 고찰」 [The Human Being's Development Viewed from Kierkegaard's Standpoint] 『교회와 신학』 [Church and Theology], vol. 26, 1994, pp. 469–97.

— 「기가(基家)의 덕성 함양론—쇠얀 키에르케고어의 교육방법을 중심으로」 [Christian Methods of Cultivating Virtues: With Special Reference to Kierkegaard's Method of Education], in 『덕성 함양의 전통적 방법론』 [Traditional Methods of Cultivating Virtues], ed. by the Academy of Korean Studies, Seongnam: The Academy of Korean Studies 1998, pp. 217–76.

— 「키에르케고어의 교육방법 고찰」 [A Study of Kierkegaard's Method of Education], 『장신논단』 [Korea Presbyterian Journal of Theology], vol. 16, 2000, pp. 683–713.

서배식 [Seo, Bae-sik], 「서양의 인간관에 관한 연구 (2): 키에르케고오르와 쇼펜하우어」 [A Study of the Western View of the Human Being (2): Kierkegaard and Schopenhauer], 『논문집』 (청주대학교) [Journal of Cheongju University], vol. 14, 1981, pp. 285–99.

신옥희 [Shin, Ock-Hee], 「키에르케고르: 실존 변증법」 [Kierkegaard: the Dialectic of Existence], in 『철학하는 방법』 [Philosophizing Methods], ed. by Gwang-seon Seo et al., Seoul: Ewha Women's University Press 1980, pp. 115–54.

—「키에르케고어의 단독자 사상의 사회·정치적 의의」 [The Socio-Political Significance of Kierkegaard's Idea of the Single Individual], 『철학과 현실』 (철학문화연구소) [Philosophy and Reality], vol. 15, 1992, pp. 360–72.

심민수 [Sim, Min Soo], 「키에르케고어의 실존적 주체성의 교육적 함의」 [Educational Implications of Kierkegaard's "Existential Subjectivity"], 『교육문제연구』 [Journal of Research in Education], vol. 21, 2004, pp. 53–73.

—「키에르케고어의 실존적 단독자 사상의 교육적 함의」 [Educational Implications of Kierkegaard's Idea of the Single Individual], 『한국교육학연구』 [The Korea Educational Review], vol. 10, no. 2, 2004, pp. 3–33.

—「키에르케고어의 실존적 교사론 연구」 [A Study of Kierkegaard's Theory of Existential Teacher], 『교육문제연구』 [Journal of Research in Education], vol. 24, 2006, pp. 1–24.

소병철 [So, Byung Chul], 「종교성과 도덕성은 조화할 수 있는가? 키에르케고르와 칸트의 종교관을 중심으로」 [Can Religiosity and Morality be Compatible? With Special Reference to Kierkegaard and Kant], 『인문과학연구』 (성신여자대학교 인문과학연구소) [Sungshin Humanities Research], vol. 31, 2013, pp. 397–420.

손재준 [Sohn, Jae-jun], 「키에르케고오르의 생애와 사상」 [Kierkegaard's Life and Thought], in Søren Kierkegaard, 『공포와 전율, 철학적 단편, 죽음에 이르는 병, 반복』 [*Fear and Trembling, Philosophical Fragments, The Sickness unto Death* and *Repetition*], trans. by Jae-jun Sohn, Seoul: Samseong Chulpansa 1976 (세계사상전집 [Great Books of the World], vol. 15), pp. 455–92.

송은재 [Song, Eun-Jae], 「키에르케고어와 비트겐슈타인의 비교연구—문제의 해소를 중심으로」 [A Comparative Study of Kierkegaard and Wittgenstein: Focusing on the "Dissolution" of Philosophical Problems], 『철학연구』 (고려대학교) [Philosophical Studies], vol. 17, 1993, pp. 147–72.

—「신앙의 정당화 문제에 대한 고찰: 키에르케고어와 비트겐슈타인의 사유를 중심으로」 [Considerations on Justification of Faith: With Special Reference to Kierkegaard and Wittgenstein], 『철학』 [Cheolhak], vol. 51, 1997, pp. 177–205.

—「키에르케고어의 전달에 관한 의미론적 고찰」 [Semantic Considerations on Kierkegaard's Communication], 『철학연구』 (대한철학회) [Journal of the Korean Philosophical Society], vol. 63, 1997, pp. 245–62.

송은재 [Song, Eun-Jae], 최춘영[Choi, Chun-yeong], 「키에르케고어의 역설과 비트겐슈타인의 '새장'에 관한 고찰: 키에르케고어의 사회성을 중심으로」 [A Study of Kierkegaard's "Paradox" and Wittgenstein's "Cage": Focusing on Kierkegaard's Sociality], 『현대이념연구』 [Studies of Contemporary Ideas], vol. 11, 1996, pp. 87–104.

송재우 [Song, Jae-Woo], 「키에르케고르적 개인적 체험의 학문적 정초 가능성: 하이데거의 해석학적 방법을 통하여」 [A Possible Scientific Foundation of Kierkegaard's Personal Experience through Heidegger's Hermeneutical Method], 『철학논총』 (새한철학회) [Journal of the New Korean Philosophical Association], vol. 55, 2009, pp. 187–208.

다카요시 야노(矢野尊義) [Takayoshi, Yano], 「透谷와 Kierkegaard의 戀愛觀」 [Tokoku's and Kierkegaard's Views of Erotic Love], 『일본문화연구』 [Japanese Cultural Studies], vol. 12, 2004, pp. 157–76.

—「透谷과 Kierkegaard의 實存」 [Tokoku and Kierkegaard on Existence], 『일본어문학』 [Korean Journal of Japanese Language and Literature], vol. 31, 2006, pp. 493–514.

—「도코쿠(透谷)와 Kierkegaard의 純潔과 原罪意識」 [Tokoku and Kierkegaard on Innocence and Consciousness of Original Sin], 『일어일문학연구』 [Journal of Japanese Language and Literature], vol. 79, no. 2, 2011, pp. 303–19.

—「기타무라 도코쿠(北村透谷)와 Kierkegaard의 성애(性愛)에 대한 죄의식(罪意識)」 [Tokoku's and Kierkegaard's Guilt-Feelings about Sex], 『일본문화연구』 [Japanese Cultural Studies], vol. 38, 2011, pp. 257–74.

—「도코쿠(透谷)문학과 인간소외(人間疎外): Kierkegaard와의 비교를 통한 분석」 [Tokoku Literature and Human Alienation: An Analysis through a Comparison with Kierkegaard], 『일본문화연구』 [Japanese Cultural Studies], vol. 40, 2011, pp. 321–40.

—「일본 근대문학에 나타난 불안과 키에르케고르의 불안 개념」 ["Anxiety" in Modern Japanese Literature and Kierkegaard's Concept of Anxiety], 『일본문화연구』 [Japanese Cultural Studies], vol. 48, 2013, pp. 265–84.

—「도코쿠(透谷)와 키에르케고르의 불안에 대한 심리학적 접근」 [A Psychological Approach to "Anxiety" in Tokoku and Kierkegaard], 『일본언어문화』 [Journal of Japanese Language and Culture], vol. 27, 2014, pp. 693–710.

양혜윤 [Yang, Hye-yun], 「S.Kierkegaard의 실존주의 미학에 관한 연구」 [A Study of S. Kierkegaard's Existentialist Aesthetics], 『미학연구』 (서울대학교) [Aesthetic Studies (Seoul National University)], vol. 5, 1998, pp. 49–75.

양승갑 [Yang, Seung-gap], 「Kierkegaard적 관점에서 본 W. H. Auden의 "The Sea and the Mirror" 연구」 [W.H. Auden's "The Sea and the Mirror," Viewed from a Kierkegaardian Perspective], 『동아영어영문학』 [The English Language and Literature Dong-A University], vol. 11, 1995, pp. 177–203.

연희원 [Yeon, Hee-weon], 「키에르케고어의 여성관 비판」 [A Critique of Kierkegaard's View of Women], 『인문과학연구』 (강원대학교) [Studies in Humanities (Kangwon National University)], vol. 12, 2004, pp. 467–90.

이진남 [Yi, Jinnam], 「아퀴나스, 키에르케고어 그리고 아브라함」 [Aquinas, Kierkegaard and Abraham], 『인문과학연구』 (강원대학교) [Studies in Humanities (Kangwon National University)], vol. 21, 2009, pp. 275–98.

윤병렬 [Yun, Byeong-yeol], 「실존하는 그리스도인—키에르케고르의 실존사상」 [The Existing Christian: Kierkegaard's Existential Thought], 『신학지평』 [Theological Horizon], vol. 17, 2004, pp. 331–62.

윤원준 [Yun, Won Jun], 「신의 음성과 책임: 레비나스와 데리다의 생각 속의 키에르케고르적 윤리」 [God's Voice and Responsibility: Kierkegaardian Ethics in Levinas and Derrida], 『조직신학논총』 [Korean Journal of Systematic Theology], vol. 28, 2010, pp. 149–76.

III. Translated Secondary Literature on Kierkegaard in Korean

Caputo, John D., 『(How to Read) 키르케고르』 [How to Read Kierkegaard], trans. by Gyu-jeong Im, Seoul: Woongjin Think Big 2008.

Sløk, Johannes, 「키에르케고르 (1813–1855)」 [Søren Kierkegaard (1813–1855)], in 『신학의 고전 II』 [Klassiker der Theologie, vol. 2, ed. by Heinrich Fries and Georg Kretschmar], trans. by Ji-seong Jeong, Seoul: The Christian Literature Society of Korea 2008.

Gardiner, Patrick, 『키에르케고르』 [Kierkegaard], trans. by Gyu-jeong Im, Seoul: Sigongsa 2001.

Heinemann, Friedrich H., 『실존철학: 살았는가 죽었는가』 [Existenzphilosophie, Lebendig oder Tot?], trans. by Mun-su Hwang, Seoul: Moonye Publishing Co. 1976.

Hubben, William, 『도스토예프스키, 키에르케고르, 니체, 카프카』 [Dostoevsky, Kierkegaard, Nietzsche and Kafka], trans. by Ji-Gwan Yun, Seoul: Kachi Publishing Co. 1983.

Hübscher, Arthur, 『헤겔에서 하이데거로』 [Von Hegel zu Heidegger], trans. by Yersu Kim, Seoul: Samsung Foundation of Culture 1975.

Jens, Walter, and Hans Küng, 『문학과 종교: 문학과 종교에 비친 근대의 출발과 와해: 파스칼, 그리피우스, 레싱, 횔덜린, 노발리스, 키에르케고르, 도스토옙스키, 카프카』 [Dichtung und Religion: Pascal, Gryphius, Lessing, Hölderlin, Novalis, Kierkegaard, Dostojewski, Kafka], trans. by Ju-yeon Kim, Waegwan: Bundo Book 1997.

Johnson, Howard A., 『키르케고오르의 실존철학: 그의 사상의 변증법적 구조』 [キェルケゴール理解の鍵その思想の弁証法的構造 [The Key to Understanding Kierkegaard: The Dialectical Structure of His Thought. A Collection of the Texts of his Lectures Given in Japan in 1952, first published in Japanese translation (Tokyo: Sogensha 1953).], trans. by Chun-gap Rim, Seoul: Hyeongseol Chulpansa 1958 (2nd ed., Seoul: Jongno Seojeok 1973; 3rd ed. Seoul: Dasan Geulbang 2005).

Le Blanc, Charles, 『키에르케고르』 [Kierkegaard], trans. by Chang-sil Lee, Seoul: Dongmunseon 2004.

Löwith, Karl, 『지식, 신앙, 회의』 [Wissen, Glaube und Skepsis], trans. by Chun-gap Rim, Seoul: Changrimsa 1961 (2nd ed., Seoul: Jongno Seojeok 1978; 3rd ed., Seoul: Dasan Geulbang 2007).

— 『헤겔에서 니체로: 시민적 기독교적 세계의 역사 연구』 [Von Hegel zu Nietzsche (Part Two)], trans. by Hak-cheol Kang, Seoul: Joyang Munhwasa 1974.

— 『헤겔에서 니체로』 [Von Hegel zu Nietzsche], trans. by Hak-cheol Kang, Seoul: Samildang 1982 (2nd ed., Seoul: Minumsa 1985; 3rd ed., Seoul: Minumsa 2006).

Lowrie, Walter, 『키르케고르: 생애와 사상』 [A Short Life of Kierkegaard], trans. by Chun-gap Im, Seoul: Changrimsa 1959 (2nd ed., Seoul: Jongno Seojeok 1979; 3rd ed., Seoul: Dasan Geulbang 2007).

Mackintosh, Hugh R., 『현대신학의 제형: 슐라이엘마하로부터 빠르트까지』 [Types of Modern Theology: Schleiermacher to Barth], trans. by Jae-jun Kim, Seoul: Hapdongdoseo 1955, pp. 352–425 (2nd ed., Seoul: The Christian Literature Society of Korea 1973, pp. 214–57).

Manheimer, Ronald J., 『키에르케고르의 교육이론』 [Kierkegaard as Educator], trans. by Hong-Woo Lee and Byung-Duk Lim, Seoul: Kyoyook Book 2003.

Martin, Harold V., 『켈케골의 종교사상』 [Kierkegaard, the Melancholy Dane], trans. by Dong-Geun Hong, Seoul: Seongam Munhwasa 1960.

Nigg, Walter, 『예언자적 사상가: 쇠렌 키에르케고르』 [Prophetical Thinker: Søren Kierkegaard], trans. by Hui-yeong Gang, Sok-zin Lim and Gyeong-seok Jeong, Waegwan: Bundo Book 1974.

Rohde, Peter P., 『키에르케고르, 코펜하겐의 고독한 영혼』 [Sören Kierkegaard in Selbstzeugnissen und Bilddokumenten], trans. by Gyu-jeong Im, Paju: Hangilsa 2003.

Thompson, Josiah, 『나의 성(城), 그 절망의 끝까지』 [Kierkegaard], trans. by Yeonghan Munhwasa, Gwangju: Yeonghan Munhwasa 1984.

Tillich, Paul, 『19–20세기 프로테스탄트 사상사』 [Perspectives on 19th and 20th Century Protestant Theology], trans. by Gi-deuk Song, Seoul: Korea Theological Study Institute 1980 (2nd ed., Seoul: The Christian Literature Society of Korea 2004).

Zuidema, Sytse U., 「키르케고르」 [Kierkegaard], in 『니체, 사르트르, 프로이트, 키르케고르: 현대사상의 거목들』 [Nietzsche, Sartre, Freud and Kierke-gaard: Great Modern Thinkers: A Collection of Translations of Nietzsche, Sartre, Freud and Kierkegaard (International Library of Philosophy and Theology: Modern Thinkers Series, Philadelphia: Presbyterian and Reformed Pub. Co.)], trans. by Chang-u Lee, Seoul: Jongno Seojeok 1983.

Index

Nagypál, Szabolcs, 22.
Nakagawa, Hideyasu, 173.
Nakahori, Hirokazu, 172.
Nakamura, Kazuhiko, 103.
Nakamura, Kenji, 141.
Nakamura, Kohei, 141, 171.
Nakao, Takashi, 141.
Nakayama, Takeshi, 141.
Nakazato, Satoshi, 98, 99, 141–2, 174, 175, 193.
Nakazawa, Hideo, 142.
Nakazawa, Koki, 98, 142.
Nakazawa, Rinsen, 142.
Nardi, Lorenzo, 72.
Nardi, Teresa, 95.
Narukawa, Takeo, 142.
Navarria, Salvatore, 72.
Ndreca, Adrian, 72–3.
Negri, Antimo, 73.
Németh G., Béla, 16.
Nepi, Paolo, 64, 73.
Neumer, Katalin, 9, 17.
Nicoletti, Michele, 63, 64, 73–4.
Nielsen, Jens Viggo, 74.
Nielsen, S. Aage, 176.
Nigg, Walter, 21, 204.
Niihata, Kosaku, 142.
Nijo, Hidemasa, 142–3.
Nishikawa, Takeo, 143.
Nishikura, Naoki, 143.
Nishimura, Eshin, 143.
Nishizaki, Toe, 143.
Niwa, Haruo, 143.
Nobile Ventura, Attilio, 74.
Nobuoka, Shigehiro, 143.
Noguchi, Yoshio, 143–4.
Noh, Heejik, 197.
Nomura, Chisako, 144.
Nordal, Sigurður, 24.
Noszlopi, László, 17.
Novák, Zoltán, 19.
Nun, Katalin, 21.
Nyman, Alf, 95.

Ochiai, Kenichi, 144.
Oden, Thomas C., 181.
Ogawa, Keiji, 100, 144.
Oggioni, Emilio, 75.
Ogiwara, Madoka, 145.
Oguma, Seiki, 133.

Oh, Sin-taek, 197.
O'Hara, Shelley, 95.
Ohara, Shin, 145.
Okabayashi, Hiroshi, 145.
Okabayashi, Katsumi, 145.
Okino, Masahiro, 145.
Okojima, Shinji, 145.
Okubo, Takayuki, 150, 171.
Okuyama, Yusuke, 145.
Ólafsson, Arnljótur, 24.
Olay, Csaba, 9–10.
Olesen, Søren Gosvig, 75.
Omine, Akira, 145–6, 150.
Omura, Haruo, 97.
Onishi, Yuka, 146.
Ono, Renmyo, 146.
Ono, Yusuke, 146.
Onogi, Satoshi, 146.
Onojima, Yasuo, 146.
Onuki, Atsuko, 146.
Ordass, Lajos, 1.
Ori, Masatoshi, 146.
Orlando, Pasquale, 75.
Orosz, László, 22.
Óskarsson, Þórir, 25.
Ota, Hironobu, 146.
Ota, Kotaro, 146.
Ota, Sanae, 103, 147.
Ota, Tomio, 133.
Otani, Hidehito, 100, 101, 102, 103, 147–8.
Otani, Masaru, 95, 98, 99, 100, 103–4, 107, 148–50, 171, 172, 173, 176, 177, 178.
Otoshi, Hiroko, 150–1, 152, 174, 175.
Ottonello, Pier Paolo, 75.
Ouchi, Atsushi, 151.
Oya, Kenichi, 150.
Oya, Toshikazu, 107, 150, 151–2, 172, 177–8.
Ozaki, Kazuhiko, 102, 103, 104, 107, 152–4, 172, 175, 176, 177.

Paci, Enzo, 29, 75–6.
Padellaro, Nazzareno, 28.
Paeg, Do-Geon, 197.
Palazzini, Pietro, 53.
Palermo, Sandra, 77.
Pálfalusi, Zsolt, 17.
Panzieri, Pucci, 29.
Papuzza, Carlo, 77.
Parente, Pietro, 77.

Paresce, Enrico, 77.
Pareyson, Luigi, 77.
Park, Bum-Soo, 199.
Park, Byoung-Jun, 197.
Park, Chang Kyun, 198.
Park, Chan-Kook, 197.
Park, Hwan-deok, 179, 198.
Park, In Cheol, 198.
Park, In-Sung, 198.
Park, Jong-hong, 198.
Park, Jong Seu, 198.
Park, Sang-hyeon, 198.
Park, Sung Eun, 198.
Park, Won Bin, 198.
Park, Ynhui, 198.
Pasqualetti, Zsófia, 17.
Pastore, Annamaria, 77.
Pastore, Annibale, 77–8.
Patkós, Éva, 22.
Pattison, George, 14, 16, 21, 37–8, 150, 174, 175.
Pedersen, Olaf, 176.
Pelikan, Jaroslav J., 176.
Pellegrini, Alessandro, 78.
Pellegrini, Giovanni, 78.
Pellegrino, Antonia, 78.
Penelhum, Terence, 78.
Penzo, Giorgio, 37, 63, 73–4, 78, 81.
Perini, Giuseppe, 78.
Perini, Roberto, 78.
Perkins, Robert L., 174, 176.
Perlini, Tito, 37, 79.
Perone, Ugo, 77–8.
Perris, Carlo, 57.
Perrot, Maryvonne, 176.
Pertici, Alessandra, 79.
Pertusati, Domenico, 31.
Petrucci, Gualtiero, 27, 34.
Pétursson, Hannes, 25.
Pétursson, Ólafur Jens, 25.
Piazzesi, Chiara, 79.
Pieretti, Antonio, 64, 79.
Pintér, Tibor, 14.
Pinto, Valeria, 79.
Piovani, Pietro, 54.
Pirillo, Nestore, 63.
Pizzorni, Reginaldo M., 79.
Pizzuti, Giuseppe Mario, 32, 45, 48, 49, 50, 56, 64, 68, 72, 78, 79–81, 89.
Plekon, Michael, 176.

Pólik, József, 17.
Polizzi, Paolo, 81.
Ponzio, Augusto, 81.
Popovics, Zoltán, 17.
Possenti, Vittorio, 37, 81.
Preti, Giulio, 82.
Prezzo, Rosella, 82.
Prini, Pietro, 53, 64, 82.
Prondoe, Grigore, 21.
Puccini, Gianni, 82.
Purkarthofer, Richard, 14.
Püsök, Sarolta, 13, 18.
Pyo, Jae-myeong, 134, 179, 180, 181–2, 193–4, 198–9.
Pyper, Hugh, 84.
Pyun, Sun-hwan, 199.

Quattrocchi, Ludovico, 66.
Quattrone, Alessandro, 33.
Quinzio, Sergio, 82.

Ra, Dong-Kwang, 199–200.
Rácsok, Gabriella, 22.
Rácz, Péter, 1, 2, 4, 18.
Rad, Gerhard von, 82.
Radnóti, Sándor, 8, 16, 18.
Rasmussen, Inge Lise, 32, 38, 74, 82.
Ravera, Marco, 71.
Redaelli, Luigi, 27.
Reggio, Pius Aimone, 29.
Regina, Umberto, 35, 38, 60–1, 74, 82–4, 86.
Ricca, Paolo, 64.
Richter, Liselotte, 176, 177.
Ricoeur, Paul, 22, 95, 176.
Riconda, Giuseppe, 71, 84.
Rim, Chun-gap, 179, 180–1, 200, 203, 204.
Rinaldi, Francesco, 84.
Ringleben, Joachim, 73.
Rizzacasa, Aurelio, 64, 84.
Rocca, Ettore, 33, 34, 75, 84, 85–6.
Rohde, H. Peter, 177.
Rohde, Peter P., 95, 107, 204.
Rollier, Mario Alberto, 86.
Romano, Bruno, 86.
Roos, Heinrich, 177.
Rosadoni, Luigi, 30, 31.
Rosati, Massimo, 86.
Rosfort, René, 86.
Rossi, Eugenio Augusto, 28.